Seeking Asylum in the UK
Problems and Prospects

Colin Harvey

Professor of Constitutional and Human Rights Law
University of Leeds

Butterworths
London, Edinburgh, Dublin
2000

United Kingdom	Butterworths, a Division of Reed Elsevier (UK) Ltd, Halsbury House, 35 Chancery Lane, LONDON WC2A 1EL and 4 Hill Street, EDINBURGH EH2 3JZ
Australia	Butterworths, a Division of Reed International Books Australia Pty Ltd, CHATSWOOD, New South Wales
Canada	Butterworths Canada Ltd, MARKHAM, Ontario
Hong Kong	Butterworths Asia (Hong Kong), HONG KONG
India	Butterworths India, NEW DELHI
Ireland	Butterworth (Ireland) Ltd, DUBLIN
Malaysia	Malayan Law Journal Sdn Bhd, KUALA LUMPUR
New Zealand	Butterworths of New Zealand Ltd, WELLINGTON
Singapore	Butterworths Asia, SINGAPORE
South Africa	Butterworths Publishers (Pty) Ltd, DURBAN
USA	Lexis Law Publishing, CHARLOTTESVILLE, Virginia

A CIP Catalogue record for this book is available from the British Library.

ISBN 0 406 89592 9

Typeset by Doyle & Co, Colchester
Printed by Hobbs the Printers Ltd, Totton, Hampshire

Visit us at our website: http://www.butterworths.co.uk

To Aidan and Sheila

Preface

This book has taken shape over a number of years. In that time I have had the benefit of working in several universities. The book started as a doctoral thesis at the University of Nottingham. From Nottingham I went to work in the University of Wales, Aberystwyth, where I managed to complete the thesis in 1996. The book has really evolved from that. At the time I thought that there was a need for a work which advanced a critical perspective on asylum law. Although the area has attracted much attention of late, there remains a need to bring this area more fully within mainstream critical debates in public law and human rights law. This book is advanced as a contribution to the critical tradition in public and human rights law scholarship. The difficulty, which I have tried to confront in this work, is how in practice one addresses the intersecting nature of modern legal and political orders. In particular, how one gives due recognition to the international and European dimensions of an area of national law. My argument in this work is that it is difficult to understand the response of one state without knowledge of international and European developments.

After Wales, I moved to Queen's University Belfast, where the bulk of this book was written. I benefited greatly in 1999 from a Visiting Research Professorship at the Program on Refugee and Asylum Law in the University of Michigan Law School. Without the encouragement and inspiration of Jim Hathaway and Chris McCrudden, I am not sure I would have ever completed this book.

One builds debts to many people in the period of a large writing project. I would like to thank the following individuals for their support and encouragement at various stages in this process: Gerry

Cross; David Dyzenhaus; Bill Fuge; Geoff Gilbert; Guy Goodwin-Gill; Brigid Hadfield; Tom Hadden; David Harris; Adrian Harvey; Mark Harvey; Joanne Harvey; Richard Ireland; John Jackson; Stephen Livingstone; John Morison; Kieran McEvoy; Jo Shaw; Ann Sherlock; Carl Stychin; Patrick Twomey; Sally Wheeler. These are only some of the people who have listened, given feedback and supported me in different ways over the years.

In particular, I would like to thank Lisa King for teaching me valuable lessons about life and for her constant encouragement.

All the errors and limitations of this work remain mine alone.

Colin Harvey
May 2000

Contents

Chapter 6

Conclusion   326

Table of statutes

Table of European legislation

List of cases

S

T

Chapter 1

Doing justice to strangers: an introduction to the law and politics of asylum

The proliferation of contextual approaches to legal scholarship makes the task of critically confronting an area of law and policy daunting. There is growing recognition that there are many voices in law's community and a multiplicity of perspectives. If one adds to this the intersecting nature of modern legal, social and political orders it is perhaps understandable that resignation has become a virtue in our postmodern age. Even a cursory glance reveals, however, that individuals and groups continue to struggle to secure recognition within states. The revelation that legal discourse is indeterminate does not appear to have halted the struggle to make the words of the law count in practice. Human rights lawyers, in particular, know that resignation is inadequate and that reconstruction must follow deconstruction. This is, however, a reconstructive effort which must accord full weight to the distortions revealed by the deconstruction of legal discourse. This critical vision is relevant for human rights lawyers. Critical scholarship in law is encouraging human rights lawyers to develop more sophisticated understandings of the nature and impact of legal discourse. The theoretical insights thus have a practical intent. The suggestion in this work is that the core of critical legal scholarship should remain the goal of emancipation. In other words, that dialectical rather than rejectionist criticism of society is the more appropriate critical response to the pathologies of modernity. This critical tradition now increasingly relies on conversational (dialogical) models of legal discourse.

The importance of the goal of emancipation remains as significant as ever for those groups most often marginalised by the mainstream discourses of politics and law. The asylum seeker experiences the force of law's symbolic and material effects in a direct way. For her the struggle to reconstruct a critical conception of legality matters. The marginalised have much to lose from the view that law is merely a 'playful game'. For asylum seekers the promises held out by the words of the law represent more than a game.

The aim of this work is to accord due recognition to the complexity of forced migration and its legal regulation, as well as to make use of a critical understanding of legality in criticising current law and practice. The critical vision of law defended in this work is one which actively contributes to the promotion of democracy. The conception of democracy sketched here is a rich one, embedded in modern understandings of postnationalism and multiculturalism. What is evident is that we are searching for a concept of law which goes 'beyond borders' but which is shaped at all levels by the input of affected groups. As this work will show, there are groups which are consistently excluded from our current legal and political conversations. The challenge in the asylum sphere is to extend the principle of inclusivity to the marginalised 'others' who have been traditionally silenced by the dominant narratives. What remains remarkable about this area of law is the extent to which affected groups are rendered invisible.

There is arguably no greater example of the interconnected nature of the modern world than the scale of migration and the capacity of some individuals to move between states and regions. While modern movements may be distinguished by reference to the increasing availability of international travel, it must be remembered that human history has been marked indelibly by migration. Exclusionary discourses which assert the homogeneity of 'nation states' might seek to deny or disguise it, but it is the case that heterogeneity is the norm in human history. The resulting diversity has enriched numerous societies. States, such as the UK, have benefited immeasurably from the contributions made by immigrants and refugees. This emphasis on increased mobility is perhaps too complacent. Globalisation has made travel more openly available, yet for many groups it has brought more rather than less restriction.[1] The process encourages greater anxiety about the mobility of some groups and thus more stringent regulation. Asylum seekers are constructed as threats to security

---

1   On globalisation see Held et al *Global Transformations: Politics, Economics and Culture* (1999). See also Habermas 'The European Nation-State and the Pressures of Globalization' (1999) 235 New Left Review 46; Held *Democracy and the Global Order: From the Modern State to Cosmopolitan Governance* (1995).

and stability, a process which legitimises harsh legislative measures. Globalisation may make the world a smaller place, but it also makes international society a more tightly regulated public space for the marginalised.

The emphasis on migration, with the benefits it has brought and the pluralism it has fostered, should not lead to a neglect of the structural factors which are the prerequisite of movement. Formal rights of free movement mean very little when structural factors make such freedom illusive. Feminist legal theory has drawn attention to the ways refugee law discourse privileges a 'male' conception of the refugee. The stereotype of the lone male political dissident contrasts sharply with the reality of modern forced migration. The emphasis on alienage is central to this construction of the refugee, which fails to capture the core of the problem from a needs-based perspective. Perhaps the most damning criticism of refugee law is that it largely ignores the real root causes of modern refugee flows.[2] As this work shows, this indicates that refugee law was designed for purposes which were not entirely humanitarian in nature. Drawing upon critical scholarship in refugee law, one of the aims of this book is to suggest that the law functions to exclude as much as it includes. It operates as a useful tool for states which wish to exercise control over migrants. Law is Janus-faced, it both coerces and enables. Refugee law, like other areas of law, both excludes and includes.

A word of caution is needed here, however. In attempting to reconcile functionalist and normativist approaches, this work emphasises the importance of multiple perspectives when analysing this area of law and policy. In order to maintain a valuable link to the post-1945 international human rights movement, it is important to recognise that, although flawed, international refugee law[3] has proved popular among states, and it still requires interpretation and application in the modern context.[4] In other words, refugee law remains important and there are a number of ways, demonstrated in the practice of some states, that it can be revitalised.[5] As a status-granting mechanism refugee law retains a significant advantage over other forms of legal protection. Interpretative

---

2 See Gilbert 'The Best "Early Warning" is Prevention: Refugee Flows and European Responses' (1997) 2 IJRL 207, 208-209.

3 All references to international refugee law and refugee law in this work are to the 1951 Convention relating to the Status of Refugees, 189 UNTS 137, and the 1967 Protocol relating to the Status of Refugees, 606 UNTS 267.

4 A good example of a work which both recognises the limitations of refugee law and its continuing relevance is Hathaway *The Law of Refugee Status* (1991).

5 Cf Fitzpatrick 'Revitalizing the 1951 Convention' (1996) 9 Harv Human Rights J 229.

strategies which emphasise, for example, the purpose of a legal regime can be helpful in advancing progressive goals. The centrality of the principle of *non-refoulement* to the refugee protection regime provides ample evidence to support this. One may therefore adopt a number of perspectives when analysing legal developments and when thinking constructively about legal and policy reform. To restrict comment to the inadequacies of refugee law would, however, be to miss the significance for asylum law (defined here as that body of law which regulates all aspects of protection in a state) of other developments in the area of human rights.

Much has been written about globalisation[6] and Europeanisation of law. This work recognises that it is no longer possible, or desirable, to neglect interdependence as reflected in these trends. More specifically, this means giving recognition to the plurality of legal forms and the way norms and values flow between legal orders. The content of this book gives recognition to the fact that the conversation about the meaning of law is increasingly transnational in nature. It is therefore necessary to examine the international legal framework as well as the Europeanisation of asylum law. Chapters 2 and 3 explore aspects of the international and European dimensions, and thus place the argument within the context of modern debates on the various challenges to the 'sovereign state',[7] and to orthodox conceptions of public law.[8] Border controls are often viewed as central to the self-understanding and definition of states. To put it simply, states define themselves by who they choose to exclude. The growing importance of international law is an acknowledgment that a number of the issues which modernity faces are being addressed co-operatively by states and other international actors. The evolution of, for example, the international law of human rights in the post-1945 period

6   See Twining *Globalisation and Legal Theory* (2000); Twining 'Globalization and Legal Theory: Some Local Implications' [1996] CLP 1.
7   Cf Himsworth 'In a State No Longer: The End of Constitutionalism' [1996] PL 639, where he makes reference to migration as one of the factors which is undermining the state and he recognises the need which arises to question the continuing validity of constitutional theory. See also MacCormick *Questioning Sovereignty* (1999); MacCormick 'Beyond the Sovereign State' (1993) 56 MLR 1.
8   See Morison and Livingstone *Reshaping Public Power: Northern Ireland and the British Constitutional Crisis* (1995) p 34, the authors argue that the orthodox approach to British constitutionalism is in serious trouble. This is traced inter alia to the failure to accommodate new forms of international and supranational order. See also Hunt *Using Human Rights Law in English Courts* (1997), for a critique of the 'traditional account of the UK's constitutional arrangements' and its inadequacy in the light of international and other developments.

demonstrates the extent to which matters previously regarded as within the domestic jurisdiction of states are now regulated by international rules and principles. To generalise, the trend (in purely formal terms at least) is to focus on personhood and not the distorting lens of nationality. In practice the symbolism of a common humanity to be found in human rights discourse is frequently undercut with sharp distinctions between citizens and others.

Chapter 4 provides a critical examination of the law and administration of asylum in the UK. It is an area which has gained a substantial measure of legal and administrative autonomy from other aspects of immigration law in recent years. This is a significant development, which reflects both the extent of asylum seeking in the UK and also recognition of the need to view it as a specific area of policy. Asylum, as an institution, challenges the instrumentalist orientation of immigration control and this should be reflected in an acknowledgment of the distinct problems which it raises. Chapter 5 examines the legal construction of refugee status and the politics of human rights as it applies in this area. The aim of this chapter is to chart refugee and human rights law as inherently connected to political struggles over the regulation of social existence. This is aided by adopting a framework which acknowledges the arguable nature of legal discourse. Asylum law, like other areas of law, is contested territory. A contextual approach should convey this sense of dynamism.

It is worth stressing at the beginning what this book is not. This work is not intended to be a detailed description of the current law of asylum. This is not an exercise in expository jurisprudence and thus not an attempt to propound yet another doctrinal reconstruction of the meaning of refugee law. The meaning to be accorded to refugee law by decision-makers has attracted intense interest. There is much competition over which rational reconstruction of refugee law is accepted by national decision-makers as correct. This work has more modest ambitions. The intention is to provide a critical examination of key aspects and themes in a legal regime which has emerged over the last decade in the UK and which is likely to assume increasing prominence. This is an exercise in critical reflection on an ongoing legal and political debate. The work is therefore advanced as a contribution to critical scholarship in human rights and public law at an important time in the UK. The process of constitutional change has sparked renewed interest in persuasive paradigmatic understandings of public law. New stories are being advanced which are clearly intended to have a practical impact. In other work I have defended the importance of social democratic legal and political theory.[9] This critical tradition in legal scholarship has undergone a revival, due mainly to a concern about the practical implications of defending some critical positions. The point to make is that this is an argument within critical legal scholarhip. My suggestion is that this is an important critical framework which might guide criticisms of the development of human rights and public law in the UK in the coming years. What it holds onto is a linkage to the political struggles which carry marginal voices into the centre of political dialogue in the public sphere. This approach brings those who make change happen back into the picture. The aim in this work is to probe what a critical understanding of legality might mean for asylum law and practice. One of my principal arguments is that it is increasingly difficult to 'fit' developments in practice into the traditional moulds in this area. As this book suggests, to understand asylum law in one state it is essential to grasp the multi-layered nature of legal discourse. I emphasise in this work the importance of remaining alive to the complex nature of interactions at the international, regional and domestic levels. The context of conversations about the meaning of law and politics has now moved 'beyond borders'. This work is a modest contribution to the effort to begin to map these complex processes in practice.

9   See Harvey 'The Politics of Legality' (1999) 50 NILQ 528; Harvey 'Governing After the Rights Revolution' (2000) 27 J Law and Soc 61.

Chapter Two

The international context: an emerging human rights framework?

INTRODUCTION

The argument in this work is that an area of public law, such as asylum law, cannot be adequately understood outside of its international and European contexts. Before consideration is given to the development of asylum law, and related issues, it is first necessary to place the question in its international legal context.[1] It is argued here that, despite the fact that refugee law is flawed from a human rights perspective, it should be viewed as a legal regime existing within an extensive body of international human rights law. This body of positive law grants rights to the individual and places duties on states toward *both citizens and aliens*. Human rights law is important for asylum seekers because the focus on *humanity* transcends nationality in the construction of protection. The discourse of human rights envisages a community of entitlement based on notions of personhood rather than status. The movement away from exclusive concern with the nationality of the individual for the purposes of international legal 'protection', which international human rights law has significantly contributed towards, is of especial importance to refugees and asylum seekers. As a group they are often the object of popular and official hostility.[2]

---

1 See generally Goodwin-Gill *International Law and the Free Movement of Persons Between States* (1978).
2 See Lillich *The Human Rights of Aliens in International Law* (1984) p 1.

The aim of this chapter is examine the international context. Globalisation is a buzzword of our times,[3] and although its novelty can be exaggerated, it has demonstrated the importance of international regulation as a way of dealing with many of the issues which afflict modernity. Forced displacement has become a pressing concern for the international community and one which requires co-operation if it is to be managed effectively. International regulation is not solely about managing the issue, however. As this chapter indicates, the turn to a human rights paradigm brings with it the aim of eradicating the root causes of flight. The human rights concern thus extends beyond exile to include the individual's right not to be displaced in the first place. This process is not about legitimising the containment policies of powerful states. It is instead a recognition of the need for comprehensive responses to the complex problem of human displacement.

The international and domestic legal arguments which traditionally dominate discussions of refugee movements, and other types of migration, are frequently framed solely in terms of a continuous reliance upon outdated conceptions of state sovereignty[4] and the connected principle in international law of domestic jurisdiction.[5] Following from these premises, the conclusion frequently reached is that states are said to have substantial discretion when it comes to their dealings with refugees, and migrants generally, in both the areas of admission and expulsion.[6] This is one of those areas that is often claimed to be 'exceptional' and thus beyond the reach of assertive international legal controls. This has also traditionally had an impact on the way that judges in domestic law approach the area. From a legal perspective, however, what does it mean to say that the state has substantial discretion in this area? To answer this question it is necessary to define what is meant by the term domestic jurisdiction in international law. This may be defined here as the conferment of power on states by international law permitting them to determine applicable standards and actions in prescribed areas of national

---

3   Cf Picciotto 'Fragmented States and International Rules of Law' (1997) 6 Social and Legal Studies 259, 260-261.

4   For some cogent criticism of this tendency, see Young 'Between Sovereigns: A Re-examination of Refugee Status' (1982) 14 Michigan Ybk Int Law 339, 340.

5   Cf Arendt *The Origins of Totalitarianism* (1958) p 278. She states that in theory it has always been true that nowhere has sovereignty been more absolute than in matters of emigration, naturalisation, nationality and expulsion.

6   Cf Nafziger 'The General Admission of Aliens Under International Law' (1983) 77 Am J Int Law 804.

policy but *within the bounds* of their international legal obligations.[7] Policy is shaped by the normative framework, but it is not beyond or outside of it. States are constrained in their actions not simply by domestic constitutional norms but also international rules and principles. Those struggling against national asylum policies tend to rely heavily on international standards when constructing their arguments. An adequate understanding of the nature of discretion is therefore only gained by possessing knowledge of the surrounding body of law. Although the admission and expulsion policies of states are matters in which international law permits the exercise of discretionary power, this discretion is not absolute (in fact the concept of discretion itself implies some background standards) and is ultimately shaped by the international legal obligations of states.[8] From a strategic perspective these norms also offer an invaluable grounding for critique of state policy. While the value of moral argumentation should not be underplayed, it is useful for those concerned with the protection of refugees that firm international standards can be appealed to. Discourses of internationalism can be useful in confronting restriction.

It has become a trite but no less relevant point that the interdependent nature of the modern international community,[9] and the continued abuse by states of individuals (which in practice often flows from unaccountable concentrations of power),[10] makes the acceptance of the absolute primacy of state sovereignty, and therefore of largely unregulated discretion, a redundant and ethically questionable conception of international affairs. In other words, no state exists as a single, wholly self-sufficient entity.[11] The movement of people, capital and technological developments contradicts any such proposition.[12] One must not, however, be blind to the existence of reactive, particularist movements. Globalisation brings with it forces of anti-globalisation. Feelings

7 See Galligan *Discretionary Power: A Legal Study of Official Discretion* (1986) p 1.
8 See Dworkin *Taking Rights Seriously* (1977) p 31. Cf Galligan, note 7 above, p 32. See Hawkins 'The Use of Legal Discretion: Perspectives from Law and Social Science' in Hawkins (ed) *The Uses of Discretion* (1994) ch 1.
9 Interdependence is not a new phenomenon: see eg Laski *The Grammar of Politics* (4th edn, 1938) p 19: 'A civil war in America may cause starvation in the cotton towns of Lancashire. The labours of a physicist who investigates the nature of ether may span the distance between London and New York. An injury to the credit-structure of Germany may involve a panic in the Bourse of Paris.'
10 McDougal, Lasswell and Chen *Human Rights and World Public Order* (1980) p 47.
11 See Pal *State Sovereignty at the Crossroads* (1962) p 1.
12 Cf Ferris *Beyond Borders: Refugees, Migrants and Human Rights in the Post Cold War Era* (1993) p xiv.

of powerless can be compensated for by rigid identification with the particular. Extreme versions of nationalism and particularism, often generated by the aggressive assertion of exclusive identities, are the obvious examples of this trend. It is the existence of these forces which has in recent times given rise to some of the largest displacements of persons.[13] The persistence of these developments does not, however, negate the argument that international society is becoming more interdependent in the ways described, and that the international community is increasingly comprised of a number of diverse actors, exerting considerable power and influence, which on occasion transcends that of the individual state.[14] This argument, from the stance of acknowledging global interdependence, may be taken too far and it is important to state that it does not assume that it provides the *criteria* for an internationally just society; any such claim is rightly condemned as facile.[15] Nor does it seek to deride the legitimate authority of states which implement international law,[16] it is used here as an expression of the inadequacy of the atomistic view of international society rather than a theoretical refutation of the notion of statehood.[17] States, like individuals, exist in a wider community within which they must co-exist. The existence of this wider community, and the need for such a community to function and possess rules to govern the interaction of participants, does not negate, necessarily, the place of the state, and in fact may facilitate that state's active participation.[18] The autonomy of states, just like

---

13   It is not improbable that the insecurities which follow globalisation have a certain role to play in this process, particularly in the often aggressive attachment of groups to exclusive forms of ethnic or national identity.

14   Cf Falk 'A New Paradigm for International Legal Studies' (1975) 84 Yale LJ 969. He argues that the changes in the international community are giving rise to a paradigm shift within international law and scholarship.

15   See Stone in Falk and Black (eds) *The Future of the International Legal Order* vol 1 (1972) pp 372, 450.

16   The interdependent nature of the international community is arguably also linked to the growth of the state itself as the chosen basis for societal organisation, evidenced in the fact that at the turn of the century there were only 50 states: see Crawford *The Creation of States in International Law* (1979) p 3.

17   Koskenniemi 'The Future of Statehood' (1991) 32 Harv Int LJ 397.

18   In the international community this is true of 'welfarist' policies and those advancing collective economic and social goals, arguably illustrated in the attempts made, inter alia, to establish a right to development: see eg Declaration on the Right to Development UNGA Res 41/128 (1986). See International Commission of Jurists *Development, Human Rights and the Rule of Law* (1981); Crawford (ed) *The Rights of Peoples* (1988). Cf Alston 'A Third Generation of Solidarity Rights: Progressive Development or Obfuscation of International Human Rights Law' (1982) 29 NILR 307. Such trends are premised on the existence of an international community based on co-operation rather than conflict or competition.

the autonomy of individuals, can be fostered by acting in concert with others. Such a collective understanding of the international community is particularly useful when thinking about refugees.

As stated above, addressing the question of global interdependence, as reflected in the evolution of the international law of human rights, means that sovereignty must be more convincingly conceptualised as a relationship between states, and other legal persons, functioning within a dynamic international legal community.[19] Sovereignty does not lend itself to precise legal delimitation and may be viewed more as a concept whose sphere has been eroded or at least more closely regulated by developments in international law.[20] This is not to deny that international law also functions to legitimise power relations in international affairs. This discussion of discretion indicates that the key to understanding the legality of state action with respect to the refugee and asylum seeker lies in a preliminary analysis of the international context. The evolution of the international law of human rights has contributed substantially to the erosion of the importance of nationality for the purpose of assessing the treatment of individuals by the state.[1] This body of law looks to the ill-treatment which is inflicted and not to her status as a citizen or migrant.[2]

---

19 See Franck *Fairness in International Law and Institutions* (1995) p 4: 'The impossibility of reconciling the notions of sovereignty which prevailed even as recently as fifty or sixty years ago with the contemporary state of global interdependence signals the profound transformation of international law which has occurred during the second half of this century. To describe this transformation is to point to a concomitant opportunity and challenge: not only to assess the extent to which international law has modified "sovereign" state behaviour, but also to examine critically whether the advance represents genuine progress, and how "progress" is to be measured.'

20 Franck, note 19 above.

 1 See GC 15/27 UN Doc A/41/40, p 117. Here the UNHRC emphasised this point with reference to the Covenant. It has stressed that as a general rule no distinction should be made between the citizen and the alien in the application of each right.

 2 However, it is notable that the attempt by the UN Commission on Human Rights to draft an instrument on the human rights of aliens met with some resistance. See UN Commission on Human Rights Res 6 29th Session 15 UNGAOR Supp 16 p 66; YUN (1972) 470; ECOSOC Res 1790 (LIV), 18 May 1973; ECOSOC Res 1871(LVI), 17 May 1974; UN Doc E/CN4/1261 (1977); UN Doc E/CN4/1296 (1978); Eg Elles *International Provisions Protecting the Human Rights of Non-Citizens*, UN Doc E/CN4/Sub2/392/Rev 1; UNGA Res 35/199, 15 December 1980; UN Doc A/C3/36/11 (1981), first report of the working group; UNGA Res 36/165, 16 December 1981; UN Doc A/C3/37/8 (1982); UNGA Res 37/169, 17 December 1982; UNGA Res 38/87, 16 December 1983; UNGA Res 39/103, 14 December 1984. See the Declaration on the Human Rights of Individuals who are not Nationals of the Country in which they Live, UNGA Res 40/144 adopted without a vote. See also the work of the recently appointed Special Rapporteur on the Human Rights of Migrants CHR Res 1994/44 E/CN4/Res/1999/44; Report of the Special Rapporteur E/CN4/2000/82.

The relevant human rights protections are mainly to be found in treaty law, both international[3] and regional,[4] but a number now derive from customary international law.[5] Given the continuing uncertainty surrounding customary international law, the focus here is on relevant provisions of treaty law. Traditionally, the responsibility of the state for the treatment of aliens was expressed in terms of injury to the alien's state of origin.[6] Vattel, for example, famously stated that the injury suffered by the individual should be regarded as an injury to the 'nation'.[7] Traditional international law could only conceive of the individual through her state of nationality. The ironic quality of this 'fiction' when applied to the refugee does not necessarily weaken the genuineness of its utility as the basis for the emerging system of state responsibility. The legal fiction of boundedness to the state was intended as a conceptual tool within this orthodox legal order. The concept had a impact, however, on how the individual was constructed within the international community. While it may constitute a logical corollary of traditional international legal theory it is open to criticism on the ground that it conflicts with notions of fundamental rights which belong to the individual and not to the state. With the evolution of the international law of human rights it has become inappropriate to view the individual exclusively through the lens of nationality. This paradigmatic shift has clear implications for the treatment of refugees and asylum seekers. Although in law the refugee retains the formal link of nationality, in practice the bond of citizenship, which constitutes the real connection, has been broken. The refugee relies on formal acknowledgment in law of her personhood. This is why the right of everyone to recognition as a person before the law is so important in this context.[8]

---

3   Eg International Covenant on Civil and Political Rights 1966 999 UNTS 171; UKTS 6 (1977), Cmnd 6702; International Covenant on Economic, Social and Cultural Rights 1966, 993 UNTS 3; UKTS 6 (1977), Cmnd 6702; International Convention on the Elimination of All Forms of Racial Discrimination 1966 60 UNTS 195; UKTS 77 (1969); Convention Against Torture and Other Cruel, Inhuman or Degrading Treatment or Punishment 1984 23 ILM 1027; Misc 12 (1985) Cmnd 9593.

4   Eg American Convention on Human Rights 1969 1144 UNTS 123; African Charter on Human Rights and Peoples' Rights 1981 21 ILM 59; European Social Charter 1961 529 UNTS 89; UKTS 38 (1965).

5   See Meron *Human Rights Law-Making in the UN* (1986) p 109.

6   See eg *Mavrommatis Palestine Concessions Case* (1924) PCIJ Series A No 2 p 12; *Danevezys-Saldutiskis Railway Case* (1938) PCIJ Series A/B No 76 p 16.

7   De Vattel *The Law of Nations, or, The Principles of Natural Law* vol iii (1964). Cf *Administrative Decision NoV (US v Germany)* [1924] 7 RIAA 119.

8   See Universal Declaration of Human Rights 1948, art 6.

REFUGEE STATUS (I): THE DEVELOPMENT OF A LEGAL CONCEPT

The term refugee has had a place in popular usage for centuries.[9] Over this period of time it has been attached, in a general way, to groups or individuals forced to flee their states of origin for a wide variety of reasons. The first widespread use of the term was in relation to French Huguenots forced to escape religious persecution in the eighteenth century. In ordinary discourse today the term tends to be applied indiscriminately to all displaced persons. In law, however, the term is strictly delimited.

Prior to the twentieth century there was generally little difficulty for those who wished to flee, and who possessed the means to do so, gaining entry into another state. The dominant nineteenth-century *laissez-faire* ideology, combined with the often inadequate administrative structures of states, meant that freedom of movement was generally secured for those with the resources to take advantage of it. It was only in the twentieth century that legal definitions of the refugee were formally drafted by the international community.[10] This concern to define refugee status coincided with the desire of most states to regulate, internally, the whole area of immigration more effectively. The rise of the administrative state brought with it increased regulation of this area and more general official anxiety about the consequences of human mobility. The distributivist nature of the modern state has resulted in much more emphasis on inclusion and exclusion. While popular usage utilises the term in all-embracing fashion, the international community required a much more specific classification of need. If protection was to be provided by states, they wished to construct as precise a definition as possible. States at the time were not prepared to issue a 'blank cheque' to the displaced. The legal definitions of refugee status which were drafted in the twentieth century were attempts at compromise.[11] A tension continues to exist between the desire of the state to regulate immigration and the needs of refugees. The difficulty has been, and remains, how to build a protection regime which concentrates on defined needs and blocks out irrelevant political or foreign policy considerations. From its inception, the

---

9 See Melander 'The Concept of the Term "Refugee"' in Bramwell (ed) *Refugees in the Age of Total War* (1988) p 7.

10 See generally Goodwin-Gill *The Refugee in International Law* (2nd edn, 1996); A Grahl-Madsen *Refugees and International Law* vol i (1966); Hathaway *The Law of Refugee Status* (1991); UNHCR *The State of the World's Refugees 1997-98: A Humanitarian Agenda* (1997).

11 Hathaway 'The Evolution of Refugee Status in International Law' (1984) 33 ICLQ 348, 349.

legal construction of refugee status evolved according to the concerns of states about their capacity to accept refugees and asylum seekers, rather than being exclusively concerned with the needs of all forced migrants. The modern legal definition of refugee status, discussed below, reflects this compromise in the variance between its provisions and the multiple types of forced migration which it does not include. If one bears the above discussion in mind, then the fact that a legal regime addressing refugees has in many instances functioned restrictively becomes less surprising. As noted, this reflects the Janus-faced nature of modern refugee law. It is both freedom guaranteeing and coercive at the same time.

Pre-1951 international agreements relating to refugee status and protection: towards a 'universal' definition of the refugee

A critical approach to the evolution of international refugee law must concern itself with the historical contingency of the definition of refugee which has gained hegemonic standing in international affairs. The definition contained in the 1951 Convention, which is so often used as the basis for labelling groups of protection seekers as 'bogus', evolved in a specific time period to address particular needs. It is important to understand how the particular became the universal and chart the paths not taken. The point is to illustrate the context in which the legal construction of the refugee was formed to provide space for critique later in this work.

The League of Nations

The first international legal instruments addressing refugee status and protection were concluded under the auspices of the League of Nations.[12] The League achieved some of its most notable successes in the field of both social and humanitarian activity.[13] Prior to the formation of the League of Nations, the assistance provided to refugees came from private organisations and voluntary agencies. The assistance supplied by these organisations was mainly in the form of relief. They were unable to offer any formal legal protection through, for example, asylum.[14] Overwhelmed by

---

12 See Henig *The League of Nations* (1973) pp 152-160. For general treatment see Zimmerman *The League of Nations and the Rule of Law 1918-1935* (1945); Scott *The Rise and Fall of the League of Nations* (1973); Pollock *The League of Nations* (1927); Walters *A History of the League of Nations* (1952).

13 Henig *The League of Nations* (1973) pp 152-160.

14 See Holborn 'The Legal Status of Political Refugees 1920-1938' (1938) 32 Am J Int L 681; Marrus *The Unwanted: European Refugees in the Twentieth Century* (1986) pp 53-61.

the numbers of those displaced in the first two decades of the twentieth century, and principally by the mass movements caused by the events following the revolution in 1917 in Russia, these private organisations made an appeal to the League to become involved in providing humanitarian assistance.[15] The Covenant of the League contained no reference to the protection of refugees, but one of the purposes of the League, which was thought to be applicable in this instance, was to 'promote international co-operation and to achieve international peace and security'. Although on a strict literal interpretation the refugee problem did not come within the League's competence,[16] the Council of the League decided in June 1921 that the refugee problem should be the subject of further investigation. In August of that year Dr Fridtjof Nansen was appointed as the High Commissioner on behalf of the League in connection with the problems of Russian refugees in Europe.[17] Concern for the plight of refugees was therefore, for the first time, brought to the attention of the international community. The mandate of the High Commissioner was gradually extended throughout the 1920s to include the refugees discussed below. In 1930 the High Commissioner was replaced with the Nansen International Refugee Office,[18] which was very much the precursor to the modern institutional structures of protection.[19]

These first arrangements were motivated by events occurring in Russia and, more specifically, the denationalisation policy undertaken by the Bolshevik government. In response to the exodus, an Arrangement with regard to the Issue of Certificates of Identity to Russian Refugees was adopted in 1922.[20] It did not contain any generalised definition of the term 'refugee' and simply applied to displaced Russians who sought it and who had not obtained another nationality. A similar Arrangement concluded in

15 See Holborn, note 14 above.
16 Holborn, note 14 above, p 687.
17 Council Resolution of 21 June 1921 LNOJ 1921 p 758. For an assessment of the contribution of Nansen to the development of structures for the protection of refugees see Scott, note 12 above, p 77. 'The League of Nations was never short of speakers to plead the case of humanity but not many of them . . . were prepared to contribute more than words. Nansen was a glorious exception. Not only did he come to Geneva to speak on behalf of the suffering; he also went to the suffering and worked with his own hands for their relief.'
18 Assembly Resolution of 30 September 1930 LNOJ Special Supplement No 83 p 48.
19 See Northedge *The League of Nations: Its Life and Times 1920-1946* (1988) p 77. 'The organisation which the indefatigable Nansen built up within the league's framework almost single-handedly formed the foundation stone for all later international relief work for refugees.'
20 13 LNTS 237, entry into force, 16 November 1922, 22 state parties.

1924 to offer some form of protection to Armenian refugees again required only that the persons displaced be of Armenian origin.[1]

In May 1926 an Intergovernmental Conference was convened in Geneva to discuss the possibility of improving upon the 1922 Arrangement discussed above. Universal application of the 1922 Arrangement was urged by some representatives but was rejected by those who saw this as too radical a departure from the traditional approach.[2] This more traditional stance mirrored international law's conception of individuals in general at that time. In addition the ad hoc approach again reflected a belief that the refugee problem was a temporary one to be 'solved' on a case by case basis. The Arrangement relating to the issue of Identity Certificates to Russian and Armenian refugees adopted at the Conference thus stated:

> 'The Conference adopts the following definition of the term *refugee: Russian refugee*. Any person of Russian origin who does not enjoy or who no longer enjoys the protection of the government of the USSR and who has not acquired another nationality.'[3]

The same definition was drafted for those of Armenian origin. There are a number of points to note about the definition. First, it concentrates on the origin of the person displaced. Second, the emphasis is on the lack of protection of the government and the requirement that the person has not acquired another nationality. The lack of protection standard is one that was repeated in later instruments. Although limited to individuals fleeing from prescribed states of origin, the definition did reflect a 'group approach' to refugee status which concentrated on this de facto lack of protection and the fact of external displacement. To this extent it differs from the more individualistic standards applied after 1945. This type of 'group approach' had the benefit of not requiring complex individual determination procedures.

In late 1926 the Council of the League resolved to extend the provisions contained in the 1926 Arrangement to other groups who were in a similar position to that of the Russian and Armenian refugees.[4] In June 1928 an Intergovernmental Conference met to discuss for the first time all aspects of the refugee question.[5] The result of the Conference is contained in the Arrangement concerning the extension to other categories of Refugees certain measures taken

1 For the extension of the High Commissioner's mandate to include these Armenian refugees see Council Resolution of 28 September 1923 LNOJ 1923 p 1349.
2 See Holborn (1938) 32 Am J Int L 681, 685.
3 Article 1 84 LNTS 2004, entry into force 14 June 1926, 23 state parties.
4 See Hathaway (1984) 33 ICLQ 348, 354.
5 Hathaway, note 4 above.

in favour of Russian and Armenian Refugees 1928.[6] The definition again was category, or more precisely, nationality specific, extending coverage to Assyrian, Assyro-Chaldaen persons of Syrian or Kurdish origin as well as persons of Turkish origin. The mandate of the High Commissioner was likewise extended to incorporate this new group.[7]

Although the above definition fulfilled its limited purposes, it was apparent at the time, and seems clear in retrospect, that a permanent and less ad hoc legal regime was required.[8] The ad hoc approach, while often, in its own terms, proving to be effective, was inadequate as a mechanism for addressing refugee movements in the long term.

Convention relating to the International Status of Refugees 1933[9]

Led by the need for a more secure grounding for refugee protection, an Intergovernmental Conference met in 1933.[10] There was general agreement that, although limited in their application, the 1926 and 1928 Arrangements were appropriate for incorporation into the Convention. Unanimity was lacking, however, as delegates from Czechoslovakia and Poland argued that the definitions were imprecise and inappropriately drafted for inclusion in an international Convention. Despite this lack of unanimity, agreement was eventually reached on a text, and the Convention relating to the International Status of Refugees was adopted. The Convention contains the definitions provided in the arrangements described above and places them together. Therefore, the comments, especially the limitations, noted there are equally applicable here.

Convention concerning the Status of Refugees coming from Germany 1938[11]

The well-documented events in Germany in the 1930s led inevitably to a large number of people being forced to flee the state. A High Commissioner for Refugees Coming from Germany had also been elected to address the problem as early as 1933.[12] Other states responded, in what was becoming the customary manner, to this exodus in 1936 by concluding a Provisional Arrangement on the

6 89 LNTS 2006, entry into force 22 September 1928, 12 state parties.
7 Council Resolution of 7 June 1928 LNOJ 1928 p 898.
8 See Hathaway (1984) 33 ICLQ 348, 357.
9 159 LNTS 3663, entry into force 13 June 1935, 8 state parties. See Hathaway (1984) 33 ICLQ 348.
10 Intergovernmental Conference for Refugees, LSC/1/1933- LSC/15/1933.
11 192 LNTS 4461, entry into force 26 October 1938, 8 state parties.
12 Assembly Resolution of 11 October 1933 LNOJ 1933 Special Supplement No 114 pp 11-14.

issue of German refugees.[13] The Provisional Arrangement defined a refugee as follows:

'any person who was settled in that country, who does not possess any nationality other than German nationality, and in respect of whom it is established that in law or in fact he or she does not enjoy the protection of the government of the Reich.'

The Provisional Arrangement formed the basis for the 1938 Convention, but the definition differs in that the rather curious phrase 'any person who was settled' is omitted. The 1938 Arrangement defined a refugee coming from Germany as follows:

'persons possessing or having possessed German nationality and not possessing any other nationality who are proved not to enjoy, in law or in fact the protection of the German government.'

The provisions of the Convention were extended in 1939 by the addition of a Protocol to address refugees coming from Austria. The substantive test of refugee status was not, however, altered and thus continued in the same vein as those in earlier periods. Nevertheless, in the agreements one may discern many of the features which were to appear in the more comprehensive agreements which emerged in the post-1945 period.

Constitution of the International Refugee Organisation 1946[14]

The period during and after the 1939-45 war represented something of a paradigm shift in defining refugee status. As noted, the previous definitions largely concentrated on groups of displaced persons, defined often with reference to their nationality and/or state of origin, with the requirement that the individual show that she lacked state protection. This approach was eventually rejected in favour of an 'individualised' conception of refugee status, which focused on the individual's relationship to her state of origin and, most importantly when considering the modern definition, her reasons for flight.[15] This was to be the initial stage on the road to the 'universal' definition of a refugee in international law which would emerge some years later.

---

13 Provisional Arrangement concerning the Status of Refugees Coming from Germany 77 LNTS 3952 entry into force 4 August 1936.
14 18 UNTS 3, entry into force 20 August 1948, 17 signatories, 18 state parties; UNGA Res 62(1) 15 December 1946. See Holborn *The IRO: A Specialised Agency of the UN* (1956).
15 Hathaway (1984) 33 ICLQ 348, 370.

The mass displacements caused by the war resulted in more intense international activity to address displacement.[16] In November 1943, before the creation of the UN itself, the United Nations Relief and Rehabilitation Administration (UNRRA) was established.[17] It was not initially formed to give assistance to refugees. The states[18] which created the organisation had done so in order to repatriate their own nationals displaced by the war.[19] It was not until August 1945 that the organisation became concerned with refugee protection as opposed to repatriation.[20] This reorientation was borne from necessity. It had become clear that many individuals did not wish to return to their states of origin because of a continuing fear that they would be subject to persecution. This extension of the organisation's competence to embrace refugee protection was attacked by the Eastern bloc countries which objected to individuals not returning to aid in the reconstruction efforts following the war.[1] Crucially, following this criticism, the competence of the organisation in this field was narrowed to include only those individuals who could show concrete evidence that they would suffer persecution upon return to their state of origin.[2] This marked a subtle shift towards the modern legal definition of a refugee by requiring that the individual demonstrate a specific likelihood of persecution by her state of origin and not simply that she possessed its nationality and lacked its protection.

This trend was consolidated in the Constitution of the International Refugee Organisation (IRO). With the dissolution of the League of Nations and the UNRRA, and the continuance of the refugee problem, there was a need for a new agency which would address the needs of the displaced. The newly formed UN provided the forum for the creation of such an organisation. The UK, the US and France argued within the UN that the problem of refugees and displaced persons was one of concern to all states. From the early years of the UN's existence, refugee protection has been of concern. In 1946, after much discussion, the IRO was

---

16 Goodwin-Gill *The Refugee in International Law* pp 5-6; Holborn, note 14 above, p 23; Marrus *The Unwanted* (1986) pp 194-295, on post-war era see pp 296-345.
17 See Holborn, note 14 above, p 24; Alister-Smith *International Humanitarian Assistance: Disaster Relief Actions in International Law and Organisations* (1985) p 35.
18 44 in number.
19 See Hathaway (1984) 33 ICLQ 348, 372.
20 See note 19 above.
 1 (1984) 33 ICLQ 348, 373.
 2 See note 1 above.

established.[3] It was created as a non-permanent specialised agency within the UN. The Constitution of the IRO offered a detailed definition of refugee status and demonstrated the shift in thinking at the time. The Constitution defined the term refugee, first, to include all victims of the nazi or fascist regimes including the Spanish regime, and, second, persons who were considered to be refugees before the war because of reasons of race, religion, nationality or political opinion.[4] In addition to this:

'the term refugee also applies to a person . . . who is outside of his country of nationality or former habitual residence, and who, as a result of events subsequent to the outbreak of the second world war is unable or unwilling to avail himself of the protection of the government of his country of nationality or former nationality.'

In this, the language that eventually found its way into the 1951 Convention is evident. The Constitution also provided for the individual to claim refugee status on the ground that she would suffer persecution upon return because of other prescribed grounds, again mirroring later developments.   Thus, persons were to become of concern to the IRO if they could be repatriated and the IRO's help was needed to achieve this end, or:

'if they have definitely, in complete freedom and after receiving full knowledge of the facts, including adequate information from the governments of their countries of nationality or former habitual residence, expressed *valid objections* to returning to those countries.'[5] (My emphasis.)

The vagueness of the term 'valid objections' meant that some clarification was required. Could any objection to return constitute the individual as a refugee? The Constitution elaborates on the term 'valid'. The most important aspect of relevance here is the following:

'(i) Persecution, or fear, based on reasonable grounds of persecution because of race, religion, nationality or political opinions, provided the opinions are not in conflict with the principles of the United Nations as laid down in the preamble of the Charter of the UN.'

One may see from the above the formative stages in what was to become the 'universal' definition of a refugee in international law. All the key elements of refugee status were essentially then in place, including what was to become the extremely problematic 'persecution standard'.

---

3   After its establishment complaints continued: see eg Report of IRO, E/1334, E/1482, E/1493, 4 ESCOR (1949) p 597. The USSR representative condemned the IRO for not carrying out its primary task of repatriation which he blamed on the involvement of the UK and the US.

4   Part I, s A 1 (c).

5   Section C 1.

In the pre-1951 period the definition of refugee status may be seen to have advanced from group specificity, the group being defined broadly in terms of nationality and lack of state protection, to a more generalised concept of refugee status, ie the constituent elements of a universal refugee definition which would be applicable to all individuals regardless of their nationality. Notably, the definitions drafted in this period were exclusively in response to European displacements. The seeds of the international legal definition of refugee status were therefore 'Eurocentric', in the sense that they evolved as a legal response to refugee movements in Europe. While the IRO Constitution is evidence of the move toward exclusive concern with civil and political rights (and thus evidence that the emerging conception of refugee status was in some sense Eurocentric in scope), this may not be said of the earlier 'group specific' approaches.

The drafting of the various refugee definitions had a number of purposes, which were often purely functional. The legal definitions allowed states to address the area of forced migration by offering the opportunity to limit the numbers of those entering their territory, while having the means to recognise refugee status in certain circumstances of defined need. From the outset, the legal regime evidenced this tension between the importance for states of immigration control and the human rights aspects of refugee protection. The 'group approach' had the benefit of offering protection to a broad class of individuals, provided that they were of the correct nationality and/or origin and were lacking the protection of their state. To this extent it avoided the need for the establishment of elaborate individualised procedural mechanisms. The problem with such an approach related primarily to its ad hoc, rather than its group specific character, and the connected difficulty of continually having to draft or re-draft agreements and extend the mandate of the High Commissioner as and when new displacements arose. As the post-1951 developments (discussed below) show, an attempt was made to remedy this by drafting a universal refugee definition, applicable to all such events. It is notable that the difficulties experienced with the narrowness of the 'Convention' refugee definition have meant that the UNHCR has encountered problems not dissimilar to those experienced by the High Commissioner in the period under examination.[6]

6   In other words, the mandate of the UNHCR has been extended, often on a case-by-case basis, to deal with groups of displaced persons who do not fulfill the 1951 Convention criteria. This is, as stated, not unlike the position faced by refugee organisations before the drafting of the 1951 Convention.

REFUGEE STATUS (II): THE CONSTRUCTION OF THE INTERNATIONAL REGIME

The international regime protecting refugees and asylum seekers is the result of a combination of international refugee law and other aspects of international human rights and humanitarian law. One of the more significant aspects of this body of law is the international legal definition of refugee status, by which the law constructs an image of the refugee which is often at variance with modern forced migration and which confines the status to a narrow band of asylum seekers. The deficiencies of the international legal definition of the refugee are recognised by states and others. As a tool to use in awarding a formal status, its adoption was nevertheless an advance over the previous response.

The post-1951 position: the 1951 Convention relating to the Status of Refugees

As was demonstrated by the creation of the IRO, the international problems resulting from displacement were of immediate concern to the newly established UN.[7] From the outset, the cold war divisions in international relations were reflected in debates within the UN when the question of refugees and stateless persons was considered. The Eastern bloc states objected strongly to measures being taken for the benefit of stateless persons without governmental consent.[8] In the case of refugees, these states advocated repatriation as the most appropriate solution to the problem. These differences of opinion were to resurface in most discussions of the refugee problem in the period.

At its sixth session, ECOSOC requested the Secretary-General to undertake a study of the situation with regard to the protection of stateless persons and the various international and national measures applied to this group.[9] It also requested that the Secretary-General report back with suggestions for possible interim measures and, additionally, make recommendations on the possibility of drafting a Convention on the subject.[10] This study was completed in 1949.[11] The Secretary-General, in drawing up his terms of reference, decided that although the term 'refugee' was not included in a literal

---

7 See eg UNGA Res 8 (I), 12 February 1946.
8 See eg E/OR (XIV) pp 491-492 Nosek (Czechoslovakia); E/OR (VI) pp 310-311; E/600 para 46, 16 UNESCOR Suppl pp 13-14.
9 See note 8 above, para 4.
10 See note 9 above.
11 UN Secretary-General *A Study of Statelessness* E/1112, Add 1, UN Series No 1949 XIV 2.

construction of his mandate, they as a group were not to be excluded from the study, primarily because many of the stateless following the war were also refugees. In this study therefore, the refugee was addressed only in so far as she was stateless.[12] The Secretary-General recommended that an international Convention be drafted to deal with what he defined as the problem of both *'de jure* and *de facto* stateless persons'. In other words, the Secretary-General viewed the refugee as an individual who was de facto a stateless person.

The discussion of the report in the ninth session of the ECOSOC was at times extremely critical.[13] The problem which the states present had was the study's lack of definitional clarity. The principal target of the criticism was the Secretary-General's classification of de facto and de jure statelessness. In particular, states objected to the categorisation of the refugee in this way. By assimilating the status of the refugee to that of the stateless person the study had, it was claimed, confused these separate and essentially distinct problems.[14] Following discussion, the ECOSOC adopted a resolution establishing an ad hoc committee to study the international status of both refugees and stateless persons.[15] The Committee was also mandated to consider the drafting of a Convention on the status of refugees and stateless persons and recommend any suggestions which would contribute to solving these problems.

Drafting

The ad hoc Committee on Statelessness and Related Problems met for its first session in January and February 1950. The Committee drafted a Convention on the status of refugees and a Protocol on the status of stateless persons.[16] The basis used for drafting the new Convention was the 1933 Convention, discussed above. At its eleventh session, the ECOSOC noted the Committee's report and requested the Secretary-General to reconvene the Committee to reconsider the two drafts in the light of comments made by states and those of the ECOSOC.[17] It decided that the preamble and art 1,

---

12 See note 11 above.
13 See eg Kulazhenkov (USSR), 4 UNESCOR (1949) p 627. The basic argument was that the study went too far. Cf Rochefort (France) p 639 arguing that the Convention should not exude 'mythic liberalism'. There appeared to be little danger of this.
14 Rochefort (France), note 13 above.
15 ECOSOC Res 248 (IX), 8 August 1949. The Committee had representatives from the following states: Belgium, Brazil, Canada, China, Denmark, France, Israel, Poland, Turkey, UK, USSR, US, Venezuela.
16 See report E/1618; draft Convention E/AC32/L32.
17 UN Doc E/1849/Add 1.

which contained the definition of refugee status, should be replaced by texts drafted by the ECOSOC itself.[18] The second session of the ad hoc Committee was held between 14 and 25 August 1950, and it carried out the changes required by the Council. In accordance with Resolution 319(IV)[19] the report was submitted to the General Assembly. The Resolution also contained the preamble and the revised art 1 as drafted by the ECOSOC.

The Third Committee of the General Assembly reviewed and amended the draft art 1 supplied by the ECOSOC at the Assembly's fifth session. In December 1950 the Assembly adopted Resolution 429(V), by which it was decided that a Conference of Plenipotentiaries was to be convened to complete the drafting and signing of the Convention relating to the status of refugees and the Protocol relating to the status of stateless persons.[20] The new draft definition, drawn up by the Third Committee, was accepted by the General Assembly and was included in the Annex to the Resolution.

The Conference of Plenipotentiaries met between 2 and 25 July 1951.[1] The dominant mood of the Conference, evident in many of the representations made by the states present, was one of general concern that they not be over-burdened. On 25 July the Convention relating to the Status of Refugees was adopted with the Final Act being signed on 28 July. The Convention entered into force on 22 April 1954.

The 1951 Convention definition

It is instructive, although hardly surprising, that more time was spent on art 1, ie the definition of refugee status, than any other article. The drafters of the 1951 Convention were essentially divided over whether 'refugee' should be defined restrictively, and limited to current displacement, or whether provision should be made for a general definition applicable into the future. This is reflected, for example, in the debates within the General Assembly Third Committee, in its consideration of the draft definition provided by the ECOSOC.[2] The views expressed throughout discussions of

---

18 See note 17 above.
19 UNGA Res 319 (IV), 3 December 1949.
20 UNGA Res 429 (V), 14 December 1950.
 1 26 states represented: Australia, Austria, Belgium, Brazil, Canada, Colombia, Denmark, Egypt, France, FRG, Greece, Holy See, Iraq, Israel, Italy, Luxembourg, Monaco, Netherlands, Norway, Sweden, Switzerland, Turkey, UK, US, Venezuela, Yugoslavia.
 2 See eg Henkin (US), E/AC/32/SR3 pp 9-10; Cha (China), E/AC32/SR5 p 2. Cf UK draft art 1 E/AC32/L2 and L3 Rev 1; US draft E/AC32/L4. See UK comment on L2 Rev 1 E/AC32/SR3 p 9.

the draft definition may be divided between those who primarily feared that liberality in this area would result in a 'blank cheque' to future refugee flows and those who wished to see a general definition applicable to all refugees. The former were concerned to make the definition as precise as possible.[4] The latter, including the UK, however, wished to see the adoption of a general definition, which, it was argued, would be more convenient for the purpose of interpretation, would protect the largest number of persons, and, most importantly, would not be confined to European refugees.[4] Despite the UK's argument,[5] the majority view at that time was that 'refugee' should be defined by listing specific categories and be confined to pre-1951 events.[6]

The final text of the 1951 Convention defines the term 'refugee' as including all those recognised as refugees under the Arrangements and Conventions discussed above. In addition, and significantly for present concerns, the Convention also included the following, core elements of which were to become the universal definition of refugee status:

'Article 1(1)(A) As a result of events occurring before 1 January 1951 and owing to well-founded fear of being persecuted for reasons of race, religion, nationality, membership in a particular social group or political opinion [he] is outside the country of his nationality and is unable or unwilling to avail himself of the protection of that country; or who, not having a nationality and being outside the country of his former habitual residence as a result of such events, is unable or owing to such fear, is unwilling to return to it.'

Difficulties had emerged at the Conference of Plenipotentiaries over whether the Convention should be applicable only to events occurring in Europe. The draft Convention submitted to the Conference, for example, specified that this was to be the case.[7] Opposing opinions were expressed at the Conference. One argument was that the Convention should apply only to events in Europe while the other was that it should apply universally.[8] A compromise was

---

3   Eg Robinson (Israel), E/AC32/SR3 p 9.
4   Hoare (UK), UN Doc E/AC32/SR6 p 3.
5   Belgium, Canada and Pakistan also argued, unsuccessfully, for a more general definition, see YUN (1950) 571.
6   Hoare (UK), UN Doc E/AC32/SR6 p 7. Cf provisional draft by working group of Ad Hoc Committee E/AC32/L6; ECOSOC Res 319 (XI) 16 (1950).
7   See note 6 above.
8   Cf Rochefort (France), UN Doc A/CONF2/SR3 p 11. See A/CONF2/SR22 pp 12-18, again Rochefort (France) stating that there needed to be restrictions if the Convention was not to become a 'blank cheque'.

eventually reached,[9] and the problem was resolved by the adoption of the following provision:

> 'Article 1(1)(B)(1) . . . for the purposes of this Convention, the words, "events occurring before 1 January 1951" in Article 1 Section A, shall be understood to mean either
>> (a) "events occurring in Europe before 1 January 1951"
>> or
>> (b) "events occurring in Europe or elsewhere before 1 January 1951" and each Contracting State shall make a declaration at the time of signature, ratification, or accession, specifying which of these meanings it applies for the purpose of its obligations under the Convention.'

States thus resolved the problem of restricting its applicability to events in Europe by offering an alternative, more geographically universal approach, which states could choose to follow.[10] Although the choice was given with respect to the geographical limitations, no such choice was offered with respect to the temporal restrictions, ie in both cases the Convention only applied to pre-1951 events. Despite this qualification, the conceptualisation was essentially regional in its functions, ie the formulation of effective solutions to the European refugee problem of the time. Although the refugee problem was widely viewed as a temporary phenomenon, states were unwilling to be parties to a treaty which would bind them unpredictably into the future. Thus, as stated above, a recurring theme in the *travaux* was the unwillingness to consent to an uncertain and ambiguous future obligation. This has been a consistent aspect of the approach of the majority of states to defining refugee status and to offering asylum to refugees since this time. The tensions which were present in the discussions at the time of the drafting of the 1951 Convention are still those which dominate debates. The arguments have continued to oscillate between familiar and tired dualisms.

The definition of the 'refugee' adopted may be described as Eurocentric in its scope. This is not entirely satisfactory as a description, but it does capture the fact that the international regime emerged as a response to specifically European patterns of forced migration. In future, the legal construction of the refugee would be confined to those fleeing violations of a band of civil and political rights, effectively excluding from consideration other aspects of forced migration, such as severe violations of economic and social rights. Reflecting the exclusionary aspect of the definition, the drafters of the Convention confined refugee status to violations

9   A/CONF2/ SR pp 13-21.
10   Cf Drago (Italy), A/CONF2/ SR19 p 15.

of civil and political rights which were, it must be stated, those rights which were gaining rapid acceptance in the period in question.

One of the points which will be made throughout this work is that when discussing the plight of the refugee and asylum seeker within a state, it is essential that the historical contingency of the original definition is drawn out. This aids in understanding the problems with refugee law and its prospects. It also demonstrates that the normative order was forged out of specific historical circumstances. The point is that the law's image of the refugee is constructed and does not represent the first, or the last word, on the persons we might wish to call refugees. This explains why so many of those who claim asylum in, for example, states such as the UK are not granted refugee status and why the distinction made between the 'genuine refugee' and the 'economic migrant' needs to be approached with caution. The definition of refugee which has gained widespread recognition was created in a particular historical period and was the result of numerous compromises. The law's image of the refugee is limited and continues to fail to capture the nature and complexity of forced migration.

The 1967 Protocol relating to the Status of Refugees

The difficulties involved in temporally restricting the application of the Convention soon became apparent as refugee movements continued in the post-war era. The location of these refugee movements also changed. From being an essentially European problem, after 1945 the location of refugee movements shifted dramatically to the developing world. The 1967 Protocol relating to the Status of Refugees removed the temporal and geographical limitations contained in the 1951 Convention, giving the definition universal applicability and thus overcoming some of the previously stated limitations.[11] The substance of the 1951 Convention definition was not, however, altered.

A number of general points may be made at this stage. Most straightforwardly, implementation of refugee law is delegated to individual states. As is argued in this work, this has proved to be a serious problem. Unlike related areas of human rights law, there is no supervisory mechanism. Interpretation of the provisions of the Convention is for appropriate authorities within states. In addition, refugee law does not include procedural requirements

11 Article 1(2), art 1(3).

which dictate the nature of the determination system which a state constructs. There are, however, legal constraints on what the state may do with an individual who has entered to seek asylum.[12] The *pacta sunt servanda* principle[13] obliges states to implement these instruments effectively and in good faith. For effective implementation of the obligations contained in international refugee law it would appear that, at minimum, the existence of an effective determination procedure is required.[14] Although the normative framework of international law is important, it is within the determination systems of states that the 'refugee' is in practice constructed. It is well known that interpretations of the Convention differ markedly. It remains the case that protection is in practice largely determined by the approaches adopted within individual states. These more realistic approaches to refugee law have not displaced the 1951 Convention.

Regional developments

States have not agreed to alter the basic refugee definition, in the form of a multi-lateral Convention, beyond that which has been described above. The 1951 Convention definition has therefore formed the basis for subsequent state practice. While there has been some significant movement at the regional level, the definition as contained in the 1951 Convention continues to dominate state practice. In regions that have experienced the most severe cases of human displacement, the exclusive use of the 1951 Convention has proved inadequate.[15] Attempts have therefore been made to draft definitions which reflect the realities in those areas.

The OAU Convention Governing Specific Aspects of the Refugee Problem in Africa 1969[16]

In the late twentieth century, Africa, in global terms, was host to some of the largest displacements of people.[17] This was not the case

12 See Goodwin-Gill *The Refugee in International Law* (2nd edn, 1996) pp 117-204.
13 Vienna Convention on the Law of Treaties, art 26.
14 Goodwin-Gill, note 13 above, p 324.
15 See Arboleda 'Refugee Definition in Africa and Latin America: The Lessons of Pragmatism' (1991) 3 IJRL 185, 186; Alexander and Berkowitz 'Hospitality or Hostility? Refugee Law in Africa' (1998) 12 I&NLP 48.
16 1001 UNTS 45, entry into force 20 June 1974, 41 state parties.
17 See generally OAU/UNHCR, Commemorative Symposium on Refugees and the Problems of Forced Population Displacements in Africa, Addis Ababa, 8-10 September 1994, (1995) IJRL Special Issue; Melander and Nobel (eds) *African*

at the time of the drafting of the 1951 Convention. At that stage, with some exceptions, the refugee problem was viewed as a European one.[18] This was to change in the post-colonial period, as mass refugee flows gradually shifted to the developing world where they were largely to remain.[19] Although 45 African states are parties to the 1951 Convention and 1967 Protocol, due to the sheer scale of the problem in Africa definitions and approaches to refugee movements have had to be adapted.[1] The root causes are various but, nevertheless, are identifiable. Factors such as colonialism, state formation and economic underdevelopment have all contributed to the problem.[2] In the 1960s the newly independent African states discovered that mass refugee flows demanded co-operation. As indicated, the 1951 Convention definition, while of use, was widely regarded as inadequate.[3] The Organisation of African Unity (OAU) was established in 1963 and was soon called upon to address the problem.[4] In 1967 the member states organised the Conference on the Legal, Economic, and Social Aspects of the African Refugee Problem in Addis Ababa.[5] The discussions at the Conference lead to the drafting of the 1969 Convention, which came into force in 1974. The adoption of the Convention was a clear recognition of the scale of the problems which the continent faced. In a joint OAU/UNHCR Commemorative Symposium in September 1994 the importance of the Convention was reiterated by the OAU member states.[6]

Refugees and the Law (1978); Eze *Human Rights in Africa* (1984) ch 7; Zolberg 'The Refugee Crisis in the Developing World: A Close Look at Africa' in Rystad (ed) *The Uprooted: Forced Migration as an International Problem in the Post War Era* (1990) p 87.

18 See Pitterman 'A Comparative Survey of Two Decades of International Assistance to Refugees in Africa' (1984) 1 Africa Today 25.

19 The displacements caused as a result of the conflicts in the former Yugoslavia and in the former Soviet Union have been a recent notable exception to this trend.

1 See Greenfield 'The OAU and African Refugees' in El-Ayaity and Zartman (eds) *The OAU After Twenty Years* (1984) ch 11.

2 Cf Nobel 'Refugees, Law and Development in Africa' (1982) 14 Michigan Ybk Int L 255.

3 See Greenfield, note 1 above, p 210.

4 See Elias *Africa and the Development of International Law* (1988) pp 121-181; Wolfers *Politics in the OAU* (1984); Sesay et al *The OAU After Twenty Years* (1984) esp chs 1 and 5.

5 See the Document of the Conference AFR/REF/CONF/1967/No 1 ff.

6 See *The Addis Ababa Document on Refugees and forced population displacements in Africa*, Adopted by the OAU/UNHCR Symposium on Refugees and Forced Population Displacements in Africa, 8-10 September 1994, Addis Ababa, Ethiopia, reprinted in (1995) IJRL Special Issue pp 301-320; UNHCR Executive Committee *Conclusion on the Recommendations of the OAU/UNHCR Commemorative Symposium on Refugees and Forced Population Displacements in Africa* UN Doc A/AC96/839 (1994).

They recommended that states that had not done so should ratify the Convention and that those that had should implement its provisions more effectively.[7]

The 1969 Convention contains a refugee definition with two branches. Article 1(1) replicates art 1(A)(b) of the 1951 Convention, thus confirming the importance of the application of the 1951 Convention standards in Africa. The difference is to be found in art 1(2), which includes:

> '[E]very person who, owing to external aggression, occupation, foreign domination, or events seriously disturbing public order in either part or whole of his country of origin or nationality, is compelled to leave his place of habitual residence in order to seek refuge in another place outside his country of origin or nationality.'

The inclusion of this expanded notion of refugee status was essential for the vast majority of African refugees, many of whom were not protected by the 1951 Convention definition.[8] By focusing on 'events seriously disturbing public order' and other situations which could be evidenced objectively the definition represents a more realistic – in terms of the evidence on mass displacement – standard than that contained in the 1951 Convention.[9]

Although the definition is a regional one, it is important for a number of reasons. First, it has been adopted by a group of 45 states which are particularly affected by the refugee problem. Second, it has been influential in discussions of the possible expansion of the refugee definition to include more relevant considerations. The UNHCR has continually stressed its importance, acknowledging that it represents in significant respects an ideal model for the provision of international protection.[10] The UN General Assembly has also given its endorsement to the provisions of the Convention,[11] recommending that:

> 'the 1969 OAU Refugee Convention, the regional complement in Africa of the 1951 Convention . . . be applied by the United Nations and all its organs as well as by non-governmental organisations dealing with the refugee problem in Africa.'

7   Recommendation Five.
8   See Kuruk 'Refugeeism, A Dilemma in International Human Rights: Problems in the Legal Protection of Refugees in W. Africa' (1987) 1 Temple Int and Comp LJ 179.
9   See Rwelamira 'Some Reflections on the OAU Convention on Refugees: Some Pending Issues' (1983) 16 Comp and Int LJ of South Africa 155, 158; Van Westerflier 'Africa and Refugees: the OAU Convention in Theory and Practice' (1989) 2 NQHR 170, 174.
10 UNHCR *Note on International Protection* UN Doc A/AC96/830 (1994) paras 34-35.
11 UNGA Res 34/61, 29 November 1979.

The Cartagena Declaration on Refugees 1984[12]

The Cartagena Declaration is one of the most recent attempts to promote a more expansive notion of the refugee.[13] The Declaration was drafted at the Colloquium on International Protection of Refugees in Central America, Mexico and Panama: Juridical and Humanitarian Problems which was held in Mexico on 19-22 November 1984. The Declaration is not a legally binding instrument, but is representative of regional thinking and has been repeatedly endorsed by the General Assembly of the OAS.[14] Latin American states have a respected tradition of granting asylum, dating back to 1889.[15] Recent years have witnessed an upsurge in the numbers of mass displacements from El Salvador and Guatemala. Again, these have placed a strain on older conceptions of the refugee.[16] In response, the 1984 Declaration was adopted, which in addition to the definition contained in the 1951 Convention defined refugees as:

> 'persons who have fled their country because their lives, safety or freedom have been threatened by generalised violence, foreign aggression, internal conflicts, massive violation of human rights or other circumstances which have seriously disturbed public order.'[17]

As with the OAU Convention, the definition is not confined to the 'persecution standard' and includes more broadly defined internal disturbances. The expanded definition does have the benefit that, as with the OAU Convention, it accords more readily with the realities of forced migration. It recognises, for example, the fact that generalised violence and internal disturbances, rather than simply individual persecution, plays a leading role in creating displacement. Further to this, it is particularly significant for its specific reference to mass violations of human rights as a ground of refugee status.

---

12 See *Annual Report of the Inter-American Commission on Human Rights* (1984-85) OEA/SER/II 66, doc rev 1, pp 190-193.
13 See Hathaway *The Law of Refugee Status* (1991) p 19.
14 See eg OASGA Res A.AG/Res 774 (XV-0/85), 9 Dec 1985, *Inter-American Yearbook of Human Rights* (1985) 1234; OASGA Res EAG/Res 838, 15 Nov 1986, *Inter American Yearbook of Human Rights* (1986) 480.
15 See eg Montevideo Treaty on International Penal Law 1889; Arboleda (1991) 3 IJRL 185, 197.
16 See eg Hey 'Human Rights and Guatemalan Displaced Persons' (1992) 10 NQHR 461.
17 Section III(3).

Mapping international refugee law

International refugee law does not solely offer a definition of refugee. It also provides certain specific guarantees. The most important of these, the principle of *non-refoulement* is, given its centrality in refugee law, discussed in more detail below. Some of the other Convention guarantees are, however, considered here. The Convention guarantees are divided into those concerning juridical status, employment, welfare, and other administrative measures. Generally, parties to the Convention are obliged not to discriminate on the grounds of race, religion or country of origin in their application of the Convention.[18] As to the standard of treatment owed to the refugee, the general rule is that parties to the Convention must accord, at a minimum, to the refugee the same treatment that is accorded to aliens generally,[19] except where the Convention contains provisions which are more favourable.[20] The more favourable standards are most favoured nation treatment[1] and the national standard of treatment.[2]

The Convention Travel Document

Article 28 of the 1951 Convention includes provision for a Convention Travel Document (CTD) to a refugee for the purpose of travel outside the territory of the state.[3] The refugee must be lawfully staying (as opposed to being lawfully resident[4]) in the territory of the contracting state for this provision to apply.[5] The format for the CTD, and various standards attaching to the renewal and extension of the document, are contained in the Schedule to the 1951 Convention. The contracting state that issues the CTD

---

18 Article 4.
19 This is the case specifically with art 13 on movable and immovable property, art 18 on self-employment, art 19 on qualifications for liberal professions, art 21 on housing, art 22 on public education.
20 Article 7(1).
1 Article 15 on the right of association; art 17 on wage earning employment.
2 Article 14 on artistic rights and industrial property; art 16 on access to the courts; art 23 on public relief and assistance; art 24 on labour legislation and social security.
3 See Executive Committee UNHCR, Conclusion No 13 (XXIX), *Travel Documents for Refugees*.
4 There are three general standards with regard to the position of the refugee. These are: first, presence which refers to the fact of presence; second, lawful presence referring to adherence to the immigration laws of the state the refugee has entered; and, third, lawful residence which may be taken to refer to a refugee who has been granted asylum on a permanent basis.
5 Article 28(1).

must, for example, readmit the refugee to its territory at any time during the validity of the document.[6] The renewal of the document is for the authority who issued it, unless the holder has established lawful residence in another state.[7] Possession of a CTD does not entitle the holder to the diplomatic or consular protection of the issuing state, nor does it confer a right of protection on this state.[8] The CTD is purely facilitative and does not affect formal nationality.[9]

There are exceptions, for example, a CTD is not required where 'compelling reasons of national security or public order apply'. The use of 'compelling' would imply that these must be serious national security and public order implications, however, this will ultimately be an issue for the individual state.[10]

Lawful entry, unlawful entry and expulsion

Taking into account the nature of refugee movements, and the fact that the persecutor is often the state, it is logical that a refugee should not be penalised for illegal entry into an asylum state. Refugee law reflects this imperative.

> 'Article 31(1) The Contracting States shall not impose penalties, on account of their illegal entry or presence, on refugees who, *coming directly* from a territory where their life or freedom was threatened in the sense of Article 1, enter or are present in their territory without authorisation, provided they *present themselves without delay* to the authorities *and show good cause* for their illegal entry and presence.' (My emphasis.)

There are a number of points to note about this provision. First, it appears to be the case that 'penalties' refers to prosecution and imprisonment following conviction but not the more common cases of administrative detention of asylum seekers upon arrival.[11] Second, it refers to those who have come directly from a territory where their lives or freedom are threatened. Those who have travelled through a safe third country are not included. Third, although the article specifically refers to the refugee, it is inappropriate to confine this only to recognised refugees. Given the declaratory nature of refugee status, any bona fide asylum seeker should benefit from the protection which this provision offers.

---

6 Schedule, para 13(1).
7 Schedule, para 6(1).
8 Schedule, para 16.
9 Schedule, para 15.
10 See Goodwin-Gill *The Refugee in International Law* (2nd edn, 1996) pp 302-305.
11 See Goodwin-Gill, note 10 above, pp 247-248.

Article 31(2) obliges states not to apply restrictions to these refugees, but, where they do, these should only be until the status of the refugee is regularised, or until she has been admitted into another state. Thus, again, measures such as administrative detention would appear to be permitted under the terms of the 1951 Convention, at least until the refugee is recognised.

Although states possess a certain amount of discretion in the area of expulsion of aliens, international law has made substantial inroads into this, particularly in cases where an individual is likely to suffer serious violations of human rights upon her return. In refugee law, art 32 of the 1951 Convention provides:

> '(1) The Contracting States shall not expel a refugee lawfully in their territory save on grounds of national security or public order.
> (2) The expulsion of such a refugee shall only be in pursuance of decision reached in accordance with due process of law. Except where compelling reasons of national security otherwise require, the refugee shall be allowed to submit evidence to clear himself, and to appeal to and be represented for the purpose before competent authority or a person or persons specially designated by the competent authority.
> (3) The Contracting States shall allow such a refugee a reasonable period within which to seek legal admission into another country. The Contracting States reserve the right to apply during that period such internal measures as they deem necessary.'

Expulsion of refugees is thus limited substantively to cases of national security or public order. Any proposed expulsion must be in accordance with due process of law and the refugee is entitled to some form of appeal, the substance of which is for the state to decide.[12]

Refugee law provides an extensive list of protections for the refugee. The principal difficulty, again, is the inadequacy of the definition of refugee status as applied by states, which in practice excludes a large number of asylum seekers from the guarantees it offers. Most of the provisions of the 1951 Convention protect the recognised refugee only. If this status is defined narrowly to include a small, exclusive, class of persons, then the wider body of refugee law simply becomes inapplicable to a considerable number of asylum seekers.

---

12 EXCOM Conclusion No 7 (XXVIII) *Expulsion*: '(c) Recommended that, in line with art 32 of the 1951 Convention, expulsion measures against a refugee should only be taken in very exceptional cases and after due consideration of all the circumstances, including the possibility for the refugee to be admitted to a country other than his country of origin.' ICCPR art 13, see UN Human Rights Committee General Comment 13 *The Position of Aliens Under the Covenant* paras 9-10.

INTERNATIONAL HUMAN RIGHTS LAW AND COMPLEMENTARITY

Refugee law differs from other areas of human rights law in significant respects. It does not reflect the specific imperatives of human rights law, and often appears securely attached to more traditional conceptions of public international law. It can, for example, prove difficult to conceptualise refugee law in purely human rights terms. Several important human rights issues raised by forced displacement are simply not addressed in refugee law. International human rights law, however, now fills many of the glaring gaps in refugee law.[13] A full understanding of the protection of asylum seekers today requires an examination of key aspects of human rights law.

Refugee law's prohibition on return is addressed elsewhere. However, it is important here to note that the international legal prohibition on return now goes beyond the confines of refugee law. The Convention Against Torture and Other Cruel, Inhuman or Degrading Treatment or Punishment 1984 provides:

'Article 3(1) No State shall expel, return ('*refouler*') or extradite a person to another state where there are substantial grounds for believing that he would be in danger of being subjected to torture.

(2) For the purpose of determining whether there are such grounds the competent authority shall take into account all relevant considerations including; where applicable, the existence in the State concerned of a consistent pattern of gross, flagrant or mass violations of human rights.'

This protection is similar in scope to both the coverage of refugee law and the jurisprudence developed by the European Court of Human Rights under art 3 of the European Convention.[14]

The Committee against Torture (CAT) has received a number of communications from asylum seekers and adopted views on

13 See Gorlick 'The Convention and the Committee against Torture: A Complementary Protection Regime for Refugees' (1999) 11 IJRL 479; Andrysek 'Gaps in International Protection and the Potential for Redress through Individual Complaints Procedures' (1997) 9 IJRL 392.
14 See ch 5.

their complaints.[15] It is worth examining some of these cases here. Although the general human rights situation is taken into account in these cases, the most important factor is whether the individual is personally at risk if returned. The existence of mass violations of human rights is not enough in itself to succeed before the CAT. In *Tala v Sweden* the author of the communication had been refused asylum in Sweden.[16] In his communication to the CAT, he claimed that his return to Iran would violate art 3, because of his involvement with the Mujahedin, and the possibility of ill-treatment by the security service of the Revolutionary Guards. While the CAT accepted that the author had been inconsistent, it made the point that 'complete accuracy is seldom to be expected of victims of torture and that inconsistencies that exist in the author's presentation of the facts do not raise doubts about the veracity of his claims'.[17] The CAT accepted that the author was suffering from post-traumatic stress disorder, as well as medical evidence relating to scars on the author's thighs. On the general human rights situation in Iran, the CAT referred to the many violations noted in the report of the UN Human Rights Commission Special Representative on the Human Rights Situation in Iran. The CAT considered that substantial grounds did exist for believing that the author would be in danger of being subjected to torture upon return. Given that many refusals of asylum are based on credibility assessments, the approach of the CAT is significant. This does not, however, mean that the CAT accepts every inconsistency; it seems that there must be a reason, such as post-traumatic stress disorder, that can account for it.[18] In

15 See *A v The Netherlands* Comm No 91/1997; *ALN v Switzerland* Comm No 90/1997; *Abad v Spain* Comm No 59/1996; *Aemei v Switzerland* Comm No 34/1995; *Ayas v Sweden* Comm No 97/1997; *EA Switzerland* Comm No 28/1995; *El Guarti, Jilali v France* Appl No 39681/97; *Falalaflaki v Sweden* Comm No 89/1997; *GRB v Sweden* Comm No 83/1997; *Haydin v Sweden* Comm No 101/1997; *HW v Switzerland* Comm No 48/1996; *IAO v Sweden* Comm No 65/1997; *Korban v Sweden* Comm No 88/1997; *JUA v Switzerland* Comm No 100/1997; *KN v Switzerland* Comm 94/199; *Kisoki v Sweden* Comm No 41/1996; *KKH v Canada* Comm No 35/1995; *Mohammed v Greece* Comm No 40/1996; *Mutombo v Switzerland* Comm No 13/1993; *ND v France* Comm No 32/1995; *PMPK v Sweden* Comm No 30/1995; *PQL v Canada* Comm No 57/1996; *R v France* Comm No 52/1996; *RK v Canada* Comm No 42/1996; *Sarialtun, Aziz and Other v Germany* Appl No 37534/97; *Tala v Sweden* Comm No 43/1996; *Tapei Paez v Sweden* Comm No 39/1996; *VV v Canada* Comm No 47/1996; *X and Y v The Netherlands* Comm No 31/1995; *X v Canada* Comm No 26/1995; *X v Spain* Comm No 23/1995; *X v Switzerland* Comm No 27/1995; *X v The Netherlands* Comm No 36/1995; *X, Y, Z v Sweden* Comm No 61/1996.

16 Comm No 43/1996.

17 Paragraph 10.3.

18 *Aemei v Switzerland* Comm No 34/1995, para 10.4.

X v Switzerland[19] the state party's argument to the CAT was based on inconsistencies in the author's account of events. The author alleged that, while in Beirut, he clashed violently with a Sudanese militia leader who told him not to return to the country. He claimed that the Sudanese embassy was involved in attempts to kidnap him and he thus fled to Switzerland, where his claim to asylum was refused. In this instance the CAT was not convinced by the author's account of events. He had never been subject to detention or ill-treatment in Sudan. His wife, who had returned to the country, had not been subjected to harassment. He had stayed in Lebanon for two years, after the threats from the militia, and the reasons for his flight to Switzerland were not detailed enough.

In *Elmi v Australia*[20] the author was a Somali national who claimed that his forced return to Somalia would violate art 3. The state argued that the torture feared would come from Somali clans and not from any state authority. The Committee stated that the warring factions in Somalia exercised functions comparable to those normally exercised by governments. Therefore, members of the armed factions fell within the meaning of the phrase 'public officials or other persons acting in an official capacity' in art 1. Given the mass violation of human rights which had been committed in Somalia, the situation of chaos prevailing in the country, and the fact that the author belonged to a small and vulnerable clan, the state had an obligation to refrain from returning him. These are illustrative examples of the relevance of the Convention against Torture to displaced persons. They are just some of the examples of communications addressed to the Committee in this area. ➡

International human rights law contains numerous other guarantees which are applicable to the asylum seeker. With reference to the obligations contained in the 'international bill of rights', *everyone* has, for example, the right to work,[1] the right to social security,[2] the right to an adequate standard of living,[3] and the right to an education.[4] With respect to civil and political rights *everyone* possesses, inter alia, the right to life,[5] equality before the law,[6] freedom of thought, conscience and religion,[7] and freedom of

19 Comm No 27/1995.
20 [1999] INLR 341.
 1 ICESCR 1966, art 6.
 2 ICESCR 1966, art 9.
 3 ICESCR 1966, art 11.
 4 ICESCR 1966, art 13.
 5 ICCPR 1966, art 6.
 6 ICCPR 1966, art 14.
 7 ICCPR 1966, art 18.

expression.[8] The UN Human Rights Committee has stated that deportation or extradition may infringe the ICCPR.[9] Further to this state parties to the CERD 1966 are obliged to ensure, again to everyone within their jurisdiction, effective protection and remedies against any acts of racial discrimination.[10]

Human rights law provides acknowledgment of the fact that while all individuals possess human rights, there is need for special provisions which address some individual's rights more specifically. This is, for example, true of women's rights and children's rights. While refugee law is applicable to everyone, it is also recognised that special care needs to be taken by states when dealing with applications made by groups such as children. The UN Convention on the Rights of the Child 1989[11] has recognised the special hardships which refugee children face. It provides:

> 'Article 22(1) State Parties shall take appropriate measures to ensure that a child who is seeking refugee status or who is considered a refugee . . . shall whether unaccompanied or accompanied by his or her parents or any other person, receive appropriate protection and humanitarian assistance in the enjoyment of the applicable rights set forth in this convention and in other human rights or humanitarian instruments to which the said States are Parties.'

Especially important for the child refugee is that those children who are deprived of a family permanently are entitled to special protection and assistance.[12] The Convention provides in this regard:

> 'Article 20(3) When considering solutions, due regard shall be paid to the desirability of continuity in a child's upbringing and to the child's ethnic, religious, cultural and linguistic background.'

The provisions of the Convention provide recognition of the fact that the needs of child refugees and asylum seekers may differ from those of adults and that due attention must be paid by states to the distinction.

NON-REFOULEMENT

> 'Article 33(1) No Contracting State shall *expel or return (refouler) a refugee in any manner whatsoever* to the frontiers of territories where his life or

---

8   ICCPR 1966, art 19.
9   See *Ng v Canada*, Communication No 469/1991. Cf *Kindler v Canada* Comm No 470/1991; *Cox v Canada* Communication No 593/1993.
10 Article 6.
11 UNGA A/RES/44/25, 5 December 1989 Annex, 28 ILM 1448 (1989); Cohen 'The UN Convention on the Rights of the Child: Implications for Change in the Care and Protection of Refugee Children' (1991) 3 IJRL 675.
12 Article 20.

freedom would be threatened on account of his race, religion, nationality, membership in a particular social group or political opinion.' (My emphasis.) Despite the much heralded erosion of state sovereignty, it has proved difficult to make inroads into the state's right to admit individuals onto its territory. Where progress has been made in the protection of the displaced is in the development of limitations on the right of the state to return protection seekers. Although states have been extremely reluctant to endorse formally the right to asylum, they are rather more open to measures which prohibit return in prescribed circumstances. One of the more significant achievements in international human rights law generally in recent times has been the restriction of state discretion, in certain instances, with respect to the expulsion of aliens. This is evident in the jurisprudence of the European Convention on Human Rights and such other human rights instruments as the Convention Against Torture and Inhuman and Degrading Treatment or Punishment 1984. Refugee law provides specific legal protection against return. Article 33 of the 1951 Convention contains the obligation which is widely considered, correctly, to be the cornerstone of modern international refugee law.[13] As other aspects

---

13 See eg UNHCR *Note on International Protection* UN Doc A/AC96/830 (1994); UNHCR *Note on International Protection* UN Doc A/AC96/815 (1993) p 3; UNHCR *Sub-Committee of the Whole on International Protection* UN Doc A/AC/96/819 (1993) p 2; EXCOM Conclusion No 6 (XXVIII) *Non-Refoulement* '(c) Reaffirms the fundamental importance of the observance of the principle of *non-refoulement* – both at the border and within the territory of a state - of persons who may be subjected to persecution if returned to their country of origin irrespective of whether or not they have been formally recognised as refugees'. See Stenberg *Non-Expulsion and Non-Refoulement: The Prohibition Against Removal of Refugees with Special Reference to the 1951 Convention* (1991) p 99; Feliciano 'The Principle of *Non-Refoulement*: A Note on International Legal Protection of Refugees and Displaced Persons' (1982) 57 Phillipine LJ 598; Goodwin-Gill '*Non-Refoulement* and the New Asylum-Seekers' in Martin *The New Asylum Seekers: Refugee Law in the 1980's* (1988) p 103; Grahl-Madsen *Territorial Asylum* (1980) p 74 ff; Henckaert 'The Current Status and Content of the Prohibition of Mass Expulsions of Aliens' (1994) 15 Human Rights LJ 301, esp 315 ff. There is widespread support for the concept in the resolutions of the UN General Assembly which address the plight of refugees: see eg UNGA 1959 (XVIII), 12 December 1963; UNGA Res 2399 (XXIII), 6 December 1968; UNGA Res 32/67, 8 December 1977; UNGA 33/26, 29 November 1978; UNGA 34/60, 29 November 1979; UNGA 35/41, 25 November 1980; UNGA Res 36/125, 14 December 1981; UNGA Res 38/121, 16 December 1983; UNGA Res 39/140, 14 December 1984; UNGA Res 40/118, 13 December 1985; UNGA Res 41/124, 4 December 1986; UNGA Res 42/109, 7 December 1987; UNGA Res 44/137, 15 December 1989; UNGA Res 45/140, 14 December 1990; UNGA Res 46/106, 16 December 1991; UNGA Res 47/105, 16 December 1992; UNGA Res 48/116, 20 December 1993. These resolutions were adopted without a vote. The principle has also been repeated in certain regional instruments eg, the American Convention on Human Rights 1969, art 22(8); Council of Europe, Resolution on Asylum to Persons in Danger of Persecution 1967, Res (67) 14.

of international refugee law, such as the definition of refugee status, have become inadequate to address the modern problems involved in forced migration, the obligation of *non-refoulement* has increasingly been relied upon to justify the continuing relevance of this body of law.[14]

The idea that an individual should not be returned to a state where she would be in danger of suffering some form of severe ill-treatment gained prominence in the late-nineteenth century, and was reflected primarily in the development of the political offence exception in extradition law. This trend, which evidenced states' unwillingness to become indirectly parties to persecution carried out by other states, or, as is often argued, their unwillingness to become involved in the political disputes of other states, had clear implications for political refugees seeking asylum. The importance of the development of a norm of non-return for refugee law was shown in the inclusion of the concept in the 1933 Convention. It was to receive further elaboration in the 1946 Constitution of the IRO, and subsequent inclusion in the 1951 Convention.

The prohibition upon expulsion and return contained in art 33 is of broader scope than that of art 32, discussed above, which prohibits the expulsion of those recognised refugees lawfully in the receiving state. The use of the words 'no contracting state' in combination with the fact that this is one of the provisions in the Convention from which no reservations are permitted[15] is evidence of its cogency. As the provision does not stipulate that the refugee be lawfully present in the state (as art 32, for example, does), the refugee may have entered the territory of the state illegally and still benefit from the protection it offers. Additional evidence for this may be gathered from elsewhere in the Convention, in particular from the provisions of art 31, discussed above. The intention behind art 31 clearly is that illegal entry should not have the effect of prejudicing the refugee's claim to recognition. The focus of the obligation of *non-refoulement*, however, is on the avoidance of the return of a refugee by a state *in any manner whatsoever*. It is apparent that it is not how this is achieved that raises the question of responsibility, but the act of return itself, ie placing the refugee in the position from which she fled. The obligation is therefore essentially negative, in that the state is prohibited from returning

---

14 Sohn and Buergenthal (eds) *The Movement of Persons Across Borders* (1992) p 123. In their statement of the governing rules relating to the movement of persons they include, as part of the principle of *non-refoulement*, the following: 'Persons invoking the rule of *non-refoulement* are entitled to temporary refuge and humane treatment pending a determination of their claim.'

15 Article 42(1).

the individual to an unsafe state, no matter what her immigration status in the host state happens to be.

Problems of interpretation have, however, arisen over whether the refugee should be recognised as such by the state before the obligation arises.[16] The UNHCR has stated that it:

'(a) Reaffirms the fundamental importance of the observance of the principle of *non-refoulement* both at the border and within the territory of a state, of persons who may be subjected to persecution if returned to their country of origin *irrespective of whether or not they have been formally recognised as refugees.*'[17] (My emphasis.)

The UNHCR argues that the *fact* of physical presence should be decisive and not formal recognition for the observance of the principle. The willingness to accept refugee status as declaratory is viewed as important by the UNHCR because of the essential focus of art 33 on non-return and not the manner of entry or presence. This position accords with a modern approach to refugee law. Nevertheless, states have shown some reluctance to accept anything which might imply for them a positive obligation of admission. The exact scope of the term return (*refouler*) has therefore been contested.[18]

Some clarification of the position is required. The French word *refouler* means to 'to drive back or repel'.[19] As stated, the principal difficulty which arises is the relationship of the obligation of non-return to the issue of non-rejection at the frontier and states' admission policies. States, it has been noted, have in customary international law the authority to decide who may enter their territory, subject to their other international obligations. Application of the principle of *non-refoulement* to all those at the frontier of state territory, who claim to be refugees, poses legal as well as practical difficulties in this regard. Some of the states involved in drafting the 1951 Convention expressed their deep concern at the possible implications for their immigration policies of liberal application of the obligation.[20] They were very aware of the potential disruptive impact of mass influxes of refugees. It was

---

16 Cf Goodwin-Gill *The Refugee in International Law* (2nd edn, 1996) p 121, he states that in principle it should not be predicated upon formal recognition.
17 EXCOM Conclusion No 6 *Non-Refoulement* (1977).
18 Cf Hailbronner 'Non-Refoulement' and "Humanitarian Refugees": Customary International Law or Wishful Legal Thinking' (1986) 26 Virginia J Int L 857, p 861. He states that the exact scope of art 33 of the Convention is unclear.
19 *Dictionaire Larousse* 631 (1981).
20 UN Doc A/CONF2/SR16, p 11 Von Boetzeler (Netherlands); UN Doc A/CONF2/SR16, p 11, Theodolis (Italy).

stated by some representatives that art 33 was not, in their opinion, applicable to large groups of refugees seeking access to state territory.[1] In this interpretation the refugee must, first, be granted permission to enter the state and only after this initial grant of admission may she evoke the protection of art 33. There have been differing doctrinal views expressed, which either contest that it should apply from the moment the refugee comes into contact with the territorial jurisdiction of the state, and that it logically should entail some form of temporary refuge, and those who state that it is only applicable when the refugee has been formally granted entry to the state territory.[2] Within the debate there is an acknowledgment that the obligation does have implications for immigration policy, although some have seen attempts to link the concept with notions of temporary refuge as a bid to circumvent the limitations of refugee law.[3] The basic tension underlying the problems here is that of the conflict between the right of the refugee not to be *refouled* and the right of the state to authorise admission onto its territory. This tension becomes most acute for states in situations of mass influx of refugees. Nevertheless, it is asserted here that the focus of the Convention obligation is upon the prohibition of the act of return itself. This is evident in the language of art 33(1), particularly in the use of the phrase 'in any manner whatsoever'. The failure to permit access to an asylum determination procedure and subsequent return is one 'manner' in which this provision may be violated. The state practice reveals that states, as a general rule, do not return asylum seekers who are physically present on their territory to unsafe countries without first giving some consideration to their claim to refugee status. Failure to consider the individual's claim to refugee status would mean that no authoritative assessment is available of whether the obligation in art 33 is likely to be violated by the state.[4]

The UNHCR, acknowledging the potential consequences of the obligation, and its importance in the protection of refugees, has consistently stated that a proper interpretation of the obligation of *non-refoulement* implies that the refugee should be admitted to state territory, and from this premise it insists that it is closely

1   Theodolis, see note 20 above.
2   See Aga Khan 'Legal Problems Relating to Refugees and Displaced Persons' (1976) 149 Hague Recueil 287.
3   See Hailbronner (1986) 26 Virginia J Int L 857.
4   See Marx '*Non-Refoulement*, Access to Procedures and Responsibility for Determining Asylum Claims' (1995) 7 IJRL 383.

connected with asylum.[5] The UNHCR's position is that if the obligation is to be effective in practice, then it must oblige states to grant some form of admission, no matter how temporary. This is undoubtedly the better interpretation of art 33, if the concern is to use the 1951 Convention as an instrument which responds to the evolving needs of refugees. In this conception the obligation of non-return does not oblige the state to offer a particular form of protection, but does imply that the state grant an asylum seeker, at minimum, temporary protection until her asylum application has been assessed. The adoption of the above interpretation of the provision would mean that the state is required to permit an asylum applicant to make a claim where no safe third country exists. Further to this, the state is required to offer the individual some form of temporary protection while this process is an ongoing one. One may therefore see how closely *non-refoulement* is linked to the right to seek asylum, discussed below.

There is another aspect of the language of art 33 that has caused some debate. It is noticeable that it contains the phrase a person whose 'life or freedom is threatened', rather than the 'well-founded fear of persecution' standard mentioned in art 1. The question arises as to whether there is a distinction between refugee status and the obligation of *non-refoulement*. Does, for example, art 33 posit a higher standard in relation to the prohibition on return than that necessary to demonstrate refugee status in art 1? Could a Convention refugee still be returned to her state of origin where it could be shown that her life or freedom was not threatened? This would be quite a bizarre interpretation of the Convention. Although some states, for example the US, draw a distinction in practice between the language of art 1 and art 33, there seems little merit in relying upon such a separation. Further to this, an examination of the *travaux* reveals that the drafters wished simply to emphasise the centrality of the prohibition on return, rather than create a separate test for instances of possible return. Nevertheless, there is clearly room for some confusion in the language adopted in this provision.

It would be natural to assume that the centrality of the obligation to refugee law would mean that there would be no exceptions to the rule. This is not the case. States were not prepared at the time to accept an unlimited obligation in this area.

'Article 33(2) The benefit of the present provision may not, however, be claimed by a refugee whom there are reasonable grounds for regarding as a danger to the security of the country in which he is, or who, having been

5 UN Doc A/AC96/815 (1993).

convicted by final judgement of a particularly serious crime, constitutes a danger to the community of that country.'

It is interesting to note that the original draft of the article contained no exceptions; art 33(2) was only added by the UK and French representatives at the Conference of Plenipotentiaries.[6] The reason was the apparent change of circumstances, relating to the cold war politics of the time, between the drafting of the Convention and the Conference, reflecting the fears of states concerning infiltration by foreign powers.[7]

THE RIGHT TO SEEK ASYLUM

In the previous section the relationship between the principle of *non-refoulement* and the right to seek asylum was discussed. Here the intention is to focus more closely on the concept of the right to seek asylum. An attempt will be made to clarify the precise status of this right and the resultant implications for the asylum seeker. A number of matters may be raised at this introductory stage, none of which is more apposite than whether this 'right' may be said to add anything to the established legal guarantees in international refugee law. In fleeing her state of origin the refugee requires admission to another state and safety from return.[8] Once she is present in the state, this form of protection is guaranteed by the principle of *non-refoulement*. The act of providing refuge is usually referred to as asylum, although each state possesses distinct mechanisms for the formal legal grant of asylum. The principle of *non-refoulement* is thus closely linked with the concept of asylum. The law of asylum, however, tends to fill the 'gaps' in the legal regime of a state by declaring the conditions under which a formal grant will be made and its precise nature and scope.

Asylum, granted by a state on its territory, has been traditionally one of the most fundamental aspects of refugee protection.[9] Both concepts, ie refugee status and asylum, are closely linked in practice, if somewhat distinct in legal theory.[10] There is much confusion about the concept of asylum. Many continue to regard refugee

6 UN Doc A/CONF2/SR16 p 7.
7 UN Doc A/CONF2/SR16.
8 See EXCOM Conclusion No 5 (XXVIII) *Asylum* (1977).
9 UN Doc A/AC96/815 (1993) p 4; UN Doc A/AC96/799 (1992), pp 5-7. See Sinha *Asylum and International Law* (1971); Grahl-Madsen *The Status of the Refugee in International Law: Asylum*, vol 2 (1972); Grahl-Madsen *Territorial Asylum* (1976); Garcia-Mora *International Law and Asylum as Human Right* (1956); Weis 'Territorial Asylum' (1966) 6 Indian J Int L 173.
10 UNHCR *Note on International Protection* UN Doc A/AC96/728 (1989).

status and asylum as synonymous when they are not. Recognition as a refugee within a state does not automatically mean an entitlement to asylum, although this does happen in practice.

As was shown above, one of the basic requirements for recognition as a refugee is that the individual be outside her state of origin. Deciphering the exact legal status of the right to asylum, and whether it may be referred to as a right of the individual, is therefore highly important for the refugee. Despite the manifest significance of this form of protection, asylum is not addressed directly in the 1951 Convention, although it is referred to in both the Final Act of the Conference and the Preamble.[11] The Final Act of the UN Conference of Plenipotentiaries requests that states:

> '[C]ontinue to receive refugees in their territories and that they act in concert in a true spirit of international co-operation in order that these refugees may find asylum and the possibility of resettlement.'

Thus, while the 1951 Convention defines 'refugee', it does not specify any obligation for the state to grant asylum to an individual recognised by a state as such.

The institution of asylum, as a moral and legal concept, has functioned for a considerable period, dating from the existence of Greek and Roman law.[12] In these differing ages the term applied to a variety of practices, but the core of the concept has always been some form of internal or external sanctuary. In the eighteenth and nineteenth centuries asylum was increasingly used to denote the act of a state in refusing extradition in cases where the individual was judged to have committed a political offence.[13] This act was, in traditional doctrine, regarded as a consequence of territorial sovereignty, ie the exclusive right of states not to extradite.[14] Asylum was thus often described solely with reference to the political offender, ie the individual dissident. While this conception of asylum has remained, and indeed flourished during the cold war, the term has also become linked with the protection offered by a state within its territory to refugees, ie those who fulfil the requirements of the 1951 Convention and other 'humanitarian refugees'. Therefore, asylum may arise in two distinct circumstances: first, where a state refuses to extradite an individual; and, second, where the state grants an individual asylum applicant

---

11 Cf Vierdag '"Asylum" and "Refugee" in International Law' (1977) 24 NILR 287.
12 See Garcia-Mora, note 9 above. Cf De Vattel *The Law of Nations, or, The Principles of Natural Law* vol iii (1964) paras 229-230.
13 See Grahl-Madsen, note 9 above, pp 17-18.
14 See Krenz 'The Refugee as Subject of International Law' (1966) 15 ICLQ 90, 91.

refugee status or some other form of humanitarian status. The reason underlying the association of asylum with refugees is therefore not difficult to grasp. As was mentioned previously, 'alienage' is central to refugee status. The requirement of 'alienage' demands that the individual be outside her state of origin. The need for surrogate protection thus arises and, if given, is often granted in the form of territorial asylum. Where the situation of the political offender and the refugee may, however, (substantially) differ is in terms of numbers. Refugee movements, on the whole, tend to be mass migrations. This is not the case with the lone political offender seeking to avoid extradition. The individualistic approach to asylum derived from this association with the political offender, while appropriate when discussing the individual refugee seeking asylum, has filtered through to almost all deliberations upon refugee protection, often when its application in these terms is impractical. This helps to explain some of the confusions which arise in debates and also perhaps why states have been so reluctant to accept binding obligations in this area.

Law and 'strangers at the gate'

The main reason why it has proved to be so difficult to advance a deontological position on refugee flows is the inescapable connection to immigration control. No matter how often the distinction between asylum and immigration is asserted, it has been difficult to retain the separation in practice. One criticism voiced of asylum policy is that it has tended to be strongly influenced by foreign policy considerations. Asylum is inexorably connected to the state's power over admission in international law. In customary international law, states possess a large measure of discretion on the admission of aliens.[15] As a general rule an alien may not assert any right of entry to a state in international law. Although states have refused to permit any erosion of this basic principle, as with other powers of the state, the discretion is ultimately shaped by international law. This last point is especially significant if the international legal position of the principle of *non-refoulement* is considered. In practice, the traditional propositions, while retaining much of their validity, can at times overstate the extent to which states are free to act in this area of law and policy.

---

15 Eg *Balalas and Balala v Republic of Cyprus* 86 ILR (1987) 126. Cf Nafziger 'The General Admission of Aliens in International Law' (1983) 77 Am J Int L 804.

The deference shown to state discretion in this area is evident in numerous judicial decisions.[16] The right of the state to regulate admission onto its territory has been repeatedly linked by the judiciary in states to the independence of the state and territorial jurisdiction.[17] The standard claim is that this is an area where the executive should possess a large measure of discretion.[18] The politically contentious nature of immigration and asylum has led to some judicial reluctance to interfere with executive decisions in national courts.[19] Asylum law, because of traditional links with foreign policy, is therefore always open to politically pragmatic policy considerations which undermine the integrity of the legal regime.

Defining asylum

There is no universally accepted definition of asylum, in terms of the standards of protection or the length of any grant. This is the inevitable result of a lack of international regulation. Unlike the concept of refugee, asylum has not been defined in an international instrument. Although the EU is now attempting to do something to address the problems that can arise as a result of this, states still tend to apply diverging criteria for the grant of asylum. As regards a working definition of the concept (both territorial and diplomatic), the following, drafted by the Institute of International Law, is usually accepted as an appropriate starting point:

> 'Asylum is the protection which a state grants on its territory or in some other place under the control of its organs to a person who comes to seek it.'[1]

For the purposes of refugee protection, the UNHCR has defined it as the sum total of protection offered by a state on its territory in the exercise of its sovereignty.[2] In its core sense the UNHCR

---

16 *Nishimura Ekiu v US* 142 US 651 (1891); *Vaaro v R* (1933) SCR 36 (Lamount J); *Re Janocka* (1932) 3 WWR 29, 1 DLR 123 (CA).
17 *Chae Chan Ping v US* 130 US 581 (1889) 630-34. *US ex rel Knauff v Shaughnessy* 338 US 537, 70 SCT 309, 94 L Ed 317 (1980): '[T]he exclusion of aliens is a fundamental act of sovereignty. The right to do so stems not alone from legislative power but is inherent in the executive power to control the foreign affairs of the nation.' The court classified the admission of aliens as a privilege and not as a right. *Kleindienst v Mandel* 408 US 753 (1972); *Harisiades v Shaughnessy* 342 US 580 (1952); *Carlson v Landon* 342 US 524 (1952); *US ex rel Turner v Williams* 194 US 279 (1904).
18 *Fong Yue Ting v US* 149 US 698 (1893).
19 Eg *US ex rel Leong Choy Moon v Shaughnessy* 21 ILR (1954) 225.
1 Institute of International Law 1950 Bath Session 1 Annuaire (1950) 167 art 1.
2 Eg UN Doc A/AC96/750 (1990) p 4.

regards asylum as including admission to safety in another country, security against *refoulement* and respect for basic human rights.[3] These definitions are helpful because they provide insight into the possible substance of a core conception of asylum detached from its differing applications in states. The lack of consensus on its precise scope has caused problems. The most persistent difficulty has been deciding on the exact limits of the term. There is a tendency, for example, to define asylum as referring to permanent settlement in the host state. In practice, however, states often grant some form of refuge on a provisional basis, leading to the development of concepts such as temporary refuge or protection.[4] It is unclear whether the term 'asylum' is intended to include temporary as well as permanent protection, and this has resulted in understandable confusion.

The 'right' to seek asylum: resistance to international regulation

While the state has the discretion in international law to regulate admission onto its territory, in conformity with its international legal obligations, it has been on occasions claimed that the individual enjoys a right to asylum.[5] This assertion is largely inspired by state practice in relation to the non-extradition of political offenders and the post-1945 'revolution'[6] in international law, particularly with regard to human rights. Despite this increased recognition of the international legality of human rights, there does not exist adequate support for the proposition that the *grant* of asylum is the right of the individual in international law. States do in fact grant asylum regularly, especially to those who they recognise as refugees under the 1951 Convention, but in doing so they emphasise that this is done as a state right and not that of an individual.[8] Asylum, viewed in this way, tends to be conceived as a humanitarian act exercised by a state, rather than an act motivated by a legal duty imposed by the

---

3   UN Doc A/AC96/815 (1993) p 4.
4   UN Doc A/AC96/815 (1993) p 11.
5   See eg UN Doc A/C3/285. The original draft of art 14 UDHR 1948. Cf Nayar 'The Right of Asylum in International Law: Its Status and Prospects' (1972) 17 St Louis Univ LJ 17, 27.
6   See McGoldrick *The Human Rights Committee: Its Role in the Development of the International Covenant on Civil and Political Rights* (1991) p 3.
7   Although several states have included a right to asylum in their constitutions.
8   Cf Whiteman *Digest* (1963) 681; De Visscher *Theory and Reality in Public International Law* (1957) pp 182-183.

existence of an individual legal right to be granted asylum. If any right does exist for the individual it is the right to *seek* asylum.[9]

The following analysis of the post-1945 legal developments is an attempt to chart the various efforts made to draft an instrument that would include a right to asylum and the present status of this right. In addition, it provides an explanation for recent developments, discussed below, which have moved away from regarding asylum as the exclusive solution or human rights issue involved in the refugee problem, towards acknowledging the root causes of displacement.

Universal Declaration of Human Rights 1948, art 14

As is well documented, the drafting of the Universal Declaration of Human Rights 1948 (UDHR) was inspired by the post-1945 concern with the promotion of human rights, reflected prior to this in provisions of the UN Charter. The idea that asylum could be conceptualised as a international legal human right was first promulgated in this period. Article 14 UDHR states:

'(1) Everyone has the right to seek and enjoy in other countries asylum from persecution.
(2) This right may not be invoked in the case of prosecutions genuinely arising from non-political crimes or from acts contrary to the purposes and principles of the UN.'

The UDHR was intended by its drafters as a non-binding instrument. As Lauterpacht has said, all the delegates who had an opportunity to express themselves stressed the absence of any element of legal obligation.[10] Its importance rests in its recognition of inalienable rights and the inspiration it provided for states drafting their own constitutions and for further developments in human rights law.[11] The fact that some of the rights of the individual contained in the Declaration are now a part of customary

---

9 The development of notions of 'preventative protection' have brought the right to *seek* asylum to the fore. By attempting to encourage the displaced to remain as close to their state of origin as possible, and in some cases in it, organisations such as the UNHCR run the risk of denying this right. See Frelick "Preventative Protection" and the Right to Seek Asylum: A Preliminary Look at Bosnia and Croatia' (1992) 4 IJRL 441; Barutciski 'The Reinforcement of Non-Admission Policies and the Subversion of UNHCR: Displacement and Internal Assistance in Bosnia Herzegovina' (1996) 8 IJRL 49.

10 Lauterpacht *Human Rights and International Law* (1968) p 365; Prakash *An Antropocentric View of Asylum in International Law* (1962) pp 91-92.

11 See Garcia-Mora *International Law and Asylum as Human Right* (1956) p 145.

international law is not relevant to considerations of a right to be granted asylum, which has not developed in this regard.

The original draft of art 14 contained a differing wording, which spoke of the right to seek and be *granted* asylum in other countries.[12] This wording, if included in the final version, would obviously have had different implications. It is testimony to the reluctance of states then to commit formally and substantively to this right. An amendment was proposed by the UK representative who wished to see the word 'granted' replaced with 'enjoy'.[13] The UK representative argued (characteristically given the dominance of this thinking among states in the subsequent Conference which drafted the 1951 Convention) that an individual right to asylum would not be acceptable due to the unpredictable consequences of such an obligation.[14] The UK would continue to grant asylum, however, it did not fall under any international legal obligation to do so.[15] This has been the approach consistently taken by states. They will frequently offer asylum and other forms of protection (often in fact on a liberal basis) but this is not viewed as the consequence of a legal right to asylum.[16] While this may, on occasion, lead states to pursue a progressive approach to human displacement, it is too often the case that it results in law and policy oriented by short term and illiberal goals.

The individual thus has the 'right' to *seek* asylum, with no corresponding duty on the part of the state to grant it. If one considers the theory that there are no rights without duties one may legitimately wonder what exactly this right amounts to. Additionally, the term 'enjoy' reflects the characterisation of the right in the UDHR as one wholly dependent on state acceptance.

UN Declaration on Territorial Asylum 1967

The Declaration on Territorial Asylum was adopted unanimously by the UN General Assembly in December 1967.[17] Article 1 of the Declaration states:

> '(1) Asylum *granted by a state, in the exercise of its sovereignty*, to persons entitled to invoke Article 14 of the Universal Declaration of Human Rights, including persons struggling against colonialism, shall be respected by other states.' (My emphasis.)

12 UN Doc A/C3/285; YUN (1947) pp 575-576.
13 See note 12 above.
14 UN Doc A/C3/SR121 pp 4-6.
15 UN Doc A/C3/SR121 p 329.
16 See Krenz (1966) 15 ICLQ 90, 108.
17 UNGA Res 2312 (XXII), 14 December 1967.

Asylum is here classified, again, as a right of the state, which it is entitled to grant at its discretion as a direct corollary of its sovereignty. The language used is weaker than that of the UDHR, making no mention of asylum as an individual right, and specifically recognising that the granting of asylum is a matter solely for the state to decide. Article 1(3) of the Declaration gives further confirmation by stating that the grounds for the grant of asylum again rest with the individual state. The text of the Declaration is a plain demonstration that states are not willing to accept the notion that an individual has a right to be granted asylum. She may have a right to seek, or to invoke, protection but it is the state which is the ultimate arbiter of who will be granted it.

Draft Convention on Territorial Asylum 1977[18]

The adoption of a Declaration by the UN General Assembly is often a preliminary step preceding attempts to draft a Convention on the subject. The Declaration on Territorial Asylum set in motion this process, which was ultimately to prove unsuccessful.[19] The Commission on Human Rights, the body which drafted the 1967 Declaration, suggested that asylum should be included in the 'international bill of rights' or else form the basis of a separate Convention. Discussions between states before the adoption of the Declaration show the expectation that the process would result in the drafting of a Convention. There was no agreement on its inclusion in the ICCPR, thus prompting attempts by other bodies to agree on a draft instrument.

In 1971 the European Office of the Carnegie Endowment for International Peace at Geneva, along with the UNHCR, convened a Conference on the issue of territorial asylum. At this meeting, and others over a period of two years, a Convention was drafted. In 1972 the Third Committee of the UN General Assembly discussed the draft.[20] The Third Committee requested the High Commissioner to pursue his activities on the issue further.[1] In 1974 the President of the General Assembly established a Group

---

18 See generally Plender 'Admission of Refugees: Draft Convention on Territorial Asylum' (1977) 15 San Diego LR 45.
19 See the Report of the UN Conference on Territorial Asylum UN Doc A/CONF78/12, 21 April 1977. See Weis 'The Draft Convention on Territorial Asylum' (1979) 50 British Ybk Int L 176; Lentini 'The Definition of Refugee in International Law: Proposals for the Future' (1985) 5 Boston College Third World LJ 183, 185.
20 YUN (1972) p 407.
1 YUN (1973) p 492.

of Experts on Territorial Asylum to work on finalising a draft. The Group of Experts subsequently submitted a report to the General Assembly, which in 1975 requested the Secretary-General to convene a Conference on Territorial Asylum.[2] Only a few articles of the draft Convention were considered by the Committee of the Whole established by the 1977 Conference.[3] The Conference was marked by much disagreement and eventually ran out of time. It is nevertheless worth briefly examining the draft articles which were discussed.

The drafting committee of the Conference proposed the following art 1 on the granting of asylum:

> 'Each Contracting State, *acting in the exercise of its sovereign rights, shall endeavour in a humanitarian spirit to grant asylum in its territory* to any person eligible for the benefits of this convention.
>
> Asylum should not be refused by a Contracting State solely on the grounds that it could be sought from another state. However, where it appears that a person requesting asylum from a Contracting State already has a connection or close links with another state, the Contracting State may, if it appears fair and reasonable require him to request asylum from that state.'[4] (My emphasis.)

The text mirrors the 1967 Declaration's rejection of any notion of an individual right to be granted asylum, again reinforcing the fact that it is a state right.[5] The grant of asylum envisaged by the draft text would be a humanitarian imperative which lacked legal enforcement. Due to disagreement among the states present, the Conference did not complete its work within the allocated time.[6] Although in the recommendation to the General Assembly the possibility of reconvening the Conference is mentioned, there is little likelihood of this happening. Most of the developed states were not in favour of its resumption. The outcome of the Conference is an example, if one is needed, of the contentious nature of this area and, more importantly, of the resistance among states to the assumption of an international legal obligation.

A future for asylum?

For a concept that is a constant source of debate within and between states in modern times, asylum remains elusive. There is

---

2 UNGA Res 3456 (XXX), 9 Dec 1975.
3 UN Conference on Territorial Asylum, 10 January – 4 February 1977, Geneva, A/CONF78/DC/R1 Annex II p 1.
4 A/CONF78/DC/R1 Annex II p 1.
5 See Grahl-Madsen *Territorial Asylum* (1976) p 63.
6 Cf Goodwin-Gill *The Refugee in International Law* (2nd edn, 1996) pp 181-182.

a tendency to assume that its meaning is self-evident. This may well be the case within individual states, which have placed a quite specific meaning on it, but it is not true generally. To equate asylum with permanent settlement is misplaced. However, this is precisely what has been happening in recent times. If asylum equals permanent settlement, it then becomes possible to talk of other forms of less secure protection. What this means in practice is that a hierarchy of protection emerges, with those who can bring their claims successfully within the 1951 Convention being granted superior forms of protection.

It is evident from the above description of the attempts to regulate asylum at the international level, that the individual does not possess a right to be granted asylum in international law. The right to *grant* asylum belongs to the state.[7] The acceptance of an individual right is seen by states as having highly unpredictable consequences and would be such a derogation from certain aspects of territorial sovereignty that they have generally found it unacceptable. This remains true, even though today substantial inroads have been made into traditional conceptions of statehood. The reasons for this are well documented. States, being fearful of mass migrations which threaten their internal order, tend to be cautious in areas such as this where they might be legally bound unpredictably into the future. As the EU member states have discovered, however, the solution does not necessarily lie in less co-operation, but may reside in more, targeted specifically towards the development of rules on international burden-sharing. States may be more willing to grant protection where there is a strong international or regional system of regulation which demonstrates a willingness to support states which have become especially burdened.

This aside, does the individual therefore possess no rights when it comes to the question of receiving asylum? As indicated, the right that the individual does possess is the right to *seek* asylum. This has, as noted above, been affirmed in the Vienna Declaration adopted at the World Conference on Human Rights.[8] This right

---

7   Eg *Public Prosecutor v Franz B* 48 ILR (1967) 155; *Political Asylum Case* 72 ILR (1969) 582. This position would appear to be confirmed in the regional instruments which mention asylum: see African Convention on Human Rights and Peoples' Rights 1981 'art 12(3) Every individual shall have the right, when persecuted, to seek and obtain asylum in other countries in accordance with the law of those countries and international conventions'; Amercian Convention on Human Rights 1969, art 22 '(7) Every person has the right to seek and be granted asylum in a foreign territory, in accordance with the legislation of the state and international conventions, in the event he is being pursued for political offences or related common crimes.'

8   UN Doc A/CONF 157/23 para 23.

to seek, as opposed to be granted, asylum is in fact rather problematic, as it does not imply any duty on the part of the state. Taken on its own, it is justifiable to question the efficacy of any such right when there is no corresponding duty in existence. Nevertheless, if this fragile right is combined with the obligation of *non-refoulement*, one may restate the position that the asylum seeker should at a minimum have her application subjected to examination, ie be physically able to seek asylum and therefore given some form of admission, no matter how temporary. Thus, while the individual does not possess the right to be granted asylum (this will occur usually in cases where she is a Convention refugee and has come directly to the host state), she may claim to be a refugee, and therefore benefit from the protection against return, which has implications for admission or protection pending consideration. The limitation within the obligation of *non-refoulement* must here be reiterated, ie the guarantee is against return to the state where the individual fears a threat to her life or liberty therefore a state may refuse asylum or protection on the ground that she may return to a 'safe state'.

THE PRAGMATICS OF SANCTUARY: THE CASE OF TEMPORARY PROTECTION

It has been argued that the 1951 Convention regime is in fact founded on the notion of temporary protection and that the attachment to permanent settlement is misconceived.[9] This may surprise some, but can be easily supported with reference to the text of the 1951 Convention. The reason why the hierarchy of protection has emerged is discussed above. As asylum was constructed as a route to permanent settlement, so other, less secure, forms of protection were conceived to deal with those who were claimed not to be Convention refugees. As asylum, refugee status and integration became entangled, so temporary forms of protection were developed to deal with other situations. The difficulty is that those who might find themselves classified as recognised refugees in more liberal times could find temporary protection being used as a tool to prop up a restrictive refugee regime.

The problems encountered for refugees and asylum seekers by the unwillingness of states to grant asylum, in the form of permanent settlement, led the UNHCR, among others, to advocate a pragmatic

---

9   Castillo and Hathaway 'Temporary Protection' in Hathaway (ed) *Reconceiving International Refugee Law* (1997) p 1.

response to the law and policy issues raised.[10] In the area of asylum, in particular, this involved support for the concept of temporary protection. The concept of 'temporary asylum' was developed in the late 1970s,[11] and the issue was debated throughout the 1980s, usually in terms of the notion of temporary refuge.[12] The basic idea is that states should, in situations where large numbers of refugees and displaced persons are involved, offer some form of protection on a non-permanent basis, pending eventual return to their state of origin or to another state proximate to it. The legality of the various notions of temporary protection derived again from an association with the obligation of *non-refoulement*. It is recognised that in situations of large-scale influx, states may simply be unable to conduct individual assessments, or that while a group does not fulfil the Convention criteria return may be inappropriate. The Executive Committee of the UNHCR has emphasised that in situations of large-scale influx, states should offer temporary refuge pending arrangements for a durable solution.[13]

The UNHCR's promotion of temporary protection arose following the displacements caused by the conflicts in the former Yugoslavia. In July 1992 an International Meeting on Humanitarian Aid to the Victims of the Conflict in the Former Yugoslavia was organised by the UNHCR in Geneva in an attempt to gain a consensus on an approach to dealing with this displacement.[14] The Meeting adopted a Comprehensive Response to the Humanitarian Crisis in the Former Yugoslavia.[15] There were a number of favoured positions at the Conference. One was the adoption of the concept of 'safe areas' combined with a concentration on containing the displaced in their region of origin. The other concerned the development of a concept of temporary protection. The large numbers of refugees and displaced persons created by the various conflicts led the UNHCR to conclude that it was not practical to

---

10 See EXCOM Conclusion No 19 (XXXI) *Temporary Refuge* (1980); Findings and Recommendations of the Working Group on International Protection UN Doc A/AC96/799 (1992) p 6; UN Doc A/AC96/815(1993) pp 9-11.

11 UN Doc A/AC 96/572 (1979); see Goodwin-Gill, note 6 above, pp 196-199.

12 See eg Group of Experts on Temporary Refuge in Situations of Large Scale Influx UN Doc EC/SCP/16; Hartman 'The Principle and Practice of Temporary Refuge: A Customary Norm Protecting Civilians Fleeing Internal Armed Conflict' in Martin (ed) *The New Asylum-Seekers: Refugee Law in the 1980's* (1988) p 87.

13 EXCOM Conclusion No 22 (XXXII) *Protection of Asylum Seekers in Situations of Large Scale Influx* (1981).

14 YUN (1992) p 903.

15 UNHCR *A Comprehensive Response to the Humanitarian Crisis in the former Yugoslavia* HCR/IMFY/1992/2.

advocate the exclusive use of individual asylum procedures in this instance, although it stressed that individuals with a valid claim should not be prevented from making one under the 1951 Convention.[16] On the substance of the concept, the UNHCR acknowledged that it would need to be elaborated upon by member states, but that at a minimum it should include admission, respect for the principle of *non-refoulement* and human rights, and repatriation when the conditions in the country of origin permitted it.[17] At the follow-up meetings to the Ministerial Conference the principle of temporary protection was accepted by 38 states.[18] EU member states accepted the concept of temporary protection with respect to vulnerable categories of people, but emphasised that large-scale displacement was not the answer to the problem and that the displaced should be encouraged to stay in the nearest 'safe area' to their home.[19] They expressed their willingness to offer temporary protection to those coming directly from combat zones who were within their borders and who were unable to return as a direct result of the conflict and human rights abuses.[20] More particularly, they specified groups who they would in principle be willing to admit temporarily: those held in prisoner of war or internment camps who could not otherwise be saved from a threat to life or limb; those injured or seriously ill who could not receive medical treatment locally; and those who were under a direct threat to life or limb whose protection could not be otherwise secured.[1] This list of vulnerable groups was further extended in June 1993[2] to include those subjected to sexual assault who could not be assisted in 'safe areas' as close to their homes as possible. The member states stressed that, while they were willing to grant protection to these vulnerable groups, it was on the basis that the persons given temporary protection would return to an area in the former Yugoslavia where they could live in safety.[3] During their stay individuals should, they stated, be permitted to live in dignity, and certain principles were elaborated such as the need for housing,

16 HCR/IMFY/1992/2 p 4.
17 See note 15 above.
18 YUN (1992) p 903.
19 Conclusion on People Displaced by the Conflict in the Former Yugoslavia, London 30 November 1992 10518/92 (Presse 230) Annex IV. See Landgren 'Safety Zones and International Protection: A Dark Grey Area' (1995) 7 IJRL 436.
20 Note 19 above.
 1 Note 19 above.
 2 Resolution on Certain Common Guidelines as Regards the Admission of Particularly Vulnerable Groups of Persons from the Former Yugoslavia, 1/2 June 1993, SN2830/93 (WGI 1499).
 3 SN2830/93, para 2.

health care and the development of children involved.[4] In practice the member states, as well as other participating states, offered temporary protection in the form of a quota system. It was not long, however, before the focus shifted to the repatriation of those who had been offered temporary protection.[5] After the cessation of hostilities, voluntary returns commenced, but later some states, notably Germany, initiated returns which could not be classified as purely voluntary.[6]

The concept of temporary protection reflects the unwillingness of states to offer permanent settlement to large numbers of individuals seeking asylum. Its deployment highlights the extent to which refugee status and asylum have become associated in the minds of states exclusively with integration and permanent settlement. This illustrates a shift in thinking among the international community, with more emphasis being placed on root causes and the human rights abuses necessitating flight.

ROOT CAUSES AND PREVENTION

Recent years have witnessed a significant 're-think' of the traditional legal approaches to the protection of refugees and asylum seekers. The 1951 Convention and the 1967 Protocol remain the principal legal instruments used by states; however, more consideration has been given, particularly beginning in the late 1970s, to the other human rights issues raised by the existence of refugee movements. One of the more notable aspects of this 'new thinking' is a questioning of the law's 'exile bias' and its neglect of the root causes of flight. The dominant theme in international refugee and asylum law, as is evident from much of the previous discussion, is the protection given to a refugee by another state. Often neglected are the violations of human rights and humanitarian law which are the underlying causes of flight.[7] This interest in focusing on the root causes of refugee movements was evident at the World Conference on Human Rights in Vienna in 1993. The Declaration from the Conference states:

---

4   SN2830/93 para 3.
5   See General Framework Agreement for Peace in Bosnia and Herzegovina (1996) 35 ILM 75 Annex 7.
6   Bagshaw 'Benchmarks or Deutschmarks? Determining the Criteria for the Repatriation of Refugees to Bosnia and Herzegovina' (1997) 9 IJRL 566.
7   See Gilbert 'Root Causes and International Law: Refugee Flows in the 1990s' (1993) 11 NQHR 327.

'23 The World Conference on Human Rights recognises that, in view of the complexities of the global refugee crisis and in accordance with the Charter of the UN . . . a comprehensive approach by the international community is needed . . . This should include the development of strategies to address the root causes and effects of movements of refugees and other displaced persons . . .'[8]

There are a number of reasons advanced for this willingness among states to approach refugee protection more holistically. In strict policy terms some states appear no longer disposed toward granting asylum (defined as permanent settlement) on a widespread basis. It is noteworthy that the new protection discourse coincided with increased resistance from states to the traditional asylum regime. Concern with prevention is no doubt admirable, even if it does come from some unlikely quarters. So long as the mechanisms and political will still do not exist to address and rectify the abuses which result in flight, talk of prevention can slide into apology for apathy and restriction. An analogy might be drawn with relative poverty within the state. All politically progressive people wish to see its eradication. But few would advocate that the current palliative welfare state system should be eroded or destroyed while the primary goal remained a long way off. The same logic holds for asylum. Prevention remains the ultimate goal but it appears to be a long way off, and should not be used as a reason to erode the institution of asylum.

There were a number of initiatives within the UN in the 1980s which illustrated the 'new thinking' among some states. In 1980 Canada made a proposal in the Commission on Human Rights that the subject of human rights abuses and mass exoduses should be placed on its agenda.[9] Following this proposal, at its thirty-sixth session, the Commission adopted a resolution on human rights and mass exoduses.[10] The General Assembly, in a number of subsequent resolutions welcomed the work of the Commission in this area, and requested the Secretary-General to report on the question at its thirty-sixth session in 1981.[11] The subsequent report of the Secretary-General gave details of the methods adopted to address human rights abuses and mass exoduses.[12] Acting upon this report, the Commission decided, at its thirty-seventh session, to appoint a Special Rapporteur to study the question.[13] The chosen

8 UN Doc A/CONF157/23 para 23.
9 See Martin 'Large Scale Migration of Asylum Seekers' (1982) 76 Am J Int L 598.
10 CHR Res 30 (XXXVI), 11 March 1980.
11 UNGA Res 35/196, 15 December 1980.
12 S-G, UN Doc E/CN4/1440.
13 CHR Res 29 (XXXVII), 11 March 1981.

Rapporteur was Aga Khan, someone with much experience in the area of refugee law. The initiative culminated in the publication in 1981 of the *Study on Human Rights and Mass Exoduses*.[14] The report was approved by the Commission at its thirty-eighth session in 1982[15] and by the General Assembly in the same year.[16] While the study initiated a welcome debate on the issue, its content contained little original analysis or insight. It recognised the need for fresh approaches in the areas of refugee and human rights law, but also stressed the continuing importance of the more traditional aspects of refugee protection, such as asylum. In considering the root causes of mass exoduses, the study emphasised the violations of human rights involved, looking specifically at the rights contained in the UDHR 1948.[17] The difficulty was that while it proved to be a welcome reaffirmation of the role of violations of human rights law in movements of refugees and displaced persons, it did little to delimit these in a precise and concrete way. Following from this work, subsequent General Assembly resolutions on the issue of human rights and mass exoduses affirmed the importance of addressing the root causes of refugee movements and called on the UN to develop ways in which these root causes might be addressed more effectively.[18] In particular, the General Assembly urged states to ensure the effective implementation of international human rights law, as this would contribute significantly to the reduction of flows of refugees and displaced persons.

Another initiative, instigated again in 1980, had similar aims. In September 1980 Germany requested that 'International Co-operation to Avert New Flows of Refugees' be placed on the agenda of the General Assembly.[19] At its thirty-fifth session the General Assembly decided to add this to its agenda.[20] In 1981 the General Assembly established a Group of Governmental Experts to study the question.[1] The resolution of the General Assembly establishing the group emphasised the importance of examining

14 UN Doc E/CN4/1503.
15 CHR Res 32 (XXXVIII), 11 March 1982.
16 UNGA Res 37/186, 17 December 1982.
17 UN Doc E/CN4/1503 para 38.
18 UNGA Res 38/103, 16 December 1983; UNGA Res 39/117, 14 December 1984; UNGA Res 40/149, 13 December 1985; UNGA Res 41/148, 7 December 1987. See Report of Secretary-General UN Doc A/43/743 and Add 1; UNGA Res 43/154, 8 December 1988.
19 YUN (1980) 940. See Lee 'The UN Group of Governmental Experts on International Co-operation to Avert New Flows of Refugees' (1984) 78 Am J Int L 486.
20 UNGA Res 35/124, 11 December 1980.
 1 UNGA Res 36/148, 16 December 1981.

the refugee's right to return and the need to address the area comprehensively with a 'future oriented approach' in mind. The group, comprising of representatives from 24 states, had eight sessions between 12 April 1983 and 2 May 1986. In assessing the scope of their mandate, the group decided to adopt a wider framework than that provided by refugee law.[2] They interpreted it to include 'coerced movements'. The term coercion –

> 'was to be understood in a wide sense covering a variety of natural, political and socio-economic factors which directly or indirectly force people to flee from their homelands in fear of life, liberty and security.'

This inclusive framework for analysis contrasts sharply with that of refugee law. In 1986 the group issued a report, the conclusions and recommendations of which were endorsed by the General Assembly.[3] The report focused particularly strongly on the issue of the root causes of displacement. These the group divided into man-made and those which were deemed natural.[4] Man-made causes were further subdivided into political and socio-economic factors. The major political causes were identified as war and armed conflict, either international or non-international, along with others such as oppression of indigenous populations and minorities.

The analysis of socio-economic factors in the movement of refugees and displaced persons has tended to be neglected. The main reason is the prominence given in this area to those suffering violations of civil and political rights. This is demonstrated within refugee law by the fact that socio-economic factors are not regarded as sufficient to establish refugee status under the terms of the 1951 Convention. It also results from the labelling of those who flee for socio-economic reasons as 'economic migrants' and therefore not in need of international protection. In general, the area is regarded as problematic, due to the inherent difficulties in attempting to distinguish voluntary from involuntary movements. The fear of some states is that to equate refugee status and violations of economic and social rights is to dissolve the distinction often drawn between refugees and economic migrants. This group drew the distinction by separating voluntary and 'traditional' movements, ie those to find employment, from economic and social factors which threaten the physical integrity and survival of individuals; one example of the latter being those who flee famine. Such

---

2   Report of the Group of Governmental Experts on International Co-operation to Avert New Flows of Refugees, UN Doc A/41/324 (1984).
3   UNGA Res 41/70, 3 December 1986.
4   Section III A-B.

conditions, indicated mainly to exist in developing states, are frequently the result of the structural inability of these states to provide for their entire populations. The difficulty here is with the establishment of legal responsibility with regard to the structural problems. What the report made clear was that socio-economic causes are a factor in the movements of refugees and displaced persons, even though in practice it may not be easy to establish their role precisely.

Having identified the major causes of refugee flows, the group addressed the question of the improvement of international co-operation in this area by examining the relevant international legal provisions.[5] It found that the legal provisions to enhance co-operation were already in existence, particularly in the light of the Declaration of Principles of International Law Concerning the Friendly Relations and Co-operation among states adopted in 1970,[6] and the relevant provisions of the UN Charter. Inadequate implementation and the lack of effective enforcement of international norms is well-charted territory in international human rights law scholarship. The report is, however, of particular importance for the acceptance, for the purposes of the study, that a wide group of individuals are affected by forced migration, and that this extends some way beyond the established legal categories.

The principal reason for addressing the root causes of refugee flows is the openly idealistic aim of prevention. As the UNHCR has stated:

'For the individual who is a potential victim of human rights abuses or armed conflict, as well as for the international community faced with a growing "refugee problem", the ideal policy and the most effective form of protection is prevention, meaning action to address and remedy conditions that could force people to become refugees.'[7]

Prevention raises challenges which go beyond the scope of this present work.[8] Here it is simply necessary to raise some of the prospects and problems within this development for the future treatment of displaced persons generally.

Once the root causes of movements of refugees and displaced persons are defined in terms of violations of international law, then any prevention strategy needs to ensure the proper implementation and enforcement of the standards of both human rights and

---

5   Paras 47-61.
6   UNGA Res 2625(XXV), 24 October 1970.
7   UNHCR *Note on International Protection* UN Doc A/AC96/815 (1993) p 14.
8   Cf UN Secretary-General *Agenda for Peace: Preventative Diplomacy, Peace Making and Peace Keeping* UN Doc A/47/277 (1992).

humanitarian law.[9] As is well known, the difficulty in this approach, for those suffering direct persecution by their state of origin, is the paradox that enforcement of rights depends upon the institution which is active in violating them. In this respect, international and regional methods of human rights promotion and protection gain in significance. A variety of mechanisms for monitoring the application of human rights law have been developed both within and outside the UN.[10] Particularly significant, besides the work carried out by the Commission on Human Rights,[11] are the treaties which specifically provide for monitoring bodies.[12] The usual form of monitoring involves state reporting, but individual complaint mechanisms are also an important feature.[13] In addition to international instruments there is an expanding regional network of human rights protection.

One of the most pressing problems for international human rights law is the divergence between the international norms and the actual practice of states with respect to human rights.[14] The present existence of large numbers of refugees and displaced persons is an indication of how relatively ineffective these measures have in the past been. The next step for the human rights movement would thus appear to be the effective realisation of rights in practice. While prevention is an aspect of a comprehensive response, this must not replace the goal of defining an adequate international legal response to the immediate needs of the refugee.[15] Prevention may therefore be characterised as a long-term aim,

---

9 In relation to enforcement there has been a resurgence of interest in post-cold war era on the question of humanitarian intervention: see eg Henkin 'Humanitarian Intervention' in Henkin and Hargrove (eds) *Human Rights: An Agenda for the Next Century* (1995) ch 14; Helton 'The Legality of Providing Humanitarian Assistance without the Consent of the Sovereign' (1992) 4 IJRL 373.

10 See Alston (ed) *The United Nations and Human Rights: A Critical Appraisal* (1992).

11 ECOSOC Res 1235 (XV11), 1967; ECOSOC Res 1503 (XVVIII), 1970. See Tolley *The UN Commission on Human Rights* (1967).

12 See Bayefsky 'Making Human Rights Treaties Work' in Henkin and Hargrove (eds) *Human Rights: An Agenda for the Next Century* (1995) ch 10; Dimitrijevic 'The Monitoring of Human Rights and the Prevention of Human Rights Violations Through Reporting Procedures' in Bloed (ed) *Monitoring Human Rights in Europe: Comparing International Procedures and Mechanisms* (1993) p 1.

13 See Schmidt 'Individual Human Rights Complaints Procedures Based on UN Treaties and the Need for Reform' (1992) 41 ICLQ 645.

14 See D'Amato 'The Concept of Human Rights in International Law' (1982) 82 Columbia LR 1110; Watson 'Autointerpretation, Competence and the Continuing Validity of art 2(7) of the Charter' (1977) 71 Am J Int L 60.

15 Cf Garvey 'The New Asylum Seekers: Addressing their Origin' in Martin *The New Asylum Seekers: Refugee Law in the 1980's* (1988) p 209, he argues that the problems illustrated by the root causes and preventative approaches are simply too overwhelming to be a pre-condition to solving refugee problems.

based around the effective implementation and enforcement of human rights and humanitarian law.

Once the root causes of refugee movements are identified then another possible policy response is the creation of early warning systems.[16] The purpose of such systems is to define areas or scenarios, through identification of causal factors and human rights monitoring, in states or regions where there is an established potential for future refugee flows. In policy terms prevention may be involved, possibly through pressure exerted by the international community, and also primarily emergency preparedness in cases where humanitarian assistance may become necessary.[17] As the UNHCR has stated:

> 'Early warning systems are intended to identify risk factors and bring them to the attention of the international community, prompting positive action to avert potential or emerging refugee flows.'[18]

In establishing root causes for use in an early warning system, there is a role for non-governmental organisations (NGOs) in the collection of information, a role which is closely intertwined with the general need for more effective human rights monitoring. The difficulties in establishing such a system relate, first, to the problem of reaching agreement, not on the root causes as such, but on the classification of causes. In this respect the use of human rights and humanitarian law as a framework, within which to act upon causes, is most appropriate. Second, there is the organisational problem of co-ordinating the approaches of inter-governmental and non-governmental organisations. This last problem is at present being addressed by the UN Department of Humanitarian Affairs, which is attempting to function as a focus for this work.[19] There is evidently much work to be done to eradicate the root causes of flight. Given this, it makes little sense to continue to undermine the right to seek asylum.

---

16 Eg Beyer 'Human Rights Monitoring: Lessons Learnt from the Case of the Isaaks in Somalia' in Rupesinghe and Keroda (eds) *Early Warning and Conflict Resolution* (1992) p 15; Beyer 'Monitoring Root Causes of Refugee Flows and Early Warning: The Need for Substance' (1990) IJRL Special Issue 71; Beyer 'Human Rights Monitoring and the Failure of Early Warning' (1990) 2 IJRL 56. Cf Ruiz 'Early Warning is not Enough: The Failure to Prevent Starvation in Ethiopia' (1990) IJRL Special Issue 83; Gordenker 'Early Warning of Disastrous Population Movements' (1986) 20 Int Migration Rev 124.

17 On humanitarian assistance see UNGA Res 46/182, 19 December 1991; UNGA Res 45/100, 4 December 1990; UNGA Res 43/131, 8 December 1988.

18 UNHCR *The State of the World's Refugees: The Challenge of Protection* (1993) p 129.

19 The Department of Humanitarian Affairs was established in 1992 for the purpose of improving the UN's emergency preparedness generally, see YUN (1992) p 575.

THE INTERNALLY DISPLACED

One of the more progressive developments, connected to the turn to prevention, is the willingness to look beyond borders in the construction of human need. If the primary concern is the eradication of the root causes of displacement, then the crossing of borders becomes less central. A focus on internal displacement is viewed as important as interest shifts to the causes of forced displacement as the principal problem. The internally displaced have thus begun to attract the attention of the international community. Globalisation also plays its part in this trend.[20] As traditional notions of sovereignty are continually eroded, so new opportunities for addressing human need present themselves. It is estimated[1] that there are between 20 and 30 million internally displaced persons, as many if not more than the numbers of refugees.[2] There is no universally accepted legal definition of internally displaced persons. The UN Secretary-General's Special Representative on Internally Displaced Persons has, however, advanced the following definition:

> '[I]nternally displaced persons are persons or groups of persons who have been forced or obliged to flee or to leave their homes or places of habitual residence, in particular as a result of or in order to avoid the effects of armed conflict, situations of generalized violence, violations of human rights or natural or human-made disasters, and who have not crossed an internationally recognised border.'[3]

The generosity of the definition contrasts sharply with that contained in the 1951 Convention. The exclusion of the internally displaced from the definition was not a deliberate attempt to rank

20 See Held *Democracy and the Global Order: From the Modern State to Cosmopolitan Governance* (1995) pp 16-27.
1 See UN Human Rights Factsheet *Human Rights and Refugees* (1993) p 22.
2 See generally Korn *Exodus within Borders: An Introduction to the Crisis of Internal Displacement* (2000); Geissler 'The International Protection of Internally Displaced Persons' (1999) 11 IJRL 451; Cohen and Deng *Masses in Flight: The Global Crisis of Internal Displacement* (1998); Global IDP Survey and Norwegian Refugee Council *Rights Have No Borders: Worldwide Internal Displacement* (1998); Global IDP and Norwegian Refugee Council *Internally Displaced People: A Global Survey* (1998); Petrasek 'New Standards for the Protection of Internally Displaced Persons: A Proposal for a Comprehensive Approach' (1995) 14 Refugee Survey Q 285; Cohen 'International Protection for Internally Displaced Persons' in Henkin and Hargrove (eds) *Human Rights: An Agenda for the Next Century* (1995) p 17; Plender 'The Legal Basis of International Jurisdiction to Act with Regard to the Internally Displaced' (1994) 6 IJRL 345; Lewis 'Dealing with the Problem of Internally Displaced Persons' (1992) 6 Georgetown Immigration LJ 693.
3 *Report of the Representative of the Secretary General* Addendum UN Doc E/CN4/ 1998/53/Add 2 para 2.

the displaced according to some unspecified conception of need, although this has been the result.[4] Those still within their country of origin often suffer the same level of ill-treatment as the refugee, and often their position is in fact more acute.[5] The drafters of the 1951 Convention were preoccupied with the immediate post-1945 refugee problem, which primarily involved external displacement. It is also the case that, in legal terms, the internally displaced are in a different position (in terms of securing protection) from refugees. Ethically, the focus is correctly upon human need. In legal terms distinctions still need to be drawn.

The predicament of the internally displaced has recently been addressed in the UN, where the gap in the present legal regime has been recognised and has been receiving attention.[6] In 1990 ECOSOC requested the Secretary-General to initiate a review of the assistance provided by the organisation to all refugees, displaced persons and returnees, and to suggest ways co-operation between the various organs might be improved.[7] Following this initiative, in 1991 the Commission on Human Rights requested the Secretary-General to consider the protection of human rights and the needs of the internally displaced in his review and to submit to the Commission, at its forty-eighth session, an analytical report on the internally displaced.[8] This the Secretary-General did.[9] At its forty-eighth session in 1992 the Commission, following consideration of the report, requested the Secretary-General to appoint a Representative to study the human rights issues raised by the existence of internally displaced persons. The Representative, Francis Deng, has since then submitted a number of important reports to the Commission and the General Assembly on the various legal and other aspects of plight of this group. This has included two useful reports on the legal norms which apply to the internally displaced.[10] In 1998 the Special Representative issued Guiding Principles on Internal

---

4 Cf Zolberg 'The Formation of New States as a Refugee Generating Problem' (1991) Annals of the American Academy of Political and Social Science 24, 27.

5 Cf Deng, note 2 above, p 3 *'The crisis of the internally displaced for the international community is that they fall within domestic jurisdiction and are therefore not covered by the protection normally accorded to those who cross international borders and become refugees.'* (My emphasis.) See also Rochefort (France) UN Doc E/AC7/SR172 p 4.

6 See eg UNGA Res 48/115, 20 December 1993; Vienna Declaration and Programme of Action, Adopted by the World Conference on Human Rights, 25 June 1993, UN Doc A/CONF157/23 para 23.

7 ECOSOC Res 1990/78, 27 July 1990.

8 CHR Res 1991/25, 5 March 1991.

9 Analytical Report of the Secretary-General on Internally Displaced Persons E/CN4/1992/23.

10 See UN Doc E/CN4/1996/Add 2 and E/CN4/1998/53/Add 1.

Displacement which represent a first step on the road to establishing specific agreed standards for the treatment of this group.[11] The Guiding Principles acknowledge that the primary duty and responsibility to provide protection rests with the national authority.[12] This includes humanitarian assistance, although they provide that international organisations have the right merely to offer their services in support of the internally displaced.[13]

In addition to reporting on the legal and factual position of the internally displaced, the Special Representative has also made a number of visits to states to examine the plight of the displaced. The states visited have included: Sri Lanka,[14] Colombia,[15] Burundi,[16] and Rwanda.[17] The reports offer insights into the plight of the internally displaced within each of the states visited and make recommendations as to possible improvements. If one examines an individual report, such as that addressing the situation in Colombia, it provides a detailed assessment of the extent of the crisis.[18] In this instance, it is of note that none of the official or unofficial organisations within the state could actually agree on the extent of the problem. The report additionally includes an explanation of the historical background to the problems faced,[19] and details of the findings of the mission.[20] A useful section here describes the human rights and humanitarian issues raised, as well as the protection concerns of the internally displaced themselves. The mission found no consensus on the definition of the term 'internally displaced person'. The government, for example, included 'natural disasters' in its definition, while NGOs in the state did not.[1] The reports provide extremely useful background material on the legal and factual position of the internally displaced in instances where this is not often readily available. It is also the case that the visits by the Special Representative aid in focusing

---

11 UN Doc E/CN4/1998/53/Add 2. For further developments see Report on *Specific Groups and Individuals: Mass Exoduses and Displaced Persons* UN Doc E/CN4/2000/83.
12 Principle 3(1).
13 Principle 25(1). See also Principle 25(2): '. . . Consent thereto shall not be arbitrarily withheld, particularly when authorities concerned are unable or unwilling to provide the required humanitarian assistance.'
14 UN Doc E/CN4/1994/44/Add 1.
15 UN Doc E/CN4/1995/50/Add 1.
16 UN Doc E/CN4/1995/50/Add 2.
17 UN Doc E/CN4/1995/50/Add 4.
18 Paras 10-16.
19 Paras 18-28.
20 Paras 33-107.
 1 Para 108.

attention on this group and add an authoritative voice to those advocating reform. The work of the Special Representative should be viewed as part of the complex network of evolving international regimes of human rights protection.

The focus on the internally displaced has not been confined solely to the Special Representative.[2] In 1994 (following the UNHCR's involvement in providing humanitarian assistance to the internally displaced in, for example, Sri Lanka, Tajikistan, Azerbaijan and Georgia under its 'good offices') at the request of the Secretary-General,[3] the UNHCR's Sub-Committee of the Whole on International Protection gave consideration to the various protection aspects of the UNHCR activity on behalf of the internally displaced.[4] This work led to the adoption by the Executive Committee, at it forty-fifth session in 1994, of a Conclusion on internally displaced persons.[5] This is the first such measure adopted by the Executive Committee and highlights the growing concern with forced or involuntary displacement itself, rather than with the geographical location of the displaced person.

One might legitimately ask at this point why, after a number of years when their plight attracted little international attention, did consideration of the internally displaced suddenly become such an

---

2 Eg UNGA Res 48/116, 20 December 1993. The General Assembly: 'Reaffirms its support for the High Commissioner's efforts, on the basis of specific requests from the Secretary-General or the competent principal organs of the UN and with the consent of the concerned state . . . to provide humanitarian assistance and protection to persons displaced within their own country in specific situations calling for the Office's particular expertise . . . Recognised the need for the international community to explore methods and means better to address within the UN system the protection and assistance needs of internally displaced persons, and call[ed] upon the High Commissioner to engage actively in further consultations on this priority issue with the Department of Humanitarian Affairs of the United Nations Secretariat and the Special Representative of the Secretary-General on Internally Displaced Persons, and with other appropriate international organisations and bodies, including the International Committee of the Red Cross.'

3 UNHCR *Note On International Protection* UN Doc A/AC96/830 (1994) para 64: 'While the situation of the internally displaced is closely analogous to that of the refugee, differing in that the former has not crossed an international border, a review of UNHCR's past and current operational activities with the internally displaced shows that in most cases it is neither posssible nor desirable, when providing assistance or protection to persons in their own country, to make distinctions between the displaced and other affected persons in the same area, except on the basis of actual need'; UNHCR *Note on International Protection* UN Doc A/AC96/821 (1993), pp 31-32 Annex, the Opening Statement of the High Commissioner.

4 UN Doc EC/SCP/87.

5 Conclusion No 75 *Internally Displaced Persons* (XLV)-1994.

imperative? In seeking to answer this, the first point is that it does appear to reflect a willingness, in the post-cold war era, to move 'beyond borders' in the consideration of human rights and humanitarian problems.[6] This demonstrates the growing confidence of international organisations in their dealings with these issues, irrespective of where the problems arise. This trend may be connected to the 'erosion' of aspects of domestic jurisdiction by international law, noted elsewhere. What it certainly does show is that international law has extended its reach to areas which traditionally would have been conceived as exclusively within the jurisdiction of the 'sovereign' state. The Special Representative on Internally Displaced Persons has illustrated admirably the underlying reason why some form of 'international' remedial action is on occasion required:

'Overwhelmingly, [the internally displaced] live under the adverse conditions of a hostile domestic environment, where their access to protection and assistance is constrained by national sovereignty.'[7]

While the internally displaced have not received the international legal attention given to the refugee, the development of international law, and more specifically human rights law, has provided a legal framework within which their treatment is to be assessed and to which states must comply. This is not, however, to state that international human rights law is the only relevant area of law which is applicable in this case; other areas, such as humanitarian law, have also provided standards of protection for those displaced in situations of armed conflict.[8]

The other major contributing factor, highlighted in this section, has been the turn to root causes. The policy of containment initiated by developed states which signalled the focus on root causes, also turned the attention of the international community to the internally displaced. If one begins from the premise that it is the root causes of displacement which are the main issue

6   Sub-Committee Report UN Doc EC/SCP/87 para 3: 'To the extent that refugee flows and internal displacement have the same causes, it makes little sense to deal only with the trans-frontier aspects of coerced population movements, either in responding to immediate humanitarian needs or in seeking solutions.'
7   UN Doc EC/SCP/87.
8   International humanitarian law is that branch of public international law which applies to situations of armed conflict both international and non-international. It is relevant to the plight of the internally displaced: see eg Geneva Convention Relative to the Treatment of Prisoners of War 1949 75 UNTS 85, UKTS 39, Cmnd 555; Geneva Convention IV Relative to the Protection of Civilian Persons in Time of War 1949 75 UNTS 287, UKTS 39, Cmnd 550. See Roberts and Guelff *Documents on the Laws of War* (3rd edn, 2000).

involved, then the precise location of the individual is no longer the central determining factor in the equation. By embracing this framework, anchored in the international law of human rights, the treatment of the internally displaced is of equal concern to that of the refugee. Jurisdictional issues still arise, but they become a secondary concern, following initial attempts to tackle causes.

The constitutive role of 'alienage' in international refugee law is open to criticism because of the distinction drawn between those displaced internally and externally in relation to their states of nationality.[9] In other words, one may argue that the system of protection is not as inclusive as it might be. While the criticism has some cogency, it must be borne in mind that the aim and purpose of the refugee definition was essentially functional in design, ie to designate to whom and when protection would be available. At the stage of development of international law in 1951 the problem was conceived to be one of external displacement. Internal displacement, however, also produces a number of novel jurisdictional problems which do not arise in the case of the refugee. In this respect the promotion of international human rights law, with its emphasis on guarantees for individuals, appears to be one way to solve the problem.

The above trends[10] have impacted upon the role of the UNHCR,[11] and those organisations which are now actively addressing the protection and assistance needs of the internally displaced. The UNHCR, in particular, has been criticised for its use of prevention discourse and a claimed movement away from its core protection function. The issue that these organisations have raised is whether the present international legal standards are adequate to address the specific needs of the internally displaced or whether a new legal instrument is needed. The terms of the debate are familiar to those with a knowledge of previous controversies within the international human rights community. Some have argued that the present arrangements do not address

---

9 Cf Shacknove 'Who is a Refugee?' (1985) 88 Ethics 274, 277.
10 Cf Cohen 'International Protection for Internally Displaced Persons' in Henkin and Hargrove (eds) *Human Rights: An Agenda for the Next Century* (1995) p 22. She states that with human rights groups, whether they be non-governmental or UN, the problem is that they tend to see the internally displaced as outside their traditional concerns. So although the problems of the internally displaced are based around the abuses of human rights which necessitate flight the trend has been to view them 'purely' as a humanitarian concern.
11 UN Doc A/AC96/815 (1993) p 13. Here the focus has moved to some extent towards notions such a preventative protection which stresses the human rights violations involved.

the distinct needs of the internally displaced as a group in an adequate manner. The opposing view holds that the problem is not the lack of available legal standards but the failure of states to enforce or comply with these areas of law.[12]

What specific needs do the internally displaced have which might be addressed by an international response? Lacking the effective protection of their state, the first need of the internally displaced is often humanitarian assistance.[13] In order to receive humanitarian assistance, the displaced person needs to reside in relative safety within the state and the organisation providing the required assistance, such as the UNHCR, must be able, with the consent of the government, to provide that assistance. This need has led recently to the creation of 'safe areas' within states, where displaced persons may be provided with humanitarian assistance and protection. This was evident as a response to the displacement caused by the Gulf War and more recently in the former Yugoslavia.[14] In the latter case the original idea was that the internally displaced would go to designated safe areas within Bosnia-Herzegovina, and be offered protection and humanitarian assistance.[15] The safe areas were envisaged as a temporary measure designed, first, to prevent the need for external displacement and, second, to facilitate the return of the displaced to their place of origin.[16] The emphasis, as has been the modern trend, is on the region or state of origin and the displaced person's right to return, coupled with the possibility of an interim right to humanitarian assistance and protection.[17] This was consistently the position of the UN Security Council on the displacement caused by the conflict in Bosnia-Herzegovina.[18]

There have been significant problems with the concept of safe areas, stemming originally from its vagueness, but largely from the substantial difficulties associated with providing protection within a state to displaced persons when there is ongoing armed conflict.[19]

12 Cf Meron *Human Rights in Internal Strife* (1987). He examines in this work human rights and humanitarian law applicable in situations of internal strife with a view to discovering gaps in coverage.
13 Cf McCoubrey and White *International Organisations and Civil Wars* (1995) ch 6.
14 See the following resolutions on events in the former Yugoslavia: UNSC Res 819 (1993), 16 April 1993; UNSC Res 824 (1993), 6 May 1993 .
15 UNSC Res 836 (1993), 4 June 1993; UNSC Res 908 (1994), 31 March 1994, possibility of extending the use of the concept within Bosnia-Herzegovina.
16 UNSC Res 836 (1993), 4 June 1993.
17 See Cohen, note 10 above, p 24.
18 See eg UNSC Res 941 (1994), 23 September 1994; UNSC Res 947 (1994), 30 September 1994.
19 Problems shown by repeated attacks on the 'safe areas' see UNSC Res 913 (1994), 22 April 1994; UNSC Res 959 (1994), 19 November 1994.

The problems experienced place a large question mark over the future utility of such measures. While the provision of assistance to the internally displaced is to be welcomed as a progression toward regarding the ill-treatment of all those displaced as a human rights issue, the practice demonstrates the continuing need to reaffirm the right of the individual to seek asylum in another state. If this legal right is curtailed, the suspicion generated is that attention to root causes is a convenient label for states to promote and implement large-scale 'containment' policies.

TOWARDS A HUMAN RIGHTS PARADIGM?

The thesis developed in this chapter is that there has been a shift in the international regime for refugee protection towards a more inclusive human rights paradigm. This does not translate into more effective protection for the forcibly displaced in practice. What it does mean is that the terms of legal discourse have been widened to include not simply the rights of asylum seekers but also the needs of the internally displaced and the importance of addressing the root causes of flight. This can be charted as a path from asylum to containment but this is to over-extend a valid partial insight and obscures the complex nature of the process that is taking place. Containment is part of the strategy of a significant number of powerful states. It is clear that prevention discourse has played a part in legitimising this. The argument here, however, is that this also reflects an attempt to view human displacement in a more inclusive sense, and embed notions of legal protection in a paradigm which more fully reflects the current governance of human need in the international community. The international context reveals the extent to which the understanding of the international system and human displacement reflected in the 1951 Convention is a partial and distorted one. An understanding of this is essential for those seeking to ground a critique of the asylum practices of individual states.

Chapter 3

Mapping the Europeanisation of asylum law

INTRODUCTION

There is much talk of globalisation of law and politics in the scholarly literature. But one of the more interesting trends in recent years is the 'Europeanisation' of asylum law and policy. In the area of refugee protection it is regionalism which is the dominant trend. To concentrate exclusively on domestic law and practice is to neglect the extent to which regionalism is shaping, and in some cases dictating, the nature of national responses. In order to understand the law and politics of asylum in the UK in the last decade it is necessary to examine the Europeanisation of asylum law in this period and the general regional context within which policy has emerged. The intention is not, however, to offer a comparative analysis of the national asylum systems in Europe. This chapter is concerned with mapping the broad trends in European practice. While protection largely depends on local legal cultures and practices, there are clear patterns in the national responses.

Many of the policies adopted on asylum now arise from broader European concerns about the creation of an area of 'freedom, security and justice'. The incremental construction of 'Fortress Europe' has led to much justified criticism of the process and the substance of policy development.[1] The aim in this chapter is to map the outline of European law and policy. Much of this policy has been clear for some time. The European Commission has on several occasions made apparent its preferences in the asylum and

---

1   See Council of Europe, Committee on Migration, Refugees and Demography *Restrictions on asylum in the member states of the Council of Europe and the European Union* (Doc 8598, 21 December 1999).

immigration fields. Progress has, however, been painstakingly slow, although this problem may be resolved in the years ahead.

Most publicity has surrounded EU policy, and rightly so, because it has made the most 'progress' on the development of a common approach. But it is important to recognise the work of both the Council of Europe (CE) and the Organisation for Security and Co-operation in Europe (OSCE). In a sense both these organisations are more representative of a European perspective, even if their work on asylum has not been as intense as the EU. What is revealed is a complex network of regional initiatives within which the approach of the UK must be situated if the evolution of law and policy is to be comprehensively understood.

ASYLUM IN THE EUROPEAN CONTEXT

Many discussions of asylum in Europe end in totalising critiques of the attempts made by the EU to construct a common policy in this area. There is little doubt about the validity of much of this criticism. For the meanness and restrictiveness of current law and practice is well documented. But the challenge in the coming years will be to construct an approach to asylum that is constructive and forward looking. Despite the concerns expressed about Fortress Europe, few suggest that the appropriate response is to abandon the project and return to a system of purely state-based regulation.

At a time when globalisation[2] is dominating discussions of the nature of international society, migration appositely presents itself as a defining issue of this era. Although it is possible to exaggerate the novelty of modern migration, few now doubt that the issue is one of growing complexity, and that the legal tools created earlier in the century to address it are increasingly inadequate.[3] The complexity of forced migration, in particular, has been recognised and met with a variety of innovative responses, including the establishment of comprehensive regional mechanisms. The new thinking that has arisen in the wake of these developments is welcome. However, there is concern that the recent trends in refugee law and policy do not pay adequate regard to important aspects of traditional international protection. In particular, in Europe the right to seek asylum has been steadily undermined.

Implicit in international refugee law is the idea that international protection is provided to a select group of displaced persons. The

2 Cf Picciotto 'Fragmented States and International Rules of Law' (1997) 6 Social & Legal Studies 259, 260-266. See also Hirst and Thompson *Globalisation in Question* (2nd edn, 1999).
3 See UNHCR *State of the World's Refugees 1995: In Search of Solutions* (1995) pp 188-189.

legal regime is not exclusively needs-based. Instead it represents a compromise between state interest in the regulation of migration and the humanitarian imperatives which flow from the continuing displacement of persons. Once it is accepted that legal regulation is required, the question then becomes one of migration management through law. This may appear to be a rather basic point. But it is not always clear, from some of the criticisms that one hears in this area, that it is accepted that legal regulation is either desirable or possible. The issue should revolve around what the substance of legal regulation should be. The next logical step, once this is accepted, is to ask at what level regulation should take place. In other words, must the legal regulation of asylum be left to individual states as is implied in the terms of international refugee law? Or is it more appropriate to envisage regional forms of regulation or co-operation? This issue is most prominent in debates in the EU. States are finding it difficult to tackle a variety of issues in Europe. Forced migration is only one in a list which includes environmental degradation and the continuing exigencies of capitalist development. Regulation can no longer be conceived within the orthodox citizen/state model, but must be analysed as a complex intermeshing of national, supranational and international legal, social and political orders. This presents formidable, but not insoluble, difficulties for those wishing to gain a comprehensive understanding of these dynamic areas.

The trend in state practice in the refugee and asylum context is to opt for enhanced, and comprehensive, regional co-operation. It is within this context that the European regional response analysed in this chapter must be seen and understood.[4] The thesis defended here is that there is potential for progressive regional regulation in Europe. This is not to deny the appalling nature of much of the regional response to asylum based on a thinly disguised policy of deterrence and restriction. The argument is that the way to remedy this in the EU is not to return to an exclusively state-regulated system but to alter the substance of EU law and practice. While acknowledging the (often extreme) limitations of past and present practice,[5] it is suggested that this should not lead to the sort of totalising critique which would ultimately result in the rejection of the process. There are indeed tensions inscribed in the move to a supranational system which do not depart significantly from those surrounding the process of state formation. A highly

---

4 Note Loescher *Beyond Charity: International Co-operation and the Global Refugee Crisis* (1993) p 197.
5 Especially in the context of rising levels of racism in Europe: see Alt 'Racism and Xenophobia in Europe' (ECRE 1994).

contentious politics of exclusion and inclusion emerges in the construction of a notion of membership for the purpose of governing through law. The suggestion here is that it is the unilateral nature (in the sense that regulation is ultimately delegated to individual states) of refugee protection which has contributed most to the development of 'lowest common denominator' strategies of regulation in Europe.[6] The 'race to the bottom' in asylum is the result of defensive reactions to migration which can be challenged within the context of more co-operative regional arrangements. The 'lowest common denominator' approach highlights the problems with a system where little or no co-operation takes place. At a time when the international community is moving incrementally towards a legal model anchored in conceptions of welfare and co-operation, refugee law remains tied to an outdated regulatory model. In international refugee law the dominant notion of responsibility remains the individual state. There are no guarantees that regionalism will necessarily result in qualitatively better forms of protection. States may adopt a highly restrictive and minimalist approach in practice. This is where it is important to consider the new political and legal spaces that have been created for transnational activism in Europe; for this activism has a part to play in the nature of the response that emerges. Too many studies of this area neglect the migrant networks that already exist in Europe and the influence that they can at times have on the process of law and policy formation. This is where the image of Fortress Europe can basically operate as an overstatement, in the sense that the metaphor can both overplay the regulatory capacities of states and underestimate the amount of organised opposition to the dominant position within the EU.

More optimistically, regional co-operation might help to overcome the atomistic nature of past approaches and encourage a policy response embedded in the principle of solidarity. The argument may seem like little more than detached utopianism to some. It is important to stress, however, that the language of solidarity is embedded within the existing practices of European states. This is about holding EU states up to their own promises.

6 See Centre for Refugee Studies, Refugee Law Research Unit 'Common But Differentiated Responsibility: A Model for Enhanced International Refugee Protection Within Interest Convergence Groups' 25 March 1996, in this paper, and other work, they advocate a new paradigm of refugee law based around the notion of interest-convergence groups. The work is an attempt to conjoin principle and pragmatism in a way that will eventually lead to more feasible regulation. See also 'The Temporary Protection of Refugees – A Solution-Oriented and Rights-Regarding Approach' 17 July 1996; Hathaway and Neve 'Making International Refugee Law Relevant Again: A Proposal for Collectivized and Solution-Oriented Protection' (1997) 10 Harv Human Rights J 115.

To talk of regulation more in tune with the concept of solidarity is to gesture at an enlightened future policy. Thus far, the European contribution to the protection of refugees and asylum seekers has been a decidedly ambivalent one.[7] The argument advanced here is that immanent critique of current policy can inspire much-needed progressive reform at the European level. The problems with the current approach should, however, not be underestimated.

In the absence of effective preventative strategies to eradicate the root causes of flight, the desire of states is to render migration manageable.[8] In other words, and as stated above, the challenge for participants in the European legal community is to develop regulatory strategies which reflect, and are responsive to, the complexities of modern migration. Policy development at the regional level is not simply based on restriction, although this has been the dominant theme thus far, but also is part of a desire to regulate this area in an effective way. This attempt has been seriously undermined by the substantial gap which has opened between policy developments and democratic and judicial accountability. Principles of accountability, transparency and participation have as yet failed to make a serious impact on the process. The EU has encouraged a climate of anxiety about the human mobility of some migrants and nurtured the steady criminalisation of asylum seeking.

As to substantive European developments, what has emerged is agreement on common concepts which will form the basis of asylum policy in the future. As yet, in the EU context, this is not reflected in common practice, but there is enough evidence to suggest that a distinctly European response to asylum is developing. Certainly, in western Europe consensus has emerged around the basic concepts which will form the basis for the future EU response. This chapter examines the policy response with specific

---

7   See Joly 'The Porous Dam: European Harmonization of Asylum in the Nineties' (1994) 6 IJRL 159, she describes the change in western European policy as one from: 'uncoordinated liberalism to harmonised restrictionism'. This has caused considerable concern for central and eastern European states, which fear that they are becoming buffer zones for migration to the west: see European Parliament *Migration and Asylum in Central and Eastern Europe* People's Europe Series 2-1997 pp 9 ff. This contains a revealing account of the often inadequate legal and practical arrangements for asylum seekers in central and eastern Europe.

8   European Commission COM (94) 23 Final para 70: 'Controlling migration does not necessarily imply bringing it to an end: it means migration management.' In drawing a distinction between asylum and other aspects of migration the Commission states para 81: 'Asylum policies are . . . different as they are aimed at managing the examination of asylum applications in such a way that every application can be considered in a fair and efficient manner.'

reference to the EU.[9] The reason for this focus is that the EU has thus far made the most progress in the direction of managing forced migration, and it is the one European regional organisation with the institutional capacity effectively to achieve this goal. The practices of the EU are having an impact throughout the region.[10]

EUROPE AND REFUGEE PROTECTION

Regional co-operation is an observable aspect of legal life in the modern international community. It has been a feature of international refugee protection for some time. But how desirable is regionalism for refugee protection in the European context? Surely one might argue that, as an international problem, it should be dealt with primarily at the international level? One answer to this, suggested above, is that the current regime for refugee protection atomises what is a collective and often mass phenomenon. Viewed from a needs-based perspective, it is mass human

9   There is ever growing literature on the subject: see generally Peers *EU Justice and Home Affairs Law* (2000); European Parliament *Asylum in the EU Member States* (2000); Bunyan (ed) *Key Texts in Justice and Home Affairs in the European Union: Volume I From Trevi to Maastricht* (1997); Guild *The Developing Immigration and Asylum Policies of the European Union* (1996); Joly *Haven or Hell? Asylum Policies and Refugees in Europe* (1996); Joly with Kelly and Nettleton *Refugees in Europe: The Hostile New Agenda* (1997); Tuitt 'Racist Authorisation, Interpretive Law and the Changing Character of the Refugee' in Fitzpatrick (ed) *Nationalism, Racism and the Rule of Law* (1995) p 45; Collinson *Beyond Borders: West European Migration Policy Towards the 21st Century* (1993); Collinson *Europe and International Migration* (1993); Coll and Bhabha (eds) *Asylum Law and Practice in Europe and N. America: A Comparative Analysis* (1992); Joly with Nettleton *Refugees: Asylum in Europe?* (1992); European Council for Refugees and Exiles (ECRE) *Asylum in Europe: An Introduction*, vol 1 (1993); ECRE *Asylum in Europe: Review of Refugee and Asylum Law in Selected European Countries*, vol 2 (1993); ECRE *A European Refugee Policy in the Light of Established Principles* (April 1994); Hailbronner 'Visa Regulations and Third Country Nationals in EC Law' (1994) 34 CMLR 969; Hailbronner 'Perspectives of a Harmonisation of the Law of Asylum After the Maastricht Summit' (1992) 32 CMLR 917; Hathaway 'Harmonizing for Whom? The Devaluation of Refugee Protection in the Era of European Economic Co-operation' (1993) 26 Cornell Int LJ 719. For comparative work on approaches within Europe, see Carlier, Vanheule, Hullman and Galiano (eds) *Who is a Refugee? A Comparative Case Study* (1997) (the study is based on national reports from Austria, Belgium, Switzerland, Canada, Germany, Denmark, Spain, France, Greece, Italy, Luxembourg, Netherlands, Portugal, UK and US); Lambert *Seeking Asylum: Comparative Law and Practice in Selected European Countries* (1995); Care (ed) *A Guide to Asylum Law and Practice in the EU* (1995); Gillespie *Report on Immigration and Asylum Procedure and Appeal Rights in the 12 Member States of the EC* (1993).

10 For an excellent description of practices in central and eastern Europe, see Liebaut *Legal and Social Conditions for Asylum Seekers and Refugees in Central and Eastern Europe* (1999).

displacement, irrespective of causes and geographical location, that is the problem facing the modern world. The plight of the individual dissident, while important, pales in comparison. In addition, the unilateral approach to regulation in the past has encouraged an irresponsible policy response in some states, resulting in inadequate management of the issue. In the light of this is not a regional answer the way forward? In this chapter, and building upon the argument that a rational asylum policy is possible, it is argued that a well-regulated regional approach, which offers mechanisms for collective action between states and burden-sharing, as well as procedures for securing the input of the regulated population, might assist in minimising restrictive practices and nurture a rational approach to forced migration. Regional co-operation can function as a device to ensure and encourage reflective practices between and within states.[11] Regionalism must, however, be supplemented by a willingness within states to restructure determination systems in line with progressive policy goals. Regional co-operation is only one part of a process intended to secure more effective protection for the displaced.

How does one account for the legitimacy of this process in the EU context? The issue is frequently avoided in the literature. One often hears reference to the democratic and judicial deficits in the EU. With regard to citizens of the EU, the solution to the problem is, comparatively, rather unproblematic. What is the position of the asylum seeker? How is a state or region to ground the legitimacy of its practices for a group that has made no input into the process of democratic law-making and connected channels of rational discussion and debate. The answer provided here is that, first, substantive law and policy at the regional level must be clear as to the groups to be protected. The process must involve the participation of affected groups (for example those already being offered some form of protection within the EU) and those who have direct experience of the needs of asylum seekers. This transparency has been notably absent from the EU process of harmonisation thus far. Once this is achieved, it is the asylum determination process which bears the heavy burden of legitimising asylum practices in Europe. Protection systems must be able to produce results which are regarded as reasonable by the majority of participants in the process if they are to be seen as legitimate. This legitimacy has been seriously called into question by the adoption of restrictive policies and practices throughout the region.

11　Some states are, however, noted for developing progressive policies in a unilateral fashion, for example, Canada.

The suggestion here is that regional solidarity can encourage more reflective asylum practices within states. It is important to remember that regional solidarity is an aspect of the wider concept of international solidarity and not connected to attempts to insulate a region from international problems. Solidarity between states should help to encourage less defensive reactions in future. The answer to current problems lies not in totalising critiques of any attempt to secure feasible regulation at the European level but in the encouragement of more inclusive co-operation tied firmly to the principles of accountability and transparency.

One of the more notable attempts to secure a comprehensive regional approach in Europe followed the break-up of the Soviet Union. The Commonwealth of Independent States (CIS) has experienced continuing instability and has had to deal with huge population movements. It is interesting to compare the reaction to the displacement from the former Yugoslavia to that in the CIS countries. What distinguishes the two situations in practice is that displacement from the former Yugoslavia spilled over into the affluent states of western Europe. In recognition of the problems they faced, the CIS called for international co-operation. A regional conference was organised by, among others,[12] the UNHCR at the request of CIS countries to address the issue.[13] The Conference took place in Geneva in May 1996 and the participants adopted a non-binding Programme of Action. The Programme of Action established, as a priority, the need to create national migration management systems and provided an outline of the principles upon which these should be anchored, as well as the administrative and operational framework. What is impressive is the attempt made in this document to think through all aspects of the problem. The comprehensive nature of the strategy is something that is lacking in, for example, the EU context. Following the Conference, the UNHCR has extended its work in the region considerably. This example illustrates the extent to which comprehensive approaches are gaining ground in the wider European context.

AMSTERDAM AND BEYOND

In the EU it is worth noting, at this introductory stage, the further developments in relation to co-operation. Progress has been incremental and yet the trends are clear. Although a process of co-operation was evident from the mid-1980s, the Treaty on European

---

12   The International Organisation for Migration (IOM) and the OSCE were also involved.
13   See UNGA Res 48/113; UNGA Res 49/173; UNGA Res 50/151.

Union (TEU) introduced the opportunity for more co-ordinated activity in the asylum context.[14] The European Commission was quick to realise the potential for the development of a comprehensive regional approach.[15] Progress has thus far been slow and disappointing. This can be attributed to an institutional structure of co-operation which was not conducive to the rapid development of common policies. Co-operation since the mid-1980s was based on complex institutional arrangements which lacked transparency and accountability.[16] Most importantly, they were also largely ineffective in developing a coherent common approach. This contributed to criticisms of the policy. It appeared that states were conscious that too much public scrutiny might impede their policy plans. The Treaty of Amsterdam (TOA) addresses this problem to some extent by amending the EC Treaty to bring asylum and immigration within the First Pillar of the EU.[17] Justice and Home Affairs came to prominence during the negotiations as a result of Austrian, French and German security concerns about enlargement, the Schengen group's insistence on incorporation of Schengen and the more flexible attitude of the UK.[18] It remained the area where there was most disagreement among states and the result, again, is that the complex and differentiated nature of the provisions are a result of this substantive disagreement. The Treaty inserts a new art 6 TEU, which proclaims that the EU is founded on 'principles of liberty, democracy, respect for human rights and fundamental freedoms and the rule of law'. One of the new objectives of the EU is to 'maintain and develop the Union as an area of freedom, security and justice, in which the free movement of persons is assured in conjunction with appropriate measures

14 Although continuing to be conducted through intergovernmentalism, the TEU made the institutional structure for co-operation more cohesive. Reflecting the well-established position that immigration and asylum go right to the core of sovereignty states have been reluctant to move rapidly in this area. However, the progress that has been made does reflect a new stage in co-operation.

15 COM (94) 23 Final para 16. Note that the previous Communication from the Commission treated the right to asylum SEC (91) 1857 Final separately from general consideration of immigration SEC (91) 1857 Final.

16 But note *Kuijer v EU Council* Case T-188/98 [2000] 2 CMLR 400. A decision by the Council to refuse access to certain documents relating to asylum on public interest grounds was annulled by the Court of First Instance.

17 See Monar 'Justice and Home Affairs in the Treaty of Amsterdam: Reform at the Price of Fragmentation' (1998) 23 Eur LR 320; Langrish 'The Treaty of Amsterdam: Selected Highlights' (1998) 23 Eur LR 3; Kortenberg 'Closer Cooperation in the Treaty of Amsterdam' (1998) 35 CMLR 833; Dehousse 'European Institutional Architecture After Amsterdam: Parliamentary System or Regulatory Structure' (1998) 35 CMLR 595.

18 Monar, note 17 above, p 321.

with respect to external border controls, asylum, immigration, and the prevention and combating of crime'. The language of human rights gains a more prominent role in the Treaty than was previously the case. The EU is drawing more intensively on the language of liberal constitutionalism, and thus raising difficult questions about constitutionalism beyond the state. The equality agenda in the EU gained further recognition through the inclusion of a new art 13 in the EC Treaty. This provides a firm legal basis for action against discrimination in the EU.

The new Title IV EC Treaty is entitled *Visas, asylum, immigration and other policies relating to the free movement of persons.*[19] It brings policy in this area within the First Pillar of the EU and represents a further step towards the formalisation of EU asylum policy. The new policy will be phased in over a five-year period. Measures are to be adopted in accordance with the provisions of the 1951 Convention and the 1967 Protocol and other relevant treaties.[20] These measures include: the criteria and mechanisms for allocating responsibility for an asylum claim;[1] minimum standards on the reception of asylum seekers;[2] minimum standards with respect to the qualification of third country nationals as refugees;[3] minimum standards on procedures for granting or withdrawing asylum.[4] Other measures adopted will deal with minimum standards for the temporary protection of displaced persons and others who are in need of international protection.[5] On burden-sharing the Treaty provides for the adoption of measures which will promote a balance of effort between member states in this area.[6] This aspect of the Treaty will not impact upon those measures which are needed to maintain law and order as well as for safeguarding internal security.[7] For the five years following the entry into force

---

19 See Guild 'After the Amsterdam Treaty' (1997) 5 Merger 8-9: 'The Community institutions have been given the power to adopt binding rules in the field of immigration and asylum . . . This is a critical step towards creating the necessary dynamic for a European immigration and asylum policy . . . On balance, the new Treaty did not confound expectations. It includes some important developments in the area of immigration and asylum which will allow community action with the benefit of democratic control by the European Parliament and some judicial control by the European Court of Justice. For the first time there is a possibility of a coherent European level approach to these issues, which most commentators would applaud.'
20 Article 63(1).
1 Article 63(1)(a).
2 Article 63(1)(b).
3 Article 63(1)(c).
4 Article 63(1)(d).
5 Article 63(2)(a).
6 Article 63(2)(b).
7 Article 64(1).

of the Treaty, the Council will act on the basis of unanimity.[8] This alters after the period of five years.[9] Provision is made for preliminary rulings from a court or tribunal against whose decision there is no judicial remedy in national law.[10]

How is all this to be carried forward? The Action Plan of the Council and the Commission on how best to implement the provisions of the TOA in an area of freedom, security and justice provides a useful guide to the proposed legislative programme. It sets out measures to be adopted within two years and others which will be adopted within the five-year period. The Action Plan recognises two weaknesses of the instruments adopted thus far: they are frequently 'soft law'; and there are inadequate monitoring arrangements.[11] The commitment to use community instruments, contained in the TOA, is viewed as an advance on this.[12] The measures to be taken in the asylum field within two years after the entry into force of the TOA are: examination of the effectiveness of the Dublin Convention; implementation of Eurodac; adoption of minimum standards on procedures for granting or withdrawing refugee status; limits on the secondary movements by asylum seekers between member states; defining minimum standards on the reception of asylum seekers; a study on the merits of a single European asylum procedure.[13] The measures to be taken as quickly as possible in accordance with the provisions of the TOA are: minimum standards for giving temporary protection to displaced persons from third countries who cannot return to their country of origin; the promotion of a balance of effort between member states in receiving and bearing the consequences of receiving displaced persons.[14] Measures to be taken within five years after the entry into force of the TOA are: adoption of minimum standards with respect to the qualification of nationals of third countries as refugees; and defining minimum standards for subsidiary protection to persons in need of international protection.[15] The Cologne European Council Presidency Conclusions included a call for the institutions to 'press ahead swiftly with the action plan's implementation'.

In March 1999 the Commission launched a discussion on asylum policy in its paper *Towards Common Standards on Asylum*

 8 Article 67(1).
 9 Article 67(2).
10 Article 68(1).
11 Paragraph 8.
12 Paragraph 8.
13 Paragraph 36.
14 Paragraph 37.
15 Paragraph 38.

Procedures.[16] The Commission has been pressing for the development of asylum law and policy for some time. In bringing forward these proposals the Commission has stated that a procedural approach makes considerable sense. In other words, that a community instrument would set out the safeguards and guarantees required but would leave room for flexibility for states. But perhaps the clearest signal yet of the seriousness with which this issue in now taken is the work carried out for the Special Council meeting in Tampere, Finland, in October 1999, in which the Presidency Conclusions reaffirmed the commitment of EU member states to a comprehensive response to asylum which includes a 'full and inclusive' approach to the interpretation of the 1951 Convention. The Conclusions state:

> 'The European Council reaffirms the importance the Union and the Member States attach to absolute respect of the right to seek asylum. It has agreed to work towards establishing a Common European Asylum System, based on the full and inclusive application of the Geneva Convention, thus ensuring that nobody is sent back to persecution i.e. maintaining the principle of non-refoulement.'[17]

The Conclusions adopted are of interest principally because of the liberality of the language on asylum. The Commission has been asked to prepare a communication on a uniform asylum procedure within one year.[18] The Commission was also invited in the Tampere Conclusions to draw up a 'scoreboard' in relation to the implementation of the TOA, the Vienna Action Plan and the Tampere Conclusions. The 'scoreboard' is intended to ensure that the progress of the member states in this area is effectively monitored. The Council adopted this 'scoreboard' at the end of March 2000. As with other such measures, this contains goals and deadlines for the establishment of an area of freedom, security and justice. These goals and deadlines follow on from the previously mentioned Action Plan.

Although there is a more secure basis for EU action in this field, problems remain. The principal one is that unanimity remains a requirement. If there is an issue that has stalled the process of co-operation it is this one, and so it is likely to continue to cause problems for those seeking to implement the ambitious agenda on asylum. Nevertheless, the Tampere Conclusions were given a relatively warm welcome by those campaigning for the protection of refugees in Europe. In particular, the encouraging references to

16 SEC (1999) 271 Final.
17 Paragraph 13.
18 Paragraph 15.

the 1951 Convention meant that, at least on paper, states were not preparing to abandon it.

On institutional reform it is worth mentioning the establishment of the High Level Working Group on Asylum and Migration. The Working Group was established in December 1998 for the purpose of developing cross-pillar Action Plans on listed states. States have welcomed the work and have extended its mandate. Cross-pillar initiatives have produced six Action Plans (Afghanistan, Iraq, Morocco, Somalia, Sri Lanka and Albania). States are particularly keen on this type of approach which promises to be comprehensive in its scope.

In addition, a Protocol to the Treaty provides a mechanism for the integration of the Schengen *acquis* into the EU.[19] In reality, the Schengen system was outside the EU in theory only (it is frequently described as a laboratory for the emerging internal market), and was the result of an attempt to accommodate dissenting voices within the Union. Although the UK, Ireland and Denmark have followed well-established practice and secured 'opt-outs'[20] from these provisions, there is little doubt that the move will result in more fully fledged European regulation in the future. The advantages of this include the potential for enhanced democratic and judicial scrutiny, something which has been notably lacking in the past. Although the provisions relating to immigration and asylum are still rather fragmentary, the Treaty will result in an improvement in the legal quality of instruments adopted in this area. This will signal a move away from the varied use of soft law measures.[1] The soft law measures that have been adopted thus far have had a practical impact which goes well beyond their formal legal status. Here again, the importance of transnational networks of activism must be stressed. For the transition from soft to hard law need not mean that the substance of the measures remains the same. States might be called upon to make good on the commitment to a 'full and inclusive' approach to the 1951 Convention.

One of the consequences of closer co-operation in the EU is a general belief that no other member state should be regarded as 'unsafe' for asylum purposes. This follows the logic of supranationalism. It can, however, be viewed as a regressive aspect

19   Protocol Integrating the Schengen Acquis into the Framework of the European Union.
20   Protocol on the Position of the UK and Ireland; Protocol on the Application of Certain Aspects of Article 7a of the Treaty Establishing the European Community to the United Kingdom and Ireland. Under Article 3 of the former Protocol the UK and Ireland have the option of taking part in the adoption and application of any proposed measure under Title IIIa.
 1   Monar (1998) 2 Eur LR 320, 326.

of the Treaty.[2] The presumption that all states are 'safe' for asylum purposes is a element of restriction which raises the problem of geographical restrictions.[3] If member states are 'safe' for asylum purposes then to what extent is this a restriction on the universal scope and applicability of international refugee law?

The European response to asylum reflects a change of mood in the region towards migration generally.[4] As member states have steadily tried to restrict migration from third states, so it was inevitable that asylum would be affected in this process. Asylum, the humanitarian exception to the general instrumentalism of immigration regulation, has suffered as a consequence of the general drive towards the reduction of immigration. To shorten the story, as a consequence of this policy the construction of the asylum seeker has undergone a transformation. During the cold war she was viewed as a heroic dissident fleeing totalitarian regimes. Now official and popular discourses address asylum seekers with barely concealed disdain.[5] EU member states compete to make themselves as unattractive as possible to asylum seekers. The 'demonisation' necessary for the legitimisation of questionable policies began in earnest in the late 1980s, and continued in the 1990s. Asylum seekers are constructed, in these discourses, as, on the whole, 'bogus' seekers after better lives rather than 'genuine refugees'. The crudity of these categories did not prevent them from having a substantial impact on the debate. In significant senses the struggle to achieve a rational discussion in this area was lost even before the process had begun. In other words, partial categories were used to shape the debate which emerged. The irony of this collective European amnesia will not be lost on those with a knowledge of modern European history.[6]

2　For criticism see UNHCR Update 20 June 1997 'UNHCR Concerned about Restricted Access to Asylum in Europe'.

3　Spain has pushed for this for some time. Not unconnected is the fact that Belgium has in the past granted asylum to Basque separatists. Cf Resolution on minimum guarantees for asylum procedures, para 20: 'The Member States observe that, with due regard for the 1951 Geneva Refugee Convention there should be no *de facto* or *de jure* grounds for granting refugee status to an asylum applicant who is a national of another Member State.'

4　See Joly (1994) 6 IJRL 159.

5　In the German context, see Schönwälder 'Migration, Refugees and Ethnic Plurality as Issues of Public and Political Debate in (West) Germany' in Cesarani and Fulbrook (eds) *Citizenship, Nationality and Migration in Europe* (1996).

6　The familiar pattern is repeating itself in Ireland at present. See Cullen *Refugees and Asylum Seekers in Ireland* (2000); Cullen 'The 1997 Border Campaign: Refugees, Asylum and Race on the Borders' in Crowley and MacLaughlin (eds) *Under the Belly of the Tiger: Class, Race, Identity and Culture in Global Ireland* (1997) p 101; Murphy 'Immigrants and Refugees: The Irish Legal Context' in Crowley

The overall trend is traceable to a variety of factors but, as noted above, most notably the falling demand for migrant labour, following the economic difficulties of the mid-1970s, and the desire to ensure that in future shortfalls in labour were dealt with intra-regionally. As Shacknove argues, there has been a distinct movement from asylum to containment in state practice.[7] In the 1980s these restrictive measures where primarily being applied to those seeking refuge from other regions outside of Europe. One of the more interesting developments in the 1990s has, however, been the extent to which mass forced migration has once again returned to Europe.[8] The conflicts in the former Yugoslavia, and those which followed the break-up of the Soviet Union, have provided added impetus to the development of a regional policy which goes beyond the narrow confines of traditional approaches to international refugee law.[9]

THE EUROPEAN HUMAN RIGHTS DIMENSION

One of the tensions that emerges in this area is between a supranationalism anchored in a version of EU citizenship and the law and politics of human rights. There has always been a tension between citizens' and human rights. But it is a tension which is often ignored or assumed to be unproblematic. The reason is that it raises serious problems for the formation of political communities. To have a political community is to possess a form of membership and belonging, whether this is acknowledged or not. Human

---

and MacLaughlin (eds) (above) p 95. See Refugee Act 1996; Lean 'Human Rights have no Borders' (1998) 1 Forced Migration Rev 17, 19: 'The 1996 Refugee Act represents a major step forward and has the potential to place Ireland at the forefront of progressive international law and practice on asylum. However, despite being passed with all-party support . . . it has been only very partially implemented.'

7   Shacknove 'From Asylum to Containment' (1993) 5 IJRL 516.

8   The fear that western Europe would be overwhelmed by migrants proved, on the whole, to be unfounded.

9   In 1994 the UN General Assembly called upon UNHCR to: 'promote and develop a preparatory process, leading to the convening, not later than 1996, of a regional conference to address the problems of refugees, displaced persons, other forms of involuntary displacement and returnees in the countries of the CIS and relevant neighbouring states', UNGA Res 49/173. For subsequent developments see UNHCR Regional Bureau for Europe, *The CIS Conference on Refugees and Migrants* (1996) 2 European Series Vol I and II. In its European regional policy UNHCR has turned its attention to the problems of central and eastern Europe. See Helton 'The CIS Migration Conference: A Chance to Prevent and Ameliorate Forced Movements of People in the Former Soviet Union' (1996) 8 IJRL 169.

rights discourse does not challenge the process of boundary drawing or the establishment of forms of membership. But in detaching entitlements from status it challenges more exclusive forms of ethnically-based theories of duties and responsibilities. Whether there is any way to resolve this tension is another matter, but there is an argument that the institutionalisation of democratic law is one way this might be achieved.

Human rights discourse has assumed a central place in legal scholarship in modern times. There are reasons to both welcome this trend and to counsel a measure of caution. On the positive side, human rights discourse is essential to the fair treatment of asylum seekers because of the shift it has engineered away from an exclusive focus on citizens' rights. Human rights discourse can, however, bring confusion with it. The moral force of the discourse can disguise the underlying values and concepts that are influencing concrete practice. Resolving disputes surrounding competing rights may involve using other values, which have validity but whose force can be lost in the rights debate. This is simply to urge a measure of caution. The legal and moral force of rights must be recognised in this context. Human rights make a difference in the asylum context even if they gain meaning in highly localised contexts and in the wake of struggles for legal and political reform.[10]

An examination of the European regulation of asylum would be incomplete without mentioning the centrality of European developments in human rights law. Rights discourse has been subjected to criticism in recent years. It can perpetuate an atomised conception of social relations to the detriment of other important societal values. The limitations of the discourse should be recognised, but this should not lead to its abandonment. The principle of legality, and the enforcement of rights through law, is important for marginalised groups. Asylum seekers, lacking the protection that often springs from the political bond of citizenship, depend upon the recognition of positivised *human* rights, ie protections which transcend citizen/stranger distinctions and attach solely to the individual's status as a human being.

10 See Plender and Mole 'Beyond the Geneva Convention: Constructing a *De Facto Right of Asylum* from International Human Rights Instruments' in Nicholson and Twomey (eds) *Refugee Rights and Realities: Evolving International Concepts and Regimes* (1999) 81; Lambert 'Protection Against *Refoulement* in Europe: Human Rights Comes to the Rescue' (1999) 48 ICLQ 515.

Human rights law is underdeveloped in EU law and practice. While the practical result may impact upon human rights protection the focus on rights is less prominent. There are sound historical reasons for this. The economic rationale of the internal market still dominates thinking on the development of the EU. The increased use of the concept of citizenship has promoted a concern with rights and raised questions about whether the EU is becoming 'constitutionalised'. This process of 'constitutionalisation' may be advanced if the proposed Charter of Fundamental Rights of the EU is adopted. At the European Council meeting in Cologne on 3 and 4 June 1999 it was decided that the rights applicable in the EU should be consolidated in a Charter. At its meeting in Tampere on 15 and 16 December 1999 the European Council agreed on the composition, working method and practical details of the body responsible for preparing a draft Charter of Fundamental Rights of the European Union. The body entrusted with the task of drawing up this Charter met for the first time on 17 December 1999.[11] At the time of writing, provision is being made for the inclusion of a right of asylum.[12] The proposed draft on the right of asylum refers to a right which attaches to persons who are not nationals of the European Union. This geographical limitation raises questions of compatibility with the 1951 Convention. It can be read alongside the new Protocol on Asylum for Nationals of Member States of the EU. This provides that asylum will not normally be granted to nationals of other member states. There are narrow exceptions to the general principle. Overall, the 'internal market' logic, and therefore economistic and instrumental thinking, dominates much of the debate in the EU. As an entity it may begin to experience a crisis of identity as its role alters. There are broader issues of where a reconstructed EU fits within the landscape of human rights protection in Europe. This brings the concept of complementarity into the picture as the various organisations attempt to complement, rather than compete with, each other.

---

11 The composition and method of work of the body established to elaborate a draft Charter is to be found in the Annex to the Tampere Presidency Conclusions.
12 Amnesty International *Comments on the right of asylum and the protection of refugees under the European Union Charter of Fundamental Rights* (March 2000).

One of the more remarkable features of modern international law is the proliferation of standards, reflected in the provisions of international human rights law. The development of human rights law has had an impact on the asylum debate. This now supplements refugee law in valuable ways, for example, remedying some of refugee law's more obvious gaps. The gap that is frequently criticised is the absence of an international monitoring body that has responsibility for making authoritative statements of the meaning of the law. The role of the UNHCR differs markedly from bodies which fulfil an adjudication role in other areas of human rights law. The absence of an international mechanism, combined with state restriction in Europe, provided the impetus to individuals to resort to the UNCAT as well as the UNHCR. In this, asylum seekers and their advocates do not differ from other groups which have made productive use of these international mechanisms for redress. What their use has highlighted is the inadequacy of the domestic enforcement of international refugee law. However, as emphasised above, one should not overestimate the value of these international mechanisms. International refugee law retains a critical importance as a status-granting mechanism which guarantees to the refugee formal recognition as a legal person.

As argued elsewhere, the most fundamental protection which law provides for the refugee is that of *non-refoulement*.[13] This norm is in a process of transition precisely because of the developments in human rights law. Human rights law has contributed to the recognition of the absolute nature of the protection. This is a position which can be contrasted with refugee law, where exceptions exist. In addition to the international standards, Europe has developed its own regional human rights mechanisms, which supplement international provisions in valuable ways. The European Convention system is rightly regarded as a highly effective mechanism for securing human rights protection. Given the enforcement problems with refugee law, it is unsurprising that it has proven useful. Again, one should not overestimate the importance of this instrument. The European Court of Human Rights takes a cautious approach to asylum, despite the fact that it has been willing to adopt an expansive interpretation of art 3.[14] For example, the evidential standards are

13 1951 Convention, art 33.
14 See ch 5.

set at a high level which makes it in practice very difficult for asylum seekers to make successful use of the mechanism. This does depend, of course, on the measure of success applied. For it is evident that the ECHR has an impact on practice which goes beyond its purely formal status. The use of the Convention system can have an impact in practice irrespective of whether a case ends up being examined on the merits by the European Court of Human Rights.

The importance of the European Convention for refugees and asylum seekers rests in its status as a *human* rights instrument. States are obliged to secure to 'everyone within their jurisdiction the rights and freedoms defined in Section I of this Convention'.[15] With some limitations the rights are equally applicable to asylum seekers. Of particular importance to asylum seekers is the guarantee in art 3.[16] Although the European Court of Human Rights has taken a cautious approach in this area (undoubtedly aware of the need to ensure that dynamic interpretation of Convention rights does not stretch the limits of its own legitimacy[17]), the European Convention now offers significant guarantees to asylum seekers. In practice, these extend beyond the scope of the 1951 Convention and remedy its gaps.[18] Other Convention rights are also important, notably art 8, Protocol 4, arts 3 and 4 and Protocol 7, art 1. The willingness of the Court of Human Rights to develop provisions such as art 3 to include the return of asylum seekers is an interesting development. It is worth remembering that this occurred at a time when many European states were in the process of constructing quite formidable obstacles to asylum seekers entering the region. The Court's approach coincided with a European trend towards increased deterrence and restriction. This reinforces the fact that these are *human* rights and apply in situations which matter to asylum seekers. It has also proved to be

---

15　Cf Commonwealth of Independent States (CIS) Convention on Human Rights and Fundamental Freedoms, 26 May 1995 (1996) 17 Human Rights LJ 159, art 1.

16　See ch 5.

17　On this issue see Mahoney 'Judicial Activism and Judicial Self-Restraint in the European Court of Human Rights' (1990) 11 Human Rights LJ 57.

18　See Harvey 'Expulsion, National Security and the European Convention' (1997) 22 Eur LR 626, 633: 'The Court of Human Rights' judgment . . . highlights the deficiencies of the 1951 Convention . . . While the prohibition on *refoulement* in art 33 is viewed correctly as the cornerstone of modern refugee law, it permits limitations on national security grounds. Viewed from the perspective of human rights law it is seriously flawed as a protection regime.'

a useful example of how a regional human rights mechanism may influence the thinking of the wider international human rights community; for the jurisprudence and thinking of the European Court of Human Rights on this issue has spread to other international human rights mechanisms. One should not exaggerate either the liberality of the approach adopted or its practical influence. I have already suggested that while expanding the reach of the European Convention, the Court has been careful, as an institutional actor within a broader European context, to delimit its availability. The concern of these human rights bodies is that they do not become a surrogate 'appeal' process used by large numbers of those who have been refused asylum.

Other instruments of note, adopted within the Council of Europe, include the European Convention for the Prevention of Torture and Inhuman or Degrading Treatment or Punishment 1987 and the Framework Convention on National Minorities 1995. They are examples of regional human rights mechanism which have contributed to struggles to secure decent treatment for those in need of protection in Europe. As will be evident from the discussion which follows, the human rights dimension now figures prominently in the refugee debate in Europe. One should not confine this to the Council of Europe only. As noted, human rights discourse is also playing an ever greater role in EU asylum law and policy.[19] And the OSCE[1] has assumed an important place in promoting human rights issues in Europe.[2] The institutions within which human rights protection arises matter and dictate the nature of the rights-based approach adopted. It is now beyond dispute that regional human rights mechanisms are having a significant impact on refugee protection in Europe.

19 See de Búrca 'The Language of Rights and European Integration' in Shaw and More (eds) *New Legal Dynamics of European Union* (1995) p 29.
 1 See generally Bothe et al *The OSCE in the Maintenance of Peace and Security: Conflict Prevention, Crisis Management and the Peaceful Settlement of Disputes* (1997); Buergenthal 'The Copenhagen CSCE Meeting: A New Public Order for Europe' (1990) 11 Human Rights LJ 217; Roth 'The CSCE Charter of Paris for a New Europe' (1990) 11 Human Rights LJ 373; McGoldrick 'The Development of the CSCE after the 1992 Conference' (1993) 42 ICLQ 411.
 2 See Wright 'The Protection of Minority Rights in Europe: From Conference to Implementation' (1998) 2 Int J Human Rights 1.

MAPPING THE BOUNDARIES OF THE EUROPEAN
REGULATION OF ASYLUM

It is beyond the scope of this chapter to provide a detailed description of the forms and substance of law and policy in its entirety. The approach adopted below is to examine the key themes which may be extracted from the European regional response thus far. Asylum law in the EU is complex. It highlights in practice the difficulties which follow from the intersection of a variety of legal orders.[3] Scanning the variety of forms of policy development, this method permits reflection on central conceptual and practical issues. It is, one might say, a map of the terrain.[4] This will help to illustrate some distinct aspects of the contribution which Europe is making to developments in this area, and point to some of the norms that are gaining acceptance as a result. This exploration of the Europeanisation of asylum law focuses on the EU because the Union has made the most progress in developing a common approach. The process of enlargement of the EU is also having an impact on those states presently on the outside. Justice and Home Affairs matters are viewed as areas where rapid progress should be made by applicant countries.

The starting point for this is the fact that all EU member states are parties to the 1951 Convention and its 1967 Protocol. While regionalism has the potential to undercut international standards, the EU has expressed a commitment to adopt measures which are in accordance with international refugee law. There is commonality in approach already because all EU member states apply the same definition of refugee status.[5] This does not mean that in practice there are common standards for asylum seekers. It is evident that some states adopt different interpretations of these common provisions. Varying recognition rates indicate that the practical construction of 'refugee' in each is also markedly

---

3   See Peers *EU Justice and Home Affairs Law* (2000) pp 106-130.
4   This is a conception of the regulatory response the validity of which is dependent upon its utility as an accessible guide.
5   See Vanheule 'A Comparison of the Judicial Interpretation of the Notion of Refugee' in Carlier and Vanheule (eds) *Europe and Refugees: A Challenge?* (1997) p 91.

different. Despite the broad similarities, and the attempts to create a common approach, it still matters which EU state an asylum seeker looks for refuge in. There are also a number of other forms of protection which attract different levels of entitlement in each state. Therefore, although broad similarities exist, the practice still varies greatly.

Root causes and prevention

As was clear in the analysis in Chapter 2, the goal of a truly comprehensive approach must be the removal of the root causes of forced migration.[6] Much attention has been directed in recent years at this aspect of the refugee debate. There are reasons to be cautious about this renewal of interest. It has come at a time when European states in particular have been engaged in an attack on the institution of asylum as it is traditionally understood. While one can welcome the discourse of prevention as belated recognition of a more comprehensive approach, there is a danger that erosion of asylum will not be met by a real commitment to prevention. There is little sign that the root causes of forced migration are being tackled effectively.

The external policy of the EU plays a part in the attempt to address the root causes of forced migration. Foreign policy straightforwardly impacts upon states of origin. It is here that development assistance, for example, contributes to reducing the factors which lead to migration.[7] Conditionality in external

---

6   In the EU see European Council Declaration on Principles Governing External Aspects of Migration Policy, 12 December 1992. Principle 1: 'They will continue to work for the preservation and restoration of peace, the full respect for human rights and the rule of law, so diminishing migratory pressures that result from war and oppressive and discriminatory government.' Also note Principle 2: '[D]isplaced people should be encouraged to stay in the nearest safe area to their homes, and aid and assistance should be directed towards giving them the confidence and the means to do so without prejudice to their temporary admission also in the territory of Member States in cases of particular need.' See Thornburn 'Root Causes Approaches to Forced Migration: A European Perspective' (1996) 9 JRS 119; Hathaway 'New Directions to Avoid Hard Problems: The Distortion of the Palliative Role of Refugee Protection' (1995) 8 JRS 288: 'The real motivation for the new found concern for the enforcement of human rights can be seen in the simultaneous and concerted action of states to throw up barricades to the arrival of refugees' (p 292). On the 'right' to remain: 'This so-called right is as ridiculous as it is evil.'

7   Peers, note 3 above, pp 106-107.

policy also has an impact on refugee issues, although this has less to do with reducing the root causes of flight and more to do with avoiding responsibility for refugees. This is evident in the inclusion of a clause on readmission agreements in the negotiations to conclude a new Lomé Convention.[8] The EU wished to include a clause requiring the readmission of non-nationals but this was rejected by ACP states.[9]

The development of measures for addressing the root causes of migration follows the emergence of EU policy generally. At the Edinburgh Summit in 1992 the European Council adopted the Declaration on Principles Governing External Aspects of Migration Policy.[10] States committed themselves to –

> 'continue to work for the preservation and restoration of peace, the full respect for human rights and the rule of law, so diminishing migratory pressures that result from war and oppressive and discriminatory government . . .'[11]

This further included the 'protection and assistance of displaced people in the nearest safe area to their homes' as well as 'targeting development aid and job creation and the alleviation of poverty'. While the language of comprehensive approaches was prevalent, in practice the concentration was on restrictive immigration and asylum polices.[12] The EU has reduced the concept of migration management to co-opting other states into a system of responsibility avoidance. The potential of prevention discourse is not being exploited to the full in current law and practice in the EU.[13] The talk of the promotion of human rights, the rule of law and democracy in the external relations of the EU is welcome. However, the clear lack of success in addressing the root causes of refugee movements means that restriction on asylum is misplaced.

The ideal toward which the human rights movement struggles is a world where oppression, and the variety of injustices which

8 *Migration News Sheet* (March 2000) p 2.
9 See note 8 above.
10 SN 456/1/92 Rev 1.
11 Principle 1.
12 See Niessen and Mochel *EU External Relations and International Migration* (1999).
13 Niessen and Mochel, note 12 above, p 70.

force people to leave their places of origin, are eliminated. Oppression of social groups involves not simply the violation of the narrow band of civil and political rights included in international refugee law, but all the other economic, social and increasingly environmental factors which cause forced migration. The causes are many and varied, and the law's image of the refugee lags some way behind modern realities.[14] The ideal is a situation whereby a full range of human rights are *effectively* protected within a flourishing deliberative political community. If refugee law is to be integrated more successfully within the wider body of human rights law, then it is the emancipation of oppressed social groups which must be the ultimate aim. As argued elsewhere in this work, this is a long-term project and can not be used to justify a restrictive approach to asylum.

As indicated, anyone approaching this area purely through the established legal categories would receive a wholly misguided picture of the root causes of forced migration. Law fails, in dramatic fashion, to reflect the real causes of forced migration (the reasons for this are discussed above).[15] In the European context there has been growing recognition that the root causes of forced migration have been neglected. For example, as part of its comprehensive migration policy, the EU has emphasised measures which address the root causes of flight.[16] As suggested here, in practice this discourse of prevention has functioned thus far to legitimise restriction in the EU context rather than resulting in practical measures to address causes.

In Europe it is the OSCE which has done the most in recent years to deal with the issue of causes in practice. Important work has been done within the institutional framework of the OSCE on issues such as crisis management and conflict prevention.[17] As the

14　Migration induced by environmental factors is not included and yet it is a factor in a number of recent forced displacements. There are estimated to be 150,000 environmental refugees in the Ukraine, 75,000 in the Russian Federation and 145,000 in Belarus, *Migration News* February 1997. Ecologists suggest that there are over 270 areas in the former Soviet Union where environmental contamination has forced people to flee their homes.

15　Gilbert 'The Best "Early Warning" is Prevention: Refugee Flows and European Responses" (1997) 9 IJRL 207.

16　European Commission COM (94) 23 Final, paras 44-54.

17　See eg CSCE Helsinki Document 1992, III. Early Warning, Conflict Prevention and Crisis Management (Including Fact-Finding and Rapporteur Missions and CSCE Peace Keeping), Peaceful Settlement of Disputes.

situation in Kosovo in the Federal Republic of Yugoslavia in 1998 showed, there is still much work to be done on this. It is correct to say that the OSCE has enjoyed a revival in the post-cold war era.[18] In a period that has witnessed the resurgence of ethnic conflict and mass displacement in Europe, the OSCE has emerged as central to attempts to promote and implement effective preventative strategies.[19] Conflict prevention, regulation and resolution are pillars upon which this institution functions. This is why its work is of such importance here. Although one might point to the non-legally binding nature of much of the OSCE documentation, this does not undervalue the role of this organisation,[20] which now plays an important part in, for example, minority rights protection in Europe. The OSCE has been involved in monitoring the refugee return process in, for example, Croatia.[1] The OSCE has also deployed civilian police monitors in Croatia.[2] Advice and assistance is to be provided in relation to, inter alia, the protection of the human rights of displaced persons and refugees.[3] In practice the OSCE has thus evolved from what was a political process to a more institutionalised body, which does, however, remain somewhat fragmented in comparison with some of the other European regional organisations. Although it lacks the cohesiveness of the EU, the OSCE has the distinct advantage of being representative as a European organisation.

Restricting access

One of the principal arguments in this chapter is that the EU is engaged in a co-ordinated exercise in deterrence. In an attempt to deter the arrival of asylum seekers in the region, use has been made

---

18 McGoldrick, note 1 above, p 66.
19 See Gilbert, note 15 above.
20 Gilbert, note 15 above, p 215.
 1 OSCE Newsletter July 1998 p 13.
 2 OSCE Newsletter June 1998 p 1.
 3 OSCE Newsletter June 1998 p 1.

of a combination of carrier sanctions and visa controls.[4] When numbers of asylum applicants rise rapidly from a state, the trend is to impose visa restrictions. The reasoning is easily grasped, and fits into the overall picture of the regulatory framework being painted in this chapter. The dominant motive for the adoption of these policies is the desire to restrict the entry of asylum seekers into the region. If individuals can not make it to Europe then they will not be able to claim asylum there, so runs the logic. In the EU carrier sanctions and visa controls are central aspects of the control strategy of member states.[5] Carrier sanctions, in particular, raise interesting questions about who should regulate this aspect of policy. Some commentators have noted that they lead to the effective privatisation of immigration control and conflict with international refugee and civil aviation law.[6] While these measures undermine the spirit of international refugee law, their influence is even more corrosive than this. For they are part of a process of extending the systemic logic of EU asylum policy into the private as well as the public spheres. They function in often subtle ways to inscribe this dominant narrative in all areas where migration management in effect takes place. What is interesting about this process is how inconsistent it

4   See Council Regulation determining third countries whose nationals must be in possession of visas when crossing the external borders of the member states, OJ 1995 L 234/1; Council Regulation of 25 May 1995 on a uniform format for visas, OJ 1995 L 164/1. There are 98 states listed here. Member states have also adopted a Joint Action concerning a uniform format for resident permits, OJ 1997 L 7/1. In March 1996 the Council adopted a Recommendation relating to local consular co-operation regarding visas, OJ 1996 L80/1. See also Joint Action on airport transit arrangements OJ 1996 L63/8, a common list of countries whose nationals are subject to airport transit visas (ten states), however, 13 member states (excluding UK and Ireland) have by Declaration undertaken to subject Bangladesh and Pakistan to the same. There is, in addition, co-operation underway in relation to training measures, exchange measures and studies and research, Joint Action of 19 March 1998 introducing a programme of training, exchanges and cooperation in the field of asylum, immigration and crossing of external borders (Odysseus programme) OJ 1998 L 99/2, on asylum see art 7. See also Proposal for Council decision on a joint action adopted by the Council introducing a programme of training, exchanges and co-operation in the field of asylum, immigration and crossing of external borders (Odysseus programme) COM 97 Final 364, OJ 1997 C 267/7.

5   See draft External Borders Convention, a version of the text may be found at OJ 1994 C11/6; Schengen Implementing Agreement Chapter Two 'Crossing External Borders'.

6   Nicholson 'Implementation of the Immigration (Carriers' Liability) Act 1987: Privatising Immigration Functions at the Expense of International Obligations?' (1997) 46 ICLQ 586. See also Danish Refugee Council *The Effects of Carrier Sanctions on the Asylum System* (1991). The UK has airline liaison officers in Dhaka, Delhi, Colombo in Sri Lanka, Nairobi and Accra: *Migration News* December 1997. In November the UK government announced the establishment of a task force to deal with alien smuggling after discovering an asylum fraud scheme in Sri Lanka.

actually is with much that states claim. The control of migration is often claimed to be central to the public function of good governance. However, in this instance we see governments prepared to 'delegate' responsibility to the private sphere when necessary. The practice has clear implications for the enforcement of international obligations. One should not neglect the value of accountability in this process. For who ultimately will hold carriers to account for the fact that they have prevented a refugee from seeking asylum in the EU?

Reshaping national asylum processes

Substantive and procedural reform of refugee and asylum law is addressed fully in the chapters on law and practice in the UK. One would, however, be left with a partial picture without recognising the extent to which this is an EU-wide trend. EU member states are engaged in a process of making themselves appear as unattractive as possible to asylum seekers. The systemic logic thus far has been towards a lowest common denominator approach. State has followed state in adopting restrictive measures ostensibly aimed at 'abusive applicants'. Institutional co-operation in regional fora has thus far not advanced the goal of a responsible and humane regionalism. What is in practice happening is that a story which emerged within the specifically national contexts of EU member states has become the dominant narrative in the region. This simplified story of the 'abusive applicant' and the 'genuine refugee' retains a grip on the debate in Europe. While reductionism is inherent in the exercise of regulating any area through law, rational debate has been stifled. A false image of the complex phenomenon of forced migration has been perpetuated in this debate.

The trend has not been exclusively in the direction of restriction. The Council Resolution on minimum guarantees for asylum procedures 1995 contains positive principles. The Resolution commits states to full compliance with the 1951 Convention and other international law obligations. It is a useful indication of the elements which should be included in national asylum procedures. For example, it states that asylum applications should be examined by an authority fully qualified in asylum and refugee matters and decisions taken independently.

A familiar feature of the many changes to the asylum policies of EU member states has been the introduction of accelerated procedures to deal with claims that are manifestly unfounded.[7] In

---

7   See European Parliament *Asylum in the EU Member States* (2000) para 3; Care *A Guide to Asylum Law and Practice in the European Union* (1995).

1992 states adopted a Resolution on manifestly unfounded applications for asylum. The measure reflects thinking that was already underway within states. The idea underlying this, and many other developments in the EU, is the belief that asylum procedures are being 'abused' by 'bogus applicants' and that these individuals should be removed from the system as rapidly as possible. A manifestly unfounded claim is defined as one which raises no substantive issue under the 1951 Convention because there is clearly no substance to the individual's asylum application or it is 'based on deliberate deception' or was 'an abuse of asylum procedures'. A connection is also made in the Resolution between the concept and the safe third country notion discussed below. Further elaboration of the potential breadth of the measure is contained in sections dealing with the meaning of the 'no substance' and 'deliberate deception' provisions. Examples of situations which are envisaged would come within the accelerated procedures include: economic migration; absence of credibility; the internal flight option; the safe country notion; use of false identity and/or counterfeit documents; and making false representations. It was evident from the scope of the measure that EU states were prepared to adopt a very liberal interpretation of the phrase 'manifestly unfounded application'. From the language adopted in the measure it was clear that the rigidly drawn distinction between the 'genuine refugee' and the 'bogus asylum seeker' was solidifying at the EU level. This reinforces arguments made elsewhere in this work that the nature of the debate was dictated by the terms of reference and the language games advanced by states. Once the terms of the debate became established, it was more difficult to advance positions which did not fit into this orthodoxy.

Reconstructing refugee status

The definition of refugee is contained in the 1951 Convention. This instrument has gained widespread international acceptance. The precise application of the Convention depends on national law and practice. This means that responses can vary between states. While one state may recognise persecution by non-state entities as coming within the definition, another may not. There is no international court or tribunal to which an asylum seeker can appeal in order to challenge this variance in national practice. The decentralised nature of refugee law is odd, given the inherently international dimension of the phenomenon of forced migration. The result is a system of regulation which is not conducive to fair or effective migration management. The inconsistency in practice raises questions about the scope and nature of international legality as this applies to the refugee and asylum seeker.

If this is a general international problem, the difficulties become even more acute when one considers the EU. For here we have an entity which functions with the systemic assumption that there is a common approach. The reality is, however, somewhat different. A real risk then arises of the unfair treatment of refugees and asylum seekers. The logical next step in the EU is to adopt a harmonised approach to the definition of refugee. This is rendered less troublesome by the existence of the 1951 Convention. In 1996 the EU adopted a Joint Position on the harmonised application of the definition of the term 'refugee' in art 1 of the Geneva Convention. This contains guidance only on the approach to the constituent parts of the definition. There is little that is new in this although the section on persecution by 'third parties' is more restrictive than the terms of the 1951 Convention would suggest it should be. It will only be considered to come within the 1951 Convention 'where it is based on one of the grounds in art 1A . . . is individual in nature and is encouraged or permitted by the authorities'.[8] The Joint Position provides that persecution 'is generally the act of a State organ'.[9]

Work has been done on trying to ensure that a common approach is taken to key elements of refugee law. There is a lack of consensus on the interpretation of some aspects of the 1951 Convention. If the EU claims to be speaking with one voice on asylum policy then it is problematic for variance to exist between national legal systems in this area. It is not evident why an asylum seeker should have her choices reduced to making one claim only in the EU if national practices continue to differ. A single European asylum system would have to function with a harmonised interpretation of the 1951 Convention before any such limitation would be fair.

On being responsible

International refugee law delegates responsibility for the substantive assessment of claims to individual states. The understanding of

8   OJ 1996 L 063/2 para 5.2.
9   Paragraph 5.1.

responsibility reflected in this body of law is an atomised one. There is no mechanism in international refugee law for responsibility sharing which would regulate a collective response. What this means in practice is that responsibility for addressing refugee movements can fall unevenly on states and regions. In the EU, for example, Germany has traditionally received more asylum seekers than other member states. This disparity can also be seen in regional context, where Europe has tended to receive a minority of the world's refugees. The question this raises is whether there should be a mechanism that would allocate refugees to states on a proportionate basis. The argument for such a mechanism is that it will result in quantitatively better protection for refugees in the long term. This raises issues from both a principled and a pragmatic perspective. The principled objection to the creation of regulatory mechanisms to allocate refugees is that they are insufficiently sensitive to individual human rights concerns. By treating refugees as means to achieving other ends, the fear is that human dignity will be compromised in the process. At its most extreme this is claimed to result in the 'commodification' of refugees. These are principled objections to this regulatory model. More pragmatically, there is a concern that these models do not work in practice. The answer to this pragmatic objection is to continue to work with the model that does exist.

In the EU attempts have been made to advance more co-operative models. In particular, there has been an emphasis on determining the state which should be responsible for assessing the individual asylum application. Both the Dublin Convention 1990[10]

10 The Dublin Convention 1990 entered into force 1 September 1997, OJ 1997 C 254/1. States have adopted a number of measures which clarify aspects of the functioning of the system. For example, there is agreement on the means of proof, OJ 1996 C 274/35, as well as a standard for determining the state responsible for examining an application for asylum, OJ 1996 C 274/44. See also Council Conclusion of 27 May 1997 Concerning the Practical Implementation of the Dublin Convention, OJ 1997 C 191/27. A number of decisions have been taken since the Convention entered into force see Decision No 1/97 of 9 September 1997 of the Committee set up by art 18 of the Dublin Convention 1990 of 15 June concerning provision for the implementation of the Convention, OJ 1997 L 281/1; Decision No 2/97 of 9 September 1997 establishing the Committee's rules of procedure, OJ 1997 L 281/26. The possible adoption of a parallel Convention has played a part in discussions between EU member states and central and eastern European states, *Euro-East* 3 June 1997. The Justice and Home Affairs Council has been keen to stress the importance of the area to the enlargement process generally.

and the Schengen Implementing Convention 1990[11] provide a mechanism for allocating responsibility for the assessment of asylum applications to one state. Although states have argued that the measures are intended to guarantee individual assessment, it is noteworthy that the provisions contain significant exceptions. The instruments do not, for example, interfere with the right to send an asylum seeker to a third state.[12] In other words, member states remain free to return an asylum applicant to a third state even before a determination is made. This appears to contradict the claims that the aim is solely to eradicate the problem of 'refugees in orbit'.[13] The instruments are drafted with a purely inter-state system of regulation in mind. On the positive side, states have, however, adopted minimum guarantees for asylum procedures which are applicable to the examination of asylum applications, as defined in the Dublin Convention.[14] As with much EU policy in this area, these guarantees are not legally binding – a fact which reduces their practical importance for asylum seekers. Serious consideration is now being given within the EU to the effectiveness of the Dublin Convention and its future replacement with a Community instrument. The European Commission has produced a working document on a future Community instrument to replace the Dublin Convention.[15] Member states have been

11 The 'Schengen system' became operative on 26 March, 1995: 'bringing to life the decades-old vision of a Europe without internal border controls . . . A new country, so called "Schengenland", has been created within Europe', see Hailbronner and Thiery 'Schengen II and Dublin: Responsibility for Asylum Applications in Europe' (1997) 34 CMLR 957. The Schengen states have agreed that the asylum provisions of the Schengen Implementing Agreement 1990 will cease to have effect when the Dublin Convention comes into force, Protocol on the consequences of the Dublin Agreement coming into effect for some regulations of the Schengen Supplementary Agreement (Bonn Protocol), 26 April 1994, cited in Bunyon (ed) *Key Texts in Justice and Home Affairs in the European Union: Volume 1 From Trevi to Maastricht* (1997) pp 134-136. See generally Meijers (ed) *Schengen: Internationalisation of Central Chapters of the Law on Aliens, Refugees, Security and Police* (1991). Problems were experienced with the practical operation of the system. For example, in January 2000 Belgium resumed identity controls at its internal borders.
12 A third state is one that is not a state party to the relevant Convention.
13 This unfortunate term refers to a common problem experienced by asylum seekers.
14 'Article 1(b) Application for asylum means: a request whereby an alien seeks from a Member State protection under the Geneva Convention by claiming refugee status within the meaning of art 1 of the Geneva Convention, as amended by the New York Protocol . . . Art 1(d) Examination of an application for asylum means: all the measures for examination, decisions or rulings given by the competent authorities on an application for asylum, except for procedures to determine the State responsible for examining the application for asylum pursuant to this Convention.'
15 SEC (2000) 522 (March 25, 2000).

critical of the practical operation of the instrument.[16] The Commission notes:

'On the basis of information which is already available, it is clear that the Dublin Convention has not operated as well in practice as its authors hoped it would.'[17]

Connected to the avoidance of responsibility, or, as some commentators have labelled it, burden-shifting, a number of re-admission agreements have been concluded between European states.[18] These bilateral agreements facilitate the return of immigrants and asylum seekers to other, notably central and eastern European states, through which they have passed on their way to seeking protection in the west. The practical result is that central and eastern European states effectively become 'buffer zones' for EU member states.

The concept of responsibility reflected in instruments such as the Dublin Convention is limited to a purely technical concern with allocating responsibility. This is perhaps best viewed as an aspect of the burden-shifting strategy in the EU rather than being a core element of a regime based on international solidarity and progressive notions of burden-sharing.

Safe countries and the internal flight option

EU member states have learned that when an asylum seeker reaches their territory they can encounter difficulties in removing her. Within the context of a general policy aimed at deterrence and restriction, there is a certain logic in trying to 'internalise' or 'regionalise' forced migration. This can be achieved directly by the use of carrier sanctions and visa controls but also indirectly by deploying concepts within the interpretation of refugee law which narrow its applicability. Rather than make these aspects of the approach to the existing definition, they have developed as 'stand alone' features of refugee law. If there is a reigning philosophy

---

16 *Migration News Sheet* (April 2000) 1.
17 Paragraph 57.
18 In response to this development the EU has adopted a number of recommendations as to the form that these agreements should take see Council Recommendation of 30 November 1994 concerning a specimen bi-lateral readmission agreement between a member state and a third country OJ 1996 C 274/20; Council Recommendation of 24 July 1995 on the guiding principles to be followed in drawing up protocols on the implementation of readmission agreements, OJ 1996 C 274/25. See UNHCR, Overview of Re-Admission Agreements in Central Europe, 30 September, 1993.

which underpins the modern approach to the regulation of forced migration in the EU, it is that asylum outside of the region of origin should be viewed as a last resort.[19] There is a marked trend towards both the 'internalisation'[20] and the 'regionalisation' of refugee movements. The concepts discussed in this section are clear evidence of this EU trend.

Much has been written about the safe country concept. As is well known, it refers to both the conditions within the state of origin of the asylum seeker and the position in a third state through which she has passed. If a state is judged to be objectively safe the rationale is that there is no reason for an individual to seek protection elsewhere.[1] This is already built into the process of assessing the merits of a claim under the 1951 Convention. An individual must have a 'well-founded fear of persecution' and thus there is a clear objective element in this test. In the EU, however, this has been put to rather different use as a way of quickly filtering out applications.

In the same vein, the presumption is that the asylum seeker must always first seek the protection of her state of origin or in another safe area within that state.[2] If there is another part of her state of origin where she would be safe, and it is reasonable to expect her to go there, then flight for the purpose of 'international protection' is unnecessary. This presumption has given rise to what is called the 'internal flight' option. This is part of the attempt to promote solutions which do not require 'external protection'. What is interesting about the development of these concepts is that these are all factors that should inform any assessment of a claim to refugee status. They have, however, been extensively promoted as 'stand alone' concepts in refugee law.

---

19 For an impressive critique of the assumptions underlying the safe country notion, see Byrne and Shacknove 'The Safe Country Notion in European Asylum Law' (1996) 9 Harv Human Rights J 185, 194-199.

20 Bennett 'Forced Migration within National Borders' (1998) 1 Forced Migration Rev 4.

 1 See Conclusion on Countries in which there is in General No Serious Risk of Persecution in Guild *The Developing Immigration and Asylum Policies of the European Union* (1996): 'This concept means that it is a country which can clearly be shown in an objective and verifiable way, normally not to generate refugees or where it can be clearly shown, in an objective and verifiable way, that circumstances which might in the past have justified recourse to the 1951 Convention have ceased to exist.'

 2 See 1951 Convention, art 1A(2), as well as including the elements discussed above the Convention also provides: '. . . and is unable or owing to such fear unwilling to avail himself of the protection of that country.'

Taking this thinking to its next logical stage of development, European states have adopted and enthusiastically (the reasons are not difficult to grasp) applied the notion of the safe third country.[3] The word 'notion' is used deliberately because it is doubtful whether it should be classified as a principle of refugee law. Again, the idea is basically the same, ie asylum is a last resort. On this occasion, however, it is trans-regional movement which is effectively being discouraged. The idea is that the individual should seek asylum in the first safe country which she reaches. As the genuine refugee is regarded as someone who is compelled to flee her state of origin, states have tried to reject the idea that she should have a choice as to where she receives protection. 'Asylum shopping' is the unfortunate label attached to this. It is worth noting, however, that the 1951 Convention makes no reference to the notion of safe third countries, and in principle does not limit the individual's choice as to the number of applications made in different states. If examined in the context of an international community where juridical equality is seldom matched by factual equality, then the application of the concept on a widespread basis by prosperous states raises several difficult problems. The first is the inconsistency of practice in Europe. Variations exist, most notably on the level of protection in the third state which will trigger return. Although there is well-known international legal protection for the asylum seeker, there is evidence, in this context, that individuals have been *refouled*.[4] A second significant problem results from what has been

3   Resolution on a Harmonised Approach to Questions Concerning Host Third Countries in Guild *The Developing Immigration and Asylum Policies of the European Union* (1996). See Fernhout 'Status Determination and the Safe Third Country Principle' in Carlier and Vanheule (eds) *Europe and Refugees: A Challenge?* (1997) p 187; Council of Europe Committee of Ministers *Guidelines on the Application of the Safe Third Country Concept* Rec No R(97) 22; UK Delegation Geneva 'Sending Asylum Seekers to Safe Third Countries' (1995) 7 IJRL 119; UNHCR 'The Concept of "Protection Elsewhere"' (1995) 7 IJRL 123; Achermann and Gattiker 'Safe Third Countries: European Developments' (1995) 7 IJRL 19; Amnesty International *Playing Human Pinball: Home Office Practice in 'Safe Third Country' Cases* (1995); UNHCR *An Overview of Protection Issues in Western Europe* (1995), p 18; Marx and Lumpp 'The German Constitutional Court's Decision of 14 May 1996 on the Concept of "Safe Third Countries" – A Basis for Burden-Sharing in Europe?' (1996) 8 IJRL 419; Shah 'Safe Third Countries: European and International Aspects' (1995) 1 European Public Law 259; Shah 'Refugees and Safe Third Countries' (1995) 9 I&NLP 3; Kjaerum 'The Concept of the Country of First Asylum' (1992) 4 IJRL 514. Cf Taylor 'Australia's "Safe Third Country" Provisions: Their Impact on Australia's Fulfilment of its Non-Refoulement Obligation' (1996) 15 University of Tasmania Law Rev 196.
4   See Amnesty International *Playing Human Pinball* (1995) p 100.

called burden-shifting.[5] By employing this concept (although the practice differs, the core concept has gained quite remarkable acceptance among states in western Europe), states may avoid accepting responsibility, and place it on others. These can be states which do not have the resources, structures and procedures required to assess asylum claims adequately. This is an example of prosperous states, within one part of Europe, employing convenient legal concepts in order to abdicate responsibility for a difficult problem. An equitable regional policy would be grounded in the idea that states in the region do not use others instrumentally as a means to achieve their own ends. The term 'burden-shifting' is, in this context, particularly apt.

The merits of the various policies aside, the pattern is plain. Asylum in another region is no longer viewed as the solution to the phenomenon of forced migration. The evolution of policy paints a coherent picture of western Europe's image of forced migration. The terms that have developed may lack normative status under international refugee law, properly interpreted, but in practice they are readily applied by states. The position may be summarised as follows: (1) states may be classified as objectively safe for the purpose of effective regulation; (2) protection must first be sought within the state of origin; (3) failing this protection should be sought in a proximate state or within that region. The assumptions underpinning this image of forced migration have already been subjected to analysis above. The principal difficulty here is that the sea change in approach in the EU has not prevented asylum seekers entering the region from elsewhere. Regardless of the ambitions of some states, refugees and asylum seekers continue to have a right to come to the region to seek refuge and protection from persecution in their states of origin. European states can not, legally and morally, decide to abdicate international responsibility for what is an *international* problem. Regionalism in this context is functioning to displace responsibility elsewhere. On many occasions this is to other non-EU states within the region. This raises troubling issues for those who advance 'European' notions of solidarity.

---

5   Cf Habermas *The Past as Future* (1994) p 131: 'Of course, the flaw of the recently concluded asylum compromise [in Germany] consists not only in its attempt to shift the burden of asylum seekers traveling overland from eastern Europe onto our neighbors – Poland, the Czech Republic, and Austria. Nor does it consist only in the introduction of problematic lists of 'persecution-free' countries . . . Above all the asylum compromise commits the error of leaving things precisely as they were with respect to naturalization rights . . .' This criticism of the 'asylum compromise' in Germany makes the important linkage to debates surrounding citizenship.

Temporary protection

It is possible to view the development of a common approach in the EU as a worthwhile venture. From a management perspective, co-operation might aid in the process of dealing with the phenomenon in a fair and effective way. The clearest example of where this thinking has been tested is in the development of the concept of temporary protection.

Whatever the precise legal issues involved in the determination of refugee status, for many EU member states recognition as a refugee is synonymous with permanent settlement in the asylum state. In this context any move, as has taken place in the EU, to meet migration needs intra-regionally was likely to impact on policies towards asylum seekers. As is evident from many of the themes in this book, the dominant mood is away from viewing refugee status as exclusively about permanent settlement. This has inspired an increased interest in temporary forms of protection. As noted, temporary protection is not an entirely new concept in international refugee law. It can be traced to discussions which emerged in the 1970s and 1980s about how to combine the recognition of the fundamental nature of the norm of *non-refoulement* with the fact that states retain the discretion to grant or refuse asylum.[6] At that time reference was made to the notion of temporary refuge.[7] In an influential paper by Coles to the UNHCR's Sub-Committee of the Whole on International Protection in 1981 the concept of temporary refuge was given comprehensive treatment. A summary of his argument is useful for the purposes of this chapter. He argued that the case for temporary refuge is based on the fact that in certain situations of large-scale influx it is neither reasonable nor desirable for the country of refuge to regard acceptance at the frontier as entailing a commitment to a

6 Luca 'Questioning Temporary Protection' (1994) 6 IJRL 535.
7 See Executive Committee UNHCR, Sub-Committee of the Whole on International Protection, *Report on the Meeting of the Expert Group on Temporary Refuge in Situations of Large-Scale Influx*, (21-24 April 1981), UN Doc EC/SCP/16. In particular see paper submitted by Coles 'Temporary Refuge and the Large-Scale Influx of Refugees' UN Doc EC/SCP/Add 1; Executive Committee UNHCR Conclusion No 19 *Temporary Refuge*. See also Goodwin-Gill *The Refugee in International Law* (2nd edn, 1996) pp 196-204. See Perluss and Hartman 'Temporary Refuge: Emergence of a Customary Norm' (1986) 26 Virginia J Int L 551, 554. They argue that a customary international law norm of temporary refuge has developed: 'The customary norm of temporary refuge prohibits a state from forcibly repatriating foreign nationals who find themselves in its territory after having fled generalized violence and other threats to their lives and security caused by internal armed conflict within their own state.'

durable solution.[8] In other words, states taking initial responsibility for the mass influx should not be expected to manage the crisis on their own. Examples highlighted to illustrate this point included Hungarian refugees in Austria in 1956, and Indo-Chinese refugees in South East Asia between 1975 and 1980.[9] An emphasis is placed in the paper on the often essential nature of international solidarity and co-operation in this context[10] and the fact that it can be 'manifested at every level – universal, regional and bilateral'.[11] From this initial discussion of temporary refuge, the language has gradually evolved to talk of temporary protection, although many of the themes addressed in Coles' paper remain relevant.

The emphasis on temporary protection and pragmatic responses to forced migration has raised the whole issue of reform of existing refugee law. Reform is certainly high on the agenda of some refugee lawyers. There is room for confusion in this debate. Most standard accounts of temporary protection present it as supplementary to refugee status. It is generally regarded as the exception to the norm for cases of mass influx where some recognition needs to be given to the genuine problems faced by states. However, a distinct argument has been advanced which disrupts this thinking. Hathaway argues that temporary protection has in fact been the rule all along.[12] In the absence of any specific reference to permanent settlement, states have, he suggests, gone beyond what they are obliged to do in international law and have thus distorted the way in which international refugee law was intended to operate. This means that one of the reform proposals advanced is based on a new temporary protection paradigm and must be very carefully distinguished from the practical developments on refugee protection in the EU.[13]

In order to understand where temporary protection lies in the broader scheme of refugee protection, it is worth noting Thornburn's argument that it is not a solution but 'a functional step towards an eventual solution'.[14] Inherent in the concept is the

8   Coles 'Temporary Refuge and the Large-Scale Influx of Refugees' UN Doc EC/SCP/Add 1 p 7.
9   UN Doc EC/SCP/Add 1 pp 8-9.
10 UN Doc EC/SCP/Add 1 p 27.
11 UN Doc EC/SCP/Add 1 p 28: 'Regional solidarity continues to be of great importance, particularly where the provision of satisfactory durable solutions is concerned.'
12 Hathaway and Neve 'Making Inernational Refugee Law Relevant Again: A Proposal for Collectivized and Solution-Oriented Protection' (1997) 10 Harv Human Rights J 115.
13 Hathaway and Neve 'Making International Refugee Law Relevant Again: A Proposal for Collectivized and Solution-Oriented Protection' (1997) 10 Harv Human Rights J 115.
14 Thornburn 'Transcending Boundaries: Temporary Protection and Burden-Sharing in Europe' (1995) 7 IJRL 459, 465.

recognition that temporary protection is part of a larger process and not an end in itself.[15] The attraction of the concept is that it permits a comprehensive perspective on forced displacement.[16] This comprehensive approach ideally includes efforts on the part of the international community to bring the conflict to an end. The logic of the temporary protection concept is that at the core of protection should be return, and thus the restoration of the citizen/state relation that has been disrupted by forced displacement. In this understanding protection is not about permanent settlement in asylum states but return when the situation warrants it. The protection that is given to the refugee is thus for the duration of the risk and is not a means to settle permanently in the asylum state.

The problems with the current international legal regime for refugee protection are well known. As stated, dissatisfaction with it has inspired some to suggest possible reformulations of the law. The concept of temporary protection has figured prominently in these debates. Hathaway is one of the leading exponents of the reformulation project and an aspect of his reform proposal has been mentioned above. It is worth exploring here his favoured approach and the criticism it has attracted.[17] At a time when serious thought is being given to reform in the EU, it is essential to explore arguments over change in refugee law.

Efforts to think pragmatically about refugee law are not new.[18] Garvey, for example, has argued that the 'humanitarian' approach to refugee protection, anchored in individual human rights, is misguided.[19] The best way to face the problem, he suggests, is by recognising the reality that refugee flows involve inter-state

---

15 UNHCR *Note on International Protection* (1994) UN Doc A/AC96/830, paras 50-51: 'One of the principal reasons for applying the term "temporary" to protection given to persons fleeing conflicts or acute crises in their country of origin is the expectation – or at least the hope – that international efforts to resolve the crisis will, within a fairly short period, produce results that will enable the refugees to exercise their right to return home in safety.'

16 See UNHCR, note 15 above, para 8: 'Comprehensive approaches do not necessarily overcome the need for refugee protection; rather, they place the problem of lack of national protection – the hallmark of the refugee regime – in its broader context.'

17 See Hathaway and Neve 'Making International Refugee Law Relevant Again: A Proposal for Collectivized and Solution-Oriented Protection' (1997) 10 Harv Human Rights J 115. Cf De Jong 'The Legal Framework: The Convention relating to the Status of Refugees and the Development of Law Half a Century Later' (1998) 10 IJRL 688.

18 See Garvey 'Towards a Reformulation of International Refugee Law' (1985) 26 Harv Int LJ 483.

19 (1985) 26 Harv Int LJ 483.

relations and working with this 'realistic' understanding of the context of refugee law. Hathaway has expanded considerably on initial tentative steps to promote a pragmatic approach. He has argued that neither humanitarianism nor human rights can adequately account for codified refugee law.[20] In this conception international refugee law functions to safeguard developed states rather than acting as a mechanism for genuine refugee protection. This critique of the premise of international refugee law has been developed with proposals for a new collectivised and solution-oriented approach advanced.[1] The aim of Hathaway's project (which he has been developing for some time) is to make a clear distinction between immigration control and refugee protection and construct the latter as a situation-specific human rights remedy. The proposal aims to take seriously the immigration control concerns of states, based on the proposition that if the institution of asylum is going to survive then the legitimate concerns of states must be taken into account. The problems with the present system are said to be the lack of a 'meaningful solution orientation' and its atomistic approach to responsibility.[2] Temporary protection in the new paradigm which Hathaway has advanced is not intended as a separate mechanism from the standard channels of refugee protection. This is intended to be the normal response to 'refugeehood'.[3] His argument is that temporary protection is in fact the norm and that the linkage made between protection and permanent settlement in the past is not based on the provisions of codified refugee law. In support of this reading it is argued that international refugee law obliges states only to avoid returning an individual to a country where she may face persecution.[4] No binding requirement to grant permanent residence exists. The reason is that this is what states were prepared to accept at the time that the 1951 Convention was drafted. Although developments in international human rights law have extended protection, there remains no right to be granted asylum. Temporary protection, according to this line of thinking, has been the norm all along.

---

20 Hathaway 'A Reconsideration of the Underlying Premise of Refugee Law' (1990) 31 Harv Int LJ 129.

 1 Hathaway and Neve 'Making International Refugee Law Relevant Again: A Proposal for Collectivized and Solution-Oriented Protection' (1997) 10 Harv Human Rights J 115. See also Schuck 'Refugee Burden-Sharing: A Modest Proposal' (1997) 22 Yale J Int L 243.

 2 (1997) 10 Harv Human Rights J 115, 137.

 3 See Castillo and Hathaway 'Temporary Protection' in Hathaway (ed) *Reconceiving International Refugee Law* (1997) p 6.

 4 Castillo and Hathaway, note 3 above, p 2.

States have chosen to make the linkage between refugee status and permanent settlement, thus interlocking refugee protection with immigration control concerns. Despite the many appeals of human rights advocates that the asylum issue is distinct from immigration, states have not been convinced.

The response proposed is based on the concept of interest-convergence groups and is aimed to encourage a collectivised approach in future. The solution which is prevalent in this approach is repatriation.[5] Once protection in the state of origin becomes viable, and certain objective conditions are met, it is argued that the host state is entitled to withdraw refugee status.[6] Hathaway rejects the assertion that refugee law requires that repatriation be voluntary, stating that this is 'wishful legal thinking'.[7] He views the resurgence of interest among states in the 'Convention's paradigm of temporary protection', which includes a right to repatriate, as arising from the 'demise of the post-War interest-convergence' between several states.[8] He recognises that the present problem is that states have failed to ensure a full range of protections to those who are offered temporary protection.[9] Despite this concern, Hathaway sees repatriation as central to the refugee protection process and as part of the attempt to encourage the development of a comprehensive approach. The key ideas for the purpose of this chapter are that this is focused on sub-global inter-state associations as the best sites for such collectivised solutions and that obligations should be distributed by common but differentiated responsibility. The fact that a particularly strict interpretation of repatriation is part of the proposed reform package is also worth highlighting as one of its more controversial aspects. In the current climate in Europe the focus on non-voluntary repatriation has the potential to be divisive. Although Hathaway is interested in thinking pragmatically about refugee law, it must be stressed that this is from a base-line of a rights-regarding protection model and a

5 See Hathaway 'The Meaning of Repatriation' (1997) 9 IJRL 552: 'Refugees are . . . entitled to benefit from dignified and rights-regarding protection *until and unless* conditions in the State of origin permit repatriation without the risk of persecution.' See also Goodwin-Gill *The Refugee in International Law* (2nd edn, 1996) pp 270-276, he notes that in recent years states have repeatedly called upon the UNHCR to do more to promote this solution.

6 (1997) 9 IJRL 552.

7 (1997) 9 IJRL 552, 553. Cf Chimni 'The Meaning of Words and the Role of UNHCR in Voluntary Repatriation' (1993) 5 IJRL 442. See also Executive Committee UNHCR Conclusion No 18 and Conclusion No 40, the emphasis in both of which is the voluntary nature of repatriation.

8 (1997) 9 IJRL 552, 553-554.

9 (1997) 9 IJRL 552, 554.

principled commitment to trying to reconcile the right to seek asylum with current political realities. What must be stressed is the difference between the reformulation Hathaway is proposing and what has been taking place in the EU. Hathaway is arguing that international refugee law was never based on anything more than the idea of temporary protection. The EU is following a model that draws a distinction between temporary protection in cases of mass flight and refugee flows. In practice this is a rejection of Hathaway's line of thinking on this issue.

The reformulation project proposed by Hathaway is an attempt to inject some pragmatic thinking into the debate in refugee law. Introducing pragmatic thinking into refugee law discourse was never going to be easy, and so it has proved. Within the EU the reform projects take on added significance because they can impact, directly or indirectly, on the substantive proposals adopted. Given the novelty of the claims made by Hathaway and others in this context, it is not surprising that concern has been expressed about the potential of this proposed reformulation project. A debate between 'realists' and 'idealists' in refugee law has been set in motion.[10] On the 'idealist' side there is a general worry that all the talk about the redundancy of refugee law simply plays into the hands of those who are seeking to erode existing legal obligations.[11] 'Idealists' in the refugee law debate are concerned with norms established in the past. It is in the very nature of lawyers to look backwards. In some contexts this makes considerable sense. For example, human rights and refugee lawyers tend to remain wedded to the existing normative framework because it is so often breached in practice. If states refuse to meet their obligations in these important spheres then this perspective is important. On this logic it is not the limitations of refugee law which are the primary problem, it is the fact that it imposes burdens which states no longer find politically acceptable. Those working from this perspective tend to stress the lack of political will on the part of states to implement refugee law fully. The focus of arguments like this is on renewal not reform; thus, the solution is that refugee law, in the EU and elsewhere, needs to be revitalised for our changing times. For those who prefer renewal over basic reform, refugee law is a site of continuing struggle where a progressive rational reconstruction of the law should be promoted and actively employed by participants.[12]

10 See Harvey 'Talking About Refugee Law' (1999) 12 JRS 101.
11 See Fitzpatrick 'Revitalizing the 1951 Refugee Convention' (1996) 9 Harv Human Rights J 229.
12 Cf Harvey 'Reconstructing Refugee Law' (1998) 3 J Civil Liberties 159.

Reference is consistently made in this literature to the importance of dynamic interpretation of the law and the fact that the 1951 Convention, in particular, is a living instrument. In this construction of the present problems of refugee law it is the failure of states to live up to their existing international commitments which is defined as the principal problem. The answer in this context is not to capitulate to state interest by promoting a 'realist' stance but for scholars to align themselves with social movements and other progressive elements of civil society to defend and uphold the rights of asylum seekers.[133] On this reading of the current crisis, the inflation of state interest and sovereignty is a negation of the fact that the international community is now constituted by a diverse range of actors, all exerting some influence on the law and policy process. This criticism emphasises the role of civil society and transnational asylum and human rights networks in continuing to 'hold the line' against the restrictionism of states. Advocates of this position argue that it is more in tune with current trends within the human rights movement.

A number of more general legal and moral objections have also been advanced against the proposal. Fear is expressed that its adoption would remove the treatment of refugees and asylum seekers from the sphere of law to that of discretion.[14] There is also concern about the possible 'commodification' of refugee movements. As noted above, this is a general argument often made against any attempt to move to an inter-state system of legal regulation. By basing the allocation of responsibility on a planned system linked to calculations of the capacity of states, some feel that the individual human rights of asylum seekers will be compromised. Human rights discourse is here celebrated as a way of confronting the proposed new regime with the humanity and 'difference' of each asylum seeker. This is an interesting example of a more general stand-off between different mindsets. The human rights-based argument is a familiar Kantian-inspired complaint against forms of utilitarianism and is indicative of deeply embedded theoretical controversies. It highlights the problem of trying to develop a regime which can deal with cases of mass forced migration adequately while ensuring that individuals are effectively protected. Underpinning these disputes are conceptual conflicts which can be linked to fundamental arguments about how law should address forced migration. It is important to

13 See generally Anker, Fitzpatrick and Shacknove 'Crisis and Cure: A Reply to Hathaway/Neve and Schuck' (1998) 11 Harv Human Rights J 295.
14 (1998) 11 Harv Human Rights J 295, 303-309.

emphasise that criticism must go beyond pure assertion. 'Commodification' may be the practical result of a certain way of thinking about refugee law, but the reasoning which underpins this must be challenged and not only the substantive result.

One of the more interesting criticisms of Hathaway's reformulation project is that it is a tactical error. In addition to principled criticism, this form of critique focuses on its pragmatic failings. When the legal rights of refugees are being steadily eroded across Europe, and elsewhere, there is concern that states will selectively appropriate this discourse to legitimise further inroads into existing protections. Taking an example from another context it is clear that the notion of a 'right to remain' has, for example, been put to highly questionable use by states to justify a restrictive approach to protection.[15] Some therefore regard this attempt to develop a feasible approach to legal regulation as a serious threat to human rights protection and as a failure of nerve. The response which this elicits is that it is a pragmatic attempt to propose constructive models of protection at a time when states are seriously considering substantive reform.

The proposed reformulation of refugee law, based on the concept of temporary protection, has given rise to much debate. There are difficult issues which arise surrounding the precise obligations owed to those seeking protection from a variety of forms of ill-treatment in their states of origin. The debate is driven by a tension between principle and pragmatism and the differing views on what is the best way to reconcile the difficult choices and decisions that must be made in this area. Commentators differ not so much over the need to ensure generous protection to displaced persons as over the best way to achieve this result given current political realities in Europe. It is too easy for human rights lawyers to dismiss pragmatism as inappropriate. Again, there are lessons here which go beyond the asylum debate. There is little that is necessarily inappropriate about pragmatism from a moral perspective. Refugee lawyers will sometimes assert that the law is the domain of principle as against the pragmatism of policy-makers. This may be superficially appealing but it is ultimately misleading. For it may in practice be more 'principled' to seek solutions which guarantee protection to the many rather than the few.

Talk of temporary protection in the EU may herald a subtle change of emphasis, but it is apparent that one underlying aim of

---

15 For criticism of the right to remain see Hathaway 'New Directions to Avoid Hard Problems: The Distortion of the Palliative Role of Refugee Protection' (1995) 8 JRS 288.

the concept is to try to find a way to reconcile priorities in public policy with the need for individual protection in cases of mass flight. More critically, the emerging EU policy on temporary protection is part of the broader picture of what has been termed the 'securitisation' of movement.[16] Asylum seekers are being steadily 'problematised' in the debate. This is not aided by the habit of placing discussion of asylum in the context of regulating transnational criminal activity. In this situation the regime that has emerged involves the construction of protection on a continuum, with return being the preferred option of states. If there is a marked trend in the EU response to forced migration, it is the turn away from integration in the EU as an acceptable solution. The avoidance of permanent settlement in host states appears as the motivating practical factor behind its adoption at present. The aim here is to chart the emergence of the concept in recent times in the EU and offer some assessment of its utility. The reasons why permanent settlement was problematised have already been examined. It is, however, important to bear in mind that this was not always the case and the practice does reflect a contemporary convergence of powerful interests around a re-think of law and practice in this area. Explorations of the 'problematisation' of forced displacement can yield valuable insights into the political and legal construction of protection.

The UNHCR has welcomed the harmonised regional response in the EU.[17] It believes that more comprehensive approaches may be facilitated by a process of progressive harmonisation. Temporary protection, when viewed in this context, can form part of a comprehensive approach to forced displacement which places protection within a continuum that begins with the outbreak of conflict in a state. The use of the concept can also be interpreted much more critically. It may be constructed as a part of the exclusionary practices of the EU and the increasing marginalisation of third-country nationals.[18] This is certainly an aspect of the EU response, but the answer, it is suggested here, lies not with a totalising critique of the process but with further and more inclusive co-operation in the future. This builds on the argument in this chapter that the substantive aspects of EU policy are not necessarily dictated by the process of 'harmonisation' itself.

---

16 See generally Chalmers and Szyszczak *European Union Law Volume II: Towards a European Polity?* (1998) pp 101-149.
17 UNHCR *Note on International Protection* (1994) UN Doc A/AC96/830 para 55.
18 Ward 'Law and Other Europeans' (1997) 35 JCMS 79.

The interest in temporary protection and responsibility sharing has been marked among some EU member states. Germany is particularly keen on the concept.[19] This is not surprising given the number of those who have sought asylum in Germany. The proposal of the German government in 1994 was to take into account population, gross domestic product as a percentage of the EU total, contributions to peace-keeping and measures taken with regard to the country of origin in assessing the responsibilities of states.[20] The intention was to distribute the displaced in accordance with a formulation of this type. It is worth keeping these proposals in mind when thinking of the solidarity mechanism which has been proposed by the Commission. Also noteworthy in this regard is the proposal to establish a European Refugee Fund to promote a balance of effort between states and deal with the consequences of reception.[1] There is a continuing dispute over the criteria to be used in distributing the fund.

The process of enlargement will have a significant impact on the protection of refugees and asylum seekers in Europe. While the extension of the harmonisation process will raise standards in some European states, existing weaknesses in the EU regime will be exported.[2] There is concern that enlargement of the EU may result in temporary protection becoming a secondary level of refugee status in the Central and Eastern European Countries (CEEC).[3] When thinking of regional solidarity it has also been emphasised that the needs of those European states which remain outside the EU must be kept in view. A regional refugee crisis in the future will not confine itself to EU member states only. This is evident in recent developments in Russia and in the former Yugoslavia.

The references to temporary protection and responsibility sharing in the TOA should be viewed as part of a shifting approach that has been evident in the EU for a number of years. There have been several measures adopted addressing the issue. Although the concept of temporary protection is not new, it was the displacement

---

19 Thornburn 'Transcending Boundaries: Temporary Protection and Burden-Sharing in Europe' (1995) 7 IJRL 459, 476, she states that the wording of a resolution on burden-sharing was a major feature of the programme of the German Presidency of the EU (July-December 1994).

20 Thornburn (1995) 7 IJRL 459.

1 COM (1999) 686. For comment see ECRE *Comments by the European Council for Refugees and Exiles on the Commission Proposal for a Council Decision creating a European Refugee Fund* (February 2000).

2 For further discussion see Harvey 'The European Regulation of Asylum: Constructing a Model of Regional Solidarity?' (1998) 4 European Public Law 561.

3 ECRE *Position on the Enlargement of the European Union in Relation to Asylum* (1998).

following the conflicts in the former Yugoslavia which heralded a rise in interest in the EU.[4] The general approach, based on a containment strategy, was to offer temporary protection to the displaced, or to encourage individuals to seek protection as close to affected areas as possible. The principal benefit to the displaced was that it offered immediate security to people whose lives and safety were at risk.[5] The advantage for states was that it relieved them of 'the need to examine many thousands of individual asylum applications – a time consuming and expensive process – and has enabled them to adopt a more generous asylum policy than might otherwise have been the case'.[6] Whatever one's view of this rather generous assessment, there were a number of problems raised in the overall 'comprehensive approach'. The deployment of 'protected areas' proved extremely problematic and interfered with the right of individuals to seek protection in other states. To add to the barriers, many states (as has become standard practice) erected visa controls, thus blocking admission. It is noteworthy that the imposition of visa controls continued after the temporary protection regime came into force. Although most states made offers of temporary protection the practice varied considerably.[7] The European Commission welcomed it 'as a positive step to deal with mass influx situations'.[8] The Commission noted that the possibility was there to build on the experience that member states had acquired in dealing with the displacement from the conflict in the former Yugoslavia and develop a uniform European scheme.[9] The UNHCR organised an international meeting in July 1992 to co-ordinate a comprehensive response to the crisis in the former Yugoslavia.[10] The concept of temporary protection figured

---

4 Koser, Walsh and Black 'Temporary Protection and the Assisted Return of Refugees from the European Union' (1998) 10 IJRL 444. See also Black and Koser (eds) *The End of the Refugee Cycle? Refugee Repatriation and Reconstruction* (1999).

5 UNHCR *The State of the World's Refugees 1997-1998: A Humanitarian Agenda* (1997) p 209.

6 Note 5 above.

7 See Joly 'The Porous Dam: European Harmonization On Asylum' (1994) 6 IJRL 159, 182; Bagshaw 'Benchmarks or Deutschmarks? Determining the Criteria for the Repatriation of Refugees to Bosnia and Herzegovina' (1997) 9 IJRL 566. See generally Selm-Thornburn *Refugee Protection in Europe: Lessons of the Yugoslavia Crisis* (1998); UNHCR *The State of the World's Refugees 1997-98: A Humanitarian Agenda* (1997) pp 203-214; Collinson *Beyond Borders: West European Migration Policy Towards the 21st Century* (1993) pp 69-79.

8 *Communication from the Commission to the Council and the European Parliament on Immigration and Asylum Policies* COM (94) 23 Final para 93.

9 Com (94) 23 Final para 93.

10 UNHCR *A Comprehensive Response to the Humanitarian Crisis in the former Yugoslavia. International Meeting on Humanitarian Aid to Victims* HCR/IMFY/1992/2.

prominently in the planned comprehensive approach.[11] The UNHCR considered it to be a pragmatic tool for meeting the international protection needs of refugees.[12] This can be viewed as part of the overall strategy of restriction, but there was also a genuine concern that facilitating displacement encouraged 'ethnic cleansing'.[13] Hard legal and moral choices had to be made. This raises interesting and difficult questions. How should states react when the active policy of one of the groups involved in an internal conflict is displacement?[14] The problem has arisen again in the response to the refugee movements from Kosovo. Here the initial response was to insist that refugees remained as close to the state of origin as possible for the purpose of facilitating safe return. The justification was that it would only aid those abusing human rights to disperse refugees throughout Europe and elsewhere. In April 1999 the Justice and Home Affairs Council agreed that the displaced from Kosovo were in need of effective protection and that this should be provided as extensively as possible in the region.[15] The Council agreed that reception in the region must be considered before any other alternative.[16] However, it recognised that protection and assistance outside of the region would be necessary for humanitarian and strategic reasons. In taking this approach the Council stressed the importance of flexibility in dealing with the changing situation in the region. The Humanitarian Evacuation Policy that was adopted is discussed in more detail below.

Further to this, there are the claims of respected organisations, such as the European Council on Refugees and Exiles (ECRE), that many of those seeking protection would probably have come

---

11 Joly 'Temporary Protection within the Framework of the New European Asylum Regime' (1998) 2 Int J Human Rights 49. See UNHCR, note 10 above, para 18: 'UNHCR agrees that temporary protection is a useful response to displacement such as, for example, the outflow from the former Yugoslavia. It is though not suitable for all situations, and should not become a substitute for the right of refugees to seek and enjoy asylum in accordance with internationally agreed standards.' The UNHCR is concerned about attempts to limit access to procedures through the use of temporary protection schemes.

12 UNHCR, note 10 above, para 45.

13 See generally Preece 'Ethnic Cleansing as an Instrument of Nation-State Creation: Changing State Practices and Evolving Legal Norms' (1998) 20 Human Rights Q 817; Zayas 'International Law and Mass Population Transfers' (1975) 16 Harv Int LJ 207.

14 (1998) 20 Human Rights Q 817, 818. Note Preece's point that this is nothing new and has been an aspect of nation-state creation since Woodrow Wilson's first statements on national self-determination in 1919.

15 *Migration News Sheet* (June 1999) p 9.

16 Note 15 above.

within the 1951 Convention definition of refugee.[17] The argument is that states can make use of temporary forms of protection to avoid granting refugee status. ECRE argues that temporary protection does not reduce the need for a supplementary refugee definition in Europe.[18] Its concern is that the increased use of temporary protection will encourage states to continue their current restrictive approach to the interpretation of the 1951 Convention. Its response is to treat temporary protection as a separate issue from the refugee definition. The complexity of these issues renders reduction of the debate into a progressive/restrictive dualism unduly simplistic. Difficult, and on occasion tragic, choices had to be made. Refugee law does not make the resolution of these issues any easier.

It is also clear that repatriation is part of the same package as temporary protection.[19] This has a human rights aspect as well as being tied to strong elements of current state interest. The human rights aspect rests on the right of individuals to return to their state of origin once conditions permit. The state interest element is that, certainly at present, states are eager to see those who have benefited from temporary protection schemes return. Reference in the Dayton Agreement[20] to the right of refugees and displaced

17 ECRE *Position on policy aspects of the European response to the emergency in the former Yugoslavia* (1992). Cf Dacyl 'Europe Needs a New Protection System for "Non-Convention" Refugees' (1995) 7 IJRL 579, at 579-580: 'The great majority of those seeking protection in Europe today do not flee individual persecution . . . Instead they flee various forms of so-called "generalized violence" (notably from internal ethnic conflicts), massive and persistent patterns of human rights violation, economic emergency, and environmental deprivation; or they are forced from their places of origin by natural catastrophes or man-made disasters.' See also ECRE *A European Refugee Policy in the Light of Established Principles* (1994) p 3, recommending that states should make use of temporary protection status and listing criteria, duration and content.

18 *Position on Temporary Protection in the Context of the Need for a Supplementary Refugee Definition* (1997).

19 See 1951 Convention, art 1C; Statute of the Office of the UNHCR 1950 UNGA Res 428(V) art 6(ii); Executive Committee of UNHCR Conclusion No 69. See also Council of Europe Parliamentary Assembly Recommendation 1348 (1997) *On the Temporary Protection of Persons Forced to Flee their Country* para 4: 'Temporary protection is by definition limited in time. It is based on the presumption of return, which must take place as soon as the conditions justifying temporary protection cease to exist. Compliance with this principle is essential if the concept is to remain credible in the eyes of the member states and to be used in the future.' The recommendation goes on to stress the need for safe and dignified return. See also Arnold 'Temporary Protection of Persons Forced to Flee their Countries' Parliamentary Assembly Report Doc 7889 (1997). Cf OAU Convention on the Specific Aspects of Refugee Problems in Africa 1969, art V.

20 General Framework Agreement for Peace in Bosnia and Herzegovina, 35 ILM 75 (1996).

persons to return freely to their homes has not been matched by the reality of repatriation practices.[1] This highlights the problem of precisely when temporary protection is to come to an end. For example, some European states felt that after the Dayton Agreement there was no longer any need for temporary protection.[2] In the context of Bosnia-Herzegovina a 'repatriation plan' was adopted which supplied benchmarks for the lifting of temporary protection.[3] Germany commenced the process of returning displaced persons in late 1996, even though it was apparent that the benchmarks had not yet been reached.[4] The legitimacy of these mandatory repatriations has been called into question,[5] as has their compatibility with the provision for safe return in the Dayton Agreement.[6] In 1997 experimental projects to facilitate the voluntary repatriation of those who had found temporary protection in a member state were also undertaken.[7] These were targeted at educational facilities for those under eighteen, vocational training, information on the economic and administrative set up with a view to reintegration, the twinning of local administrative areas and aid to transport.[8] The UNHCR began organising the repatriation of refugees to Croatia and Bosnia-Herzegovina in 1996, not long after the signing of the Dayton Agreement.[9] Under Annex 7 of the Dayton Agreement one of the main roles of the UNHCR was to facilitate negotiations between governments to encourage the safe return of refugees.[10] For example, in April 1998 a Protocol was signed between the Federal Republic of Yugoslavia and Croatia which outlined a workable procedure for repatriation.[11]

As noted, this was in the general context of a particular fondness among some for repatriation. The problem which this has highlighted is when precisely temporary protection may be ended,

---

1   Annex 7. See Bagshaw 'Benchmarks or Deutschmarks? Determining the Criteria for the Repatriation of Refugees to Bosnia and Herzegovina' (1997) 9 IJRL 566.
2   Arnold 'Temporary Protection of Persons Forced to Flee their Countries' Parliamentary Assembly Report Doc 7889 (1997) para 28.
3   (1997) 9 IJRL 566, 572-573.
4   (1997) 9 IJRL 566, 579.
5   (1997) 9 IJRL 566, 581.
6   Annex 7.
7   See Joint Action concerning the financing of specific projects in favour of displaced persons who have found temporary protection in the Member States and asylum-seekers OJ 1997 L 205/3.
8   Article 1.
9   UNHCR *UNHCR Federal Republic of Yugoslavia Information Bulletin* (January 2000) p 7.
10 Note 9 above.
11 Note 9 above.

when repatriation is legitimate and who decides. The practice in this context is revealing and indicates that significant pressures can be brought to bear on those who benefit from temporary protection regimes to return in inappropriate circumstances. This is not to underestimate the fact that, for most refugees, return is the solution they want. For example, by July 1999 the UNHCR estimated that more than 740,000 of the 800,000 refugees in countries surrounding Kosovo had returned home.[12]

As noted, the concept of temporary protection began to re-emerge in this period and can be found in a number of EU measures adopted. The Conclusion on people displaced by the conflict in the former Yugoslavia was adopted at the meeting of Immigration Ministers in London, 30 November to 1 December 1992. The Conclusion clearly expressed the position that large-scale and permanent displacement would encourage ethnic cleansing and would not assist in resolving the problem.[13] Further to this, 'displaced persons should be encouraged to stay in the nearest safe areas to their homes' and the focus should be on helping the displaced to remain in these safe areas. Reference was also made to sharing the financial burden of the relief activities. Member states agreed on the adoption of guidelines for the operation of these activities.[14] As to temporary protection there was agreement on the temporary admission of listed groups, specifically those held in prisoner-of-war or internment camps who could not be saved from a threat to life or limb, those who were seriously ill and who could not obtain local treatment and those who were under direct threat and could not secure protection in any other way. The policy was further developed in the Resolution on certain common guidelines as regards the admission of particularly vulnerable persons from the former Yugoslavia. This confirmed that the overall aim was to grant temporary protection to individuals on the basis that they would return 'to an area in the former Yugoslavia in which they can live in safety'.[15] The Resolution contained a list of principles to be respected by member states in the implementation of their policy. These included access to resources allowing individuals to live in decent conditions. The Resolution suffered from familiar problems associated with this approach to policy-making. The vagueness of the principles of protection combined with the equivocal language made this a

---

12 UNHCR *UNHCR Kosovo Information Bulletin* (August 1999) p 3.
13 Paragraph 1.
14 Paragraph 4.
15 Paragraph 2.

particularly weak set of guidelines. This approach was again reflected in the Resolution on burden-sharing with regard to the admission and residence of displaced persons on a temporary basis.[16] The resolution applied to 'persons whom Member States are prepared to admit' on a temporary basis 'in the event of armed conflict or civil war'.[17] It was not applicable to those displaced persons admitted prior to the Resolution. This included persons who had already left their state of origin to go to another state.[18] The Resolution made reference to a number of listed groups: those held in prisoner of war camps or internment camps who could not be saved from a threat to their life; the injured or seriously ill who could not obtain medical treatment locally; those under 'direct threat' who could not secure protection in their region of origin; those subjected to sexual assault, but only where possible assistance was not available as close to their homes as possible; and those who came directly from conflict zones who could not return because of the conflict and human rights abuses. The Resolution did not apply to a person where there were 'serious reasons for considering' that she had committed crimes against peace, a war crime, or crime against humanity, or a serious non-political crime before entry on a temporary basis.[19] The need for harmonised action in the context of mass influx was recognised and mention was made of consultation with the UNHCR. Again, there was a clear emphasis on help in the region of origin first of all. There was also agreement expressed on the principle that temporary protection 'could be shared on a balanced basis in a spirit of solidarity'.[20] Criteria were listed linking this to the contribution that each member state was making to the prevention or resolution of the crisis and all the 'economic, social and political factors which may affect the capacity of a member state to admit an increased number of displaced persons under satisfactory conditions'.

It was soon accepted that the Resolution needed to be supplemented. Council Decision on an alert and emergency procedure for burden-sharing with regard to the admission and residence of displaced persons on a temporary basis set out a more detailed description of the procedure to be followed.[1] The procedure

16 OJ 1995 C 262/1. See generally Kerber 'Temporary Protection: An Assessment of the Harmonisation Policies of the European Member States' (1997) 9 IJRL 453. For critical comment see ECRE *Comments on the 1995 "Burden-Sharing" Resolution and Decision Adopted by the Council of the European Union* (1996).

17 Paragraph 1(a).

18 Paragraph 1(a).

19 Paragraph 1(b).

20 Paragraph 2(4).

 1 OJ 1996 L 63/10.

could be initiated by the Presidency, a member state or the Commission deciding that a meeting of the K4 Coordinating Committee was necessary to discuss whether a temporary protection regime should be initiated.[2] After this, the Presidency was charged with periodically supplying a report on the situation to be forwarded to member states. The Decision lists possible items for the agenda of this meeting including the adoption of a timetable for anticipated admission requirements.[3] The Coordinating Committee was to prepare a proposal to be submitted for the Council's approval.[4] If there was delay, the Council might apply its procedural rules on urgent cases. The Decision stated that the 'detailed arrangements for admitting displaced persons shall be decided on by each member state'.[5] Criticism of the legality of the measures goes to the core of the legitimacy of these arrangements, but in practical terms can disguise the fact that they highlight the incremental emergence of serious thinking about the development of co-operative mechanisms for managing human displacement.

The minimal nature of these measures indicated that there was a need for more detail on the precise mechanism to be adopted for the duration of temporary protection. The process of trying to find an adequate temporary protection mechanism and place it on a more secure footing is still ongoing in the EU. There has, however, been some progress, notably in the work of the European Commission on this matter, which is worth examining in some detail here. A point of departure is that the Commission views a temporary protection regime as an exception to the normal mechanisms of refugee law. It is recognised as a useful tool, to be used by states in emergency situations to protect specific categories of persons, without giving them immediate access to the refugee determination process.

The Commission's original proposal for a Joint Action on the temporary protection of displaced persons went some way toward meeting concerns about the deployment of the concept.[6] A temporary protection regime is defined as 'an arrangement . . . offering protection of a temporary nature to persons in need of international protection'.[7] Persons in need of international protection refers to third country nationals or stateless persons

---

2   Paragraph 1.
3   Paragraph 2.
4   Paragraph 3.
5   Paragraph 4.
6   OJ 1997 C 106/13. See ECRE *Comments on the Proposal of the European Commission Concerning the Temporary Protection of Displaced Persons* (1997).
7   Article 1(a).

whose 'safe return under humane conditions is impossible in view
of the situation prevailing in that country'.[8] In particular, this
included persons who fled from areas affected by the armed
conflict and persistent violence, and those who were 'under a
serious risk of exposure to systematic or widespread human rights
abuses', specifically those compelled to leave because of ethnic or
religious persecution.[9] A mass influx is defined as the arrival in the
EU of a 'significant number of persons who are presumed to be in
need of international protection'.[10] The temporary protection
regime envisaged would only be established to deal with cases of
mass influxes and after taking into account whether adequate
protection can be found in the region of origin.[11] The Commission
would submit a periodic report to the Parliament and the Council
on the situation in the state of origin and the application of the
temporary protection regime.[12] When deciding on the phasing out
of the regime and on return, priority would be given to the
furtherance of voluntary repatriation in co-operation with, for
example, the UNHCR.[13] On the basis of the Commission report,
the Council would examine the best way to aid a member state
which has been particularly affected by the mass influx.[14] As to the
individuals involved, the member states would issue a residence
authorisation for the duration of the temporary protection regime.[15]
Member states would ensure the right to family reunion with
respect to spouses and minor and dependent children and the
absence of documentary proof of the marriage would not be
thought of as an impediment to family reunification.[16] On welfare
rights, the member states would ensure that individuals have
permission to work and are given equality of treatment with
recognised refugees for the purpose of pay, social security and
other working conditions.[17] On housing, member states would
endeavour to provide housing similar to that provided to recognised
refugees, although they would be permitted to use temporary
housing for one year at the start of the regime.[18] Provision is also

---

8 Article 1(b).
9 Article 1(b).
10 Article 1(c).
11 Article 3(1).
12 Article 4.
13 Article 4.
14 Article 5.
15 Article 6.
16 Article 7.
17 Article 8.
18 Article 9(1).

made for medical care and for public education.[19] Controversially, an examination of an asylum application may be postponed during the regime but this may not exceed five years.[20] There are exclusion clauses which would prevent persons who there are serious reasons for considering have, for example, committed a crime against peace or a war crime or who are regarded as a danger to the security of the state, from benefiting from the regime.[1] The proposed Joint Action was welcomed enthusiastically in some quarters.[2]

After consultation the Commission amended its original proposal.[3] The proposed Joint Action is now linked to another on solidarity, which is discussed below. The definitions have been considerably altered. The regime now includes reference to persons requesting international protection 'in the event of mass flight'[4] with the arrangement specifically being without prejudice to the recognition of refugee status under the 1951 Convention.[5] On the 'persons in need of international protection', their safe return under 'dignified' and humane conditions must be impossible.[6] This refers in particular to those who have fled 'armed conflict or persistent violence'.[7] As indicated, 'mass flight' has replaced 'mass influx'.[8] One gap in the previous proposal was the absence of any reference to the ECHR. This is remedied by a provision which states that arts 3 and 4 shall be given effect in compliance with the ECHR.[9] Additional reference is made also to ensuring that member states are free to adopt their own arrangements until the implementing measures are in place.[10] There is much 'tightening

---

19 Article 9(2) and (3).
20 Article 10.
1 Article 11.
2 ECRE *Comments on the Proposal of the European Commission Concerning the Temporary Protection of Displaced Persons* (1997): 'It is ECRE's principled position that temporary protection should be a flexible tool to provide, on prima facie grounds, protection to all in need of it in emergency situations.' See also ECRE *Position on Temporary Protection in the Context of the Need for a Supplementary Refugee Definition* (1997).
3 The amendments are not as extensive as those proposed by the European Parliament: see OJ 1997 C 339/146. The Parliament, for example, proposed a new art 2(3)(a): 'This joint action is a complement to the Geneva Convention and may be invoked only if there is a sudden mass influx into the European Union of persons in need of international protection.'
4 Cf ECRE, note 2 above, p 3.
5 Article 1 (a).
6 Article 1(b).
7 Article 1(b).
8 See Article 1(c).
9 Article 2(2).
10 Article 2(4).

up' in evidence in the amendments. For example, art 3(2) now provides that the decision to establish a regime shall, at minimum, determine the specific groups to which it is applicable and the duration of the regime (it will not exceed five years[11]). As to the Council's consideration of the Commission's report, further reference is made to possible amendments, in particular in relation to duration and the persons to be protected.[12] Provision in relation to assistance to member states in art 4 has been renamed 'Solidarity in the application of the temporary protection regime'. The Commission report should 'refer to all future means for implementing solidarity in the application of the temporary protection scheme'. This will be implemented in accordance with the other Joint Action discussed below.

Provision on authorisation to remain has been altered with reference now to a document issued under national law permitting a person to remain during the duration of the scheme.[13] It is notable that additional provision has been made for withholding authorisation on grounds of public policy or public security. On family reunification, specific measures are to be provided to address the plight of particularly vulnerable categories, such as women and unaccompanied minors. The measures on welfare rights remain largely unaltered in substance, although there is now a specific link to the authorisation document mentioned in art 6.[14] The measure dealing with asylum is much more specific. Thus, the examination of an asylum claim is to be dealt with in accordance with the national law of a member state.[15] Suspension of the claim in line with national law is not to exceed three years and may be deferred for a further two years if measures have been adopted to phase out the scheme.[16] Another addition is that while an asylum seeker's claim is being examined she cannot benefit from rights under a temporary protection regime.[17] An individual must therefore either come under the asylum regime or the temporary protection regime, she cannot benefit from the protections which flow from both at the same time. Where an asylum seeker is refused refugee status and she is eligible under the temporary

---

11 ECRE, note 2 above, arguing that the period of temporary protection should not exceed two years and if the need for protection continues after that then it should be transformed into a permanent status.
12 Article 4(2)(a).
13 Article 6.
14 Articles 8–9.
15 Article 10(1).
16 Article 10(1).
17 Article 10(2).

protection regime, she would enjoy the guarantees under it until eventual phasing out.[18]

A significant development which followed the Commission's consultations was the linkage to the concept of solidarity.[19] Reference to solidarity in the wider international context of protection is not new. The 1967 UN Declaration on Territorial Asylum provides:

'Where a State finds difficulty in granting or continuing to grant asylum, States individually or jointly or through the United Nations shall consider, in a spirit of international solidarity, appropriate measures to lighten the burden on that State.'[20]

This provision envisages a linkage between international solidarity and responsibility sharing. The connection is not novel from the perspective of international refugee protection. In 1981 the Executive Committee of the UNHCR observed that large-scale influxes caused problems for certain states and noted the move away from permanent settlement.[1] It stressed, however, that basic minimum standards needed to be reaffirmed pending a durable solution and 'to establish effective arrangements in the context of international solidarity and burden-sharing for assisting countries which receive large numbers of refugees'.[2] The conclusion sets out a number of principles which should apply in cases of large-scale influx.[3] On responsibility sharing and solidarity, the Conclusion indicates that this may take place on a bilateral or multilateral basis at the regional or international levels and in co-operation with the UNHCR. In another conclusion on International Solidarity and Refugee Protection it 'stressed that the principle of international solidarity has a fundamental role to play in encouraging a humanitarian approach to the grant of asylum and in the effective implementation of international protection in general'.[4] These measures can, however, remain aspirational, the difficulty is trying to make these abstract commitments to solidarity concrete in practice. There is also the problem of ensuring that regional solidarity does not undercut both international solidarity and the existing obligations of individual

18 Article 10(3).
19 See Coles UN Doc EC/SCP/Add 1.
20 UNGA Res 2312 (XXII) art 2(2).
1 Conclusion No 22.
2 Paragraph 3.
3 The minimum basic standards outlined include: the provision of all necessary assistance; respect for family unity; all possible assistance for the tracing of relatives; provision for the protection of minors and unaccompanied children; and the facilitation of voluntary repatriation.
4 Paragraph 3.

states.[5] This might occur if, for example, states decide to reinterpret refugee law on a region-wide basis.

The proposed Joint Action concerning solidarity in the admission and residence of beneficiaries of the temporary protection of displaced persons[6] is bound closely to the proposal on temporary protection.[7] The proposed measure acknowledges the need to ensure that the principle finds concrete expression through financial assistance. These are termed 'solidarity mechanisms' which might follow the Commission's report mentioned above.[8] The Council must act unanimously in this area and before a decision is taken the Council is required to consult with the UNHCR.[9] The decision taken relates to financial assistance from the Community budget for the purposes of, for example, provisional accommodation, medical assistance, social assistance and education.[10] The decision may also define rules for distributing individuals between member states.[11]

The debate on temporary protection has stalled because of a lack of consensus in the Council on the issue. At the informal Justice and Home Affairs Council meeting in Berlin on 11–12 February 1999, the German government put forward a paper on burden-sharing.[12] The proposed plan was for a more flexible

5   See Executive Committee UNHCR Conclusion No 85: '(p) Recognizes that international solidarity and burden-sharing are of direct importance to the satisfactory implementation of refugee protection principles; stresses, however, in this regard, that access to asylum and the meeting by States of their protection obligations should not be dependent on burden-sharing arrangements first being in place, particularly because respect for fundamental human rights and humanitarian principles is an obligation for all members of the international community.' See also OAU Convention on the Specific Aspects of Refugee Problems in Africa 1969 1000 UNTS 46 art II(4): 'Where a Member State finds difficulty in continuing to grant asylum to refugees, such Member State may appeal directly to other Member States and through the OAU, and such other Member States shall in the spirit of African solidarity and international co-operation take appropriate measures to lighten the burden of the Member State granting asylum'; Council of Europe, Committee of Ministers Resolution on Asylum to Persons in Danger of Persecution 1967, art 4, 'Where difficulties arise for a member State in consequence of its action in accordance with the above recommendations, Governments of other member States should, in a spirit of European solidarity and of common responsibility in this field, consider individually, or in co-operation, particularly in the framework of the Council of Europe, appropriate measures in order to overcome such difficulties.'
6   OJ 1998 C 268/23.
7   Article 14 provides that the Joint Action on temporary protection will enter into force on the same day as the Joint Action on solidarity.
8   Article 2(1).
9   Article 2(2).
10   Article 3(a) and (b).
11   Article 4.
12   *Migration News Sheet* (March 1999) p 6.

arrangement than that proposed by the Commission, but even this has met with criticism.[13] The Commission plan is viewed by some states as too generous to the displaced. The Action Plan discussed above and the new Scoreboard provide further details of the envisaged way forward. The Commission has stated that after the entry into force of the TOA it intends to revise its proposals on temporary protection and re-present them as a draft Community instrument with appropriate modifications.[14]

This examination of the development of the concept in the EU is revealing. The suggestion is that while states may be prepared to indulge in progressive rhetoric, it can prove more difficult to secure agreement on concrete legal mechanisms for responsibility sharing in practice. This has become evident in the failure to reach consensus in the Council on this matter. Temporary protection has emerged in the context of a general shift in thinking in the EU and elsewhere on the most appropriate way to regulate forced migration. Although deployed in the specific context of forced displacement it can be viewed as part of the 'securitisation' of the migration debate in the EU. This raises issues surrounding the governance of migration in Europe which go beyond the bounds of this chapter. Increasingly, mass flight is being constructed on the basis of a continuum, beginning with the causes of conflict and ending in return. This shift away from integration as the primary 'solution' to forced displacement is having serious implications for the treatment of a variety of groups in Europe.

One way to address the problems that arise is to insist that its use is minimised. In other words, that it only be deployed in exceptional cases of mass flight. An alternative is to call for the abandonment of its use entirely. States would then be encouraged to return to the use of refugee law. However attractive this option might be for some, it is unlikely to gain widespread acceptance among states. A practical alternative may be a concrete proposal which would encompass:

- an independent and objective assessment of when there is a situation of mass flight;
- periodic review of assessment;
- a clear statement of entitlements;
- strict and appropriate time limits;

---

13 Note 12 above.
14 Commission Working Document *Towards Common Standards on Asylum Procedures* SEC (1999) 271 Final. For positive comments on the willingness of the Commission to enter into dialogue and criticisms see Amnesty International *Comments by Amnesty International on a Document from the European Commission* (21 May 1999).

- access to refugee status determination after a designated time period;
- appropriate use of art 1(C).

The Academic Group on Immigration-Tampere (AGIT) has advanced practical proposals on the issue.[15] AGIT recognises the ad hoc nature of current arrangements and suggests that the EU return to the drawing board and devise a new collective strategy.[16] In this new strategy it recommends that particular attention be paid to the 'management perspective'.[17] As the Group acknowledges, migration management is the reason states feel compelled to use the concept of temporary protection.[18] It addresses this concern with a proposal for a form of 'Conditional Protection' to last for a period between six months and one year.[19] During this period, both the state and the protected person would have certain duties. The state would have to resolve the management problem and the protected person would have the duty to remain in the state and be prepared to return when conditions permitted.[20] Other practical suggestions include the use of a reserve service of immigration staff and possibly the borrowing of trained staff from other EU states. The EU, as well as the individual state, would guarantee to the protected person that she is not *refouled* during the 6- to 12-month period. After 12 months the state is required to process the asylum application. Those adjudged to be fleeing the conflict could then be granted 'unlimited protection' (Convention status) or time-limited protection.[1] The 'time-limited protection' would offer the individual all the guarantees of Convention refugee status but would be limited to two years. The duty of the protected person during this period is to prepare for return. In the proposal this is linked to art 1C. The suggestion is that states adopt a time limit to art 1C. If the condition mentioned in art 1C5 were to be met within these two years, and with the concurrence of the UNHCR, then the status would be withdrawn. After the two-year period the normal rules on cessation would apply. If return is not possible in the two years, then the state has a duty to confer on those individuals time-limited protection.

---

15 AGIT, *Efficient, Effective and Encompassing Approaches to a European Immigration and Asylum Policy*, (June 1999) subsequently published in (1999) 11 IJRL 338.
16 Note 15 above, p 11.
17 Note 15 above.
18 Note 15 above.
19 Note 15 above, p 12.
20 Note 15 above.
 1 Note 15 above.

The proposal tries to address the concerns of all participants and in this sense is rather novel. The refugee and asylum debate is polarised around partial perspectives that on occasion fail to acknowledge the validity of these differences. There are good reasons why this level of contestation exists, but on many occasions it is counterproductive to the overall goals of refugee protection. This reform proposal appears to recognise this problem. For states, the Group argues that this will ensure better management of the issue. The EU would also gain from the experience of collective decision-making. Protection seekers benefit from the promise of secure protection and the reassurance that the notion of return is being kept alive. As with any proposal on temporary protection, the accepted problem is that the decision on status is postponed. These proposals will attract criticism from advocacy groups irritated by the rejection of fundamentalist positions. There is, however, already enough literature containing abrasive criticism of EU policy while there is insufficient serious thought on how these regulatory mechanisms can be made to work in the interests of all. It may take time for EU law and policy to emerge fully but this will come to pass. Proposals which fail to engage with the realities of regulatory contexts make little or no positive contribution. The assessment of what is the reality of this regulatory context is, of course, contested. But if one still believes that an 'objective' or 'impartial' assessment of events on the ground is possible, then this must be the touchstone for critique. Legal regulation can be made to work and proposals which demonstrate how this might be achieved are useful. The proposal covers all the main problems with temporary forms of protection. Whether or not states that already disagree on the substance and procedures of temporary protection would agree to this is another issue. It does have the considerable merit of advancing a constructive way forward. There will no doubt be a number of other such proposals available for consideration by states as they begin to move from 'soft' to 'hard' law in this area.

Rights and protection in the EU

The EU is currently sending confusing signals to the international community on refugee protection. While the importance of 'full and inclusive' interpretation of refugee law is stressed, the reality is that states are avoiding the spirit and the letter of refugee law. What is in effect taking place is a process of 'de-formalisation', whereby states are opting out of the international legal framework.

It is a de-formalisation process that has ironically moved states back, at the regional level, to elements of formalism, essentially by bringing aspects of immigration and asylum policy under the EU 'First Pillar'. Whatever critics who use the Fortress Europe metaphor believe, states clearly view international refugee law as imposing onerous burdens on them. Refugee law is frequently described as a relatively weak mechanism of protection and yet many states find it excessively demanding. States have been creative in their attempts to secure a paradigm shift in the language of refugee protection. The pragmatic results can leave protection seekers with inadequate protections compared with those they might have accessed if accorded formal refugee status. It is beyond the bounds of this work to explore broader EU debates. However, it is precisely at this point that moves towards postnational forms of membership become important. Protection seekers in the EU will increasingly need to draw on human rights discourse in order to challenge law and policy developments. By using rights mechanisms that attach to personhood, and not status, protection seekers will be making a concrete connection between the regional and the universal. This argument is not meant to offer legitimacy to current state practice in this area. Rather it is to emphasise that, regardless of the precise status of those who are granted some form of temporary protection, they can only benefit from the strategic deployment of rights discourse. This is where consideration of postnational forms of membership becomes important. If EU member states are serious about creating an inclusive area of 'freedom, security and justice', aspects of the postnational critique will have to be accepted. Irrespective of the numbers and varieties of new migration categories created, states are required to achieve their objectives with reference to rights that attach to personhood.

The re-emergence of the concept of temporary protection provides the opportunity to think holistically about the protection of displaced persons. It constructs displacement as a process and not an end in itself. As argued in this chapter, this new protection discourse constructs displacement as a point on a continuum beginning with flight, and initial protection, to safe return under humane and dignified conditions. At present, states are keen to emphasise return over integration in the context of temporary protection regimes.[2] In practice, those states willing to offer temporary protection in the context of the former Yugoslavia did

---

2   ECRE *The State of Integration in the European Union: A Working Paper* (1998). For a defence of the importance of integration see ECRE *Position on the Integration of Refugees in Europe* (1999).

so on the understanding that return was part of the package. The movement away from integration as a 'solution' is ethically questionable and is difficult to implement in practice, and there is concern that integration is being seriously neglected at the EU level.[3] As is argued here, this trend is directly traceable to broader currents in migration regulation in Europe. While internal movement by EU citizens is being actively encouraged, the price is being paid for by refugees, asylum seekers and others. Movement by certain 'strangers' has been steadily 'problematised' and presented as an 'irritant' and threat to the identity of the emerging European polity. Areas that should be clearly distinguished, such as crime and migration, have been constructed in European debates as connected. There is little evidence that this damaging trend is abating.

The use of temporary protection in the EU differs from proposals advanced by some of the commentators discussed in this chapter. Although quantitatively it may become the rule in refugee protection, in theory it is intended to be the exception to protection under the 1951 Convention, applicable only in cases of mass flight. The concept of temporary protection being discussed is distinct from the legal regime established under the 1951 Convention, although connections do exist, notably on eventual access to refugee status determination procedures. It is intended to be a flexible and pragmatic tool to address the realities of migration management in the context of large-scale influxes of displaced persons in need of protection. Protection under the 1951 Convention has become linked to permanent settlement and thus states do not see this as an appropriate way to deal with the totality of the problem.[4] There is little that is new in this: European states have offered forms of supplementary protection for some time. What is novel in Europe is the attempt to develop this policy on a regional basis.

If implemented effectively as envisaged, with due regard to appropriate guarantees, then there is reason to believe that temporary protection regimes could function as adequate mechanisms for reaching a compromise between principle and pragmatism in this context. One can, of course, reject this trend in

---

3 Note 2 above.
4 This is not confined to Europe: see Frelick 'Afterword; Assessing the Prospects for the Reform of International Refugee Law' in Hathaway (ed) *Reconceiving International Refugee Law* (1997) p 147. 'However, even those societies most open to immigration, such as the United States and Canada, have signaled their unwillingness, as a matter of course, to be open to the arrival of asylum-seekers'

state practice. In this chapter it is argued that the 'de-formalisation process' must be challenged. There remain a number of dangers that call the use of the concept into question. Restrictive approaches to the 1951 Convention definition may be reinforced and effective access to determination processes undermined. The human rights of asylum seekers might be seriously eroded in the new informal processes of protection that have emerged in the EU. While there may be pragmatic reasons to welcome informalism in this area, it is doubtful whether such practice will ultimately benefit refugees and asylum seekers. The fact that those who are protected under the temporary protection regime benefit from important human rights guarantees must be acknowledged, but they will remain effectively excluded from the important guarantees contained in refugee law. In practice it is the issue of return that will prove most divisive. There will be a strong temptation for states to seek to begin the process of return before it is safe to do so. This will focus attention on the 'voluntary' nature of returns under the regime and the need to ensure that those who benefit from temporary protection have ways to challenge hasty decisions taken by some states. The potential for the polarisation currently endemic in this area to intensify is clearly there. In a world of widespread inequality and continuing oppression, individuals (with the means to do so) will respond as they always have, by moving elsewhere. States can seek to evade this by constructing walls of exclusion, and legal regimes of responsibility shifting, but the basic fact will remain. Until EU member states learn to accept this, and build legal regimes with long-term plans in mind, then progress in this area can not be made.

At the core of the new regime in the EU must be the recognition of the views of affected groups. What is missing in the schemes designed thus far is the participation of refugees and asylum seekers. This is perhaps the most serious flaw in the existing arrangements. What is remarkable about the refugee debate is the way the voices of the displaced are silenced in a process that will have serious implications for their protection needs. When the importance of participation is being stressed in so many other fields, is it not time for serious thought on how it can be ensured in the EU refugee debate?

INTERNATIONALISM AND THE PROTECTIVE STATE

There is no attempt in this chapter to be comprehensive. Key developments in EU asylum law and policy are used to illustrate a more general argument. This chapter has mapped the development and broad outline of the European regulation of asylum, as well as the philosophy underpinning it. Before the mid-1980s one could not really speak of a 'European' asylum policy. Although movement has been slow, it is now apparent that the regulation of asylum in the EU has transcended the individual state and been transplanted to the supranational level. This raises numerous problems, perhaps most straightforwardly on issues of democratic and judicial control. On this the changes resulting from the TOA are an advance. It will, however, be worth watching whether the shift from 'Third' to 'First' Pillar makes any substantive difference in practice. The culture surrounding decision-making in the asylum area is still firmly embedded.

Although developments thus far have not been encouraging, the argument here is that there are possibilities as well as problems. This chapter rejects totalising critiques of the process of harmonisation. Criticism of 'Fortress Europe' can lend weight to simplistic stories of a 'totally administered legal world' in which the humanity of the individual is repressed. Just as legal regulation can be part of the problem, it can also be a major factor in the solution. The answer still lies in winning the legal and political arguments over the substance of EU asylum law and policy. In addition to this, the inclusion of human rights in EU law and policy may help to promote values other than market-based ones. The question now is: who really owns human rights law in Europe?

In concluding, it is apt to mention what is one of the major difficulties stressed throughout this chapter: the absence of participation by the regulated community. The exclusion of refugees and asylum seekers from the debates surrounding legal regulation is marked. Although the contribution of 'representative groups' may help, this does not negate the need for imaginative institutional reform with a built-in deliberative component. The challenge for the EU will be to construct a regime which includes the voices of refugees and asylum seekers and is based on respect for human rights and human dignity.

Chapter 4

Regulating asylum (I): the law and politics of asylum in the UK

INTRODUCTION

The transnational nature of the legal conversation about the terms of refugee protection is evident from the analysis thus far. The UK is part of a web of international legal relations. National asylum law must be located within these intersecting legal orders. The end result is a complex set of conversations among a number of participants in law's community about the future of refugee protection. The UK's reputation as a state with a well-established tradition of granting asylum to refugees has increasingly been called into question in recent years. Following many of the broadly European trends, examined elsewhere in this work, the UK has constructed a legal regime which has been subjected to sustained criticism from a variety of quarters.[1] In response to a significant increase in the numbers of those seeking asylum in the UK a legal regime specifically addressed to the asylum issue has emerged. It is a regime which has been subject to constant revision. The Immigration and Asylum Act 1999 is the most significant legislative change in this area since the Immigration Act 1971.[2] It is questionable whether it resolves the many problems which afflict asylum law in the UK, and it is the latest in a line of legislative

---

1   Travis 'Fortress Europe's Four Circles of Purgatory' *Guardian* 20 October 1998: 'Britain's procedure for coping with refugees and asylum-seekers is breaking down.'
2   See Home Office *Fairer, Faster and Firmer – A Modern Approach to Immigration and Asylum* Cm 4018 (27 July 1998).

measures.[3] There will be more alterations to the regime in the coming years, both to adjust to internal concerns of public administration and the changes in asylum policy at the European level. The aim of this chapter is to explore the law and politics of asylum in the UK. For this purpose key themes in the asylum debate are examined. The argument developed here is that the UK, like many other European states, has advanced a policy anchored in the principles of deterrence and restriction.

SITUATING ASYLUM LAW

Public law has undergone a transformation recently. Values are back in vogue and there is a renewed concern with constitutional principle and the protection of human rights. Domestic politics has played a leading part in this, but it also reflects the increasing globalisation and Europeanisation of law and politics. As with public law generally, it is no longer adequate (if it ever was) to ignore the international and European dimensions of the issue. This is especially true of asylum law, where refugee movements must be viewed as an inherently 'international' problem. The international dimension includes both the normative constraints upon state action, contained in, for example, international human rights law and insights derived from a knowledge of the practical reality of international refugee movements. As I have emphasised in this work, in relation to international human rights law, there are guarantees which are directly applicable to refugees and asylum seekers (even if at present they remain, in formal terms, unenforceable in UK courts). When focusing on international refugee law (and its inherent limitations), it is vital not to lose sight of this fact.[4] This is especially important at a time when a growing number of public lawyers are recognising the inadequacy of traditional conceptions of the subject. Refugee and asylum lawyers can fairly be said to be ahead of the rest on this issue. For they have been drawing upon international standards in domestic legal argumentation for some time. Asylum law and practice is ineluctably shaped by internationalism. As we have seen, European practices are exerting a strong influence also. Human rights lawyers have lessons to learn from refugee lawyers.

---

3   Refugee Council *The Immigration and Asylum Act 1999* (January 2000): '. . . we are concerned that the opportunity to develop a fair and efficient asylum process has been wasted.'
4   See Goodwin-Gill 'Who to Protect, How. . ., and the Future?' (1997) 9 IJRL 2, 2-3.

In addition, there is the familiar problem of the way in which the law constructs 'refugee identity'.[5] The debate in the UK oscillates between conceptions of the 'genuine' and 'abusive' asylum applicant which bear little relation to the complex realities of human migration. Refugee law is recognised to include a limited conception of the refugee. It is, in essence, a legal term of art designed for particular purposes.[6] The difficulty is that, conceived from a needs-based perspective, it is entirely inadequate as an inclusive legal tool for refugee protection (if this term is applied more holistically to embrace all those coerced into fleeing their places of residence).[7] A vast number of individuals, forced to flee their homes, do not come within the 1951 Convention definition. However, they undoubtedly remain in need of some form of legal protection. This is often lost in the heated debate around asylum in the UK. This reality is reflected, for example, in the widespread application of a variety of 'humanitarian' categories, which states employ in often ill-defined ways in their domestic law.[8] The centrality of the concept of alienage is also problematic.[9] It continues to privilege boundaries in the classification of need at a time when some have noted a tendency to move 'beyond borders' in the treatment of such international problems.[10] This has had a particularly damaging impact in relation to gender issues, where the focus on exile, combined with the limited definition of refugee status, has resulted in, for example, the neglect of the plight of women refugees.[11] In practice European states are reluctant to

5   For a critique of the way the law constructs the refugee, see Tuitt *False Images: The Law's Construction of the Refugee* (1996).

6   Goodwin-Gill *The Refugee in International Law* (2nd edn, 1996) p 3.

7   Cf Shacknove 'Who is a Refugee?' (1984-1985) 95 Ethics 274, he argues that neither persecution nor alienage captures what is essential about refugeehood, and focuses instead on, inter alia, a conception constructed around basic needs and a social contractarian model.

8   See Lambert *Seeking Asylum: Comparative Law and Practice in Selected European Countries* (1995) pp 126-144. Cf Dacyl 'Europe Needs a New Protection System for "Non-Convention" Refugees' (1995) 7 IJRL 579.

9   See Hathaway *The Law of Refugee Status* (1991) p 29.

10   See Ferris *Beyond Borders: Refugees, Migrants and Human Rights in the Post Cold War Era* (1993); Collinson *Beyond Borders: West European Migration Policy Towards the Twenty First Century* (1993).

11   The gender-neutrality of international refugee law has come under attack. The 1951 Convention does not, for example, include reference to persecution on grounds of gender. In recognition of this gap, attempts have been made recently to draft guidelines on gender-based claims to asylum. See generally Daoust and Folkelius 'UNHCR Symposium on Gender-Related Persecution' (1996) 8 IJRL 180; Kelly 'Gender-Related Persecution: Assessing the Asylum Claims of Women' (1993) 26 Cornell Int LJ 625; Kelly 'Guidelines for Women's Asylum Claims' (1994) 6 IJRL 517; Greatbatch 'The Gender Difference: Feminist Critiques of

embrace a more inclusive definition of refugee. They wish to remain wedded to relatively clearly defined obligations in this area. For states, refugee law remains a tool which continues to balance their domestic and international responsibilities in a reasonable way.

With respect to the realities of international refugee movements, there has been some new thinking in recent times, inspired by the willingness to view the problem within a more comprehensive framework.[12] This has impacted on asylum law and practice by highlighting the other human rights guarantees which apply in this area. The result is that those who do not receive refugee status can be offered other forms of protection. The premise for this is that individuals manage to reach the state of asylum in the first place. There has, for example, been criticism of the exclusive concentration on exile. As noted above, refugee law's focus on alienage and exile has been criticised largely because of the resulting tendency to ignore the root causes of flight. Given the turn to prevention discourse in the international community, asylum has been presented as an outdated response to the problems of the forcibly displaced. This causes a problem for asylum lawyers, who find themselves faced with a human rights argument for essentially restricting access to the solution of asylum. It is a truism that asylum and migration are not the answers to the political, social and economic inequalities which fuel the policies of repressive governments, and which contribute towards the creation of refugee movements. Refugee and asylum law are the products of realism as well as idealism. The law emerged from a realistic assessment of the conflictual nature of international and national societies. This

Refugee Discourse' (1989) 4 IJRL 518; Johnsson 'The International Protection of Women Refugees: A Summary of Principal Problems and Issues' (1989) 1 IJRL 221; Neal 'Women as a Social Group: Recognizing Sex-Based Persecution as Grounds for Asylum' (1988) 20 Col Human Rights LR 203; Oosterveld 'The Canadian Guidelines on Gender-Related Persecution: An Evaluation' (1996) 8 IJRL 567; Wallace 'Making the Refugee Convention Gender Sensitive: The Canadian Guidelines' (1996) 45 ICLQ 702; Wallace 'Considerations for Asylum Officers Adjudicating Asylum Claims from Women: American Guidelines' (1996) 9 I&NLP 116. In October 1993 the UNHCR Executive Committee adopted Conclusion No 73 on Refugee Protection and Sexual Violence. See also UNHCR *Sexual Violence against Refugees: Guidelines on Prevention and Response* (1995). The introduction states: 'The Guidelines provide basic advice on appropriate action, particularly preventive, and are also intended to encourage active reflection and discussion between colleagues. They seek to promote attitudinal changes in relation to sexual violence where these are an obstacle, to improve or initiate services that address psychosocial as well as health needs, and, overall, to create an awareness and sensitivity to the special needs and concerns of refugees who have been subjected to sexual violence.'

12 UNHCR *The State of the World's Refugees: In Search of Solutions* (1995) ch 1.

argument may surprise those who seek to cast asylum lawyers as idealists, refusing to face the reality of human migration. Asylum lawyers, in particular, are aware of the fact that there has been a persistent failure to address the root causes of forced migration and that is why a clear commitment to international 'surrogate' protection remains necessary.

With the ensuing turn to root causes, and focus on prevention, there has been a willingness to develop new strategies, and thus a number of the past problems and deficiencies are beginning to be addressed.[13] While this is a welcome development, an element of caution is required. The study of refugees and asylum seekers is not an either/or issue. A more inclusive approach demands genuine recognition of all aspects of the problem. What it should not do is allow states to evade responsibility for protecting refugees on the basis of highly abstract (and ultimately hollow) commitments to concepts such as prevention and the 'right to remain'.[14] In other words, the 'turn to root causes' should not distract attention excessively from the fact that there is still a pressing need to ensure that asylum determination procedures within states are as fair and effective as possible.

The European dimension of asylum law has already been mentioned. Any analysis of the international dimension must be supplemented with consideration of the European aspects of the issue. Although progress has been sluggish,[15] it is apparent that there has been a steady 'Europeanisation' of asylum and immigration law. EU member states have adopted a number of measures in an attempt to secure common practice in this area. The concepts which have been agreed upon at EU level are discussed above. The general trend is the adoption of what is best described as a 'lowest common denominator' approach to asylum. Critiques of national law and practice are frequently now met with the argument that this is common practice in the EU. If a practice is normal in the EU, then it should be acceptable in the UK, so the logic runs. The issue which the human rights movement is having to address is that policy formation is effectively moving beyond the national level. Keys concepts in asylum law are being formed within international fora. This raises the issue, which I will return to later, of developing

---

13 Note 12 above, p 19.
14 Cf Goodwin-Gill 'The Right to Leave, the Right to Return and the Question of the Right to Remain' in Gowlland-Debbas (ed) *The Problem of Refugees in the Light of Contemporary International Law Issues* (1996); Cf Hathaway 'New Directions to Avoid Hard Problems: The Distortion of the Palliative Role of Refugee Protection' (1995) 8 JRS 288.
15 Giving rise to calls for reform of the present institutional arrangements.

strategies for transnational legal activism. Asylum lawyers must be able to engage with states at the levels on which policy formation is taking place. As we have seen with the example of the EU, this can be a serious problem when there is no mechanism available to challenge problematic aspects of law and policy.

The evolving EU process is having a substantial impact on the nature of the legal changes in the UK. While it is certainly possible to be highly critical of developments thus far at EU level, there is also room for more imaginative approaches in the future. There is recognition, for example within the UNHCR, that a harmonised regional response to refugee movements may have advantages. In practice, concepts such as responsibility sharing and international solidarity should be central to any morally defensible asylum regime.[16] By developing co-operation, the EU may help to avoid short-termist reactions to refugee movements. While such an approach is eminently desirable in theory, it has proved rather harder to develop in practice. It appears that it will take some time before the requisite level of trust is established for them to explore more progressive joint policies in this area. For the asylum seeker the reality of protection is often essentially state based.

In attempting to situate asylum law in the UK, this chapter argues that one cannot neglect the international and European dimensions. It is no longer possible to view this area of public law separately from its wider contexts. It is only when the contextual dynamics of the issue are understood that more clarity may be gained in considering what the asylum determination system in a state may be expected to achieve, and how improvements may be made. There is a paradigm shift in thinking about public law in the UK. Any analysis of asylum law is necessarily implicated in this process of reconstruction. In particular, the gradual emergence of a positive human rights law agenda in the UK has fundamental implications for how we consider the future of the institution of asylum.

THE PURPOSE AND FUNCTION OF ASYLUM LAW

In assessing UK asylum law it is essential to have an understanding of its purpose and function. There is little general understanding of why this legal regime exists and what purpose it is intended to serve. At the core of the institution of asylum rests the proposition

---

16 See EXCOM Conclusion No 52 (XXXIX) *International Solidarity and Refugee Protection;* EU Council (JHA) Resolution on Burden-Sharing, Bull EU 6-1995 132; Harvey 'Restructuring Asylum: Recent Trends in UK Asylum Law and Policy' (1997) 9 IJRL 60, 70.

that states have a right to exclude non-citizens.[17] Asylum is thought to be the humanitarian exception to this general right of states. While there is much erosion of the traditional notion of sovereignty, states still insist on adopting a highly instrumental approach to migration control. The ability to regulate migration is central to the self-understanding of most modern states and is linked to internal notions of self-determination. Although some are prepared to enter associations which permit the free entry of other nationals, this is regarded as exceptional rather than the rule and is tightly regulated. There is little sign that states are prepared to abandon this position. Asylum thus remains an important exception to the general rule. The law and politics of this exception do, however, provide an insight into wider questions about the 'constitution' of modern states.[18]

The protean nature of the concept of asylum may give rise to a number of problems. Its association with the lone political offender tends to highlight an individualistic bias, which functions at the expense of a neglect of the group nature of most refugee movements. This springs from an association with extradition law and, in particular, cases where extradition is refused because of the applicability of the political offence exception. In these cases the individual is a lone political dissident, who may operate in association with others. What is distinctive is the individualised nature of the process. This is in marked contrast to the reality of refugee movements, which tend to be mass migrations of peoples. The association of these with the traditional view of asylum is problematic. It also highlights a tension in asylum law. In cases of mass flight it may not be feasible to offer everyone an individual assessment of their claim. The difficulty is whether this logic necessarily compromises the right to effective access to a refugee status determination process. There is a pragmatic tension between the practical problems which surround managing human migration and the more principled consideration of the legal rights of the individual.

A further issue is the association of asylum with permanent settlement in a host state. It is not often noted that, despite the inherent weaknesses of international refugee law, many states have insisted on associating asylum with permanent settlement. Given that asylum is largely defined in the law and practice of individual

---

17 See *Chae Chan Ping v US* 130 US 581 (1889); *Nishimura Ekia v US* 142 US 651 (1892); *Musgrove v Chun Teeong Toy* [1891] AC 272.
18 See Gibney 'Liberal Democratic States and Responsibilities to Refugees' (1999) 93 Am Political Science Rev 169; Walzer *Spheres of Justice: A Defence of Pluralism and Equality* (1983) ch 2.

states, it is arguable that there is nothing necessary about this conclusion. In the UK the term has been exclusively linked to the 1951 Convention, which is unfortunate in the light of other developments in human rights law relating to the prohibition on expulsion. The fact is that refugee law does not require a state to grant permanent settlement to refugees. It was designed to offer temporary protection until the conditions in the state of origin made return possible. The failure to recognise this fact has been one of the reasons for the turn away from refugee law in recent times. There is no necessary connection between refugee law and permanent settlement in an asylum state. This is not a new observation, but it is one that should be reconsidered in asylum law in the UK. This suggests that the concept of temporary protection is neither novel nor dangerous. States have failed to recognise that refugee law legislates for this area in a way which would enable them to address the area effectively. Human rights law is, however, not silent on the issue.

There are good reasons why refugee law contains an individualistic bias, and this is a definite advantage when arguing against some of the recent excesses in state practice. Historical analysis reveals that the states which drafted the 1951 Convention were concerned not to grant a 'blank cheque' to the displaced of the future. There remains an unwillingness in the international community to assume an unlimited future obligation. There is a basic fear that underpins this which goes to the core of thinking on sovereignty. It is the fear of being overwhelmed by human migration. While this is a reality for some, there is little evidence that European states do not have the legal and administrative capacity to manage refugee flows fairly and effectively.

The history of the various attempts to conclude an international instrument on asylum reveals again a marked reluctance to commit to binding obligations in this area. While art 14 of the Universal Declaration of Human Rights refers to 'the right to seek and enjoy asylum from persecution', as noted, this is a non-binding instrument. The right to grant asylum remains a right of the state. It is nevertheless important to note that while international law does not oblige the state to grant asylum, it now contains specific prohibitions on return in a number of defined contexts. It no longer makes sense to continue to refer solely to the absence of a duty upon the state to grant asylum when there is now such a strong and well-defined obligation of *non-refoulement*. The concepts are so intertwined that drawing rigid boundaries becomes rather artificial, although states continue to insist on making such distinctions in practice. The argument is reinforced if one considers that the prohibition on *refoulement* applies when the refugee presents herself at the frontier of the state. It is in fact the principle of *non-refoulement* which grounds the human rights orientation of refugee law, and provides the link to the obligations of states to respect fundamental human rights. If there is a primary purpose of asylum law, it is to ensure that individuals have a solid guarantee that they will not be returned to a state where they will suffer sufficiently serious human rights violations. It recognises that in the modern state-based system the citizen-state relationship can breakdown. States can fail to protect citizens from persecution by other groups in society as well as actively persecute individuals themselves. Asylum law is the legal expression of a moral commitment. It is the legal reflection of the moral commitment to protect those who are likely to suffer sufficiently serious human rights violations in other states. It is the concrete manifestation within a state of a universal commitment to human rights protection. States, through law, are being asked to honour the practical implication of their use of human rights discourse.

It has been argued above that asylum law in the UK must be studied within its international and European contexts. However, this does not exhaust the demands of a contextual approach. Asylum law, as with any other social institution, serves certain purposes. In administering and/or adjudicating in the area, it is possible to neglect the fact that purpose must be ascribed, in the sense that when we interpret a text we are all situated participants in the law and policy community. While historical analysis might reveal the limited original purposes of the drafters of the 1951 Convention, it is a document whose meaning is far from unambiguous. One can argue that it is a 'living instrument' and thus should be interpreted in a dynamic way. This does not, however, overcome the problem of offering a defensible reconstruction of law. For even a living instrument must be interpreted in such a way as to give it meaning and practical effect. The argument here is that the Convention must be interpreted in a way that makes it practical and effective. It is only by adopting this approach that the commitment to human rights protection can be made meaningful. When imposing an interpretation upon the text it is therefore important to view it purposively as a living body of law. In other words, if the 1951 Convention is not to become irrelevant to the world's refugees, then it does need to be interpreted in the light of contemporary developments and trends. The difficulty is that, unlike the European Convention on Human Rights, it does not have a body attached to it charged with giving authoritative guidance on its precise meaning. This means that the

1951 Convention is left to national decision-makers to interpret and apply. It is fair to state that national decision-makers can have other considerations in mind than refugee protection. Refugee law has arguably suffered as a result, although it is worth noting that some national judges and decision-makers have been prepared to take an inclusive approach to the Convention provisions. National decision-makers are, however, often not in the best position to impose a reconstruction of refugee law which reflects a primary commitment to the value of refugee protection. This is not, however, to suggest the simple imposition of the values of the interpreter. The text has its own inherent limitations, which purposive interpretation cannot overcome. As we will see in the next chapter, there are distinct limits in the Convention which no purposive approach will be able to overcome. This is where to assert an overly expansive approach may well cause practical problems. The legal regime is already being questioned by states and they might be tempted to abandon it altogether if it lost any connection to what they thought they had agreed to. The evidence from the European Convention system might suggest otherwise.

The reason for the emphasis on purpose is the well-founded belief that policy factors may lead to a restrictive interpretation being applied to, for example, art 1 of the 1951 Convention, if due regard is not paid to the overriding imperative of refugee protection.[19] Following this line of argument, asylum law must function so as to ensure the fair, effective and efficient assessment of asylum claims. The law should facilitate this process and not follow a purely exclusionary regulatory strategy. The enabling aspects of law have been neglected in this area thus far.

TOWARDS LEGALITY

Asylum law, as a distinct field of legal study, is of fairly recent origin. There has been an evolutionary movement towards legality in this area of social practice. What began as an area dominated by discretion has gradually seen the encroachment of legal regulation. This has placed asylum law and practice on a more secure footing and this process of formalisation is to be welcomed. There has also been a greater degree of openness surrounding the process, with steps being taken to consult affected groups and make public some previously unpublished guidance. This has not blunted the criticism

---

19 Even the former Home Secretary, Michael Howard, insisted that the principal aim of the legal changes which he introduced was to enable genuine applications to be dealt with more quickly: HC Hansard Vol 268 col 702, 11 December 1995.

that the current system is a 'shambles' and the substance of the current law is the object of sustained criticism.

In response to the increase in asylum applications, the UK has made a number of alterations to its system of refugee protection. The overriding policy objective has been control orientated, with the emphasis on the reduction of the number of those seeking asylum, and the acceleration of the asylum process. In seeking to achieve these aims, measures have been adopted which are not confined solely to the asylum determination system. The end result of the process is that the case-by-case assessment of applications on their individual merits has been compromised in the drive to deal with the delays in the system. In 1996 there was a substantial reduction in asylum applications, leading the Conservative government to claim success for its policy of deterrence.[20] However, the numbers of applications rose again in 1999, suggesting that applications for asylum will fluctuate from year to year. The argument that the UK is being overwhelmed by 'abusive' claimants must confront the fact that the majority of asylum applicants in the UK come from states with a record of serious human rights violations.

The UK's oft-cited liberalism on granting asylum is an overstatement which masks a much more complicated reality. Immigration control in the UK has been characterised by a number of dominant trends. The most significant, and recurring problem, is the ad hoc and reactive nature of legal regulation. Little explicit attempt was made to pursue a principled, comprehensive and open approach. When governments did act, they were frequently inspired to legislate in an unsystematic way and with questionable motives in mind. The legal regime has emerged pragmatically and in piecemeal fashion and is well known for its complexity. Whether it is any more complicated than other areas of law and practice may be doubted. It is possible that the argument of 'complexity' masks other purposes.

It is difficult to speak of a legal regime existing to deal with asylum prior to the 1980s. This is not to say that the practice of granting asylum was non-existent but that no detailed legislative framework was in place.[1] It was only in the 1980s and 1990s, with the rising number of asylum applicants, that a system of regulation began to emerge more fully. The 1951 Convention was referred to

---

20 HC Hansard Vol 290 cols 1030-1031, 20 February 1997.
 1 See generally Stevens 'The Case of UK Asylum Law and Policy: Lessons from History?' in Nicholson and Twomey (eds) *Current Issues of UK Asylum Law and Policy* (1998) p 9.

in the 1980 immigration rules but no mention was made of a specific procedure to address refugee claims. There were particular problems with the asylum procedure as it then existed. The introduction of the Immigration (Carriers' Liability) Act 1987,[2] and the increased use of visa requirements, resulted in concerns in the late 1980s about restricted access to the asylum procedure. Problems also persisted in the 1980s on the limitations placed upon appeal rights. Even at this stage, it was clear that there was an intention to try to undercut the right to seek asylum by preventing individuals reaching the UK.

It was not until the 1990s that the asylum debate led to focused legislative action. The legislative response in the UK followed a pattern that had become familiar from elsewhere in Europe. Rising numbers of applicants sparked calls for reform of the system. Those seeking asylum in the UK were constructed as 'bogus' seekers after better lives, as opposed to 'genuine refugees'. The reductionism inherent in this language has already been criticised above, but it has been a prominent aspect of the debate none the less. The rise in the number of applicants led to increased government action. Given the developments in the EU, a more solid basis for UK law and practice was a likely result of the harmonisation process also.

There are problems with the terms in which the debate has been conducted. The simplistic nature of many of the labels used stands in sharp contrast to the complexity of modern migration. The debate on asylum became polarised around competing policy positions tied to the particular perspective of participants in the debate. Official discourses portrayed the majority of those seeking refuge as economic migrants. The narrative was often one of tragic realism. Asylum law and practice became the legal mechanism for policing the borders of membership in an inherently unjust world. In official discourses the gaze of authority was directed at the asylum seeker and the individual nature of her claim and behaviour. This had the disciplining function of deterrence. The conclusion reached by government was that the system needed to be reformed in order to exclude those abusing it and remove them as quickly as possible from the system. The 'genuine refugee' would then be facilitated in making her application. The problem became not the system's inability to distinguish properly between refugees and economic migrants but individual 'abuse' of the system. Recognition was given to global inequalities but the government

---

2   See Ruff 'Immigration (Carriers' Liability) Act 1987' [1987] PL 222. See also IND *Charging Procedures: A Guide for Carriers* (revised edn, 1996).

repeatedly stated that the asylum regime was designed to protect only those who could bring their claims within the 1951 Convention. This is a fair argument to make. State parties to the 1951 Convention accept only a limited exception to the general rules of migration control. An inclusive interpretation can be adopted, but in order to protect the existence of the regime, limits must be acknowledged.

If the debate could be reduced only to this, then things would indeed be straightforward. The most intense arguments have tended to be within refugee law. General world-views about the nature of refugee protection are reflected in the politics of interpretation within refugee law. In other words, it is not always certain where the lines should be drawn within refugee law. In practice significant numbers of those not granted refugee status were given Exceptional Leave to Remain (ELR). The existence of this 'humanitarian' status was an implicit acceptance of the fact that other individuals required protection, even if they did not come within the 1951 Convention as interpreted in the UK. This interpretation of what has been happening in practice is not universally shared by all commentators. An alternative position is that there is a pervasive 'culture of disbelief' within the Home Office, which has a severe impact on the way that the claims of applicants are classified and assessed. Rather than looking to label applicants in advance, this approach focuses attention on institutional context and how the asylum regime constructs the refugee in practice. This points to the fact that asylum law is applied in practice by officials whose rational decision-making is unavoidably shaped by the social and institutional context. What is eventually validated as the legal construction of the refugee is ultimately the product of a process which has shaped the result in ways that can not be exclusively captured by a purely deductive model of legal reasoning. The culture of decision-making is as important as the definition of refugee status currently used by states. To make this claim is not to assert that all those who make asylum applications in the UK are necessarily 1951 Convention refugees. It would be surprising, given the inequality which exists in and between states, if individuals did not wish to seek better lives elsewhere.

What reasons may be given by way of explanation for the increased interest in asylum law in the UK? A series of prominent factors help to explain. This catalogue of explanatory factors is intended to be indicative of the predominant themes, rather than an exhaustive account of the reasons underlying the formation of recent law and policy. The first is the *government's interpretation* of the rise in the number of asylum applicants since the mid-1980s.

In 1999 the figure stood at 71,158[3] compared with 4,256 in 1987.[4] This is second only to Germany in the EU, which received 95,113 applications for asylum in 1999.[5] This can be compared with the US, which received 43,677 applications and Canada, which received 29,868 applications in 1999.[6] There has clearly been a sharp increase in the number of applications in the UK. Disputes have arisen, not over this fact, but over the interpretation to be placed on the increase in numbers. The reason for placing the emphasis on the government's interpretation of the statistics is that it has not claimed that the number of applicants alone has determined the legal and policy response. Instead, it has relied on the familiar argument that the majority of applications are 'bogus'.[7] Thus, it is important to note that the official justification for the measures adopted is based not on the quantity of applications but on the official interpretation of the increase. One would suspect, given the centrality of the argument to the justification of policy, that quite detailed empirical evidence existed to support such claims. The level of evidence required to support the claim has not been forthcoming: reliance has, however, been placed instead on the consistently low refugee recognition rates in[1] the UK. A second influential factor is the EU harmonisation process discussed in Chapter 3.[8] A third element in this picture is possibly less tangible than the others, but is nevertheless important. This is the general movement away from regarding asylum as the exclusive solution to refugee movements, borne from new policy objectives formulated by western European states (among others) in the post-cold war era.[9] In the western European context, the attitudes which motivated legal restrictions on the entry of migrants from outside the region (initiated in the mid-1970s) have filtered into assessments of the appropriate responses to

3 *Migration News Sheet* (March 2000) p 9.
4 Home Office Statistical Bulletin *Asylum Statistics United Kingdom 1995* 9/96.
5 *Migration News Sheet* (March 2000) p 9.
6 Note 5 above.
7 Michael Howard (former Secretary of State for the Home Department); HC Hansard Vol 268 col 699, 11 December 1995: 'Britain has a proud record of giving refuge to those fleeing genuine persecution, but we cannot ignore the fact that our procedures are being abused.'
8 See eg Hathaway 'Harmonizing for Whom? The Devaluation of Refugee Protection in the Era of European Economic Co-operation' (1993) 26 Cornell Int LJ 719; Joly 'The Porous Dam: European Harmonization on Asylum in the Nineties' (1994) 6 IJRL 159; Hailbronner 'Perspectives on a Harmonisation of Asylum Law after the Maastricht Treaty' (1992) 29 CMLR 917; Loescher 'The European Community and Refugees' (1989) 65 International Affairs 613.
9 See Shacknove 'From Asylum to Containment' (1993) 5 IJRL 516.

refugees and asylum seekers.[10]   While this has necessitated some consideration of the development of more efficacious preventative strategies, it is arguably the deterrence and containment aspects which have dominated in practice. This has perhaps inevitably lead to claims that concepts, such as prevention, provide a cloak of humanitarian legitimacy for the introduction of policies which conflict with the traditional approaches to refugee protection.

The legislative framework is contained in the Immigration Act 1971, the Asylum and Immigration (Appeals) Act 1993, the Asylum and Immigration Act 1996 and the Immigration and Asylum Act 1999. The legislation has followed the trends established in the early 1990s.[11] The legislative activity in the 1990s is quite remarkable if viewed in the context of the relative neglect in the past. Overall, an impressive array of legal and policy tools are now in place to implement government policy. The asylum debate provoked discussion of more general constitutional questions about the ability of Parliament to protect the rights of minorities and familiar controversies surrounding the role of the courts. The courts have recently shown a willingness to defend concepts of basic fairness at a time when government seemed more concerned with administrative expediency.[12] Poor management of the rise in the number of asylum seekers and an unwillingness to invest properly in the creation of a fair and effective overall system, combined with abuse of the system, has resulted in a backlog in dealing with applications, which the Labour government has also failed to address satisfactorily.[13]   In March 1999 there were almost 65,000 cases in the backlog and by November 1999 this had reached 98,000.[14] There is a sense in which dealing with this backlog in an equitable way clouds every other

10   Castles and Miller *The Age of Migration: International Population Movements in the Modern World* (1993) pp 77-80; Collinson *Europe and International Migration* (1993) pp 46-63.
11   See Stevens 'The Asylum and Immigration Act 1996: Erosion of the Right to Seek Asylum' (1998) 61 MLR 207.
12   Eg *R v Secretary of State for Social Security, ex p JCWI; R v Secretary of State for Social Security ex p B* [1996] 4 All ER 385, [1997] 1 WLR 275. See Harvey 'Asylum Seekers, *Ultra Vires* and the Social Security Regulations' [1997] PL 394.
13   See Home Office Annual Report (1996) para 17.18: '[The] dramatic increase in the number of applications has resulted in a large backlog of outstanding asylum applications, currently around 50,000, which has congested the whole system. The cross departmental study of the asylum process (part of the Comprehensive Spending Review) is considering how best to reduce the backlog, as well as looking at how new applications should be handled'. In 1996 39,000 decisions were made, due largely it seems to the introduction of a new short procedure and various other changes as a result of the 'spend to save' initiative. The attempt to increase the overall numbers of decisions taken has continued.
14   Refugee Council *The Immigration and Asylum Act 1999* (January 2000).

issue. This trend is not confined to the UK. Goodwin-Gill has, for example, noted that the majority of those seeking asylum in Europe today are trapped in a state of limbo and thus a 'sort of non-existence'.[15] The backlogs and delays in the UK are only one further example of this general trend. In a concerted move to address this issue, the Home Office has attempted to speed up decision-making. In March 2000, for example, 11,340 asylum decisions were taken.[16]

The courts on this occasion, in effect, stepped in to breach the gap that was opening up between the instrumental pragmatism of government and the principles upon which a humane refugee regime should operate.[17] In practice the political struggle over the basic terms of asylum policy shifted into the courts,[18] with some success for those concerned about the human rights implications of government policy. Why were the courts so responsive? There are a number of interpretations which might be placed on this interventionist policy. Perhaps the most convincing reconstruction of this practice, with regard to defensible modern, procedural justifications of judicial review, is that the courts were attempting to ensure equal access to procedures for the determination of asylum applications in a substantive sense. This can be phrased in terms of a right to effective access to the determination procedure, with the aim being that all those with an arguable case are in practice able to make use of the available procedures. The more familiar theme of protecting minorities against the dangers of majoritarianism also, it is suggested, played a part. On a more general level, however, there seems to be a new mood among members of the judiciary which is conducive to intervention and, among some, there is a willingness to adopt human rights discourse.[19]

---

15 Goodwin-Gill 'Refugees and Security' (1999) 11 IJRL 1, 3.

16 *The Guardian* 26 April 2000.

17 Eg *R v Hammersmith and Fulham London Borough Council, ex p M; R v Lambeth London Borough Council, ex p P; R v Westminster County Council, ex p A; R v Lambeth London Borough Council, ex p X* (1997) Times, 19 February; *R v Secretary of State for the Environment, ex p Shelter and the Refugee Council* (23 August 1996, unreported). See also *R v Newham London Borough Council, ex p Gorenkin* (1997) 30 HLR 278. See generally, for criticism of the policy, The Glidewell Panel *The Report from an Independent Enquiry into the Implications and Effects of the Asylum and Immigration Bill 1995 and Related Social Security Measures* (16 April 1996) pp 37-38. Cf *Report by the Social Security Advisory Committee under Section 174(1) of the Social Security Administration Act 1992*, Cm 3062, January 1996; Amnesty International *Slamming the Door: The Demolition of the Right to Asylum in the UK* (1996) pp 10-21.

18 *Guardian*, 6 May 1997.

19 Note 18 above. See also Sedley 'The Constitution in the Twenty-First Century' in Nolan and Sedley *The Making and Remaking of the British Constitution* (1997) p 79; Laws 'Is the High Court the Guardian of Fundamental Constitutional Rights?' [1993] PL 59; Sedley 'Human Rights: a Twenty First Century Agenda' [1995] PL 386.

Whether this is viewed as a strategic and self-serving attempt to expand the judicial canvas, or a natural and welcome development of the common law, ultimately depends on the choice of framework adopted.[20]   Arguments over asylum seekers tend to fit with the judicial self-understanding of their role as protectors of vulnerable minorities. There is evidence to suggest that some measure of success has been achieved for refugee advocates by adopting this argumentative strategy. What is evident is that for a period in the 1990s the politics of asylum entered the courts and led to disputes between the judges and the executive. Both the Labour and Conservative governments have made explicit criticisms of the judges over their approach to this area. Although this formed part of more broadly based arguments in public law, it is on the asylum issue that some members of the judiciary were prepared to make a stand against the government. This judicial activism provides the background to the successes of the human rights movement in arguing for legislative change in the UK.

CONSTRUCTING ASYLUM LAW AND POLICY

The asylum system is governed by a legislative framework, administrative rules, official instructions and the broad principles of public law. The adoption of immigration rules[1] reflects broader developments on the rise of administrative rule-making,[2] and there has been some debate over their precise legal status. The immigration service is also issued with detailed instructions, some of which were made publicly available in 1998. In the past these instructions have leaked out to representatives but now some of the internal guidance issued to staff in the Asylum Directorate can be accessed.[3]   The treatment that asylum seekers receive in practice does not depend solely on the asylum legislation. As argued above, the UK government has been creative in seeking to achieve its objectives. The treatment of asylum seekers in practice has been affected by a variety of aspects of, for example, welfare law; most notably, in recent years, social security law and housing law. The National Assistance Act 1948 proved to be useful in the struggles that were waged against Conservative government policy

---

20 For a convincing account of a defensible framework, see Dyzenhaus 'The Politics of Deference: Judicial Review and Democracy' in McTaggart (ed) *The Province of Administrative Law* (1997) pp 279-307.

1 Immigration Act 1971 s 3(2). The asylum rules are contained in paras 327-352.

2 See generally Baldwin *Rules and Government* (1995); Baldwin and Houghton 'Circular Arguments: The Status and Legitimacy of Administrative Rules' [1986] PL 239.

3 http:\\www.homeoffice.gov.uk.

from 1996 onwards. In reality, asylum seekers have depended on political struggles waged against hostile government action. On some occasions the courts have shown a willingness to intervene in defence of their rights. The point to note is that developments in asylum law are linked to wider trends in public law in the last decade. To finish the story here would be to give a misleading impression of what happens in practice. Asylum law reflects the wider changes which are happening in the field of public law. Although the significance of globalisation and Europeanisation can be exaggerated, it does appear to be having some impact in this area. Asylum law is distinct in this respect, as all participants are trying to resolve what is at core an internationalised phenomenon. Decision-makers and representatives are required to make judgments about conditions in other states based upon a wide number of sources. Refugees and asylum seekers benefit from an 'international regime' of protection. Thus, states are required to co-operate with the UNHCR.[4] In the UK, for example, the UNHCR can become a party to an appeal. The UNHCR has published a *Handbook on Procedures and Criteria for Determining Refugee Status.*[5] This provides useful guidance and carries considerable weight in practice among representatives and decision-makers, regardless of its precise legal status. Although it is at times imprecise (notably with respect to the 'particular social group category'), it does offer a step-by-step guide to the interpretation of the Convention. The Executive Committee of the UNHCR has issued a considerable number of conclusions which again have proved to be useful when attempting to distil international standards and practices.

PROCESSES OF PROTECTION

The institutions and structures of protection shape the practical implementation of legal standards in this area. The institutional context of refugee law matters and, in practice, 'the refugee' emerges from the concrete and contextual application of rules. The structure of the asylum interview and the credibility assessments made by decision-makers have a fundamental impact on the way the refugee is constructed in practice.[6] As has been noted:

4   1951 Convention, art 35.
5   On its legal status, see *Bugdaycay v Secretary of State for the Home Department* [1987] AC 514; *R v Secretary of State for the Home Department, ex p Sivakumaran* [1988] 1 AC 958.
6   See Kälin 'Troubled Communication: Cross-Cultural Misunderstandings in the Asylum Hearing' (1986) 20 Int Migration Rev 230.

'Law and legal systems are cultural products . . . The cultural basis of law deeply influences the behaviour of persons participating in legal procedures.'[7]

If, for example, the interviewing process is not gender sensitive, then key information (essential to the evaluation of an application) may be lost. The problems continue to the appeal stage. For example, Weston notes:

'What often remains unacknowledged is the vulnerability of an asylum applicant who is unable to obtain direct corroborative evidence and the concomitant burden of fairness this places on the examiner.'[8]

As she states, 'the "culture of disbelief" is alive and well, although not omnipresent'.[9]

Although, in formal terms, the Home Secretary is responsible for the determination of asylum claims, it is the Asylum Directorate (AD) which has the practical task of administering the asylum process. The 1999 Act does, however, further extend the administrative reach of central government in this area, notably in the new support arrangements. The substantial changes to the administration of asylum reflect an administrative response to the rise in numbers of asylum seekers since the mid-1980s. A notable development has been the increase in the numbers of staff employed in the AD. In recent times there has been a move towards an integrated casework system in the IND in order to try to make the process more efficient. The computerisation of immigration, asylum and nationality casework was intended to be part of a general streamlining of the system.[10] Under a PFI contract, awarded in 1996, Siemens Business Services were appointed to develop a new computerised casework system within the IND to replace the paper-based system.[11] A new Integrated Casework Directorate has been created to deal with casework that was previously handled by five different directorates. There are continuing problems with the system, which has been criticised for its inefficiency. The backlog in decision-making is a persistent administrative problem. This has raised the issue of a possible amnesty for asylum seekers. The word 'amnesty' is out of place in this context. It further extends the symbolic criminalisation of asylum seeking. However, this is the term of choice in the debate.

7 (1986) 20 Int Migration Rev 230.
8 Weston 'A Witness of Truth' – Credibility Findings in Asylum Appeals' (1998) 12 I&NLP 87, 87.
9 (1998) 12 I&NLP 87, 89.
10 Paragraph 6.11.
11 Paragraph 7.2.

While the government is unwilling to use the language of amnesty, in effect this is the practical result. It is accepted that the asylum system in the UK is deeply flawed. There was much discussion during the passage of the 1999 Act of the importance of front loading decision-making. The 1999 Act makes provision for a restructured appeal process and it will be seen whether this leads to a significant re-think on the importance of primary decision-making. What distinguishes the passage of the 1999 Act from previous legislation was the establishment of a Special Standing Committee which was able to give more extensive consideration to the process than usual. The practical result was that the 1999 Act was debated intensely compared with previous legislative measures.

The administration of asylum has moved beyond the AD. The privatisation of immigration control in practice extends the reach of governmental policy beyond its traditional confines. The underlying rationale of government is that it is best to ensure that individuals cannot arrive in the UK. If individuals cannot make it to the UK then this avoids concerns about the procedures of the determination process. The usual response is to impose visa requirements on nationals of refugee-producing countries. Those refugees seeking to flee their state of origin are unlikely to go through the formality of acquiring a visa prior to departure. It may be unsafe for them to do so. The rules are another way to deter the arrival of asylum seekers. The UK, like other European states, is prepared to go beyond the refugee status determination process in an effort to achieve its policy objectives. This is another mechanism through which the state can attempt to abdicate responsibility.

On adjudication, the pre-1960s history of the regulation of immigration and asylum reveals a remarkable void in legal protection. No comprehensive appeal rights existed until the Immigration Act 1969. In the post-1945 period a number of attempts were made to re-think various aspects of administrative law. The new thinking was reflected in the recommendations of the Franks Committee 1957,[12] leading to the enactment of the Tribunals and Inquiries Act 1957 (now 1992). The area of immigration control was no exception to this trend. The Wilson Committee (established to examine whether appeal rights should be available to aliens and Commonwealth citizens who were refused admission or were required to leave the UK) reported in 1967.[13] It made some critical comments on the absence of appeal

---

12 Cmnd 218.
13 Cmnd 3387.

rights. While the Committee praised the work of the immigration service, it recognised that in some cases decisions may have been made differently if made by an appellate authority 'after a dispassionate review of the relevant evidence'.[14] The Committee was particularly influenced by the criticism that, as the system stood, justice was not seen to be done.[15] It recommended the establishment of a two-tier appellate authority with a central tribunal and 'subordinate judicial officers', to be known as adjudicators. Following from their concerns about symbolic justice, the Committee was keen to ensure that the appeal process was viewed as essentially separate from the administration. The Immigration Act 1969 reflected the recommendations of the Committee and its provisions were effectively replicated in the Immigration Act 1971. A two-tier appellant structure was created, consisting of adjudicators and the Immigration Appeal Tribunal (IAT). This is the same basic structure as exists today. Prior to 1987, and in contrast to the Committee's recommendations, special adjudicators and members of the IAT were appointed by the Home Secretary. Since then, however, the Lord Chancellor has assumed this function.[16] The Lord Chancellor appoints the Chief and the Deputy Chief Special Adjudicators.[17] The 1999 Act also provides for the appointment of regional adjudicators.[18] In the past it was for the Lord Chancellor to designate those special adjudicators who would deal with asylum cases. This power is now vested in the Chief Adjudicator.

The Labour government's attempts to reform the system have included a review of the appeals process which resulted in new legislation. In a consultation paper issued in July 1998 it set out possible options for reforming the system.[19] The appellate system was clearly encountering considerable difficulties. The backlog and the subsequent delays in the system were simply the symptoms of deeper problems. The proposals for reform mapped a number of possibilities for restructuring the system. The consultation document listed three main problems with the appeal system: inconsistent decisions; too many decisions overturned by the courts; and too many remittals from the IAT to special adjudicators.

14 Cmnd 3387, para 83.
15 Cmnd 3387, para 84.
16 Immigration and Asylum Act 1999, s 57. Previously, this was regulated by the Transfer of Functions (Immigration Appeals) Order 1987, SI 1987/465.
17 Immigration and Asylum Act 1999, s 57(2) and Sch 3, para 1.
18 Schedule 3, para 1.
19 Home Office/Lord Chancellor's Department *Review of Appeals: A Consultation Paper* (July 1998).

Lack of resources was not directly referred to. The document also made no reference to the clear need for a comprehensive legal aid scheme in this area.[20] The suggested solutions included boosting the status and capability of the IAT, or creating a single-tier system. The government favoured the option of enhancing the role and status of the IAT by making it into a Court of Record.[1] A further suggestion was that appeal hearings might be on the papers only. This does raise the issue of how credibility is to be properly assessed in this context.[2] Also, there are principled concerns about the appellant's sense of fairness in seeing and hearing that justice is being done.[3] The 1999 Act substantially alters the appeal system and will be discussed in more detail below. However, it is worth noting here that the two-tier system remains in operation, although some restructuring has taken place. The government has opted for a process of reform of the internal dynamics of the existing system rather than a rejection of this approach. The institutional context for adjudication has, however, been altered.

A prominent aspect of government criticism of this area is interference by the courts. The consultation document, and subsequent comment, indicate a concern with the judiciary's approach to asylum law.[4] It is an area where in recent years there has been a large number of applications. The government has expressed the view that the need for judicial review should be rare. It is possible to be extremely critical of this thinking, with its focus on delay. It is important to stress, however, that judicial review has an important place. The government has indicated that the reduction in judicial review applications should be achieved by creating a more effective appeals mechanism, which has the respect of the appellants, the public and the court. A restructured and 'enhanced' appellate authority might encourage what one

20 ILPA *Response to the Home Office/Lord Chancellor's Department Review of Appeals: A Consultation Paper, and to Relevant Parts of the White Paper* (1998) para 1.4. This is of particular significance in Northern Ireland, where a clear gap existed in provision for the representation of appellants, see Law Centre (NI) *Response to Fairer, Faster and Firmer-A Modern Approach to Immigration and Asylum* (1998).

1 Home Office/Lord Chancellor's Department *Review of Appeals* (1998), para 7.18; ILPA, note 20 above, para 17.2: 'ILPA would respectfully suggest that these deficiencies are the result of operational inefficiency internal to the IAT; they are problems of constitution and personnel rather than power or status.'

2 *Review of Appeals*, para 10.3. See generally Ruppel, 'The Need for a Benefit of the Doubt Standard in Credibility Evaluations of Asylum Applicants' (1991-92) 23 Columbia Human Rights LR 1.

3 *Review of Appeals*, para. 10.6.

4 See Blake and Sunkin 'Immigration Appeals and Judicial Review' [1998] PL 583.

author has, in a different context, called 'deference as respect'.[5] In the longer term, this is the only way that resort to the courts should be addressed. As with other individuals in the UK, asylum seekers have the right to access to the courts. At its core this is about rebuilding trust in a system which, as has been suggested here, at present lacks legitimacy and moral authority at all stages. This will depend on reform of the IAT which goes beyond the surface and looks instead to its internal functioning. It is also worth emphasising that improved first instance decision-making, combined with properly funded and competent legal representation at an early stage, is as important as a well functioning appellate system. Front loading the system is the only appropriate way to reduce judicial review applications. It remains to be seen whether the new legislative provisions will remedy the serious problems with the present process of refugee protection in the UK. The concern is that the political calls for more speedy decision-making may have a negative impact on the quality of decisions.

CRITICAL VOICES IN ASYLUM LAW AND POLICY

Thus far this book has focused on providing a guide to the framework of asylum law. It is essential also to address the critical scholarship which has begun to emerge in this area.

The asylum process in the UK has attracted much critical attention. The debate continues nevertheless to oscillate between familiar positions, without erosion of the traditional narratives of asylum seeking. For critical lawyers this will not do and it is essential that critical insights are imported into the area of asylum law. As Fraser has argued, a critical social theory should operate with its eye firmly fixed on the work of those oppositional social movements with which it has 'a partisan, though not uncritical, identification'.[6] In refugee and asylum law the main dissenting voices have focused on the blindness of the law to the specific experiences of women refugees.[7] It is this gender critique of asylum law which will be the focus of this section.

---

5   Dyzenhaus 'The Politics of Deference: Judicial Review and Democracy' in McTaggart (ed) *The Province of Administrative Law* (1997) p 279.

6   Fraser *Justice Interruptus: Critical Reflections on the 'Postsocialist Condition'* (1997) p 21.

7   See generally Indra (ed) *Engendering Forced Migration: Theory and Practice* (1998); Crawley *Women as Asylum Seekers: A Legal Handbook* (1997); Bhabha and Shutter *Women's Movement: Women Under Immigration, Nationality and Refugee Law* (1994); Spijkerboer 'Women and Refugee Status: Beyond the Public/Private Divide' (1995) 7 IJRL 756.

The gender critique of asylum law has had some measure of success, because of the ability of critical theorists to combine with activists to attempt to bring about meaningful change. There are wider lessons here for the human rights movement in the UK, and for critical scholars approaching human rights law and practice. It is too easy to neglect the groups in society which make social change happen. Human rights NGOs, as well as refugee and human rights lawyers, play a vital role in the process of protecting refugees in the UK. The point is the importance of political struggle in achieving any practical advances for this group. There is a tendency in human rights law in particular to neglect context, or more sophisticated understandings of law being developed in other realms of legal scholarship. One of the principal arguments in this work is that this is an inappropriate response.

One of the more dynamic trends in this area of late is the contribution made by feminist theorists and activists to ongoing debates about the future of refugee and asylum law. There is now, belatedly, an acknowledgment that asylum law in the UK is not the purely neutral edifice it is often claimed to be. This merges with growing concern, from a variety of perspectives, that both its substance and its practice may disguise partial perspectives on the totality of the human experience. It is now evident that the traditional narratives told about the process of seeking asylum mask the more complicated picture of the refugee experience. A number of writers have begun to expose refugee law's one-sided nature and the ways its substance and its practical application neglect the specific experiences of women refugees.[8] This work seeks to demonstrate that the promise of universalism held out by the words of refugee law is not fulfilled in practice. Feminist legal theory, in particular, may be employed in this area of public law to show how reconstructive critique can help to bring about legal and policy reforms. It is now a trite point, but law is argumentative in nature, it is contested terrain. This should be of interest to those who wish to see how theoretically informed critique of the law might be transformed into constructive practical proposals for concrete change. It is suggested that this essentially reformist agenda is an appropriate way forward. To be critical in this sense is to test the law on its own ground. However, this model draws into the picture individuals and groups who are frequently excluded. By highlighting the distortions in the perspectives of those tasked with law and policy making and application law may be reinterpreted and designed to fit the new picture that emerges of the experience of the refugee.

8   Eg Tuitt *False Images: Law's Construction of the Refugee* (1996) pp 33-35.

Law's diverse community

Law functions in both material and symbolic ways. The material aspect of the law is connected to its coercive and instrumental character. Regulation in the area of immigration and asylum law straightforwardly excludes on its face and functions in order to sanction, for example, the deportation of individuals from the UK. This is the brute face of the law. Law does, however, also function symbolically to reproduce dominant images of regulated populations.[9] The images which law produces both shape and reflect distorted and partial perspectives, which can be challenged by drawing upon work that exposes this and tries to reshape doctrine and the practice of law accordingly.

That the slogan 'the personal is the political' may be unpalatable to some should not lead to a rejection of the core of truth which it contains. A worthwhile contribution of feminist theory is to have decisively undermined the traditional conception of the public/private divide.[10] The story is now very familiar, but worth re-telling, if only in outline form. In general terms, classical liberal political theory was committed to the division of the public and private spheres.[11] The private was that sphere which was not subject to legal regulation: in other words, a space where society and its norms would not intrude. These theories were linked to individualism and had their corollary in a conception of autonomy which was reliant on negative liberty or 'freedom from' rather than 'freedom to'.[12] Classical liberalism thus tended towards an anti-

---

9   Cf O'Donovan *Sexual Divisions in Law* (1985) pp 19-20; Cotterrell *Law's Community: Legal Theory in Sociological Perspective* (1995) pp 221-248.

10 See Lacey *Unspeakable Subjects: Feminist Essays in Legal and Social Theory* (1998) pp 71-97; Young 'Impartiality and the Civic Public: Some Implications of Feminist Critiques of Moral and Political Theory' in Benhabib and Cornell (eds) *Feminism as Critique: Essays on the Politics of Gender in Late Capitalist Societies* (1987) p 74.

11 Cf Lacey, note 10 above, p 72.

12 See Berlin *Four Essays on Liberty* (1969) p 171: 'Pluralism, with the measure of 'negative liberty' that it entails, seems to me a truer and more humane ideal than the goals of those who seek in the great, disciplined, authoritarian structures the ideal of "positive" self-mastery by classes, or peoples, or the whole of mankind'; Mill *On Liberty* (1974) p 63: 'Society can and does execute its own mandates; and if it issues wrong mandates instead of right, or any mandates at all in things which it ought not to meddle, it practises a social tyranny more formidable than many kinds of political oppression, since, though not usually upheld by such extreme penalties, it leaves fewer means of escape, penetrating much more deeply into the details of life, and enslaving the soul itself.' Cf Raz *The Morality of Freedom* (1986) p 425: 'Three main features characterize the autonomy-based doctrine of freedom. *First*, its primary concern is the promotion and protection of positive freedom which is understood as the capacity for autonomy, consisting of the availability of

perfectionist view of the state.[13]   Its purpose was not to make individuals good but simply to create the framework whereby individuals could pursue their freely chosen ends. As with a number of classic theories of liberalism, the model of human nature adopted was that of the abstracted, or disengaged,[14] subject defined in universalist language (although abstracted from context, this 'individual' was often driven by highly specific and all-too-human instrumentalist goals). The emergence of the social sciences in the nineteenth century lead to scepticism about the idealism implicit in much political philosophy. Confronted with empirical knowledge of everyday oppression and exploitation, normative political theory seemed naïve. A split (which continues to this day) between a normative political philosophy (always open to criticism for being abstracted from reality) and social science (always open to the accusation that it submerges or fails to acknowledge its normative commitments) began to open up. For those concerned with tackling the root causes of disadvantage and inequality, normative political philosophy was (and continues to appear) much too cosy and on occasion seemed to slide in the direction of apology.[15] The difficulty, which is still with us, and which all those

an adequate range of options, and of the mental abilities necessary for an autonomous life. *Second*, the state has the duty not merely to prevent denial of freedom, but also to promote it by creating the conditions of autonomy. *Third*, one may not pursue any goal by means which infringe people's autonomy unless such action is justified by the need to protect or promote the autonomy of those people or of others.'

13 See Barry *Political Argument* (1964) p 66.

14 For an examination of the background to the rise of 'disengaged reason' and the distortions which it has wrought, see Taylor *The Sources of the Self: The Making of Modern Identity* (1989) pp 143-158. Taylor is interested in why people adopt naturalism when trying to explain human behaviour. He recognises the attractiveness of notions of disengagement, particularly its picture of freedom. Unlike a number of others, he does not wish to reject the scientific outlook; his concern is that it is not used to define the totality of our lives. In addition, the moral grounds of naturalism need to be drawn out.

15 See Dewey *Reconstruction in Philosophy* (1957) pp 191-192: 'Rationalistic logic formerly made men careless in observation of the concrete in physical philosophy. It now operates to depress and retard observation in specific social phenomena. The social philosopher, dwelling in the region of his concepts, "solves" problems by showing the relationship of ideas, instead of helping men solve problems in the concrete by supplying then hypotheses to be used and tested in projects of reform.' Dewey's distrust of 'conceptualism' and its distortions goes to the heart of the pragmatist disposition. Although a more general argument it does hint at the irritation with normative political philosophy evident in much empirically-inclined work and also in some feminist theory. See also Dewey *Liberalism and Social Action* (1935), he argues that coercion and oppression are not the product of science and technology but of the perpetuation of old institutions and patterns which remain untouched by scientific method. Dewey's optimistic liberalism, with its emphasis on an experimental mind-set, contains valuable insights which remain important.

concerned with human rights protection, including feminist theorists, inherit, is how to give due recognition to two things. First, the situated nature of our lives and thought and, second, the structural factors which drive the tension between legal and factual equality, as revealed by the social sciences. Is this possible while at the same time holding onto the universalism, and normativity, of, for example, human rights law discourse? The politics of difference, while vital in recognising the pluralism of modern societies, is an insufficient response to this dilemma.

Having placed this discussion in context, it is necessary to extract core elements of feminist theory which are relevant to the argument developed here. The straightforward starting point is that feminist theory can not be reduced to any one particular insight. Feminism displays the same diversity in its scholarship as anyone living in a pluralist society would expect to find in any branch of modern legal and political theory. For the purposes of this chapter, it is enough to trace some of the core themes: deconstruction of the public/private divide; distrust/rejection of universalist moral, political and social theory; suspicion of normative political philosophy and the disengaged image of the self; emphasis on context and the situated nature of our practical reasoning; and explorations of the structural factors which contribute to the gap between legal and factual equality. As this discussion has sought to show, these themes are part of the ongoing conversation of modernity. It was not long before the insights of feminist theory began to impact upon refugee law scholarship,[16] and eventually on asylum law and practice in the UK. One of the first gaps exposed is the absence of specific reference to gender as an enumerated ground of persecution. It is worth noting that the guidelines which have been adopted, and that are discussed below, do not alter the basic position that gender is not included as a ground of persecution in refugee law. In addition, the systematic neglect of the experiences of women is highlighted.[17] This is now combined with recognition of the problems fostered by a distorted view of the refugee

---

16 See UNHCR Executive Committee (UNHCR EXCOM), Conclusion No 39 (1985) para (k), which: 'recognised that States, in the exercise of their sovereignty, are free to adopt the interpretation that women asylum seekers who face harsh or inhuman treatment due to their having transgressed the social mores of the society in which they live may be considered as a "particular social group" within the meaning of Article 1A(2) of the 1951 United Nations Refugee Convention.' Greatbatch 'The Gender Difference: Feminist Critiques of Refugee Discourse' (1989) 1 IJRL 518; Johnsson 'The International Protection of Women Refugees' (1989) 1 IJRL 221.

17 Note 16 above.

experience. The structural factors which dictate who migrates and to where have also been explored. This has fed into a general theme in critical refugee law scholarship, one aspect of which is the questioning of refugee law's traditional focus on asylum. The fact is that the majority of the world's refugees are women and yet the majority of asylum seekers – in, for example, Europe – are men. Another result of this criticism is that the internally displaced now receive much more international attention than was the case in the past.[18] It is evident that feminist theory has much to contribute to critical explorations of refugee law.

It is time to move from the necessary abstraction of the previous section to examine how the gender blindness of refugee law is being addressed. At the centre of the current gender critique of refugee law lies concepts of equal treatment and equal access to determination systems within states which connect with proceduralist understandings of public law. It is suggested here that the challenge in refugee law at present is to reconstruct law and practice on the basis of this norm of substantive equality.

One scholar has advocated the deployment of a cultural jurisprudence as suited to the demands of the area:[19]

'Cultural jurisprudence aims to explore ways in which the development of the law can be informed by an understanding of culture so that values of justice can be enhanced and expanded to apply to all populations that come within the jurisdiction of the law.'[20]

Although broadly defined, it is welcome recognition of an existing problem and provides a framework for future research. The emphasis placed on a heightened measure of cultural sensitivity on the part of all those tasked with law application is particularly relevant to the concerns of this book.[1] While the focus of Juss's work is on the fostering of pluralist democratic values in racially and ethnically diverse societies, the gender dimension should also be recognised. 'Race', ethnicity *and* gender must be central concerns of any 'new' cultural jurisprudence. The issue addressed in this section is how the insights revealed by the critique can be translated

18 See *Report of the Representative of the Secretary-General on Internally Displaced Persons* UN Doc E/CN4/1998/53.

19 Juss *Discretion and Deviation in the Administration of Immigration Control* (1997) pp 10-39.

20 Note 19 above, p 5.

1 Note 19 above, pp 18-19: 'Cultural jurisprudence is vital where the actors operate in a relatively unconstrained legal field, laying emphasis on the exercise of wide discretionary power, which require cultural training and sensitivity.'

into meaningful institutional change in the light of this 'new' cultural jurisprudence.[2]

Engendering the asylum process

When considering the landscape of refugee law today, one of the more significant developments is the adoption of gender guidelines by a number of states. The attempt to mainstream a gender perspective in law and policy development is now a familiar theme in European and public law.[3]   Within the EU, a number of innovative new strategies are being employed in order to achieve the aim of equal opportunity for men and women. It appears that the critique which underlies such new thinking is beginning to have an impact on asylum law. The reason this has occurred is because of active social movements and political struggle.

In recognition of past failure to address adequately the experiences of women within the asylum determination process, some states have decided to adopt measures which will encourage a less distorted approach to refugee determination in the future. The UNHCR played a significant role in this process. In 1991 it issued *Guidelines on the Protection of Refugee Women*[4] and the Executive Committee of the UNHCR has adopted several Conclusions on the problems they encounter.[5]   The UNHCR guidelines are particularly useful. For example, they recognise that:

> 'International protection goes beyond adherence to legal principles. Equally important, the protection of refugee women requires planning

---

2   For some thoughts on how this might be addressed in the interviewing process in asylum cases, see Hinshelwood 'Interviewing Female Asylum-Seekers' (1997) Special Issue IJRL 159.

3   See European Commission *Incorporating Equal Opportunities for Men and Women into all Community Policies and Activities* COM/96/97/Final; Commission *Progress Report on Equal Opportunities* COM/98/122/Final. These outline new structures that have been put in place and ones that are recommended in order to mainstream equal opportunities, this includes: awareness-raising; training; preparation of guidelines; tools for gender impact assessments; and gender proofing. See also Council Resolution on integrating gender in development co-operation, 20 December 1995; Council Conclusion on gender issues in development co-operation, 18 May 1998.

4   EC/SCP/67, 22 July 1991. See also UNHCR *Interviewing Applicants for Refugee Status: Training Module* (1995) ch 4, 'Interviewing Women Refugee Applicants'; UNHCR *Guidelines on Preventing and Responding to Sexual Violence Against Refugees* (1995). See also UN Fourth World Conference for Women *Beijing Platform for Action*, UN Doc A/CONF177/20 (1995) para 149(i).

5   UNHCR EXCOM Conclusion 73 *Refugee Protection and Sexual Violence*; UNHCR EXCOM Conclusion 64 *Refugee Women and International Protection*; Conclusion 60 *Refugee Women*; Conclusion 54 *Refugee Women*; UNHCR EXCOM Conclusion 39 *Refugee Women and International Protection*.

and a great deal of common sense in establishing programmes and enforcing priorities that support their safety and well-being.'[6]

While such guidelines from the UNHCR have no formal legal status, they are often more useful in practice than some general legal standards. The reason is that they provide practical guidance on a range of specific issues. They may aid the process of mainstreaming protection principles. One criticism of such measures is that their informal nature makes them less useful when it comes to contentious areas, or when protection principles collide with other priorities. Without effective internal or external enforcement mechanisms, it may be difficult to achieve the required changes in the decision-making 'culture'. This criticism attaches not only to these guidelines from the UNHCR but the use of guidelines more generally.

Following the UNHCR's lead, Canada, the US and Australia have adopted gender guidelines which seek to embed a gender perspective within the determination process.[7] In order to explore the nature and scope of these guidelines, the Canadian Immigration and Refugee Board (IRB) Guidelines will serve as an illustrative example for the purpose of this chapter.[8]

6 Guidelines p 9.
7 Australian Department of Immigration and Multi-Cultural Affairs 'Guidelines on Gender Issues for Decision-Makers' July 1996; US Immigration and Naturalization Service 'Considerations For Asylum Officers Adjudicating Asylum Claims From Women' 26 May 1995; Canadian Immigration and Refugee Board, 'Guidelines on Women Refugee Claimants Fearing Gender-Related Persecution' 9 March 1993, updated November 1996. See Anker 'Rape in the Community as a Basis for Asylum: The Treatment of Women Refugees' Claims to Protection in Canada and the United States (Part I)' (1997) 12 Bender's Immigration Bulletin 476, 478: 'The Canadians did more than issue the guidelines. The IRB took active steps to implement and monitor them. . . the IRB has conducted ongoing educational programs designed to educate immigration officials on fundamental human rights principles and gender issues in asylum claims . . . As a result of this monitoring, when critical issues have been identified the IRB has been able to respond with specific training.' As she notes, there have, however, been resource problems. For a useful analysis of the gender guidelines in context, see Macklin 'Refugee Women and the Imperative of Categories' (1995) 17 Human Rights Q 213. See also Oosterveld 'The Canadian Guidelines on Gender-Related Persecution: An Evaluation' (1996) 8 IJRL 569; Wallace 'Making the Refugee Convention Gender Sensitive: The Canadian Guidelines' (1996) 45 ICLQ 702.
8 Note that other Guildelines have now been adopted by the Chairperson: *Guidelines on Detention* (March 1998); *Guidelines on Civilian Non-Combatants Fleeing Civil War Situations* (March 1996); *Guidelines on Child Refugee Claimants: Procedural and Evidential Issues* (August 1996). In the US in December 1998 the *Guidelines for Children's Asylum Claims* were adopted. For comment, see Bhabha and Young 'Not Adults in Miniature: Unaccompanied Child Asylum Seekers and the New US Guidelines' (1999) 11 IJRL 84.

First, a brief outline of the Canadian asylum determination system. Few would disagree with the proposition that Canada has shown the way in designing a respected asylum determination system. The system is not without its serious problems. However, it has stood for some time as a useful example of a more defensible approach to the area. In contrast to the UK, the Canadian system has gained a marked level of legitimacy among those who participate in it. This is not to exaggerate the strengths of the system, it is subject to continuing criticism within Canada; however, it offers a useful model for comparison.

The IRB was created in 1989 and it is Canada's largest tribunal. It is an independent administrative tribunal with quasi-judicial functions. It consists of three divisions, one of which, the Convention Refugee Determination Division (CRDD), assesses asylum claims. It sits usually in two-person panels with assistance from a Refugee Hearings Officer (RHO). Initially, a claim is assessed by a Senior Immigration Officer in order to determine whether the claim is eligible to be heard by the CRDD. If eligible, the claim may be advanced to the CRDD for determination. The RHO is responsible for conducting background research into the claim. The process is specifically designed to be inquisitorial. Members of the CRDD are required to write reasons, even for positive applications in gender-related cases, though in law reasons are required only for negative decisions.[9] There is no appeal from a decision of the CRDD but it may be judicially reviewed if the leave of a Federal Court judge is obtained. The Federal Court has held that in relevant cases it is an error of law to ignore the guidelines.[10] The Immigration Department is not a party to the proceedings, unless the issue of exclusion arises. The CRDD does not have the power to grant asylum; this is the responsibility of the Immigration Department. If a positive decision is made, the applicant is granted refugee status and may then apply for permanent residence status. Refugee recognition rates are markedly higher

---

9 See Bernier (Special Advisor to the Chairperson, IRB, and Senior Advisor on Gender Equality, Department of Justice, Canada) 'The IRB Guidelines on Women Refugee Claimants Fearing Gender-Related Persecution' (1997) Special Issue IJRL 167-168: 'We do . . . require that the Members write reasons even for positive decisions on gender-related claims (by law only negative decisions must always be given in writing), and we expect Members to justify any departure from the Guidelines.' She cites the following from the decision of the Federal Court of Canada in *Narvaez v Minister of Citizenship and Immigration* FC-TD, 9 February 1995, p 6: 'While the Guidelines are not law, they are authorized by subsection 65(3) of the [Immigration Act] and intended to be followed unless circumstances are such that a different analysis is appropriate.'

10 *Mohamed v Secretary of State for Canada* (1994) 73 FTP 159.

than in the UK. This suggests that despite the fact that both states apply the same formal legal definition of refugee, the practical construction of protection differs considerably. This reinforces the argument that the 'refugee' emerges within the institutional context of determination procedures.

The Chairperson of the IRB has the power to issue guidelines.[11] Gender guidelines were adopted by the Chairperson in March 1993 and updated in November 1996. Although they are not legally binding (this fact has attracted criticism[12]) they are generally regarded as having had a progressive impact on the determination system.[13] As to content, they promulgate a step-by-step analysis of the refugee definition, highlighting precisely when and where a gendered perspective should inform the decision-making process. The General Proposition is worth citing:

> 'Although gender is not specifically enumerated as one of the grounds for establishing Convention refugee status *the definition of Convention refugee may properly be interpreted* as providing protection for women who demonstrate a well-founded fear of gender-related persecution by reason of any one, or a combination of, the enumerated grounds.' (My emphasis.)

Although a woman's claim must go through the same process as a man's, she is permitted, if a request is made in writing, to have women CRDD members present, a woman RHO and a woman interpreter. On procedural matters, emphasis is placed on sensitivity to the specific experiences of women, with appropriate training provided to officials. In addition, on substantive issues of refugee law, the guidelines promote a gendered perspective on all important aspects of the interpretation of the law.

---

11 Immigration Act, s 65(3).
12 Oosterveld (1996) 8 IJRL 567, 580-83.
13 See Anker, note 7 above, p 482. She does, however, note some problems: 'not all the decisions reviewed have demonstrated the same sensitivity to women. Moreover, there is reason for concern in the termination of the working groups and termination of the internal reports on gender reasons . . . But the Canadians are clearly "ahead of the rest" and their example has had a remarkable effect outside Canadian borders.' JUSTICE, ILPA, ARC *Providing Protection: Asylum Determination in Canada, Supplementary Report 2* (1997) pp 14-15: 'The guidelines issued by the Chairperson are extremely important in informing good decision-making . . . The guidelines are important not only because they state (and arguably expand) the definition of refugee; but also because they provide the decision-maker with a series of necessary steps and relevant questions, as the building blocks in satisfying themselves as to whether the definitional criteria have been met. This assists a rigorous and consistent approach to decision-making, which applicants and their representatives can expect to rely on (the guidelines are publicly available).' Macklin (1995) 17 Human Rights Q 213, 275

The success of the guidelines can not be attributed solely to their formal enactment. A further factor is the willingness of the relevant authorities to try to ensure that they become meaningful in the culture of decision-making through the use of working groups and training programs. As to matters of adjudication, the position has also been advanced by the willingness to connect interpretations of refugee law to other developments in the international law of human rights.[14] A human rights paradigm has emerged which attempts to keep refugee law relevant. The Canadian example illustrates the use that may be made of guidelines in promoting a gendered perspective on asylum law. Guidelines have also been used for other purposes in Canada, and there is no reason why they need to be confined to the gender dimension. Formal adoption is only a first step in the effort to promote an institutional culture which is conducive to the effective interpretation and application of refugee law.[15] It is evident that the legal construction of the refugee within states is dependent on the community of interpreters of refugee law in important ways. While the law's image of the refugee has undoubted rhetorical and symbolic power, it is within the administrative and adjudicative systems of individual states that the 'refugee' emerges.[16] The culture of decision-making, and therefore the context within which the community of interpreters of refugee law operates, is central. One of the arguments advanced by critics of the UK system is that there is a pervasive culture of disbelief or suspicion. Rather than continue to lament the clearly narrow definition of refugee law, what this suggests is that more attention needs to be paid to the 'social construction of protection' in its legal setting. The point is to examine the institutional factors which define protection *as well as* the principles of protection. A project of reform must keep in view both institutional design and the norms of human rights and refugee law. Although the Canadian model has problems, it does provide a useful starting point when thinking about the challenges of reform.

14 Eg *A-G of Canada v Ward* (1993) 2 SCR 689, 103 DLR 4th.
15 Bernier (1997) Special Issue IJRL 167, 168-169: 'Essentially, our Guidelines seek to remove the blinkers that too often cause us to approach refugee claims by women according to the more familiar situation of men refugees. This was achieved moreover, within the terms of the 1951 Convention.'
16 This helps to shift attention away from an exclusive concern with the legal rule and toward empirical work on, for example, the culture of public administration. The point is *not* to discourage a focus on rules but to encourage a more comprehensive approach to analysis.

THE POLITICAL STRUGGLE IN THE COURTS: ASYLUM, RIGHTS AND THE JUDGES

Can the courts play a role in the promotion of values conducive to the fair assessment of asylum claims? The evidence from the UK is that the courts are willing to adopt a relatively assertive approach in this area. Law can make a difference in the struggle to protect refugees and asylum seekers. However, it is important to understand why law makes a difference and the circumstances within which it will work to constrain power. The courts can fulfil an important role in ensuring that principles of legality are a part of the asylum decision-making process. The courts have shown a willingness to intervene in defence of the rights of asylum seekers. This action can conflict with standard accounts of immigration and asylum law which stress judicial deference in this field. If this was once the case, it is not a completely accurate reflection of the picture now.[17] It is worth charting the struggles that have developed between the courts and the government over the terms of asylum policy. As I have argued, in practice the politics of asylum entered the courts.

The background to judicial intervention was the ever more restrictive approach to the treatment of asylum seekers by the Conservative government. In particular, the restrictions on the economic and social rights of asylum seekers attracted considerable criticism. Taking into account the nature of the changes, and the amount of adverse publicity, it was unsurprising that a challenge to Conservative government policy was mounted by the Joint Council for the Welfare of Immigrants and an asylum applicant in the important case of *R v Secretary of State for Social Security, ex p Joint Council for the Welfare of Immigrants, ex p B*.[18] At the core of the challenge was the argument that the regulations restricting access to welfare benefits were ultra vires the enabling statute because Parliament could not have intended to permit such a degree of interference with statutory rights in the Asylum and Immigration Appeals Act 1993 and/or with fundamental human rights.

The judgments in the case are illustrative of the clashes that can occur between two distinct ways of approaching this aspect of judicial review when basic human rights are at issue. Simon Brown LJ, delivering the judgment of the majority, accepted, as a preliminary point, that the aim of seeking to remove economic migrants from the asylum process was a valid one and could not be called into

---

17 See Harvey 'Refugee law, the judges and a "new" human rights culture' (2000) 14 I&NLP 5.

18 [1996] 4 All ER 385, [1997] 1 WLR 275.

question by the court. Thus, the central purpose of the government's asylum policy was not at issue in the case. However, he did identify a relevant problem with the policy: that genuine asylum seekers found themselves faced with an onerous choice of either remaining destitute and homeless while their claims were being determined, or returning to their state of origin to face persecution. On this interpretation, the policy appeared to contradict the stated intention of the government to facilitate the effective assessment of genuine claims. With the above discussion in mind, the reasoning is worth examining in detail.

After outlining the asylum and social security law context, and noting the deleterious impact of the regulations, Brown LJ looked to the substance of the applicant's arguments. The first was that the regulations were inconsistent with the 1993 Act, s 6, which protected the asylum applicant from removal pending determination of her claim to asylum. It was claimed that in creating various sub-categories of asylum seekers not envisaged by this legislation, the regulations were ultra vires. The applicants argued that the 1993 Act made no distinction between 'in-country' and 'after-entry' applicants as the regulations did. Brown LJ rejected this argument, stating that the Secretary of State for Social Security was under no obligation to align the benefit scheme with the approach adopted under the 1993 Act. In other words, the Secretary of State was not prevented by the terms of the 1993 Act from creating various sub-categories of asylum seekers for social security purposes.

The stronger argument advanced by the applicants was one based on the concept of the right of access to the determination process. They argued that the right of access was fundamental to the protection afforded by the 1951 Convention. The argument was that the removal of benefits would constitute a serious impediment to this right of access. Brown LJ stated that a conflict between the regulations and the 1993 Act did not arise solely because the intention was to reduce the number of those invoking rights of appeal under the 1993 Act. He did, however, acknowledge that genuine refugees would also be affected by the measures. In advancing this argument, the applicants relied upon *Leech (No 2)*.[19] Brown LJ accepted that the decision in *Leech (No 2)* was of assistance to the applicants, but stated that the analogy was not a precise one. He had no difficulty in accepting the right of the Secretary of State to discourage economic migrants by restricting their benefits. The regulations were not invalid simply because of

19　*R v Secretary of State for the Home Department, ex p Leech (No 2)* [1994] QB 198.

their 'chilling effect'. The claim made here by the applicants effectively pushed the *Leech* principle a step further. In this case there had been an interference with the right of access of an asylum seeker to the determination process. The interference in question, however, related to the economic and social context of seeking asylum. This is a broadly based form of proceduralism which takes into account the factors which are constitutive of autonomy. In other words, this involved accepting the argument that the Secretary of State owed a positive duty towards asylum seekers with regards to the provision of benefit and a facilitative understanding of autonomy. This was a step (following his reassurance that parliamentary sovereignty was not in issue) that Brown LJ was prepared to take in this case. In defending this conclusion, he reasoned that Parliament had demonstrated in the 1993 Act a commitment to the UK's 1951 Convention obligations. Further to this, he noted that:

> '[S]o basic are the human rights here at issue that it cannot be necessary to resort to the Convention for the Protection of Human Rights and Fundamental Freedoms to take note of their violation.'[20]

To support this contention, he referred to a statement made by Lord Ellenborough, extolling the virtues of the law of humanity which was 'anterior to all positive law'.[1] In the light of broader debates in public law, it is worth noting that the conclusion reached was, however, anchored solidly in an interpretation of parliamentary intent. In other words, the necessary parliamentary intent of primary importance was that expressed in the 1993 Act, where a central place had been given in this area of law to the right of access to the asylum process. Brown LJ concluded that the benefit regime had been altered so drastically as to defeat this statutory right of asylum seekers to gain access to refugee status.[2] This is an important conclusion on what has long been a problematic aspect of the law. The lack of procedural rights in the 1951 Convention is often referred to as one of its chief defects. The majority judgment in this case is therefore a welcome recognition of a valuable principle. In securing this right of access, Brown LJ stated that prior to recognition it was necessary that basic provision should be made if the statutory right of refugees to claim asylum was not to be defeated.[3] He noted, obiter, that although it was not

20 [1996] 4 All ER 385 at 401.
 1 [1996] 4 All ER 385 at 401.
 2 See also *R v Secretary of State for the Home Department, ex p Jammeh* (1997) Times, 11 September.
 3 [1996] 4 All ER 385 at 401.

for the court to advise the Secretary of State on the best way to address claims which lacked merit, a number of other European countries had introduced voucher schemes to tackle the problem and to secure basic provision. While the principal concern was the right of access, this was linked to the economic and social plight of asylum seekers. The reasoning is important because it links the process of seeking asylum to its economic and social context. Contained within this reasoning is a substantive vision of autonomy linked to a rich understanding of proceduralism.

In his judgment Waite LJ concurred with the above approach. The basic principle, which he accepted, was that when deciding upon the validity of subordinate legislation the presumption was that Parliament did not intend it to conflict with statutory rights protected by other primary legislation.

These judgments may be contrasted with the dissent of Neill LJ. Adopting a more traditional approach, anchored in a different reconstruction of legislative intent, Neill LJ dissented from the majority. He argued that when deciding whether secondary legislation was ultra vires the enabling statute, it was necessary to consider the primary purpose and the main effect of the legislation. The primary purpose of the legislation was to deter economic migrants and not genuine refugees. In assessing the primary purpose, Neill LJ looked to the stated intention of the government and was not, unlike Brown LJ, prepared to delve any deeper than this. This may be contrasted with the majority approach, where an assessment of the practical impact of the policy shaped the decision. In a clear reference to the policy implications of its decision, he noted that the court should be conscious that it was considering a matter which involved the allocation of public funds. For his part, he stated that it was apparent that the legislation was not aimed at genuine refugees: the Secretary of State was entrusted by Parliament to strike a balance, and this he had done; it was therefore not the place of the courts to intervene. For Neill LJ, where secondary legislation enacted under one statute impacted upon rights conferred in another, the court had to look at the extent of the impact and, provided the secondary legislation was prima facie within the enabling powers, to examine the stated objects which the secondary legislation sought to achieve. Looking at these factors, Neill LJ did not believe the threshold of legality had been crossed. As indicated above, the majority of the Court of Appeal were not convinced by this argument.

The events which followed the judgment are now well known by public lawyers and demonstrated that legal victories can be symbolic only. The government immediately acted to reinstate the regulations by amending the Asylum and Immigration Bill as it was going through its parliamentary stages in the House of Lords.[4] However, this Court of Appeal judgment remains important principally because of the weight attached by the majority to the right of access to the asylum determination procedure. This case forms part of an emerging common law jurisprudence of human rights. It offers an insight into the role of judicial interpretation in the reconstruction of intent. The judgment is another example, if one is needed, of the willingness of some members of the judiciary in judicial review proceedings to intervene in defence of human rights. The majority were clearly concerned to uphold the statutory right to effective access to refugee status determination procedures and to prevent its erosion through the use of a punitive regulatory strategy. The decision was further recognition by the courts of the importance of human rights protection. The swift reaction of the Conservative government provided an example of the difficulties with the traditional approach to human rights protection in the UK. By amending the Asylum and Immigration Bill to reinstate the regulations, the government signalled its lack of concern for principle in the face of its own public policy imperatives.

The story did not end there. In *R v Hammersmith and Fulham London Borough Council, ex p H*[5] the Court of Appeal held that the National Assistance Act 1948, s 21(1)(a) should be interpreted in the light of current developments. It thus placed a responsibility on local authorities to provide assistance to asylum seekers who fulfilled the relevant criteria. The court held that Parliament could not have intended that those in need be without recourse to assistance. The willingness of the court to intervene against government policy was again demonstrated, and the burden of provision therefore shifted from central government to local authorities.[6] One of the reasons for the creation of the new

---

4   HL Hansard Vol 573 col 596, 24 June 1996. For concern about the speed of this
    process, see HL Hansard Vol 573 cols 1016-1017, 27 June 1996.

5   (1997) Times, 19 February. See also *Lismane v Hammersmith and Fulham London
    Borough Council* (1998) 31 HLR 427.

6   Some London authorities have been particularly displeased with this result. From
    an early stage Westminster Council, for example, proposed to move hundreds of
    asylum seekers to Liverpool in order to cut the cost of feeding and housing them,
    Guardian 16 May 1997. See also HC Hansard Vol 291 cols 837-858, 5 March
    1997, a debate on the problems faced by a number of London boroughs; HC Hansard
    Vol 292 cols 268-269, 12 March 1997, local authorities to be reimbursed for
    reasonable costs that have followed the judgments. See *R v Newham London Borough
    Council, ex p Gorenkin* (1997) 30 HLR 278, where the court held that the council had
    no power to issue food vouchers to asylum seekers under the 1948 Act unless they were
    also being provided with residential accommodation by the council.

support arrangements was the burden that was thus imposed on some local authorities.

Other cases can be used to illustrate the argument that the move towards 'taking right seriously' in the UK has had some impact on asylum jurisprudence. The judiciary will be empowered even further when the Human Rights Act 1998 enters into force in October 2000.[7]

The legal construction of refugee status will be dealt with in more detail below. However, a case which involved an important aspect of asylum law and practice will be examined here. The case highlights again the results of political struggle by social movements and others. The House of Lords' ruling in *R v Immigration Appeal Tribunal, ex p Shah; Islam v Secretary of State for the Home Department* is welcome for the liberal and progressive approach adopted by the majority to an important area of refugee law.[8] It is a judgment which must, however, be contextualised. For it is no coincidence that it was delivered in a climate of intense discussion of domestic human rights protection. The case raises fundamental questions about the role of the judges in asylum law. Their various interventions have not gone without critical comment. The Home Secretary, Jack Straw, has been critical of the liberality of the judiciary in this area. First, however, we will look at the broader context.

The debates in refugee law over the precise interpretation of 'particular social group' can seem odd in two distinct senses. First, as was noted in Chapter 2, developments in international human rights law are leaving refugee law behind on this issue. For example, the prohibition on return in art 3 of the European Convention on Human Rights includes no reference to any grounds of ill treatment. The protection against return is absolute. From this perspective, painstaking dissection of aspects of the law of refugee status appears as a distraction. This is a mistake. While it is essential to recognise that there is now a broad range of individuals entitled to international protection, refugee law remains of vital importance. As argued throughout this book, primarily this is because refugee law operates as a status-granting mechanism. Those entitled to protection under refugee law gain concrete and specific guarantees and protections. One of the principal problems with the current popularity of differentiated forms of protection is that individuals are often left in an insecure position. This is part of what is termed in this work the 'de-formalisation' process in refugee protection. What is meant by this is that states, even

7   See ch 5.
8   [1999] 2 All ER 545, [1999] INLR 144.

though offering rhetorical commitments to refugee law, are in practice steadily undermining it. This is achieved by interpretations and the development of 'concepts' which are contrary to the letter and spirit of the law and by a refusal in some contexts to make reference to legality. This is part of a process of moving from legality to the arbitrary exercise of discretion which human rights lawyers must avoid unwittingly contributing to. In other words, there are both principled and pragmatic reasons for retaining faith in refugee law even when, and if, a 'new human rights culture' emerges.

In relation to the *Shah/Islam* judgment, it is increasingly open to question whether the claims of refugee women should be so concentrated on the particular social group category. The obvious, and much repeated starting point, is that gender is not listed as a ground of persecution. However, as Hathaway has noted, it is 'properly within the ambit of the social group category'.[9] This is not the only way to think about the claims of women refugees. If awareness of the experiences of women is to be mainstreamed in the refugee protection process, this should, where appropriate and possible, be based on the established categories such as 'political opinion'.[10] The social group category must not become the excuse for a failure to reinterpret all aspects of refugee law. Refugee law must be reconstructed or reinterpreted in a way which reflects the specific experiences of women refugees.[11] This is because the feminist critique of refugee law has exposed how present interpretations are based on a partial and distorted perspective on the totality of the refugee experience. To accept this argument is to acknowledge the blind spots in our own interpretations and the necessity of having an inclusive concept of 'refugee'. As I suggest, while we might welcome the House of Lords' ruling in *Shah/Islam* for its human rights-based approach, we should, however, be cautious about conniving in the construction of a highly inappropriate image of women refugees. This is all part of constructing a human rights culture in this area. In this, refugee lawyers can both learn from the current debate in human rights law in the UK, as well as lend their considerable experience to nurturing a human rights culture. And it is this point which has

9 Hathaway *The Law of Refugee Status* (1991) p 162.
10 See Stanley and Tennant 'Women asylum seekers: an alternative approach' (1998) 12 I&NLP 54; Harvey 'Mainstreaming Gender in the Refugee Protection Process' (1998) 129 NLJ 534. There is now extensive literature on the subject: see eg 'UNHCR Symposium on Gender-Based Persecution' (1997) Special Issue IJRL; Macklin 'Refugee Women and the Imperatives of Categories' (1995) 17 Human Rights Q 213.
11 Harvey 'Reconstructing Refugee Law' (1998) 3 J of Civil Liberties 159.

been neglected in the human rights debate thus far. For refugee lawyers have grappled with rights-based interpretations of existing law for some time.

The extensive use made of comparative jurisprudence in this debate highlights its essentially international nature. While comparative jurisprudence does not solve all problems, it does aid in the process of encouraging a measure of consistency and certainty in the area. It is important that the interpretation of 'refugee' within the terms of the 1951 Convention is relatively consistent. As those with knowledge of empirical studies of the refugee protection process will know, it is difficult to ensure that this consistency is translated into concrete practice on the ground. The social group category has continually managed to avoid precise interpretation and it has proved difficult to gain international consensus. There is, however, what might be termed an 'international judicial conversation' going on about this and other aspects of refugee law. In addition, there is another international context that is worth noting. This is the international network of non-governmental groups dedicated to improving the protection of refugees. In this specific context the political networks for legal reform are worth studying on their own. It is enough here to note the new political spaces being opened up in Europe and elsewhere by these social movements.[12] In a sense, the judges, lawyers and various non-governmental entities are engaged in a transnational conversation about the meaning of refugee law. To focus exclusively on the legal construction of 'refugee' in cases such as the one under examination is to miss the human element involved in ensuring that refugee law remains a site for continuing interpretative struggle. It is necessary to view *Shah/Islam* not purely as a landmark ruling on the particular social group category, but also within the context of national, regional and international attempts to explore refugee law's past distortions and hopefully amend them in future. The ruling is thus part of an ongoing dialogue about the legal treatment of women refugees and one that should not end as a result of this ruling. Although problems remain with the approach that has been adopted, this is an example of how ideas can be brought from the periphery to the centre of legal reform debates.

Many scholars have begun to question the suitability of the liberal model of human rights-based reasoning. The result, it is suggested, is that some are now searching for a social democratic conception of human rights suitable to modern times. Such a social

---

12 See Favell 'The Europeanisation of Immigration Politics' (1998) 2 European Integration On-line Papers http://eiop.or.at/eiop/texte/1998-010a.htm.

democratic understanding of law and democracy recognises that other forms of power need to be tackled if human rights abuses are to be eradicated. Take, for example, Sedley LJ's reference to the street children in Southern America in *Shah*.[13] As he noted, these children are in constant danger from armed groups beyond the control of the state, yet it is hard to imagine that the framers of the 1951 Convention would have intended that they should be excluded. The reality is that in some societies human rights abuses primarily spring from the actions of non-state actors. The public/private divide is increasingly open to question, especially if the primary concern is to see the eradication of human rights abuses from whatever quarter. Feminist theorists thus contribute to a broader trend which brings, for example, multi-national corporations under the scrutiny of human rights lawyers.

The *Shah/Islam* case involved domestic violence in the general legal and societal context of a society (Pakistan) where there was a lack of state protection. Both cases were heard by the Court of Appeal. In *Shah* the High Court had quashed the IAT's refusal of leave and in *Islam* the IAT found that her claim did not come within a Convention ground, with the Court of Appeal reaffirming the decision of the IAT. As Waite LJ noted in the Court of Appeal, the Swedish delegate who introduced the phrase at a late stage in the drafting process could not have imagined the amount of trouble it would later cause for lawyers the world over.[14] He regarded the *Savchenkov*[15] principles (1), (2) and (4) as sound and approved them for use in these 'difficult cases'.[16] On the form of

13 *R v Immigration Appeal Tribunal, ex p Shah* CO 4330/95, 25 October 1996.

14 *R v Immigration Appeal Tribunal, ex p Shah; Islam v Secretary of State for the Home Department* [1998] 1 WLR 74 at 80.

15 *Secretary of State for the Home Department v Savchenkov* [1996] Imm AR 28. '(1) The Convention does not entitle a person to asylum whenever he fears persecution if returned to his own country. Had the Convention so intended, it could and would have said so . . . (2) To give the phrase "membership of a particular group" too broad an interpretation would conflict with the object identified in (1) above . . . (4) The concept of a "particular social group" must have been intended to apply to social groups which exist independently of persecution. Otherwise the limited scope of the Convention would be defeated: there would be a social group, and so a right to asylum whenever a number of persons fear persecution for a reason common to them.'

16 Contrast this with Lord Steyn, [1999] 2 All ER 545 at 554: 'The judgments in that case contain references to *Sanchez-Trujillo's* case but no adoption of its reasoning on the element of cohesiveness. The ratio of *Savchenkov's* case is that the alleged group (Russian security guards at a hotel who feared victimisation by the mafia) did not exist independently of the persecution . . . Paragraph (1) was not explicitly adopted by the Court of Appeal but it was also not rejected. In these circumstances *Savchenkov's* case cannot assist the argument of the Secretary of State. Counsel for the Secretary of State informed the House that [he] no longer supports his submission in para (1).'

the third principle, he turned to the position supported by the majority in *A v Minister of Immigration and Ethnic Affairs*[17]

> 'The Convention emphasizes that the group must be a "particular" and "social" group. This means that the members of the group must share something which unites them, and which sets them apart from the rest of society and is recognised as such by society generally.'

Waite LJ had difficulties with the idea that the attributes should exist independently of the feared persecution. He argued that once the persecution was removed, so the group disappeared. It is notable that he did not accept the concepts of 'cohesion' and 'homogeneity', regarding them as too vague. Henry LJ agreed that the group needed to exist independently of the persecution feared. Unlike Waite LJ, he did regard cohesiveness as relevant but 'there will exceptionally be those who though recognised by society as a social group lack any "cohesion" with their homogeneous fellows and remain disparate individuals'.[18] Therefore, although relevant, it was not necessary in every case. The immigration control concerns raised are most obviously revealed in Staughton LJ's judgment. His remarks are evidence, if any is still needed, of the importance of anchoring the interpretation of refugee status in international human rights and other objective standards. If this is not done, decision-makers can easily lose sight of the specificity of the task before them. The ruling of the House of Lords in the case is evidence that the judiciary has not lost sight of this primary aim. Lord Steyn outlined the general position of women in Pakistan. As he noted, the defining factual framework in the case was state-tolerated discrimination. The fact that the phrase was added at a late stage, he stated, tells us nothing about its contextual meaning. It is notable that he found the relevant preambles important. These were important in two senses. First, they demonstrated that the premise of the Convention was that all 'human beings shall enjoy fundamental rights and freedoms'. Second, and more importantly, they demonstrated, he argued, that counteracting discrimination was the primary purpose of the Convention. In this Lord Steyn made direct reference to the first preamble of the Universal Declaration of Human Rights 1948. He acknowledged that it was common ground that the group must exist independently of the persecution feared. The next issue which he addressed was whether cohesiveness was a requirement for the existence of the group. Here he cited, at some length, from the decision of the US

17 (1997) 142 ALR 331, HC of A.
18 [1998] 1 WLR 74 at 91.

Board of Immigration Appeals in *Re Acosta*.[19] He demonstrated that there was not a clear line of authority in the US on this issue and that the 'preponderance of US case law does not support *Sanchez-Trujillo*'. He cited a number of other authorities in his questioning of *Sanchez-Trujillo*.[20] The reference to the cohesiveness of the group was not justified:

> 'In 1951 the draftsmen of article 1A(2) of the Convention explicitly listed the most apparent forms of discrimination then known, namely the large groups covered by race, religion, and political opinion. It would have been remarkable if the draftsmen had overlooked other forms of discrimination . . . the draftsmen of the Convention provided that membership of a particular social group would be a further category . . . Loyalty to the text requires that one should take into account that there is a limitation involved in the words "particular social group". What is not justified is to introduce into that formulation an additional restriction of cohesiveness.'

His reference to the New Zealand case *Re GJ*[1] is important, accepting as he did that the reasoning there was essentially correct. The point, as he noted, is that homosexuals do not constitute a cohesive group, yet were held to be a social group in this case. This provided added ammunition for his argument against *Sanchez-Trujillo*. The restrictive view was also important because in international law a treaty ought to be interpreted in a purposive sense.

What is perhaps most striking about the judgments of Lords Steyn and Hoffmann is their willingness to accept the argument that women in Pakistan constitute a particular social group. Lord Steyn stated that 'there is no satisfactory answer to the argument that the social group is women in Pakistan'. If he had not accepted this point, he stated that he would have accepted it as a more narrowly defined group on the basis of the gender of the applicants, the suspicion of adultery and their unprotected position in Pakistan. His adoption of Sedley J's remarks on the humanitarian purpose of the Convention is significant. Lord Hoffmann's explanation for why domestic violence was regarded as persecution in Pakistan, and not necessarily in the UK, is interesting. He noted that in the UK women could take action in the courts, while in Pakistan women lacked effective protection from the state. There is a slight confusion here. The fact that women lack protection does not make the activity persecution. It can amount, as one part of refugee status, to building a successful claim. As with Lord Steyn, he

19 (1985) 19 I & N 211.
20 See also Goodwin-Gill *The Refugee in International Law* (2nd edn 1996) pp 358-359.
 1 [1998] 1 NLR 387

viewed the general intention of the drafters of the Convention as clearly connected to the concept of 'discrimination in matters affecting fundamental rights and freedoms . . .' He offered his understanding of discrimination. On social group, he stated: 'rather than an enumeration of specific social groups, the framers of the Convention were in my opinion intending to include whatever groups might be regarded as coming within the anti-discriminatory objectives of the Convention.' In assessing what social group they belonged to, he adopted a notably liberal interpretation, stating that women in Pakistan were a social group. It is worth observing that he questioned the attempt to develop sophisticated sub-categories and he made reference to the Refugee Women's Legal Group guidelines.[2] As argued, underpinning many of these cases is a political struggle to protect human rights and Lord Hoffmann's reference is an acknowledgment of this fact. Some comments of the Chairman of the IAT are specifically mentioned by Lord Hoffmann. They are comments from a position of cultural relativism which he took issue with. The expressed fear by the Chairman, that the overt criticism of Pakistani society led to the granting of refugee status because of a disapproval of social mores in non-western societies, is odd. On this it is worth stressing that the victims of persecution seldom accept this imputation. One of the constant themes in the interpretation of refugee status is that it, and the grant of asylum, should not be perceived as an unfriendly act. To import this concern into the process would be to apply irrelevant considerations that could damage the system of refugee protection. As Lord Hoffmann noted, the activity is contrary to both the constitution of Pakistan and to international human rights instruments. Lord Hope's judgment is in line with this progressive approach. Relying on the reasoning of Lord Steyn, he agreed that although uniform interpretation of the provisions of the Convention was desirable, this had not emerged in the US, Australian and Canadian case law. He stressed the importance of having regard to the 'evolutionary approach which must be taken to international agreements of this kind'.[3] This allowed the court to take into account factors that may not have been obvious to the framers of the Convention. The notion of social group he regarded as an 'open-ended one' and thus he concluded that the 'reason why the appellants fear persecution is not just because they are women. It is because they

---

2   Refugee Women's Legal Group *Gender Guidelines for the Determination of Asylum Claims in the UK* (July 1998). See also Crawley *Women as Asylum Seekers: A Legal Handbook* (1997).

3   [1999] 2 All ER 545 at 568.

are women in a society which discriminates against women'.[4] Referring to *Re Acosta*[5] and *A-G v Ward*[6] he stated that this position was consistent with previous authority. Again, the emphasis here was on the need not to confine the group more narrowly. Lord Hutton was more cautious preferring to allow the appeals on the 'narrower ground' outlined in the judgment of Lord Steyn.

Lord Millett, in his dissent, placed great store by the fact that the Convention was not intended to offer refugee status to all victims of discrimination. He was not willing to accept the proposition that those who refuse to conform to norms are persecuted because of membership of a particular social group. They are, he stated, persecuted as individuals because of their failure to conform, not because they belong to a social group.

The ruling of the House of Lords is based on an inclusive interpretation of a key phrase in refugee law. The judgments are peppered with references to the need to adopt a humanitarian and evolutionary interpretation of the Convention provisions. In reaching this conclusion they draw impressively on comparative jurisprudence and international standards. This helps to place refugee law much more securely within the context of other human rights standards, and thus draws decision-makers away from the temptation to allow immigration control concerns to dominate their interpretation of this phrase. There is one note of criticism that can be sounded. It does not necessarily apply to this case but is part of a wider critique of the mechanisms for dealing with the claims of women refugees. The tendency to argue women's claims within the social group category must be questioned. Often the 'political opinion' ground is much more appropriate to these types of cases. We must be careful to mainstream a gendered perspective in law and practice. Care is needed in order to ensure that the dynamic and proactive nature of women refugees' lives are not downgraded in an attempt to place them within a social group. Often women are expressing by their actions political dissent directed against the dominant norms in society. This needs to be more widely recognised in structuring the response of representatives and decision-makers to asylum cases.[7]

---

4   [1999] 2 All ER 545 at 568-569.
5   Note 19 above.
6   (1993) 103 DLR (4th) 1.
7   Cf Goodwin-Gill *The Refugee in International Law* (2nd edn, 1996) p 363: 'it is argued [that] being a woman is a sufficiently political statement in itself, so far as violence against women, domestic, sexual or public, is part of the process of oppression . . . [w]ithin the scheme of international protection offered by the 1951 Convention relating to the Status of Refugees and its national counterparts, such an approach has found no support.'

The ruling of the House of Lords took place in the context of ongoing debates about human rights protection in the UK. It has already been suggested that this and other rulings are best viewed as part of the wider political struggles of the human rights movement. Another example of this trend is *R v Secretary of State for the Home Department, ex p Adan*.[8] Here the issue was whether Germany and France could be regarded as safe third countries given their approach to the interpretation and application of the 1951 Convention. The material factor was that both states adopt the 'accountability' interpretation, which limits refugee status to persecution by the state. An argument which found favour in the Court of Appeal was that the 1951 Convention has an 'international meaning'. It was to the application of the true meaning of the Convention that the Court of Appeal looked. The court had 'no doubt' that those fearing persecution by non-state agents were entitled to the protection of the 1951 Convention.[9] In the UK this interpretation was adopted and applied by the House of Lords in *Adan v Secretary of State for the Home Department*.[10] In *ex p Adan* the following is telling:

> 'In our view the convention has to be regarded as a living instrument: just as, by the Strasbourg jurisprudence, the European Convention on Human Rights is so regarded. Looked at in this light, the Geneva Convention is apt unequivocally to offer protect[ion] against non-state agent persecution, where for whatever cause, the state is unwilling or unable to offer protection itself.'[11]

The reference to social rights at the conclusion of the judgment is reminiscent of Brown LJ's comment in *R v Secretary of State for the Home Department, ex p JCWI*, discussed above.[12] The court did not

8   [1999] 4 All ER 774.
9   [1999] 4 All ER 774 at 795.
10 [1998] 2 WLR 702.
11 [1999] 4 All ER 774 at 795.
12 [1996] 4 All ER 385 at 401: 'And yet these regulations for some genuine asylum seekers at least, must now be regarded as rendering these rights nugatory. Either that, or the 1996 regulations necessarily contemplate for some a life so destitute that, to my mind, no civilised nation can tolerate it. So basic are the human rights here at issue, that it cannot be necessary to resort to the Convention for the Protection of Human Rights and Fundamental Freedoms (Rome, 4 November 1950; TS 71 (1953); Cmd 8969) to take note of their violation. True, no obligation arises under art 24 of the 1951 convention until asylum seekers are recognised as refugees. But that is not to say that up to that point their fundamental needs can properly be ignored. I do not accept they can. Rather, I would hold it unlawful to alter the benefit regime so drastically as must inevitably not merely prejudice, but on occasion defeat, the statutory right of asylum seekers to claim refugee status.'

rule out the possibility that destitution in a third country might raise questions as to the safety of that country.[13] This willingness to at least give consideration to economic and social rights should be noted beyond the confines of asylum law. In the appropriate context some members of the judiciary are evidently prepared to have due regard to the protection of economic and social rights. Similar humanitarian concerns in safe third country cases were also evident in *R v Secretary of State for the Home Department, ex p Gashi*.[14]   Here the Secretary of State was held not to have discharged his duty of anxious consideration with reference to actual refugee recognition rates in Germany, as opposed to simply examining the German jurisprudence.

One way that states can seek to deter asylum seekers is through the use of penalties for illegal entry. With the widespread use of visa controls and carrier sanctions, it can be difficult for asylum seekers to reach the territory of another state legally. As UK practice shows, it can also be problematic for those engaged in facilitating the entry of asylum seekers. From 1994 onwards, asylum seekers were being stopped at airports and charged under the Forgery and Counterfeiting Act 1981. Again, when given the opportunity, the courts intervened to uphold the fundamental importance of art 31 of the 1951 Convention in *R v Uxbridge Magistrates' Court, ex p Adimi*.[15] In a context where the applicants had been charged with offences relating to the possession of false documents, the court was willing to accept that art 31 of the 1951 Convention applied to those seeking asylum in good faith, and

13   [1999] 4 All ER 774 at 798-799: 'In our judgment the Secretary of State, in administering s 2(2)(c) of the 1996 Act, is only concerned with the question whether there exists a real risk that the third country will refoule the putative refugee in breach of the convention: that is in breach of art 33. This follows, in our judgment, from the words of the subsection. The Secretary of State is not concerned to see that the claimant will or may not enjoy the social rights to which we have referred if he is permitted to stay in the third country. We would not, however, exclude the possibility that such a claimant might in the third country be faced with so destitute an existence, if he were wholly excluded from the right to work and from any access to social provision, and possessed no other resources upon which he might call, that he would be driven to return to the country of feared persecution even though he had successfully claimed such rights of residence in the third country as are offered by these other forms of protection.'

14   [1999] INLR 276.

15   [1999] INLR 490. See the New Zealand case *Eiji v A-G* Judgment of 29 November 1999.

whose quest for asylum involved them in, for example, the use of false documents.[16]

On the purpose of art 31, Brown LJ stated:

> 'Self-evidently it was to provide immunity for genuine refugees whose quest for asylum reasonably involved them in breaching the law . . . That art 31 extends not merely to those ultimately accorded refugee status but also to those claiming asylum in good faith (presumptive refugees) is not in doubt . . .'[17]

His judgment ends with the following:

> 'It must be hoped that these challenges will mark a turning point in the Crown's approach to the prosecution of refugees for travelling on false passports. Article 31 must henceforth be honoured.'[18]

The court's decision lead to a change in practice by the Crown Prosecution Service and detailed guidance has since been issued on the application of art 31.[19] The legislative response can be found in s 31 of the 1999 Act. The provision reflects the language of the 1951 Convention, although it is inserted as a defence and not a bar to prosecution. The difficulty which these cases highlight is that an asylum seeker may have no other legal way of entry into the UK. However, if the asylum seeker should not be prosecuted in these circumstances, should the same principle apply to those who in good faith bring asylum seekers to the UK?

These cases are not used to make overstated claims for the judiciary. What is, however, suggested is that they challenge unreflective statements about judicial deference in this area of law and practice. The judges have demonstrated that in certain circumstances they will be responsive to human rights arguments. This judicial activism in asylum law is part of a changing legal landscape. For human rights lawyers this is evidenced most clearly by the Human Rights Act 1998, but it is also one part of a general package of constitutional reform. The legislation raises very directly

---

16 Brown LJ [1999] INLR 490 at 494: 'It must be appreciated that these three cases – grouped together for a single hearing because they raise different facets of a wider problem – represent but the tip of the iceberg of aggrieved asylum-seekers. In the papers before us are various studies demonstrating clearly that since 1994 there has been a significant increase in the number of refugees arrested whilst seeking transit on forged travel documents through the UK to the USA, or, more commonly Canada, and this despite there being no apparent rise in the number of passengers stopped.'

17 [1999] INLR 490 at 496.

18 [1999] INLR 490 at 506.

19 Webber and Harrison 'Criminal Prosecution and Article 31 of the Refugee Convention' (2000) (February) Legal Action 23.

familiar controversies about the judicial role. As one commentator has noted:

> 'The incorporation of the European Convention on Human Rights . . . by the Human Rights Act 1998 raises many interesting questions concerning how deeply it will penetrate the United Kingdom's domestic legal orders. However, perhaps the most central is how British judges will respond to the interpretive challenges posed by broadly-drafted Convention rights and, in particular, the need to determine the limits to those rights.'[20]

There may well be lessons for human rights lawyers in the way that the courts have approached the interpretation of the 1951 Convention. Many claims have been made for the Human Rights Act 1998.[21] There is general consent for the idea that it should herald the emergence of a new human rights culture. One should, of course, be cautious about claims to novelty, but there does now appear to be momentum on this issue. There must be clarity on what we mean by a 'human rights culture'. A human rights culture worth the name is connected to the values of openness, transparency and participation. In other words, the ability of representatives and decision-makers to be receptive to innovative and creative ideas and thinking in the legal sphere.[1] As Hunt has observed, this does mean that we have to examine the prevailing legal culture of the legal profession and the judiciary to see if it is conducive to the development of a human rights culture.[2] In the refugee and asylum sphere, this can be extended to include the administration. The evidence reveals the severe difficulties in making human rights effective in practice. While some judges may reveal a willingness to adopt a rights-based approach to asylum, mainstreaming this in law and administration is an onerous task.

Whatever view one takes on the judicial role in a social democracy, there is now clear evidence of judicial openness in asylum law. For groups, such as asylum seekers, which lack a strong base in the democratic process, the judicial role takes on added significance. Asylum seekers will benefit from a more activist judiciary inspired by the Human Rights Act 1998. But perhaps with cases like *Shah/ Islam* this process has in fact already begun.

---

20 McHarg 'Reconciling Human Rights and the Public Interest: Conceptual Problems and Doctrinal Uncertainty in the Jurisprudence of the European Court of Human Rights' (1999) 62 MLR 671.

21 For a note of scepticism, see Ewing: 'The Human Rights Act and Parliamentary Democracy' (1999) 62 MLR 79.

1 See Hunt 'The Human Rights Act and Legal Culture: The Judiciary and the Legal Profession' (1999) 26 J Law and Soc 86, 102.

2 (1999) 26 J Law and Soc 86.

DETAINING AND DETERRING ASYLUM SEEKERS

The detention of asylum seekers is one of the most questionable aspects of asylum policy in the UK and elsewhere.[3] If there is a practice which nurtures the image of the 'criminalisation' of asylum seeking it is this. The UNHCR has stated that detention should normally be avoided,[4] however, it remains a common aspect of asylum law and practice throughout Europe.[5] The policy has been heavily criticised in recent years, and there have been a number of disturbances in the centres.[6] There are clear international standards which are applicable to the conditions of detention, its length and the adequacy of supervision.[7] The government has responded in the 1999 Act with increased regulation of detention centres, combined with further judicial involvement and a presumption in favour of bail.[8] There will be up to two routine bail hearings. The first will take place within nine days of the initial detention and the second about one month later.[9] The Home Secretary has the power to direct where these bail hearings will take place.[10] For example, this might be in a detention centre, prison or an IAT hearing centre. In March 2000 a former military camp at Oakington in Cambridgeshire, which was converted into a reception centre, was opened.[11] This reception centre has room for up to 400 persons and would appear to herald the increased used of reception centres in the UK.[12] The Oakington centre is intended as a base to fast-track asylum claims and make decisions within seven days.[13]

---

3 Refugee Council *The Immigration and Asylum Act 1999* (January 2000): 'The detention of asylum seekers is a national scandal. The UK detains more asylum seekers than any other European country. Over 9,000 asylum seekers are detained every year – most are not charged with any criminal offence and around half are held in prisons. Many asylum detainees go on to get refugee status or exceptional leave to remain.'

4 UNHCR Conclusion No 44 (XXXVII) *Detention of Refugees and Asylum Seekers* para (b).

5 See UNHCR *Detention of Asylum-Seekers in Europe* (1995); Hughes and Liebaut (eds) *Detention of Asylum Seekers in Europe: Analysis and Perspectives* (1998).

6 A number of asylum seekers were charged with rioting after disturbances at the Campsfield Detention Centre in 1998. The trial collapsed in June 1998 when the CPS decided to drop the case. One of the individuals has sued the Home Office and the security company, Group 4, for being wrongfully accused of rioting: see *Migration News Sheet* (January 2000) p 13.

7 See eg UNHCR *Guidelines on Detention of Asylum-Seekers* (1999)

8 Immigration and Asylum Act 1999, Pts III and VIII.

9 Immigration and Asylum Act 1999, s 44.

10 Section 45.

11 *Migration News Sheet* (April 2000) p 15.

12 *Migration News Sheet* (April 2000) p 15.

13 Refugee Council *Briefing* (14 March 2000).

Although it is the case that in international law states have competence to detain asylum seekers,[14] international standards also offer valuable protections.[15] The government has indicated that, although it is 'regrettable', it is 'necessary to ensure the integrity of our immigration control'.[16] The White Paper proposed criteria for when detention would be justified in future. The provision of a statutory framework for the management and administration of detention centres is marked change from previous practice.[17]

An asylum seeker may be detained by an immigration officer while her application for asylum is being examined or pending appeal and/or removal.[18] Macdonald and Blake accurately describe the power of detention as ancillary to other decisions: in other words, it is a holding power while other measures are being considered. It is apparent that while the detention of asylum seekers may be desirable from the perspective of public administration, it is inappropriate and arguably disproportionate to the administrative goals which it seeks to achieve. In recognition of this, it is generally used in the UK as a 'last resort' where the claim is held to be without foundation, and/or the identity of the applicant or her attendance at subsequent interview is in doubt.

Administrative detention is legally permissible in cases of illegal entry.[19] There is no conflict with refugee law if an asylum seeker

14 Goodwin-Gill *The Refugee in International Law* (2nd edn 1996) p 247.
15 See 1951 Convention, art 31; UNHCR EXCOM Conclusion 44 *Detention of Refugees and Asylum-seekers*: 'that in view of the hardship which it involves, detention should normally be avoided. If necessary, detention may be resorted to only on grounds prescribed by law to verify identity . . . or to protect national security or public order'; UNHCR *Guidelines on the Detention of Asylum-Seekers*; UN Body of Principles for the Protection of All Persons under Any Form of Detention or Imprisonment 1988; International Covenant on Civil and Political Rights 1966, art 9; *A v Australia* UN Human Rights Committee, Communication No 560/1993; European Convention on Human Rights 1950, art 5(1)(f); *Amuur v France* (1996) 22 EHRR 533; *Chahal v United Kingdom* (1996) 23 EHRR 413. See also JUSTICE *Response to the White Paper: Issues Relating to Detention* (1998); Amnesty International *Cell Culture: The Detention and Imprisonment of Asylum-Seekers in the UK* (1996); Amnesty International *Prisoners without a Voice: Asylum-Seekers Detained in the UK* (1994).
16 Paragraph 12.3.
17 Paragraph 12.18.
18 Immigration Act 1971, Sch 2, paras 2 and 8. See Macdonald and Blake *Immigration Law and Practice in the United Kingdom* (4th edn, 1995) p 266; Witherow 'Detention of Asylum Seekers: A Continuing Cause for Concern' (1995) 9 I&NLP 59; Ashford *Detained Without Trial: A Survey of Immigration Act Detentions* (1993). For the position in the US see Bhabha 'Deterring Refugees: The Use and Abuse of Detention in US Asylum Policy' (1992) 6 I&NLP 117.
19 Immigration Act 1971, Sch 2, paras 9 and 16(2).

is also classified as an illegal entrant. Conflicts do arise where the state deliberately penalises the asylum seeker in the form of criminal prosecution for illegal entry. Cases where this has occurred have already been discussed above.

The criticisms of detention have resulted in increased legal regulation. This includes the regulation of detention centres as well as more judicial supervision. The 1999 Act makes detailed provision in relation to the functioning of these centres. It places detention centres on a statutory footing,[20] and provides that the Home Secretary must make rules for their operation and management.[1] There must be a detention centre manager in each facility,[2] and the Home Secretary has the power to intervene in the management of a centre.[3] Visiting Committees have an important role in inspecting the conditions in detention centres.[4] After severe problems, the government has responded with increased legal regulation of the practice of immigration detention. There remain problems with the detention of asylum seekers in particular and on this the general presumption in favour of bail may improve the situation.

It is apparent that although there has been some improvement in the regulatory framework, the arrangements with regard to the detention of asylum seekers are open to question. As a preliminary point, it is worth considering whether, as a general issue, the detention of asylum seekers is a proportionate response on the part of the state, given the conditions from which an asylum seeker has sought to flee, and the fact that seeking asylum is a legitimate way to seek to enter the UK. While the detention policy raises numerous ethical questions, it is necessary to consider whether it complies with the relevant provisions of international human rights law.

Compliance with the European Convention on Human Rights is considered in the next chapter. With respect to international refugee law, it may be recalled here that art 31 of the 1951 Convention obliges states not to penalise refugees on account of their illegal entry or presence, provided that good cause is shown for this illegal entry and that they present themselves without delay to the relevant authorities. The crucial term here is the word 'penalise'. Does the administrative detention of asylum seekers by the UK constitute a 'penalty'? It appears to be the case that

20 Part VIII.
 1 Section 153.
 2 Section 148.
 3 Section 151.
 4 Section 152.

administrative detention alone would not suffice to constitute a 'penalty' unless there was some further action taken, such as a criminal prosecution for the use of false documents. It is notable that the rationale for administrative detention is also not that the individual has entered the UK illegally but that the immigration officer believes that she may abscond or not adhere to other aspects of her grant of admission. The Executive Committee of the UNHCR has, however, expressed its deep concern at the number of asylum seekers in detention throughout the world. It recommends that detention should normally be avoided, and that where it is used that it should be subject to administrative or judicial review.[5] In its comments on the UK's report, the UN Human Rights Committee[6] has been critical of the policy of detaining asylum seekers, with reference to art 9(1) and (4) ICCPR. The detention of asylum seekers in the UK has also been of concern to the European Committee for the Prevention of Torture and Inhuman or Degrading Treatment or Punishment. Under art 2 of the 1987 Convention, state parties are obliged to permit visits by the Committee to any place within its jurisdiction where persons are deprived of their liberty by a public authority.[7] For example, in November 1999 the Committee visited Northern Ireland. The purpose of these visits is to enable the Committee to examine the treatment of persons deprived of their liberty 'with a view to strengthening, if necessary, the protection of such persons from torture and from inhuman or degrading treatment or punishment'.[8] Given the remit of the Committee, it is clear that the detention of asylum seekers is within its mandate. A legitimate question would be whether the detention of asylum seekers amounts to inhuman or degrading treatment. There is certainly a risk for the state, inherent in the act of detaining this particular group of individuals, that the treatment may raise this issue. Confirming widespread concern about the treatment of this group of detainees,[9] between 15 and 31 May 1995 the Committee visited five immigration

---

5   UNHCR Executive Committee, Conclusion No 44 (XXXVII) *Detention of Refugees and Asylum Seekers* (1986).

6   *Comments of the Human Rights Committee*, CCPR/C/79, Add 55. See King, Starmer and Weir 'The British Way of Doing Things: The UK and the ICCPR 1976-94' [1995] PL 504.

7   The Committee first visited Northern Ireland to investigate the treatment of prisoners in 1993: see *Report to the Government of the UK on the Visit to Northern Ireland*, CPT/Inf (94) 17; *Response of the Government of the UK*, CPT/Inf (94) 18.

8   Article 1.

9   *The Times* 5 March 1994; *The Times* 6 June 1994.

service detention facilities in the UK.[10]   As stated above, the UK government has made efforts, following this visit, to improve the conditions of asylum seekers in detention.

The above analysis indicates that the continued policy of detaining asylum seekers while examining their applications raises a number of issues for the UK's compliance with international human rights law. The suspicion is that detention exists for external as well as internal consumption. Although it is often denied, detention has a deterrence effect. The government aims, even with well regulated detention centres, to send a message to those intending to seek asylum in the UK.

RESTRUCTURING ASYLUM

The UK is not alone in substantially altering its asylum system. The restructuring of asylum processes has been a notable feature of legal developments in Europe. All changes in the formal framework of asylum law in the individual state must eventually find their way into administrative practice if the aims and objectives of government policy are to be achieved. For the asylum applicant who has arrived in another state and who requires some form of protection, the real issue is how legal norms are translated into the administration of asylum within the state.[11] The end result of the 'new thinking' in this area may be seen in the substantial restructuring of asylum administration and adjudication which has taken place in the last decade. Since the 1993 Act, the emphasis in the administration of asylum has been on the removal of the extensive delays in decision-making and on the importance of speeding up the entire process. Evidence for this may be found in the substance of, for example, the earlier 'Spend to Save' initiative of the Conservative government. This involved the recruitment of extra case workers but also an increase in the number of presenting officers to deal with appeals. A significant development here has been the introduction of 'shortened asylum procedures' to process

10 Campsfield House, Oxford; The Beehive, Gatwick; Holding Room, Gatwick Airport; The Queen's Building, Heathrow; Holding Rooms at Terminal 1, 2, 3, Heathrow Airport, European Committee for the Prevention of Torture and Inhuman or Degrading Treatment, 5th General Report, CPT/Inf (95) 10, 3 July 1995.

11 This is initially dependent on state acceptance of the relevant instruments of international refugee and human rights law. For the refugee and human rights lawyer, however, it is with adequate implementation of international legal rules that attention must then focus. This requires some consideration of institutional context.

applications from listed states.[12]   The procedure differs from previous practice in that all asylum applicants whose claims are dealt with under this procedure may be interviewed from the moment they state their intention to apply. In in-country cases this could be within a few days and in port of entry cases within hours of arrival. This was introduced as a 'pilot scheme' in 1995 with the intention of speeding up decision-making in applications involving individuals from Ghana, India, Nigeria, Pakistan, Poland, Romania and Uganda. Applicants were given an interview at the time of making the application and required to make further representations within a period of five days. After this, a decision was taken on the claim. The scheme has been extended since then.[13]   It is worth noting that, under the original scheme, all of the applicants were refused asylum. The importance of eradicating delays in the asylum process cannot be overstated; ideally the applicant requires a decision on her application as quickly as possible. The problem which the shortened procedures raise is whether effective decision-making within the determination system is being compromised for the sake of administrative efficacy. Without more detailed empirical evidence, an assessment is undoubtedly hampered; however, the evidence which is available does suggest that there is cause for concern.

CONCEPTS AND CONSEQUENCES

One of the arguments in this book is that there is a 'de-formalisation' process in operation in refugee and asylum law. States, including the UK, are making use of questionable concepts with the aim of undermining legality as it applies in this area. For many western governments, the central aim of their restructured asylum law and policy is the removal of claims which lack merit through the use of expeditious asylum procedures.[14] Beginning from the premise that their asylum systems are being used by those who wish to enter their territory for other, usually economic, reasons, states have attempted to construct legal regimes whereby such claims are removed efficiently without prejudicing the applications of genuine 1951 Convention refugees. As with other EU member states, this has been a core aspect of UK developments. The means generally adopted to achieve this aim have not involved 'blanket' rejections

---

12 Amnesty International *Slamming the Door: The Demolition of the Right to Asylum in the UK* (1996) pp 8-9.
13 Note 12 above.
14 See Hailbronner 'The Concept of 'Safe Country' and Expeditious Asylum Procedures: A Western European Perspective' (1994) 5 IJRL 31.

of certain applications – a move that would violate aspects of both international refugee and human rights law – but the use of accelerated procedures. How sound are some of the concepts which have been adopted? The safe country concept, in the form in which it was promulgated in the 1996 Act, was not novel in refugee law. As to the countries which were designated as safe, the issue was debated in Parliament between 15-16 October 1996.[15] Agreement was reached on the first list of safe countries which were: Bulgaria; Cyprus; Ghana; India; Pakistan; Poland; and Romania.[16] It is interesting to note the inclusion of India on this list in the light of the judgment of the European Court of Human Rights in *Chahal*.[17]

Developments in Europe played a part in the domestic adoption of this rule. The Conclusion adopted by the EU on this was influential for the UK government. The language of the relevant section of the 1996 Act was very similar. When introducing the Asylum and Immigration Bill, the Home Secretary listed the criteria to be adopted when applying the concept: there must be in general no serious risk of persecution; the country must generate large numbers of applications; and a large proportion of the applications must be unfounded.[18]

The government stressed that certification in this context would not lead to 'blanket' refusals for applicants coming from these states. In theory, the commitment to case-by-case assessment remained. It was, however, difficult to see how such an initial presumption would not seriously impact on the individual application. Refugee law is often accused of possessing an individualistic bias. In this context, however, this alleged 'bias' is an undoubted advantage. The criticism of this provision had some success and the relevant rule has since been repealed by the 1999 Act.

It is apparent from the legislative framework and the immigration rules that there is a deep-seated suspicion surrounding the stage at which an application is made. The assumption underlying these measures is that claims may be made in order to try to remain in the UK, rather than on the basis of a well-founded fear of persecution. Care is needed here, however, primarily because the focus of refugee law is on preventing *refoulement*, and not the stage

---

15   HC Hansard Vol 282 col 691, 15 October 1996; HL Hansard Vol 574 col 1690, 16 October 1996.
16   The Asylum (Designated Countries of Destination and Designated Safe Third Countries) Order 1996 SI 1996/2671.
17   (1997) 23 EHRR 413.
18   HC Hansard Vol 268 col 703, 11 December 1995.

at which an asylum application is made. There are good reasons why an asylum applicant may seek to delay making a claim.

The 'white list' was an example of a concept imported unnecessarily into asylum law and practice. There is a reason why it has proven attractive. If an asylum seeker is from a state on the 'white list', then her claim could be effectively dismissed and thus dealt with more speedily. The adoption and application of this concept had clear implications for refugee status determination. The fact that it has been repealed does not, however, prevent decision-makers from applying similar assumptions, but in more informal ways.

PUNISHING ASYLUM SEEKERS

One of the principal arguments in this chapter is that various UK governments have been prepared to be creative in their attempts to promote a restrictive approach to asylum law and policy. In attempting to secure their aims, governments have utilised a wide number of measures extraneous to the asylum determination process itself. As part of the more general project of deterrence and criminalisation, asylum seekers began to be punished for coming to the UK to seek asylum. At its most crude this policy has involved the reduction or elimination of welfare entitlements; the rationale being that the majority of those seeking asylum are abusive applications. These individuals and groups are said to be attracted to the UK by its welfare system. Socio-economic rights protection for asylum seekers is thus cast as one more 'pull factor' for future asylum seekers. The removal of a variety of welfare entitlements from certain groups of asylum applicants is another element of this. The measures again stem from the view that the asylum process is the object of sustained 'abuse' by economic migrants. The logic is that, by removing these benefits, economic migrants will be deterred from claiming asylum in the future. This branch of government policy attracted considerable criticism.[19] As we have seen, the courts have shown a willingness to intervene to quash aspects of it. These legal victories can, however, be purely symbolic.

The policy has evolved to the stage where a new bureaucracy has been created to implement it. Underpinning the approach is the

---

19 See Report by the Social Security Advisory Committee, January 1996, Cmnd 3062; Amnesty International *Slamming the Door* (1996) pp 10-21; Glidewell Panel *The Asylum and Immigration Bill 1995: The Report of the Glidewell Panel*, 16 April 1996; Harvey 'The UK's New Asylum and Immigration Bill' (1996) 8 IJRL 184, 185-186.

belief that distinctions can be made on socio-economic rights between nationals and non-nationals. The government thinking is that non-nationals, precisely because of this status, are not entitled to the full range of socio-economic benefits which attach to nationality.

Initially, the measures were targeted at 'in-country' applicants with the basic intention being the withdrawal of welfare payments to some asylum seekers. Provision was, however, made for reclaiming these benefits in cases where the individual was subsequently recognised as a refugee.[20] It is beyond the bounds of this work to examine the complex new support system in place for asylum seekers.[1] However, it is possible here to outline the ambitious exercise in 'social engineering' that the government has embarked on. The overall aim is to create a new regime of welfare provision which will apply to 'persons subject to immigration control'.[2] Between enactment and entry into force of the 1999 Act, interim arrangements were in place.[3] The 1999 Act provides a skeletal framework for the system only. Support for asylum seekers[4] is regarded as a national responsibility by the government and, in line with this thinking, a new support system has been established.[5] The underlying principle is that the responsibility for the provision of support to destitute asylum seekers lies with the National Asylum Support Service (NASS) within the Home Office.[6] The

20 Asylum and Immigration Act 1996, s 11(2).
1 For an early outline of the proposals, see Home Office *Asylum Seekers Support* (March 1999) p 5: 'The system which the Government inherited was a shambles which places unplanned burdens on local authority social services departments. . . The longer term aim is to introduce new support arrangements separate from the main benefit systems. Under the new system, only asylum seekers in genuine need will receive support and this will be mainly in kind with accommodation offered on a 'no-choice' basis.'
2 Section 115. See Persons Subject to Immigration Control (Housing Authority, Accommodation and Homelessness) Order 2000, SI 2000/706.
3 Asylum Support (Interim Provisions) Regulations 1999 SI 1999/3056. See also Home Office *Asylum Seeker Support: Proposed Interim Arrangements Under Schedule 8 of the Immigration and Asylum Bill* (1999) at para 3: '. . . the Government is of the view that the current arrangements under which local authorities support asylum seekers are under severe strain in some parts of the country. They therefore wish to make early provision to modify local authorities' duties towards asylum seekers to redistribute the burden between local authorities, from shortly after the Immigration and Asylum Bill receives Royal Assent.' For current position see Asylum Support Regulations 2000, SI 2000/704.
4 For the purposes of this Part of the 1999 Act, a claim for asylum includes European Convention and well as 1951 Convention cases, s 94(1).
5 Immigration and Asylum Act 1999, Pt VI.
6 See NASS *Consultation Document on the Main Regulations Under Part VI of the Immigration and Asylum Act 1999* (November 1999). The document set out the regulations which would be introduced to give effect to the secondary legislation provisions contained in Pt VI of the Immigration and Asylum Act.

NASS will have overall responsibility for the support system, will assess claims for support and will contract with public, private and voluntary sector partners who will provide the actual support services to asylum seekers. This does not mean that it will assume responsibility in all cases. There is provision for the Home Office to contract with local authorities, housing associations, private sector landlords and the voluntary sector. The Home Secretary can make payments to local authorities where they have incurred expenditure in relation to asylum seekers and their dependants.[7] He may also make grants to voluntary organisations for the provision of support to asylum seekers.[8] In providing support, the Home Secretary may attach conditions which could depend on, for example, the behaviour of the applicant.[9] The support provided includes accommodation, or the provision of essential living needs or both.[10] The intention is that support should not normally be given by way of cash payments.[11] For example, asylum seekers would be given vouchers which could be used in certain shops in exchange for food.[12] The problem with the support arrangements is that they do little to aid in the struggle to eradicate social exclusion. It is arguably the case that one of the reasons for the measures is precisely to achieve a form of social exclusion.

The introduction of a policy of dispersal highlighted government concern about the burdens imposed on some local authorities in London. Some councils in the south east of England had begun their own form of dispersal by transporting asylum seekers to private landlords in the north of England.[13] Before the full implementation of the 1999 Act, the government introduced a voluntary interim dispersal scheme to relieve the pressure on local authorities in London and the south east. This was intended to operate from 6 December 1999 until 31 March 2000. The 1999 Act provides that one factor that the Home Secretary must have regard to is the desirability of providing accommodation where there is a ready supply.[14] He is prevented from having regard to the

---

7   Section 110.
8   Section 111.
9   Section 95(9).
10 Section 96.
11 Section 96(3).
12 In January 2000 the contract to provide vouchers was awarded to a French company called Sodexho Pass International. Disputes have arisen with supermarket chains over the provision of change when the vouchers are used by asylum seekers: *Guardian* 15 March 2000.
13 *Guardian* 26 February 2000.
14 Section 97.

preference of the asylum seeker.[15] As argued in this chapter, this is another aspect of the denial of the asylum seeker's autonomy. In particular, there is a risk that, if not managed properly, it might lead to asylum seekers being denied essential services. For example, problems can occur with access to legal representation, language support and specialist health provision, which can often only be found in London. There is a lack of good legal representation for asylum seekers outside of London. The full implementation of the dispersal and voucher schemes to include 'in-country' as well as 'port of entry' cases was delayed because of a lack of accommodation offered by private landlords and local authorities outside of the South East of England.[16] The IND decided that a phased implementation process was appropriate.

There may be instances where a local authority refuses to co-operate with the Home Secretary. In such cases he may designate an area as a reception zone and he could, for example, direct the local authority to make a specified amount of housing accommodation available to him.[17] This may raise issues under the devolutionary arrangements in the UK. While immigration and asylum are excepted matters, housing is not. Any exercise of his powers under this section would have to follow extensive consultation with the devolved administrations. This raises more general questions about how the process of constitutional change will impact upon the treatment of asylum seekers. While central government retains control over immigration and asylum law, it will not have responsibility for all aspects of the treatment of asylum seekers.

The 1999 Act makes detailed provision for an appeals mechanism against decisions relating to support. Asylum support special adjudicators hear appeals against a refusal of support.[18] There is a chief asylum support special adjudicator as well as a deputy. When an special adjudicator makes a decision, there is no further appeal and the asylum seeker cannot make another application for support under Pt IV unless there has been a material change of circumstances. It is an offence for a person to give information which she knows to be false for the purpose of gaining assistance.[19] In more serious cases of fraud, an individual may be guilty of the offence of dishonest representations.[20]

---

15 Section 97(2).
16 *Guardian* 7 March 2000.
17 Section 101.
18 Section 102 and Sch 10.
19 Section 105.
20 Section 106.

This is an outline of the changes contained in the 1999 Act. The legislation signals an attempt to distinguish the treatment of asylum seekers from citizens in the UK. Destitute asylum seekers are thus subjected to what amounts to an experiment in differential treatment. There are serious risks involved in removing asylum seekers from the existing welfare regime. At a time when the government has legislated specifically for human rights protection, this drawing of distinctions in the economic and social sphere is odd, but consistent with the policies of successive governments in the UK.

Another way that states can punish asylum seekers for exercising the right to seek asylum is through prosecution for illegal entry. As already noted, in some cases illegal entry is connected to the use of false documentation. However, there are cases were more creative means have been used. For example, individuals have hijacked airplanes and diverted them to London. In February 2000 a Boeing 727 which had been hijacked by Afghan nationals landed in London.[1] Some of those involved sought asylum in the UK. This was not the first time that this had happened. In 1998 the Court of Appeal quashed the convictions of six Shi'ites from southern Iraq who had applied for asylum after hijacking an aircraft of Sudan Airways. Rose J compared their plight with that of Anne Frank in concluding that they had acted under 'duress of circumstances'. These are exceptional cases, but they indicate the lengths which individuals are prepared to go to gain access to the asylum system in the UK.

The struggle in the courts over this issue and the subsequent legislative reform is examined above. What has occurred in the UK is a steady criminalisation of asylum seeking. This is a part of the general stress on deterrence. To understand the trend one must grasp that it is now difficult for asylum seekers to gain entry to the UK legally. The closure of legal access, and the general climate of restriction in practice, can force refugees and asylum seekers to use traffickers and thus rely on clandestine methods of entry.[2] Not only is there a regime for punishing those official carriers who bring asylum seekers to the UK, there is also now in place a strict regime for punishing those engaged in human trafficking.[3] While there is a genuine need to address the trafficking problem, this can have an indirect impact on the ability of asylum seekers to reach the UK. The rules on punishing those who carry clandestine entrants[4]

1   *Migration News Sheet* (March 2000) p 13.
2   See Morrison *The Cost of Survival: The Trafficking of Refugees to the UK* (July 1998).
3   See Harding *The Uninvited: Refugees at the Rich Man's Gate* (2000).
4   Immigration and Asylum Act 1999, ss 32–39 and Sch 1.

and the charges levied against carriers[5] will impact upon asylum seekers. Human traffickers are, in one sense, a consequence of the policies being pursued by European governments. There is a measure of balance in the legislation. For example, those bona fide organisations which assist asylum seekers will not be prosecuted for facilitation of illegal entry.[6] The new defence, based on art 31, of the 1951 Convention has already been mentioned. These suggest some awareness of the problems faced by asylum seekers.

A COMPREHENSIVE RESPONSE? ASYLUM AND THE KOSOVO CRISIS

Mass movements of refugees returned to Europe in the 1990s. The post-cold war era has seen the rise of the internal armed conflict as an important source of forced displacement in the region. This has led to the creation of procedures designed to accommodate situations of mass flight. The refugee crisis in Kosovo in 1998-99 was the largest refugee movement in Europe since the second world war. As with many modern refugee movements, the closest neighbours were some of the poorest countries in Europe. In response the UK participated in the Humanitarian Evacuation Programme (HEP) of Kosovar refugees. The concept of humanitarian evacuation was a new response promoted by the UNHCR initially on a regional basis.[7] It can be traced to earlier, and more pragmatic solutions, promoted by the UNHCR in Europe. The Macedonian authorities had expressed concern that a mass influx of refugees would destabilise their country. In the rush to evacuate, it appears that little thought was given by the UNHCR to the precise legal status of these refugees.

Initially, the response in the UK was co-ordinated by the Refugee Council, which led a multi-agency response. However, because of the size of the programme the Home Office eventually took responsibility for it. Reception centres were established in Leeds, the East Midlands, Scotland and the North West. These centres offered accommodation for about 1,000 people. The government committed the UK to receiving up to 1,000 refugees a week. Under the HEP, the government announced a special concession which permitted family reunion. This was withdrawn from 13 September 1999. The HEP ended on 15 June 1999. The final flight to the UK was on 25 June and in total the UK accepted

---

5   Immigration and Asylum Act 1999, s 40.
6   Immigration Act 1971, s 25(1C).
7   Amnesty International *The Protection of Kosovo Albanian Refugees* (May 1999) p 13.

4,345 people under this programme.[8] Overall, it is estimated that 850,000 Kosovars fled and, following the peace deal of 15 June 1999, almost 90% returned.[9] In order to facilitate the process of return, the UK government offered an assistance grant and allowed people to embark on an 'explore and prepare' visit to examine conditions at home. As to claims to asylum, the Home Office granted all Kosovars 12 months' ELR. Those who arrived on the HEP did not have their leave curtailed.[10] By 1 March 2000, 1,111 of the Kosovars accepted by the UK had returned. The rest of those who entered the UK under the evacuation programme were entitled to remain in the UK until 22 April 2000. Of the 335 Kosovars who accepted the Home Office's 'explore and prepare', scheme 202 returned to the UK.

CHALLENGING RESTRICTION: THE POLITICS OF APPEAL RIGHTS

The role of the courts in the asylum process has been referred to above. It is now time to examine the politics of appeal rights in asylum law. These rights have been fundamentally affected by the changes contained in the 1999 Act.[11] As with the other aspects of the asylum process, it is essential to understand the context. For example, the backlog in first-line decision-making is also reflected at the appellate level. One of the more important aspects of asylum law and practice in the UK for the applicant is the availability of appeal rights against a negative asylum decision. To ensure that an asylum applicant is protected as effectively as possible from *refoulement*, she must have an opportunity to appeal against the initial decision to an impartial and independent body. The serious implications of return mean that any mistake of law or fact must be remedied while the applicant is in the UK. It is the right to life of the individual which is ultimately at stake in these cases. This places an onerous responsibility on decision-makers, but it also means that asylum seekers require effective legal advice and legal representation. The provisions of the 1999 Act on the regulation of immigration advisers may play a part in ensuring that those who

8 The Refugee Council *Update on the Kosovo Crisis No 5* (August 1999).
9 Amnesty International *Humanitarian Evacuation and the International Response to Refugees from Kosovo* (June 1999).
10 IND *Public Guidance on the Humanitarian Evacuation Programme: Consideration of Asylum Applications and Family Reunion Policy from the Kosovo Region* (1999).
11 Immigration and Asylum Act 1999, Pt IV and Sch 4.

advise asylum seekers are competent to do so.[12]   The Refugee
Legal Centre (based in London) and the Immigration Advisory
Service have both played an important role in this regard.[13]   It is
therefore necessary in this section to explore and evaluate the
adequacy of the appellate structure which does exist, as well as
examining the role of judicial review in these cases. This will reveal
the politics which underpins the dynamics of asylum adjudication.

It is worth recalling that a full appellate structure in this area of
administration was only introduced in the UK as recently as 1969
and subsequently incorporated, with minor changes, in the 1971
Act. In the period from 1914 to 1969 there were no effective legal
guarantees of due process for the immigrant and asylum seeker.
The construction of the appellate structure in this area in the late
1960s was a consequence of the 'new' thinking in administrative
law, as well as a response to the difficulties which the UK experienced
under the European Convention on Human Rights. While the
creation of the appellate structure represented a progressive step,
the *scope and nature* of the appeal rights in the period which has
followed have been a recurring problem. Even after 1969, the
appeal system was for many immigrants and asylum seekers simply
not as extensive as it might have been. In a number of instances
individuals whose claims to asylum had been refused were only
permitted to appeal against the decision from the state of origin.
This left judicial review as the only 'in-country' method of
challenging a decision. A number of organisations concerned with
the plight of refugees, including the UNHCR, had called for this
anomalous position to be rectified.[14]   One of the positive aspects
of the 1993 Act was the introduction of the possibility of an 'in-
country' right of appeal for all asylum applicants to a special
adjudicator. The extension of appeal rights must be viewed in the
light of the increasing resort to 'fast-track' procedures and other

---

12 Immigration and Asylum Act 1999, Pt V and Schs 5-7. The Act provides for the
    establishment of an Immigration Services Commissioner and an Immigration
    Services Tribunal.
13 As have bodies such as the Immigration Lawyers Practitioners' Association.
14 For pre-Asylum and Immigration Appeals Act 1993 rejection of these calls, see
    HC Hansard Vol 159 col 184, 1 November 1991 (Peter Lloyd, Home Office, the
    then Minister Responsible for Immigration): 'In a variety of contacts over a
    number of years UNHCR officers have made their preference for an in-country
    right of appeal for all asylum applicants. The government have responded by
    explaining the risk that we see by encouraging abusive asylum applications from
    passengers who have been refused leave to enter for other purposes in order to
    benefit from delays inherent in an extended appeal system.' Cf Amnesty
    International *Deficient Policy and Practice for the Protection of Asylum Seekers* (1990).

elements of restriction.[15] The extension of rights of appeal has been followed with significant limitations on those rights. The stated aim is to streamline the appeals process. The factors underpinning this are the delays in the system and the general backlog of cases.

From their inception, the appellate authorities have had a number of recurrent difficulties. Possibly the most frequent (but certainly not the only) problem has been the delays which have traditionally been a part of the system's operation, and which the government have been concerned to eradicate.[16] The delays with respect to the asylum appellate procedures have been of particular concern to the Council on Tribunals, since the rapid increase in applications in the late 1980s.[17] In the early 1980s the adjudicators received approximately 9,000 immigration and asylum applications annually.[18] By 1993 this figure had risen to 25,244 appeals.[19] In 1997 the immigration adjudicators received 33,927 appeals.[20] The figures for the IAT are deceptive, as they deal with a large number of applications for leave which are on occasions not recorded, but again there was a notable increase in the number of appeals which they received; thus, in 1984 this figure stood at 831,[1] in 1993 it was 6,559,[2] in 1996 it was 13,157,[3] and in 1997 it was 17,250.[4] The figures reveal that this is an appeal system which is dealing with a growing number of cases.

One may see from the above that there is a problem regarding the number of appeals. This, combined with the government's concern to speed up the process does, however, raise important issues relating to the proper regulation of the work of special adjudicators in asylum cases. This point is reinforced if one considers that, for an increasing number of asylum seekers, the only appeal right they possess is to a special adjudicator. Prior to the 1999 Act, it was noted that the most prolific source of remittals from the IAT to special adjudicators was the failure to apply the

15 See Gillespie, 'The Asylum and Immigration Appeals Bill: A Review of the Proposed Appeal Rights' (1993) 7 I&NLP 68.
16 Cf *Annual Report of the Council on Tribunals* HC 13 (1971-72) p 20; HC 64 (1981-82); HC 234 (1986-87) p 28.
17 Eg *Annual Report of the Council on Tribunals* HC 97 (1990-91).
18 *Annual Report of the Council on Tribunals* HC 64 (1981-82), 9,284 applications; HC 129 (1982-83), 9,676; HC 42 (1983-84), 9,428.
19 *Annual Report of the Council on Tribunals*, HC 22, (1993-94).
20 *Annual Report of the Council on Tribunals*, HC 45 (1998-99).
 1 *Annual Report of the Council on Tribunals*, HC 54 (1984-85).
 2 *Annual Report of the Council on Tribunals*, HC 22 (1993-94).
 3 *Annual Report of the Council on Tribunals*, HC 376 (1997-1998).
 4 *Annual Report of the Council on Tribunals*, HC 45 (1998-1999).

proper standard of proof to asylum claims.[5]   Given this, one can only speculate on the number of questionable assessments where IAT scrutiny is specifically excluded.

Members of the IAT are appointed by the Lord Chancellor.[6] He is empowered to appoint both legally qualified and other members.[7] The Lord Chancellor appoints both the President and the Deputy President of the IAT.[8] The Lord Chancellor is also responsible for the appointment of special adjudicators.[9] Provision is made for the appointment of a Chief and Deputy Chief adjudicator as well as Regional adjudicators.[10] The qualifications for appointment are the same as for IAT members.[11]

The role of special adjudicators

The special adjudicator has an important role in the asylum process. The 1999 Act replaces and re-enacts much of the previous system and detailed rules of procedure regulating appeals are issued by the Lord Chancellor. There is a substantial body of case law on the general principles which should govern the work of special adjudicators which will still be relevant. However, a study conducted by the Asylum Rights Campaign during debates on the Asylum and Immigration Bill in 1995-1996 revealed serious problems in the work of special adjudicators.[12]

The duty of the special adjudicator is to assess the decision 'de novo'.[13] This means that she may review any determination in relation to the facts. She is therefore not limited in this assessment to the facts which were available to the Home Office decision-makers when the original decision was taken. She must assess the asylum application with reference to the events which exist at the time of the hearing.[14] The special adjudicator will therefore, unlike the High Court in judicial review proceedings or statutory appeals, be evaluating the facts 'afresh'. The IAT has set out what

---

5 See McKee 'Recent Trends in Asylum Appeals' (1995) 9 I&NLP 52.
6 Immigration and Asylum Act 1999, Sch 2, para 1(1).
7 Schedule 2, para 1(2). The phrase 'legally qualified' is defined in Sch 2, para 1(3).
8 Schedule 2, para 2.
9 Immigration and Asylum Act 1999, s 57.
10 Schedule 3, para 1.
11 Schedule 3, para 2.
12 Asylum Rights Campaign *The Risks of Getting it Wrong* (April 1996).
13 There is a long line of case law relating to the requirement that adjudicators are responsible for approaching the decision 'afresh' on the facts, eg *R v IAT, ex p Davesh Desai* [1987] Imm AR 18; *Rohima Bibi v ECO, Dacca* [1986] Imm AR 103.
14 *Sandralingham v Secretary of State for the Home Department* [1996] Imm AR 97.

it considers to be the proper approach of a special adjudicator[15] in dealing with an asylum appeal. It has stressed the need for the special adjudicator to assess whether the claim is well founded, based on an assessment of the evidence as a whole (going to the past, present, future), with reference to the criterion of the 'reasonable degree of likelihood' test. The IAT has stated that the special adjudicator should refer in her decision to the test, as set out in the ruling of the House of Lords in *Sivakumaran*. This is important because it can be difficult to ensure that the lower standard is mainstreamed in all aspects of the process. The High Court has held, however, that the special adjudicator is not required to set out this standard in every case, it is enough for her simply to mention *Sivakumaran*.[16] There has been a difference of view on this issue between the IAT and the High Court in the past. In support of a more prescriptive approach, there is, for example, evidence of inconsistency in the application of this standard by special adjudicators in practice. For example, in *Valeriu Banica v Secretary of State for the Home Department*[17] the applicant was arrested and detained in a psychiatric hospital in Romania and diagnosed as unfit for military service. He was subjected to numerous assaults by police and staff in the hospital. In his determination the special adjudicator stated that he had not been *convinced* by the applicant's evidence. The IAT was critical of the approach adopted by the special adjudicator, stating that the word 'convinced' imported an unnecessarily high standard and remitted the application to the special adjudicator for consideration de novo. This demonstrates the importance of the role of the IAT in ensuring that a special adjudicator is applying proper standards to individual appeals. The inconsistency evident in past determinations is of concern, particularly given the increasing importance of their role in the appellate system.

In making her determination the special adjudicator is required to supply reasons which deal with the evidence in an adequate way and give an assessment of, for example, the credibility of witnesses where she has heard oral testimony.[18] In *Amin* Schiemann J stated

---

15 *Koyazia Kaja v Secretary of State for the Home Department* [1995] Imm AR 1.

16 *R v IAT, ex p Sanjeev Kumar; Joga Singh* [1995] Imm AR 55.

17 (10770) IAT, reported in (1994) 8 I&NLP 147.

18 *R v Secretary of State for the Home Department, ex p Toko Kasanga Makombo* [1995] Imm AR 548, per Judge J at 550-551, 'It is trite law that reasons should always be given. They must be clear. They must explain why a particular adjudicator has reached the conclusion he has'; *R v IAT, ex p Mohd Amin* [1992] Imm AR 367; *R v IAT, ex p Chang Yang* [1987] Imm AR 568; *R v IAT, ex p Sukhjeevan Singh* [1994] Imm AR 513.

that special adjudicators should indicate 'with some clarity': the evidence accepted, the evidence rejected, any evidence upon which she is undecided, and the evidence which she regards as irrelevant. The claim that a special adjudicator has not given due weight to an aspect of the applicant's evidence is frequently the basis upon which individuals seek to challenge these decisions by way of judicial review proceedings.[19] The importance of supplying reasons for credibility assessments by special adjudicators can not be overstated. First, credibility assessments are central to a large number of asylum cases, second, the adjudicator is the only appellate body which will have an opportunity to hear oral evidence, and finally, detailed reasons provide an individual with the opportunity to rectify an incorrect decision or errors of law on appeal or review. The IAT and the courts are reluctant to attack credibility findings by special adjudicators. It has been stated that it would require 'something overwhelming' before the IAT or a court would set aside or review the findings of credibility made by a special adjudicator who had seen and heard witnesses.[20]   In *Horvath v Secretary of State for the Home Department* the IAT set out the general principles applicable in these cases. The appellant was a member of the Roma community in the Slovak Republic. His appeal against refusal was dismissed by a special adjudicator on the basis of an adverse credibility assessment. The IAT restated the position that it would be reluctant to interfere with findings on credibility. If it was to interfere it had to be shown that the special adjudicator had made a fundamental error in her approach. In evaluating the evidence of an asylum seeker, her assertions had to be related to the background human rights situation. In this case the special adjudicator had not done this. She had applied the wrong approach and in such instances the IAT was entitled to re-examine the facts of the case.[1]

---

19 See eg *Stella Mondi Mageto v IAT* [1996] Imm AR 56. The applicant was a citizen of Kenya who argued that the special adjudicator had failed to give proper weight to a report by a clinical psychologist stating that the applicant was suffering from post-traumatic syndrome. The Court of Appeal dismissed the renewed application for leave stating that the finding of the special adjudicator could not be faulted. Simon Brown LJ stated that the issue raised was so obvious that it did not need to be spelt out in the determination. This would, he said, place an unnecessary burden upon special adjudicators.

20 *R v IAT, ex p Mohammed Dauda (No 2)* [1995] Imm AR 600.

1 Note that the decision of the IAT was the object of an unsuccessful appeal to the Court of Appeal see *Horvath v Secretary of State for the Home Department* [2000] INLR 15. The judgment of the Court of Appeal was affirmed by the House of Lords in *Horvath v Secretary of State for the Home Department* (2000) Times, 7 July.

The courts have shown a willingness to intervene. For example, in *R v IAT, ex p Ahmed* the special adjudicator did not find the applicant credible.[2] The court distinguished between a review of the special adjudicator's finding on credibility from the requirement that she place these assessments in the context of findings about the prevalence of the conduct complained of. There was an absence in this case of any general findings of fact in the special adjudicator's determination. The credibility assessments had not been placed in the context of the general picture of human rights violations in Pakistan. As a result she had erred in law. The reasons provided by the special adjudicator must bear upon the point at issue in the case and indicate the basis of fact upon which the decision has been reached.[3] This does not, however, mean that the special adjudicator is required to isolate every piece of evidence. It is sufficient for her to demonstrate these matters have been taken into account. During the hearing the special adjudicator is entitled to ask questions of witnesses, where the representative has failed to ask questions which the special adjudicator believes to be of importance.[4] As the principal fact-finding body within the appellate system, the special adjudicator is ultimately responsible for the weight attached to the evidence submitted by the applicant.[5] In the past both the IAT and the courts have recognised that special adjudicators are often the best placed to decide on issues of fact, particularly, as stated above, when she has had the opportunity to hear witness testimony.[6] The IAT[7] and the courts, in judicial review proceedings,[8] have traditionally, however, exercised some measure of control of the decisions of special adjudicators, and the scope of their legal powers. In *Lawrence Assah v IAT*[9] the special adjudicator and the IAT differed fundamentally in their assessment of the facts in the case. The appellant was a Ghanaian citizen who feared persecution because of his past work as a polling booth assistant who, during an election campaign, had complained to the authorities of 'ballot rigging'. Although the special adjudicator,

---

2   [1999] INLR 473.
3   *R v IAT, ex p Iram Iqbal* [1993] Imm AR 270.
4   *Rothman Bahar v IO, Heathrow* [1987] Imm AR 334.
5   *R v IAT, ex p Naushed Kandiya* [1989] Imm AR 491; *R v IAT, ex p Aurangzeb Khan* [1989] Imm AR 524.
6   Eg *R v IAT, ex p Mahendra Singh* [1984] Imm AR 1; *R v IAT, ex p Kwok On Tong* [1981] Imm AR 214. Although it may be argued that the courts are moving in a similar direction on the issue of the review of facts as they have done on errors of law.
7   Eg *ECO, Bombay v Vali Patel* [1991] Imm AR 147; *Oberoi v Secretary of State for the Home Department* [1979-80] Imm AR 175.
8   Eg *R v IAT, ex p Tazzamil Hussain* [1982] Imm AR 74.
9   [1994] Imm AR 519.

who heard the oral testimony of the appellant, stated that he had 'impaired credibility', he nevertheless accepted some of his claims. The IAT, however, held that none of the events put forward by the appellant were true. On appeal to the Court of Appeal it was argued that the IAT should not have interfered with the special adjudicator's finding of primary facts. The court, while acknowledging the importance of the fact-finding role, held that where a special adjudicator's finding of fact was not sustainable the IAT was entitled to reverse her findings. The IAT had thus not erred in law in reaching this conclusion. Therefore, although the special adjudicator has considerable power to weigh up the evidence and establish the primary facts,[10] the IAT has, in exceptional cases, the power to reverse these findings of fact in instances where the original decision is 'not sustainable'.

The courts and procedural restriction

As with other areas of the asylum process, the struggle over appeal rights was also fought in the courts. One of the purposes of the 1993 Act was to reconcile the extension of appeal rights with the government's expressed desire to prevent abuse. One common way of trying to reconcile these twin objectives is the creation of accelerated procedures. In asylum law this was achieved through the creation of a 'fast-track' procedure for certain asylum appeals. The 1993 Act, Sch 2, para 5 set out special appeal procedures for claims which were certified by the Home Secretary to be without foundation. This included claims that did not raise any issue as to the UK's obligations under the Convention or were otherwise frivolous or vexatious. The 1996 Act extended the list of instances where this special procedure would apply. A struggle was, however, to ensue over what precisely some of these legal terms meant. As the government began to realise, it could not always rely on the courts to facilitate its work. In *R v Secretary of State for the Home Department, ex p Senay Mehari*[11] the High Court held that the true construction of Sch 2, para 5(3)(a) was that an application did not raise an issue as to the UK's obligations unless on the facts it was incumbent on the Home Secretary to consider the claim substantively. Therefore, on the court's construction, para 5(3)(a) applied *only* to safe third country cases. The interpretation to be given to para 5(3)(b) by a special adjudicator was addressed in *R v Special Adjudicator, ex p Alves Paulino*.[12] The special adjudicator

10 Eg *R v Secretary of State for the Home Department, ex p Arthur Kingo* [1994] Imm AR 539.
11 [1994] Imm AR 151.
12 [1996] Imm AR 122.

in this case had agreed with the Home Secretary's decision to certify the asylum application as frivolous within the meaning of para 5(3)(b). He did so because he agreed with the negative credibility assessment. Rose LJ stated that while a lack of credibility which was fundamental to the claim could be regarded as frivolous, this was not so where it was a fringe matter. This, he stated, was clearly the position here, and it was thus inappropriate to regard the applicant's claim as frivolous. The court thus revealed its willingness to intervene on this aspect of the asylum process.

Judicial recognition of the purpose behind the 1993 Act was evident in the House of Lords' ruling in *Abdi v Secretary of State for the Home Department*.[13] The applicants were Somali nationals, who had come to the UK via Spain to seek asylum. The Home Secretary issued certificates that their claims were without foundation and that they should be returned to Spain. The special adjudicator agreed with the certification of the Home Secretary, and thus dismissed their appeal. The applicants sought judicial review to challenge the Home Secretary's certification and the decision of the special adjudicator. They argued that the Home Secretary was obliged to make available to the special adjudicator the material upon which he based his decision to issue the certificates. Lord Lloyd stated that the purpose of the new procedure was to ensure the rapid return of applicants in safe third country cases.[14] There was no duty of discovery placed upon the Home Secretary by the asylum procedure rules. It was not the case, he stated, that justice required discovery in asylum appeals, and, further to this, such an obligation would conflict with the specific provisions of the procedural rules which specified in clear terms what the Home Secretary must provide to the special adjudicator:

> '[I]f the courts were to supplement the rules by imposing some such obligation . . . there would be a risk of frustrating the evident legislative purpose that "without foundation" appeals should be considered with all due speed.'[15]

The majority ruled that no such obligation of discovery could be placed by the courts on the Home Secretary. The case highlighted again the struggle over the terms of asylum policy waged in the courts. In this instance the court was not prepared to side with the asylum seeker and instead chose to give higher priority to the objective of the Home Secretary.

13 [1996] 1 All ER 641.
14 [1996] 1 All ER 641 at 657.
15 [1996] 1 All ER 641 at 657.

A feature of the UK asylum system is tight time-limits for certain appeal processes. These can be problematic in cases where an individual is deemed to have received notice of determinations in the relevant procedural rules. *R v Secretary of State for the Home Department, ex p Saleem* is a useful example of such a problem.[16] By virtue of the Asylum Appeals (Procedure) Rules 1996, the applicant was deemed to have received notice of determination the second day after it was sent.[17] This rule applied regardless of whether it was received. The applicant had not received notice and thus missed the five-day deadline for appeals. Her application for judicial review was successful and the court held that the rule was ultra vires the enabling provision. The court held that the 1971 Act did not authorise a rule of 'such draconian consequences'.[18] It was not within the reasonable range of responses that Parliament could have intended the Lord Chancellor to make. In *R v IAT, ex p Jeyeanthan; Ravichandran v Secretary of State for the Home Department* a special adjudicator had allowed the appeals of both applicants.[19] The Home Secretary wished to appeal against this decision to the IAT but he failed to provide the proper application as required by the procedural rules. He applied by letters which did contain all the relevant information except the declaration of truth contained in the prescribed form. In only one of the cases was this challenged and the IAT rejected the argument. In both cases the appeal of the Home Secretary was allowed. The Court of Appeal restated the general principles applicable to these cases and held that in this case there had been substantial non-compliance. However, the non-compliance could be cured by the IAT under its procedural rules. Given that the rule was there to protect asylum seekers who might make many procedural errors, it should be given a broad interpretation. Lord Woolf MR stated that this interpretation was of general importance in protecting asylum seekers against injustice.[20]

---

16 [1999] INLR 621. Affirmed by the Court of Appeal in *R v Secretary of State for the Home Department, ex p Saleem* (2000) Times, 22 June.
17 Rule 42 (1)(a).
18 Per Hooper J, note 16 above, p 627.
19 [1999] 3 All ER 231.
20 [1999] 3 All ER 231 at 242: 'If in these appeals you concentrate on what the rules intend should be the just *consequence* of non-compliance with the statutory requirements as to the contents of an application for leave to appeal I would suggest the answer to these appeals is obvious. Neither J nor R have in any way been affected by the omission. It was as far as they were concerned a mere technicality. Other than to discipline the Secretary of State there could be no reason well after the event to treat his successful application for leave as a nullity. Both the discretion and consequences questions should be answered in the Secretary of State's favour.'

The structure of appeal rights

The current position is set down in the 1999 Act but must be viewed in the context of the above struggles over appeal rights. In particular, the rules on rights of appeal reflect the attempt to reconcile expeditious procedures with the extension of appeal rights. The rules reflect a clear focus on speed, evident in, for example, the introduction of the 'one-stop' appeals system. There are extensive limitations in place on the rights of appeal in immigration and asylum law with the intention being to facilitate the speedy resolution of asylum and other cases. The provisions of the 1999 Act follow an extensive consultation over the effectiveness of the appellate system in this area.[1] The government was concerned to streamline the process and was actively considering a number of options. This included restructuring the appellate authority and the possibility of moving from a two-tier to a single-tier system.[2]

The asylum seeker has the right, in response to action taken against her under immigration law, to an appeal on the ground that this would be contrary to the 1951 Convention.[3] Provision is made for the removal of appeal rights in national security and other cases.[4] If, for example, there is a refusal of leave to enter because of the provisions of art 1F of the 1951 Convention, and the Home Secretary has certified that the disclosure of material would be contrary to the interests of national security, no appeal to a special adjudicator will lie.[5] The option available in these cases is an appeal to the Special Immigration Appeals Commission.[6] However, in these cases there are restrictions which follow the determination of the Commission which are intended to limit the availability of a human rights based appeal against the decision. In cases determined by the Commission the Home Secretary may, for example, certify that in his view the claim that human rights had been violated was to delay the removal of the individual.[7] The rules recognise the importance of the distinction between refugee status

1 Home Office/Lord Chancellor's Department *Review of Appeals: A Consultation Document* (July 1998).
2 Review of Appeals, note 1 above, para 5.7. The Home Secretary successfully appealed to the Court of Appeal in *Secretary of State for the Home Department, ex p Rehman* (2000) Times, 31 May.
3 Immigration and Asylum Act 1999, s 69.
4 Section 70.
5 Section 70(4).
6 Special Immigration Appeals Commission Act 1997. See *Rehman v Secretary of State for the Home Department* [1999] INLR 517. The Home Secretary successfully appealed to the Court of Appeal in *Secretary of State for the Home Department, ex p Rehman* (2000) Times, 31 May.
7 Section 73.

and other forms of protection. Thus, an appeal is available where an individual has gained leave to enter or remain on other grounds.[8]

In safe third country cases an appeal can be made to a special adjudicator, but only on the ground that the conditions attached to the certificate of the Home Secretary were not satisfied.[9] Where return is to a member state, or other designated state, then there is no 'in-country' right of appeal if the Secretary of State has certified that the claim of a human rights violation is manifestly unfounded.[10] In other cases, if the certificate is not set aside by a special adjudicator then the individual is not permitted an appeal under the 1999 Act before her removal from the UK.[11] No appeal is permitted in these cases if the prescribed rules of procedure are not followed.[12] While an 'in-country' right of appeal does exist in some of these cases, it is a limited one. The clear intention behind the rules is that there be no 'in-country' appeals in some cases involving safe third country removals and a strictly limited appeal in others. The rules reflect governmental concern with excessive delay in the system of removals in these cases.

Several aspects of the rules reflect the commitment to expeditious determination. The duty of disclosure on the appellant is intended to facilitate the practical operation of the one-stop shop appeals process. The IAT is given the power to issue a notice stating that the appeal is of no merit before final determination.[13] The clearest example of the trend is the restriction of appeals to special adjudicators only in certain cases. In this the 1999 Act follows the trend set in earlier legislation, although it is worth noting that in certification cases 'contrary to the Convention' refers to the 1951 Convention and the European Convention on Human Rights.[14] The cases in which no appeal is available to the IAT include: the use of false or invalid passports without a reasonable explanation; where a 1951 Convention fear of persecution is not shown; where there is a fear but it is manifestly unfounded or the circumstances which gave rise to the fear no longer subsist; where no right under the Human Rights Convention is disclosed or where it is but the case is manifestly unfounded; manifestly fraudulent cases; and frivolous or vexatious claims.[15] This restriction will not apply if the

8 Section 69(3).
9 Section 71(2).
10 Section 72(2).
11 Section 72(1).
12 Section 72(3).
13 Section 79.
14 Schedule 4, para 9(8).
15 Schedule 4, para 9.

evidence adduced in support of the asylum claim establishes a reasonable likelihood that the appellant has been tortured in the country to which she is to be sent.[16] There is, in addition, provision for the removal of appeal rights in certain cases where the asylum application is made after a prescribed period.[17]   The Home Secretary must certify that one purpose of the claim was to delay removal and the applicant had no other legitimate purpose.

The Human Rights Act 1998 has had an impact on the reform of asylum law. Under the 1999 Act a special adjudicator or the IAT is empowered to allow an appeal if it considers that the relevant authority[18] has acted in breach of the appellant's human rights.[19] An authority acts in breach of human rights if she acts, or fails to act, in a way which is unlawful under s 6(1) of the Human Rights Act 1998.[20]

The rules surrounding appeal rights have been carefully drafted to facilitate limitations and overall restriction. This may make sense as part of an attempt to address the backlog in decision-making, but at what cost to the asylum seeker?

The determination of appeals

The argument thus far is that the rules on appeal rights are an attempt to balance competing interests. The suggestion is that the rules privilege expedition in asylum and other cases. It is time to examine the powers of the appellate authorities in asylum cases. The powers of the special adjudicator and the IAT are essentially the same. It has already been noted that the government decided to retain the two-tier appeals system.

'Not in accordance with the law or the immigration rules'

The principal difficulty associated with the interpretation of this phrase is the meaning of the term 'the law'. Is the phrase intended to refer only to immigration and asylum law, or to law in general? If one looks to immigration and asylum law for a decision to be in accordance with the law, this will primarily, but not exclusively, mean that it accords with the existing legislative framework. The

16 Schedule 4, para 9(7).
17 Section 76(5).
18 An authority means: the Secretary of State; an immigration officer; a person responsible for the grant or refusal of entry clearance, s 65(7).
19 Section 65(5).
20 Section 65(2).

trend has been, however, to view the law as being of wider scope than this, although there has been some conflict within the IAT on this. Macdonald and Blake have noted that the problem encountered for the appellate authority is not which aspect of immigration and asylum law to apply, but the extent to which the general principles of administrative law should be applicable.[1] In a number of asylum cases the appellate authority has decided the issue with reference to the general principles of administrative law. Thus an asylum seeker (either in this instance or in cases of discretion discussed below) may argue that the Home Secretary has acted illegally, or irrationally, or that the decision was infected with procedural impropriety.[2] In *Oberoi v Secretary of State for the Home Department*[3] the special adjudicator had not informed the appellant's representative of the importance he attached to an aspect of the immigration rules which had not been relied on by the Home Secretary in his decision. The IAT held that this violated the rules of natural justice, as the appellant should have been given the opportunity to make representations on this point. Although in this case the IAT held that the rules of natural justice were applicable, there have been conflicting approaches adopted by the IAT in the past, determined often by the individual who is chair of the tribunal.

The role of the appellate authority in these cases is the essentially judicial one of deciphering the interpretation of the law and applying it to the particular facts of the case. For example, in asylum cases the Home Secretary may be seeking the deportation of an individual whose asylum application has been rejected. In this instance the appellate authority will be able to determine whether a rejected asylum applicant is a refugee, and/or whether her return would be contrary to art 33 of the 1951 Convention, which has been made, in practical terms, a part of UK law. In asylum cases 'in accordance with the law' will primarily mean that the appellate authority must decide the case with reference to the law of refugee status. However, there is the additional issue of compliance with the Human Rights Act 1998 to take into consideration. As is argued here, this legislation will impact significantly on asylum law and practice.

The immigration rules have an ambiguous status, even though many appeals rest on their proper interpretation. As is well known, it is through the 1971 Act, s 19 that the rules gain their legal status

1   *Immigration Law and Practice in the United Kingdom* (4th edn, 1995) p 578.
2   Eg *Patel* [1990] Imm AR 478; *Jinnah Rahman* [1989] Imm AR 325.
3   [1979-80] Imm AR 175.

in immigration and asylum law. Any examination of the rules attests to the fact that they are drafted in a general way. However, the development of the legal regime surrounding immigration and asylum has witnessed the gradual evolution of the rules, which have become steadily more comprehensive in language and scope. One would assume that the appellate authorities would possess some established and relatively clearly defined method for the interpretation of the rules. But, as Evans has noted, it is difficult to state precisely the interpretative principles which are used. In the case law one finds varying, and at times inconsistent, approaches adopted. An analysis of the case law suggests that it is the context and merits of the case which play a significant, if not determinative, part in the approach ultimately adopted. Thus, in some a teleological approach to their interpretation[4] is advocated, while in others there is a tendency to emphasise literalism.[5] In these cases context is everything. In *R v IAT, ex p Takeo and Takeo*[6] the High Court and the IAT disagreed on the proper approach to the interpretation. The IAT had applied a literal interpretation which in this case, involving the omission of permit-free employees from the rules relating to remaining in the UK after entry, had in effect denied the applicant a right of appeal. The court, rejecting the approach taken by the IAT, stated that there was a need to apply a 'common-sense' approach to the rules. This case may be contrasted with *R v IAT, ex p Rahman*,[7] where the Court of Appeal stated that although the rules should be interpreted in a 'common-sense' fashion,[8] where the language was plain and unambiguous the specific requirements of a rule could not be ignored. In this case the respondent's father, who had settled in the UK, died. He was a successful businessman who had left the respondent a large amount of his capital. The respondent wished to enter the UK but could not, as he was required by the relevant rule to show that capital raised on the sale of the business would be capital he had brought into the UK with him. However, as he had inherited this he could not fulfil the requirement in the rule. The Court of Appeal rejected the approach of the Divisional Court, which had sought to interpret the rules 'in the round'. Here it held that there was a specific requirement in the rules, derived from a literal interpretation, which had not been fulfilled. Where the rule was

4 Eg *Nisa v Secretary of State for the Home Department* [1979-80] Imm AR 20.
5 Eg *ECO, Dacca v Armat Ali* [1981] Imm AR 51.
6 [1987] Imm AR 522.
7 [1987] Imm AR 313.
8 Eg *Alexander v IAT* [1982] Imm AR 50; *R v IAT, ex p Peikazadi* [1979-80] Imm AR 191.

as specific as it was in this case the Court of Appeal held that the requirement could not be circumvented by adopting a purposive interpretation. Again, this case may be contrasted with another entry case, *R v IAT, ex p Bibi*.[9] The applicant (62) was a citizen of Pakistan, dependent on her son, who was resident in the UK. She had separated from her husband but she was not a widow; which was a specific requirement of the rules for entry of dependent relatives under 65. The court held that the rules had a certain amount of ambiguity and to avoid absurdity they should be interpreted purposively.[10] Adopting this approach to interpretation, the applicant was entitled to enter the UK, provided the other aspects of the rule were complied with. It is clear from the case law that interpretation of the immigration rules is often inconsistent and highly context dependent. Important factors in deciding on the interpretation to be adopted are the facts and merits of the individual case, and the ambiguity of the rule. This flexibility in the approach to interpretation may be subject to some criticism; however, it reflects the nature of the rules which are not strictly rules of law. It also reflects the indeterminacy of much legal interpretation generally. Any criticism of this adjudicative pragmatism may be met by the assertion that flexibility may ensure fairness in the individual case.

The exercise of discretion in asylum cases

It is argued in this chapter that there has been a movement 'towards legality' in asylum law. However, this increased legal regulation of asylum does not mean that we should underestimate the extent of discretion in this area. As is now widely recognised in public law scholarship, discretion is a rather more complicated entity than traditional approaches would have us believe. It is more a case of reshaping discretion to secure the core values of an area of social practice than of seeking its eradication. The traditional rule of law model is thus a misleading guide to addressing discretion in asylum law and practice.

In asylum cases a decision-maker can allow an appeal if the decision or action involved an exercise of discretion and 'that the discretion should have been exercised differently'.[11] In assessing the exercise of discretion, and whether she would have exercised it differently, the decision-maker must determine: first, whether

---

9 [1987] Imm AR 392.
10 Cf *ECO, Bombay v Stanley Noronha* [1995] Imm AR 341.
11 Schedule, 4 para (1)(b).

the decision actually involved the exercise of discretion; and, second, whether this discretion should have been exercised differently. What this means is that she does not simply ask whether the decision was *Wednesbury* unreasonable, as the courts are limited to in judicial review proceedings, but whether she would have exercised it differently.

When a special adjudicator allows an appeal she must issue any directions for giving effect to the determination which she thinks are required and may make any other recommendation relating to immigration and asylum law which she thinks should be taken.[12] In asylum cases one type of determination might be that she considers the individual to be a refugee within the meaning of the 1951 Convention.

ASYLUM SEEKERS AND JUDICIAL REVIEW

There has been a considerable renewal of interest in judicial review. The justification of the practice has traditionally attracted much interest. At present those concerned with the promotion of progressive political values are concerned with how it might be reconciled with social democratic principles. Many of the issues which underpin this general debate have already been considered in this chapter. To understand the importance of judicial review to the debate on asylum one must grasp the context of the arguments. Judicial review applications by asylum seekers have attracted the attention of government. For example, a consultation document on restructuring the appellate system states:

> 'Judicial review is an important mechanism for maintaining the rule of law and subjecting executive decisions to proper scrutiny. The need for such review should, however, be rare and limited to resolving important, novel or complex points of law. In order to ensure this, an effective appeal system needs to carry the confidence of the appellants themselves, the public and the Courts.'[13]

Blake and Sunkin were critical of the proposals advanced by the government.[14] They argued that the changes had not been fully thought through. Concern has been expressed about delay in the process, caused by resort to judicial review, as well as the substantive judgments of the courts. For a government concerned to address a backlog in the decision-making process, judicial review can

---

12 Schedule 4, para (5).
13 Home Office/Lord Chancellor's Department *Review of Appeals: A Consultation Document* (July 1998) para 6.1.
14 Blake and Sunkin 'Immigration: Appeals and Judicial Review' [1998] PL 583.

appear as another delaying factor. The argument advanced in this chapter is that the only appropriate way to address the issue of judicial review is by the creation of an appeals system which will command the respect of the courts. The courts will be more inclined to defer to other stages in the process where the decision-making is capable of commanding their respect.

One of the most significant developments in public law in the past three decades has been the much heralded 'rise of judicial review'. Whether one regards this as overstated or not, it has impacted on the asylum debate in the UK. In this period, the courts have slowly extended their jurisdiction,[15] resisted parliamentary attempts to exclude review,[16] and exercised close control over the operation of broad discretionary powers.[17]   Combined with a willingness to draw upon the language of human rights, this has meant a considerable alteration in the terms of the debate.[18]   The courts have not, however, been prepared to go as far as the High Court of Australia in *Minister for Immigration and Ethnic Affairs v Teoh*.[19]   The High Court held that ratification of an international Convention was a positive statement by the executive that it would act in accordance with the Convention. The positive statement was enough to ground a legitimate expectation that decision-makers would act in accordance with it.

With the onset of increased judicial activism, judicial review has taken on a more high profile role. Whether one views this in quantitative or in purely symbolic terms there is little doubt that judicial review of administrative action has undergone something of a revival. Connected to this revival of interest there has been much recent discussion on the possibility of procedural reform, partly motivated by the work undertaken on the issue by the Law Commission, but primarily because of the numerous difficulties which have arisen since the reforms of the late 1970s.[20]   A number of writers have, however, sought to stem this enthusiasm somewhat,

---

15   *Council of Civil Services Unions v Minister for the Civil Service* [1985] AC 374.
16   Eg *Anisminic Ltd v Foreign Compensation Commission* [1969] 2 AC 147.
17   *Padfield v Minister of Agriculture, Fisheries and Food* [1968] AC 997; *Laker Airways Ltd v Department of Trade* [1977] QB 643. See Marshall 'Lions Around the Throne: The Expansion of Judicial Review in Britain' in Hesse and Johnson (eds) *Constitutional Policy and Change in Europe* (1995) p 178.
18   See eg *R v Ministry of Defence, ex p Smith* [1996] QB 517.
19   [1995] 128 ALR 353.
20   See Law Commission *Administrative Law: Judicial Review and Statutory Appeals* (1994) (Law Com No 226); Cane 'The Law Commission on Judicial Review' (1993) 56 MLR 887; Emery 'Judicial Review and Statutory Appeals: Options for Reform' [1993] PL 262.

with a reminder that there are still a number of practical barriers which face the applicant seeking judicial review.[1]

As a preliminary point it is worth stressing that, ultimately, the asylum applicant seeks good administrative practice whereby her application is given comprehensive expert assessment by individuals who have taken due regard of the evidence she has submitted. Where an asylum claim is rejected, there is no substitute for the availability of an appeal on the merits of the decision to a special adjudicator and/or the IAT. Judicial review (the inherent supervisory power of the High Court), in theory at least, does not offer an appeal on the merits,[2] rather the emphasis is on an examination of the decision-making process and the legal basis for the decision, and thus how a decision is reached rather than its essential correctness. It was noted above, that a special adjudicator, for example, reviews a decision de novo in relation to the law and the facts. Judicial review simply does not offer the asylum applicant the same level of scrutiny of the original decision.[3]

Traditionally the constitutional foundation for judicial review has been the ultra vires rule, which states that the courts in judicial review proceedings are simply 'policing' parliamentary intent, and thus ensuring that public bodies do not exceed their legal powers. It has become clear that this justification is problematic and generally unsatisfactory as an explanation of judicial practice.[4] In reality, the distinction between appeal on the merits and review is somewhat nebulous. The courts remain, however, understandably keen, given the constitutional implications of their rulings, to stress their awareness of its existence, and the constitutional limitations under which they are placed in judicial review.[5] Within

---

1 See Sunkin 'The Problematic State of Access to Judicial Review' in Hadfield *Judicial Review: a Thematic Approach* (1995) p 1. He raises the question of whether it is possible to talk of a right of access when one must seek the permission of a judge which may be granted or refused as a matter of discretion; Birkinshaw *Grievances, Remedies and the State* (2nd edn, 1995) pp 257-259. He notes that there are still in existence significant practical barriers for the applicant in making use of the courts.

2 *Chief Constable of North Wales Police v Evans* [1982] 1 WLR 1155.

3 See *Turgut v Secretary of State for the Home Department* [2000] Imm AR 306. While the Court of Appeal recognised that it had an obligation to subject the Home Secretary's decision to rigorous examination by considering the underlying factual material, his judgment in this case was held not to be unreasonable.

4 See Beatson 'The Scope of Judicial Review for Error of Law' (1989) 4 OJLS 22.

5 *Nottinghamshire County Council v Secretary of State for the Environment* [1986] AC 240, per Lord Scarman at 250-251. *Sashir Singh v IAT* [1995] Imm AR 500, per Sir T Bingham MR 506, 'The present field [special adjudicator's assessment of evidence] is one in which it is tempting for the court to stray into taking its own view of the facts. That is an imputation which the court must resist. A court's function is limited to a review of the challenged decision on one or more of the familiar grounds.'

the extensive case-law on judicial review there is a notable tension between two conflicting purposes. While the judiciary, following the ultra vires model, theoretically seek to 'police' the boundaries of existing legal powers and enforce legislative intent, this often directly conflicts with their other expressed aim of protecting the individual from abuse. In other words, it is evident in the jurisprudence that the doctrines of the rule of law and parliamentary supremacy clash in practice. Thus, when one examines the grounds of judicial review, and their application by the courts, it is evident that one would have to strain the ultra vires model considerably to accommodate the decisions which have been made. The problems and mystifications of justifying judicial review by the use of the ultra vires concept have led some to argue, convincingly, that the court should, on the basis of intellectual honesty at the very least, base its reasoning upon substantive principles of judicial review, rather than relying on vague grounds for intervention such as unreasonableness.[6]   The argument is based on a belief that the courts in judicial review proceedings do not simply examine the decision-making process but form their judgments on the substance of the case. The argument finds ample support in the history of the judicial review of administrative action. This approach would dispel the present widespread, and frequently justified suspicion, that judicial intervention functions in a purely instrumental fashion, a conclusion aided by the opaque nature of the grounds of review. Perpetuating the essentially Diceyan tendency to emphasise remedies over rights the judiciary has been, as yet, unwilling to expound substantive principles of review. In terms of the relevance of this for the asylum seeker, it is at least arguable that, by elaborating substantive principles of review, the administration would stand in a surer position as to the legality of its actions. Further to this, the existence of such principles may aid in attempts to improve administrative practice. Given the trend towards increasing restriction, the courts can, by elaborating the principles which apply to everyone within the jurisdiction of the state, offer a much-needed defence of legality in this sphere. Asylum seekers require recognition as persons before the law and a clear statement of the applicability of the principles of legality to their cases. The development of a jurisprudence of human rights can, for example, only aid in the political struggle to achieve protection for this vulnerable group.

6   Eg Jowell and Lester 'Beyond Wednesbury: Substantive Principles of Administrative Law' [1987] PL 368.

Although judicial review has become more significant, its inherent weakness as a independent remedy has led some to question its relevance for asylum seekers and argue that it is ultimately of marginal significance.[7] This argument cautions against a 'court-centred' approach to areas where judicial review may be of little practical utility for promoting good administrative practice. The ultimate validity of such criticism is dependent upon the criteria of significance which the observer adopts. If it is based on the utility of judicial review as a remedy, then there is little doubt that on its own it is not an effective one for an asylum seeker. If it is the number of cases which are brought, then immigration and asylum have traditionally accounted for a large proportion of judicial review cases.[8] It is, however, arguably unwise to focus excessively on the quantitative aspects of judicial review, for it fulfils an important symbolic role in ensuring that the principle of legality applies in asylum cases. At a time when governments throughout Europe are applying different standards of treatment to asylum cases, the courts have a role in promoting the equal protection of the law. A useful example of the readiness of the courts to defend the principle of legality is *M v Home Office*.[9] The facts of the case reveal a series of exceptional administrative mistakes resulting in a Zairean citizen, who had been refused asylum, being returned to his state of origin, while a further application for leave was still pending. This case gives a revealing insight into the processes which an asylum applicant experiences. The facts may be summarised as follows. M, having been refused asylum, also had his application for leave to move for judicial review refused. His renewed application to the Court of Appeal was also refused. Following this, a new solicitor for M applied to the High Court again, but on this occasion on fresh grounds. Garland J ordered the postponement of removal pending the hearing of the new application. There then followed a misunderstanding by which the judge believed he had received an understanding by the representative of the Home Secretary that this would be carried out. This was not the case, and the applicant

---

7   See Hutchinson 'The Rise and Ruse of Administrative Law and Scholarship' (1985) 48 MLR 293, 318. Cf Hutchinson *Dwelling on the Theshold: Critical Essays on Modern Legal Thought* (1988) p 86. Here he argues that the gap between the rhetorical role of judicial review and the reality is large.

8   Sunkin 'The Judicial Review Case-Load 1987-1989' [1991] PL 490. The number of judicial review proceedings involving asylum was particularly large in 1987. Sunkin 'What is Happening to Applications for Judicial Review?' (1987) 50 MLR 432.

9   [1994] 1 AC 377.

was returned to his state of origin via Paris. The judge ordered that the Home Secretary ensure that the applicant be returned in safety. On the day following the removal, Home Office officials attempted to secure the applicant's return but the Home Secretary, following legal advice to the effect that the court's mandatory interim injunction had been made outside its jurisdiction, cancelled the return arrangements. One of the main issues in the case was whether the courts had jurisdiction in prerogative proceedings to grant coercive orders against officers of the Crown given the provisions of the Crown Proceedings Act 1947. The case was significant in terms of the applicability of the application of the principles of legality. The issue centred on the proper construction of s 31(2) and (3) of the Supreme Court Act 1981 and the almost identical provisions of RSC Ord 53, r 3(10). Lord Woolf, opposing the narrow interpretation offered by Lord Bridge in *R v Secretary of State for Transport, ex p Factortame*,[10] concluded that the section, and the rules, did permit interlocutory injunctions against officers of the Crown. This was the case even where, as here, leave to apply had not yet been granted.[11] Having stated this, Lord Woolf acknowledged that this jurisdiction should only be exercised in limited circumstances against officers of the Crown.[12] The reason for this was straightforwardly that a declaration would usually suffice, as the Crown could normally be trusted to comply. Lord Woolf had some sympathy with the view that an interim declaration might be advantageous in these cases. It is clear from the facts of the case that the Home Secretary normally does not seek removal when an application for leave is pending, but that here there was a serious administrative error, compounded by what subsequently proved to be inaccurate legal advice. The case is a significant clarification of the law and in its defence of the rule of law aids in the judicial protection against the return of an asylum applicant.

The criticism expressed about judicial review has some validity, in its cautioning against a 'court-centred' approach and in encouraging public lawyers to think about practical impact. On this, judicial review has had some impact on the politics of asylum in the UK. This stands in marked contrast to some of the negative assessments of the judicial role in the past. For example, Evans,

10 [1990] 2 AC 85.
11 [1994] 1 AC 377 at 423: 'The injunction was granted before he had given the applicant leave to apply for judicial review. However, in a case of real urgency, which this was, the fact that leave had not been granted is a mere technicality. It would be undesirable if, in the situation with which Garland J. was faced, he had been compelled to grant leave because he regarded the case as an appropriate one for an interim injunction.'

noting a tendency towards judicial conservatism in this area, has suggested a number of reasons for this. First, he argues that initially the legislative scheme was regarded as experimental, being passed as it was, in 1914 and 1919, in times of national emergency. Second, the widespread existence of executive discretion necessitated against intervention, particularly in an area where the royal prerogative was still alive and well. Third, aliens were generally not regarded as being capable of possessing rights. The courts, for example, have continually stressed that there are no common law rights of entry to the UK.[13] Vincenzi has added weight to this assessment, stating that the motivating factors have been the absence of legal rights and the existence of prerogative powers in this area.[14] Despite judicial concern about 'politically sensitive' areas of national policy, there seems to be no principled reason which justifies any substantive difference in approach. This position is now recognised in asylum cases, where the courts have emphasised the fundamental importance of subjecting asylum decisions to close scrutiny. In *Bugdaycay* Lord Bridge stated that in asylum cases the courts in judicial review were entitled to:

> 'subject an administrative decision to the most rigorous examination; to ensure that it is in no way flawed, according to the gravity of the issue which the decision determines. The most fundamental of all human rights is the individual's right to life and when an administrative decision under challenge is said to be one which may put the applicant's life at risk, the basis for the decision must surely call for the most anxious scrutiny.'[15]

Further to this, there are judicial pronouncements in the strongest terms that the individual's status as an non-citizen is of no importance for judicial scrutiny of administrative action. Thus, in *Khawaja v Secretary of State for the Home Department*[16] Lord Scarman stated emphatically that everyone within the jurisdiction of the UK had the equal protection of the law. One must compare these statements with those of Evans regarding immigration law, when he argues that:

> 'the legislature and the judiciary, apparently assuming that a high degree of administrative discretion is essential for effective implementation of immigration policy have proved so unwilling to restrict the discretion of the administration in this area that the latter has been left with considerable

12 [1994] 1 AC 377 at 422.
13 *Musgrove v Chun Teeong Toy* [1891] AC 272; *Schmidt v Secretary of State for Home Affairs* [1969] 2 Ch 149.
14 Vincenzi 'Aliens and the Judicial Review of Immigration Law' [1985] PL 93, 95; Peiris 'Judicial Review and Immigration Policy: Emerging Trends' (1988) 8 LS 201.
15 [1987] 1 AC 514 at 531.
16 [1984] AC 74.

scope to take arbitrary action against all persons subject to immigration laws.'[17]

While this may have been the position in the past it is not evidently the case in the UK at present.

This debate surrounding the willingness of the court to intervene has premises which some who favour a 'functionalist' approach to administrative law might not raise.[18] Those who operate within the functionalist 'mind-set' tend to be suspicious of the existence of judicial review in a democracy. Further to this, in the functionalist conception of public law the demands of each individual area differ. Thus, one cannot impose precisely identical principles on areas as far removed as social security law and asylum law. Such reasoning also cautions us against an exclusively 'court-centred' approach to administrative law. The suggestion in this literature is that extensive judicial discretion is as problematic as administrative discretion.[19] Increased judicial activism is thus a cause for concern and not necessarily for celebration. Conclusions on the role of judicial review tend to follow previously defined normative stances in public law. Views may differ depending on whether a functionalist, normativist or other approach is adopted.[20] The functionalist arguments are based on a legitimate distrust of judicial intervention springing from the essential dilemma, noted by Cappelletti,[1] of how judicial review is reconciled with the principles of democracy.[2] Such avowed pragmatism in the approach to differing areas operating within administrative law, and the rejection of the 'generalist' method in public law (only one part of the functionalist argument), has raised some questions for the

---

17 Evans 'UK Immigration Policy and the European Convention on Human Rights' [1983] PL 91.

18 Eg Cranston 'Reviewing Judicial Review' in Richardson and Genn (eds) *Administrative Law and Government Action* (1995) pp 45-80; Arthurs 'Re-thinking Administrative Law: A Slightly Dicey Business' (1979) 17 Osgoode Hall L J 1. Cf Allan 'Dicey and Dworkin: The Rule of Law as Integrity' (1988) 8 OJLS 266, 268: he argues that there is a need for over-arching principles on a rights-based theme. For an excellent analysis of the different styles of public law thought see Loughlin *Public Law and Political Theory* (1992).

19 See Griffith 'Administrative Discretion and the Courts – The Better Part of Valour?' (1955) 18 MLR 159.

20 For a Weberian 'ideal-typical' classification of public law thought see Loughlin, note 18 above, pp 58-62.

1   Cappelletti *Judicial Review in the Contemporary World* (1971) pp 1-20.

2   Cf McAuslan 'Administrative Law, Collective Consumption and Judicial Policy' (1983) 46 MLR 1. Perhaps the most consistent exponent of this distrust is Griffith: see eg Griffith *The Politics of the Judiciary* (5th edn, 1997).

integrity and consistency of this legal regime.[3] While accepting the need for administrative agencies and tribunals to function within a defined area, in the final analysis, it is often groups such as asylum seekers which are disadvantaged by inconsistency in the application of principle, particularly as their rights are so frequently jeopardised by administrative expediency. It is no coincidence, for example, that those who mount strong theoretical defences of constitutional review do so on the basis of their concerns about the protection of minority rights.[4] This work can, however, be misleading. It is not to the common law that we most often look for the promotion of progressive political values. The welfare state in the UK is, for example, a creature of legislation and its rise met with judicial resistance. The intention is not to promote an unreflective view of the judicial role. The history of immigration and asylum law and practice demonstrates that aliens are on occasion particularly disadvantaged as a minority in the UK. For this reason there is considerable merit in the argument that the judiciary should adopt a rigorous approach in reviewing these cases. Close scrutiny by the judiciary, combined with the encouragement of good administrative practice, would clearly be justifiable in terms of both 'universalist' or functionalist arguments. Judicial review can play a part in the promotion of the core values of good governance. A further point is that it is possibly too simplistic to divide public law scholarship rigidly in this way. This may explain why elements of both approaches have proved to be desirable in the asylum law context. The descriptive methodological insight that functionalism brings is welcome, but at times normatively deficient, particularly if considered in the present post-empiricist times. There is no deep-seated conflict between utilising the results of functionalist-inspired empirical work in public law to advance or advocate normativist-inspired alterations or reforms. It is important to understand the intricacies of an area such as asylum law and practice *as well as* elaborating the principles upon which judicial intervention may be based. Therefore, it may be the case that public law scholarship is not in fact as 'bifurcated' as has been claimed.[5] All theories of public law require some anchor in normative principle.

3   On the issue of law as integrity, see Dworkin *Law's Empire* (1990) pp 225-275.
4   See eg Cappellati *The Judicial Process in Comparative Perspective* (1989) p 131; Allan 'The Limits of Parliamentary Sovereignty' [1985] PL 614. There has been much written on the scope of constitutional review in the US and the protection of minorities: see Ely *Democracy and Distrust: A Theory of Judicial Review* (1980) pp 131-179; Wolfe *The Rise of Modern Judicial Review* (1986). Cf Tushnet *Red, White and Blue: A Critical Analysis of Constitutional Law* (1986).
5   See Loughlin *Public Law and Political Theory* (1992) p 394.

On the practical level of adjudication, while the courts have shown an acknowledgment of the vulnerable plight of the asylum seeker and the importance of rigorous judicial review, they must acknowledge and reconcile their own approach with the expertise of special adjudicators and the IAT, and the need to encourage better administrative and adjudicative practice in future. An analysis of judicial review in this area must therefore be seen in the light of the above discussion and based upon an acknowledgment of its limitations and well as its potential.

Illegality

Possibly the most straightforward (and deceptively simplistic) statement of the ground of 'illegality', is that a body which exercises public law functions must act in accordance with its legal powers.[6] Thus, one key aspect of the ground of 'illegality' is ensuring that the Home Secretary and the administration remain within the law. By giving the 1951 Convention primacy over the immigration rules, UK law creates the possibility that the rules themselves could be regarded as ultra vires where they were not in accordance with the 1951 Convention. As indicated, the recent developments in public law, noted above, particularly the move towards defining all errors of law as open to review, have substantial implications for tribunals such as the IAT. The post-*Anisminic* case law has demonstrated a willingness to disregard the distinction between errors of law which go to jurisdiction and those which do not.[7] The most obvious implication for tribunals of defining all errors of law as jurisdictional is the potential for the expansion of judicial intervention.[8]

'Simple ultra vires' represents only one aspect of this ground of review. There are a number of other situations which will be held to amount to 'illegality'. The constraints of the principle of legality when fundamental rights are involved are of particular relevance to the asylum seeker. The public body must not use its power for an improper purpose and must take all relevant considerations into account.[9] It must also disregard irrelevant considerations when it is making its decision. In *Re Musisi*[10] the House of Lords addressed

---

6 For extended analysis see De Smith, Woolf and Jowell *Principles of Judicial Review* (1999) pp 151-243.

7 Eg *Page v Hull University Visitors* [1993] 1 All ER 97; *Re Racal Communications Ltd* [1981] AC 374, per Lord Diplock at 383.

8 See Gould 'Anisminic and Jurisdictional Review' [1970] PL 358.

9 See eg *R v Secretary of State for the Home Department, ex p Dinesh* [1987] Imm AR 131.

10 [1987] AC 514.

the question of whether the Home Secretary had failed to take relevant considerations into account in an asylum case. M had been temporarily admitted to the UK pending a decision on his leave to enter as a visitor. His application was refused and he subsequently made an asylum claim. He alleged that if he was returned to Kenya he would not be permitted re-entry, but would instead be sent back to Uganda, where he claimed to have a well-founded fear of persecution. The Home Secretary did not seek verification of that statement, but simply refused M leave on the ground that he was not a refugee. Evidence was produced during the judicial review proceedings which showed that Kenya had in the past been guilty of returning people to Uganda. The court held that the Home Secretary failed to take this matter into account and had a misplaced confidence in Kenya's willingness to perform its 1951 Convention obligations. Thus, a consideration of the utmost relevance to the individual's case had not been taken into account by the Home Secretary and the refusal was therefore quashed. In *ex p Allaa Hashem*[11] the applicant had applied for asylum one year after his arrival in the UK, when he had originally sought to enter the UK as a visitor. The court held that the Home Secretary was entitled to take this deception into account when considering the application. Article 31(1) of the 1951 Convention did not apply here because of the applicant's delay in requesting asylum.

Asylum applicants seeking judicial review often claim that the Home Secretary has taken an irrelevant consideration into account. In *Conteh v Secretary of State for the Home Department*[12] the Home Secretary had exercised his discretion in this safe third country case not to consider the applicant's claim for asylum. He had been a member of the government of Sierra Leone which had been responsible for, and implicated in, widespread corruption in the state. The applicant argued, however, that this was an irrelevant consideration for the purposes of an asylum claim. The Court of Appeal rejected this argument noting that the 1951 Convention made explicit reference to exclusion from refugee status and therefore it was a relevant consideration for the purpose of a refusal.

Irrationality/unreasonableness

The term 'irrationality' is possibly inappropriate in this context, given that it overstates what in practice will be regarded as

---

11 [1987] Imm AR 577.
12 [1992] Imm AR 594.

unreasonable by the courts.[13] Nevertheless, both terms have been used by the courts to describe this ground of review. The ground applies specifically to the abuse of discretionary power and is one of the most frequently contested grounds of review in asylum cases. It focuses on the reasonableness of the actual exercise of the discretion, offering something akin to a rather weak judicial 'safety net' when other grounds can not be found. It is within this category that the traditional ultra vires doctrine is most seriously strained in order to function as a justification for review.[14] In *Associated Provincial Picture Houses Ltd v Wednesbury Corpn*[15] Lord Greene stated:

> 'It is true to say that, if a decision on a competent matter is so unreasonable that no reasonable authority could ever have come to it, then the court can interfere.'[16]

Lord Greene defined the requirements to fulfil this ground of review as particularly high, stating that it would require something 'overwhelming'.[17] Lord Diplock in the *GCHQ* case[18] discussing 'irrationality' stated that it applied to a decision which was 'outrageous in its defiance of logic' and one that 'no sensible person who applied his mind to the question to be decided could have arrived at'.[19] Lord Scarman made a similar pronouncement in *Nottinghamshire County Council v Secretary of State for the Environment*,[20] stating that the decision must be so absurd that the decision-maker may be held to have 'taken leave of his senses'. It is evident from the language used by the courts that this is viewed as dealing with exceptional cases.

Some examples are necessary, in order to provide an indication of instances where a challenge based on unreasonableness has been mounted. In *ex p Yurekli*[1] the court held that it was not unreasonable for the Home Secretary to take into account the fact that the applicant could live in another part of his state of origin without being persecuted (which represented initial judicial approval of a concept which has since been included in the immigration rules).

---

13 *R v Devon County Council, ex p G* [1988] 3 WLR 49.
14 The courts utilise a construction of presumed parliamentary intent, ie Parliament is presumed to intend that all discretionary power is exercised reasonably.
15 [1948] 1 KB 223.
16 [1948] 1 KB 223 at 230.
17 [1948] 1 KB 223 at 230.
18 *Council of Civil Service Unions v Minister for the Civil Service* [1985] AC 374.
19 [1985] AC 374 at 410.
20 [1986] AC 240 at 247.
1 [1990] Imm AR 334.

In other words, the court held that it was not unreasonable for the Home Secretary to operate the 'internal flight option' policy. In *ex p Alupo*[2] the applicant for asylum failed to make a claim for asylum on arrival in the UK. The court held that it was not unreasonable for the Home Secretary to take this matter into account when assessing the credibility of the applicant. In *Hamieh v Secretary of State for the Home Department*[3] the applicant, a citizen of Lebanon, produced further information regarding his claim to asylum, following the original rejection by the Home Secretary. The Court of Appeal held that it had not been unreasonable for the Home Secretary to reject the asylum application on the basis of this new information.

This has been used in the past by those who wish to challenge the reasonableness of the Home Secretary's decision to send them to a safe third country. In *Khaboka v Secretary of State for the Home Department*[4] the applicant, a citizen of Congo, claimed that it was unreasonable for the Home Secretary to conclude that France was a safe third country in the light of evidence presented relating to the return of asylum applicants to Congo in the past. The Court of Appeal held, however, that the Home Secretary had not acted unreasonably.[5] What is notable from the case law is that while the ground is frequently raised, a decision is rarely held to have been unreasonable. This provides support for the proposition that only in the most exceptional cases will a decision of the Home Secretary be held to be unreasonable.

Procedural impropriety

The ground of 'procedural impropriety' includes statutory procedural requirements as well as the common law rules of natural justice. While natural justice may be divided between the 'rule against bias' and the 'right to a fair hearing', it is the latter which is principally of concern here. The creation of 'new' appeal rights for asylum seekers reduces the likelihood that natural justice will constitute a successful ground of review in asylum cases. This does not discount the possibility that special adjudicators and the IAT may be responsible for breaches of natural justice.

2   [1991] Imm AR 538.
3   [1993] Imm AR 323.
4   [1993] Imm AR 484.
5   See also *R v Secretary of State for the Home Department, ex p Murali* [1993] Imm AR 311.

In general terms the rules of natural justice, as they apply to the concept of a fair hearing, require a decision-maker to supply notice of a decision to those affected by it and to give those persons the opportunity to make representations. There is no general duty in administrative law to give reasons,[6] although exceptions to this have been developed by the courts.[7] For the asylum applicant this lack of a general duty to give reasons is problematic where she is granted ELR rather than asylum, given the general lack of information available on the criteria used to grant this status.

One of the main difficulties has been with respect to the types of decisions which are subject to the rules of natural justice. Judicial and quasi-judicial type decisions have usually been thought to be the most appropriate for subjection to these rules, although there have been questions raised concerning the need to maintain such distinctions.[8] It is questionable whether the focus should be on the type of decision taken if, in a particular case, it seriously affects the rights or interests of a group, such as asylum seekers.

As with other areas of judicial review, natural justice has undergone something of a revival.[9] This revival has been marked with a considerable amount of terminological confusion. Particularly interesting has been the debate surrounding the 'duty to act fairly'. The use of the term a 'duty to act fairly' was first mentioned in *Re HK*, an immigration case.[10] Here the applicant, who was settled in Bradford, sought to bring his 15½-year-old son, HK, into the UK. The immigration officer at the port of entry was suspicious, as he believed that his son was older than claimed. After further examination the immigration officer concluded that he was to be refused admission as he was older than the permitted age of entry. During the course of the habeas corpus hearing, the applicant was given leave to apply for certiorari to quash the decision to refuse admission. Lord Parker CJ, while acknowledging that the official was not required to act in a judicial or quasi-judicial capacity, stated that he had a duty to act fairly. Nevertheless, in this case it was held that the official had not violated this duty.

What of asylum cases? As indicated in the previous discussion on the role and significance of judicial review in asylum cases, the courts have tended, unsurprisingly given the interests at stake, to apply a high standard of procedural fairness. The need for such a

---

6 See generally Richardson 'The Duty to Give Reasons: Potential and Practice' [1986] PL 437.
7 Eg *R v Secretary of State for the Home Department, ex p Doody* [1993] 3 All ER 92.
8 *Schmidt v Secretary of State for Home Affairs* [1969] 2 Ch 149, Lord Denning.
9 Arguably precipitated by *Ridge v Baldwin* [1964] AC 40.
10 [1967] 2 QB 617.

rigorous approach to judicial review was most clearly demonstrated by the House of Lords in *Bugdaycay*. However, the courts are also aware of governmental concerns about delay and there is again a balance to be achieved. In *ex p Frank Yemoh*[11] the Home Secretary appeared not to have accepted the applicant's account of physical ill-treatment, nor the account of how he left his country of origin. The court held that fairness in this instance required that the applicant should have been given the opportunity of considering and seeking to refute these two points, which led the Home Secretary to conclude that the applicant was being untruthful. In *Gaima v Secretary of State for the Home Department*[12] the appellant was an overstayer who claimed asylum while detained pending removal. She alleged that she had been unable to put her case fully during her asylum interview; the Home Secretary, however, had refrained from re-interviewing her. The practical effect of this failure to re-interview was that a factual issue had been raised, upon which the applicant did not have an opportunity to comment. Referring to both *Re HK* and *Bugdaycay*, May LJ stated:

> '[I]n these refugee, asylum cases the court is entitled to, and should, subject administrative decisions to rigorous examination. The court should ensure that the decision-making process has been *wholly fair throughout*.'[13] (My emphasis.)

The court stated that in this case an adverse assessment had been made of the applicant's credibility and that she had not been given an opportunity to comment upon it. The court held that there had been procedural impropriety. The case is important for the emphasis which it places on the need for the Home Secretary to allow the applicant to respond to adverse credibility assessments, but also for the prominence given in the judgment to the importance of a high standard of procedural fairness. In other cases the courts have, however, shown an awareness of the problems experienced by the administration, and a willingness to acknowledge the need for some flexibility in the operation of the asylum determination system.[14]

---

11 [1988] Imm AR 595.
12 [1989] Imm AR 205. Cf *R v Secretary of State for the Home Department, ex p K* [1990] Imm AR 393.
13 [1989] Imm AR 205 at 209.
14 Eg *Shahib Al-Mehdawi v Secretary of State for the Home Department* [1990] Imm AR 140, reversing the decision of the Court of Appeal, which had held that the rules of natural justice could be violated through default by the advisers of the applicant. The House of Lords stated that the position of the Court of Appeal would 'open a wide door' and would seriously undermine the principle of finality in decision-making.

Some of the procedural problems experienced by applicants in past asylum cases have since been remedied. Thus, in *Secretary of State for the Home Department v Pathmakumar*[15] the problem experienced by the respondents has since been rectified by the Home Secretary.[16] In that case the respondents had claimed asylum on arrival from Sri Lanka. This was refused, as was leave to enter. The respondents claimed that there had been unfairness in the process. Specifically, they pointed to the fact that they had not been reminded on re-interview of the answers which they had given in the previous interview, and they had not been told the reasons why the Home Secretary had been provisionally inclined to take a decision. The Court of Appeal agreed, stating that there had been a breach of the rules on natural justice in the procedure, for the reasons indicated by the respondents. Following this decision, the Home Secretary decided to introduce 'minded to refuse' notices, which invite comments from the applicant on his initial decision.[17] The 1999 Act further develops the law in this area.

The approach of the courts on this issue is illustrated again in *R v Secretary of State for the Home Department, ex p Santigie Sesay*.[18] The applicant claimed asylum on arrival in the UK. During his interview he felt disorientated and unwell. He stated that, because of the threat of detention, he continued with the interview, but did not 'do justice' to his application. On the basis of the interview he was refused asylum. The court held that any procedural unfairness evident at the interview stage had been remedied by the nature of the appeal to the special adjudicator.

Another aspect of procedural impropriety which raises points of interest here is that of legitimate expectation.[19] As noted above, there has been an attempt to develop the law in this area in line with international human rights obligations in recent years. These developments clearly have implications for asylum seekers. In *A-G of Hong Kong v Ng Yuen Shiu*[20] Ng, who was an illegal immigrant from Macau of Chinese origins residing in Hong Kong, was subject to a removal order from Hong Kong. A statement had been read outside Government House which included an

---

15 [1989] Imm AR 402.
16 This is evident also of the usefulness of judicial review, on the occasions when it leads to a change in administrative practice.
17 See eg *R v IAT, ex p Joseph Williams* [1995] Imm AR 518.
18 [1995] Imm AR 521.
19 See generally Craig 'Legitimate Expectations: A Conceptual Analysis' (1992) 108 LQR 79.
20 [1983] 2 AC 629.

undertaking to interview those threatened with removal, and that each individual case would be considered on its merits. He challenged this on the basis that he should have been given an opportunity to submit for consideration all the circumstances of his case. The Court of Appeal of Hong Kong had made an order prohibiting the Director of Immigration from implementing the order before the applicant had an opportunity to make representations. The Attorney General appealed to the Privy Council against this decision. Lord Fraser stated that when a public authority makes a promise it was in the interest of good administration that it should abide by this so long as this did not interfere with its statutory duty.[1] The Court of Appeal in *R v Secretary of State for the Home Department, ex p Asif Mahmood Khan*[2] found the reasoning in the case persuasive. Here the issue was policy guidance issued by the Home Office on the question of admission of foreign children for the purposes of adoption. The Home Office stated that while this would normally not be permitted, there were certain exceptions which they listed in a circular letter. Parker LJ stated that the letter did afford the applicants in the case a reasonable expectation that the procedures would be followed and thus quashed the decision to refuse entry clearance. In *Oloniluyi v Secretary of State for the Home Department*[3] the Court of Appeal held that there was a legitimate expectation where the applicant had been given a personal assurance by officials from the IND that she would have no problems re-entering the UK having travelled abroad during her current period of leave.

It is apparent from the case law that a legitimate expectation will arise with respect to both a personal assurance to an individual and where there is a general policy which is not followed in her case. In a number of past asylum cases legitimate expectation has been raised only to be held not to apply on the facts. Thus, in *R v Secretary of State for the Home Department, ex p Kyomya*[4] the court held that the issuance of a Standard Acknowledgement Letter did not give rise to a legitimate expectation that an asylum application would be considered on its merits. In *R v Secretary of State for the Home Department, ex p Biljana Sop*[5] (a safe third country case) the special adjudicator disagreed with the Home Secretary's certification. The Home Secretary stated that if he lost the appeal

1   [1983] 2 AC 629 at 639.
2   [1984] 1 WLR 1337.
3   [1989] Imm AR 135.
4   [1993] Imm AR 331.
5   [1994] Imm AR 204.

he would consider the application on its merits. However, shortly after the special adjudicator's determination the High Court clarified the law on the matter, and the Home Secretary successfully appealed to the IAT. The court rejected the applicant's argument that the previous statement had given rise to a legitimate expectation.

HUMAN RIGHTS, ASYLUM AND THE POLITICS OF MEMBERSHIP AND BELONGING

This chapter has focused on the law and politics of asylum in the UK. It is clearly contested legal and political terrain, within which important issues in public law and human rights law are being regularly tested. The asylum seeker challenges legal systems to demonstrate that their principles are universal and that entitlements attach not only to citizenship but also to personhood. With increasing discussion of postnationalism in Europe, it makes considerable sense to construct a system which attaches entitlements to personhood and not to status. However, practice in the UK suggests that the distinction between citizens and non-citizens matters in concrete terms. The support system designed to move away from cash payments and the use of dispersal shows that the human rights of asylum seekers are tied in practice to their legal status in the UK. Boundaries are being drawn in the UK and those who are not included can be subject to highly restrictive measures. This suggests that more attention needs to be paid in public law and human rights scholarship to the law and politics of membership and belonging.

What is the future then of the right to seek asylum in the UK? As noted, the right was given explicit recognition in the Universal Declaration of Human Rights 1948.[6] That it was promulgated in an international instrument is highly appropriate because the future of asylum in the UK is now intimately connected to international developments. There was a failure, in the period which followed the Declaration, to solidify this right in international human rights law. Its status has remained open to question since. The problem for human rights lawyers is that the right clashes with the interest of the state in regulating entry. It can be stated with some confidence that states are still unlikely to accept a positive obligation. However, as is clear from the UK's experience, once within the jurisdiction of a state the asylum seeker has legal and other avenues open to her which can address the risk of return.

6   Article 14.

While states may not be willing to bind themselves formally to a right to asylum, the practice in Europe suggests that they will permit a diverse range of protection seekers to remain on their territory. In the absence of an international regulatory mechanism, the institution of asylum remains tied to the systems of individual states. This may be changing fundamentally with the development of a supranational order in the EU.

The developments in UK asylum law and policy are illustrative of the problems which may arise when a state allows public policy imperatives to overwhelm human rights considerations in the treatment of individuals. Constructed upon claims which were often not adequately proven, the UK government has adopted measures which many correctly regard as highly questionable. The right to seek asylum has been steadily eroded and undermined. This chapter has sought to reject a purely instrumental view of asylum law, on the basis that such an approach may contribute to the neglect of consideration of the humanity of the 'other'. The key to a critical perspective on asylum law is to encourage learning processes inside and outside of the institutions of protection. Participants in the asylum debate should be reminded not to lose sight of the humanitarian imperative in the interpretation and application of law and policy. The other instrumental factors can often cloud and seriously distort the effective assessment of the claims of asylum seekers. The challenge is to nurture a communicative model whereby the asylum seeker's human dignity is respected. This is not aided when, for example, provocative slogans and labels are used in the debate.

It is the argument of this chapter that deterrence and restriction are key elements of the UK's asylum law and policy. Insufficient attention has been paid to the potentially enabling role of law. The functional and enabling aspects of asylum law are necessarily linked to the humanitarian purpose ascribed to the law in the above analysis. Asylum law must therefore primarily facilitate the fair, efficacious and efficient consideration of the claims of those who seek protection. Asylum seekers must be guaranteed *effective access* to a proper decision-making process which is sensitive to the asylum context. The serious error in recent law and policy has been to target the act of asylum seeking itself by adopting restrictive measures unconnected to the asylum determination process. If there is a conviction that the system is being 'abused', then the way to address this is through a fair and expeditious determination system. The practices described in this chapter have perhaps inevitably led many to conclude that deterrence has been at the heart of UK asylum law and policy for at least the last decade. The challenge for the UK is to construct a principled approach to refugee and asylum law which pays rather more attention to the needs of the forcibly displaced, and the advances made in other areas of human rights law, than has been the case in the past. The key to the future of asylum law may lie in the full recognition of the fact that the asylum seeker is a person before the law.[7] The emphasis on personhood and not status should be at the core of human rights and asylum law in the UK.

---

7   See International Covenant on Civil and Political Rights 1966, art 16; Universal Declaration of Human Rights 1948, art 6.

Chapter 5

Regulating asylum (II): the legal construction of refugee status and human rights protection in the UK

INTRODUCTION

The legal construction of refugee protection is of fundamental significance for those seeking asylum in the UK. Law's image of the refugee has both a symbolic and a material significance. The 1951 Convention holds out the prospect of a form of surrogate 'international' protection until circumstances permit the safe return of the refugee. This 'international' protection finds concrete expression in the law and practice of states. The law has an image of those entitled to protection which has significant implications for the asylum seeker. In the UK this protection extends beyond the 1951 Convention to include those entitled to protection under the European Convention on Human Rights. This is significant because, as was noted in earlier chapters, human rights law remedies some of the deficiencies of refugee law without necessarily replacing it. It is best viewed as offering a form of complementary protection. In the UK, as in other states, one challenge will be to manage complementary forms of protection fairly.

The aim in this chapter is to examine the law of refugee status and human rights law from a critical perspective. The purpose is to show how legal discourse constructs the entitlement to protection and explore the subtle distortions which can inform this process of legal interpretation. The intention is to explore the law's image of the refugee as well as the applicable provisions of human rights law. Even where the 1951 Convention does not apply, human rights law may be used and one objective here is to assess its significance. The future of refugee protection in the UK will rest on the ability to make refugee and human rights law effective in practice.

THE RECONSTRUCTION OF REFUGEE STATUS

The international development of the legal concept of refugee was examined in Chapter 2. For an individual to qualify as a refugee she must possess a:

> 'well-founded fear of being persecuted for reasons of race, religion, nationality, membership of a particular social group or political opinion'.[1]

She must be outside her state of origin and be unwilling or unable to avail herself of state protection. There are clearly several distinct elements of the legal definition of refugee. As Goodwin-Gill has noted, the definition is 'highly individualistic'.[2]

> 'It supposes a dispassionate case-by-case examination of subjective and objective elements, which may well prove impractical in the face of large numbers, although they too require the benefit of certain minimum standards.'[3]

The purpose in this section is to examine how the meaning of 'refugee' has been reconstructed in UK law and practice. If an individual claims asylum in the UK, she has already overcome one hurdle contained in refugee law. A person can only be a refugee, for legal purposes, if she is outside of her state of origin. The term 'reconstruction' is used deliberately in this chapter. This springs from the belief that participants are involved in a process of rational reconstruction of the meaning of refugee law. This links the meaning of refugee to the normative framework adopted by participants as well as the comparative jurisprudence in the field. Decision-makers are not involved in a purely deductive exercise in rule application, rather they are using the available materials in an attempt to reconstruct a coherent vision of refugee status.

'Well-founded fear'

The application of the test to establish a well-founded fear is crucial to the determination of refugee status. The usual approach is to suggest that it comprises of two basic elements. First, the objective element looks at the objective basis of the claim and, second, the subjective element looks to the existence of a fear of the

1 Article 1A(2).
2 Goodwin-Gill *The Refugee in International Law* (2nd edn, 1996) p 325.
3 Note 2 above.

objective conditions. Hathaway has rejected this in strong terms.[4] He argues that the well-founded fear aspect of the definition 'has nothing to do with the state of mind of the applicant for refugee status...'[5] He suggests that the concept is 'inherently objective' and stresses that the focus is on prospective risk rather than what has happened in the past.[6] There is merit in this argument if refugee law is to be understood as part of a wider body of human rights law. It is the objective element of the test which creates the link between the individual claim and the human rights situation in the applicant's state of origin. This objective element is clearly the most important aspect of the test. It effectively 'internationalises' asylum decision-making and requires decision-makers to be open-minded in their assessments of the conditions which exist in other states. The term 'fear' does, however, remain an aspect of the 1951 Convention. It is therefore essential to understand how the subjective (fear) and objective (well-founded) elements are interrelated in UK law and practice.[7] The UNHCR has emphasised the existence of two distinct aspects of the test. In describing the subjective element, the UNHCR notes the need for an assessment of the personality of the individual and her credibility where the claim is not clear on the available facts.[8] With respect to the objective aspect, it recommends that it be evaluated with reference to the statements of the applicant viewed in the context of the background situation in her state of origin. The recommendations of the UNHCR focus on the significance of considering each claim on its individual merits and not solely in the light of the general situation in the individual's state of origin. 'Blanket' assessments of particular states leading to an automatic rejection of the application are not appropriate. However, the UNHCR accepts that in some cases 'group determination', where the need for protection is urgent and individual determination of each claim is simply not practical, may be acceptable.[9] This suggestion has

4   Hathaway *The Law of Refugee Status* (1991) p 65.
5   Note 4 above.
6   Note 4 above.
7   Melander 'The Protection of Refugees' (1974) 18 Scandinavian Studies in Law 153, 158.
8   UNHCR *Handbook* para 40.
9   UNHCR *Handbook* para 44. The immigration rules provide for group determination in certain instances: '344. Cases will normally be considered on an individual basis but if an applicant is part of a group whose claims are clearly not related to the criteria for refugee status in the Convention and Protocol he may be refused without examination of his individual claim. However, the Secretary of State will have regard to any evidence produced by an individual to show that his claim should be distinguished from those of the rest of the group.'

generally been neglected, but it is a sound one. If it is evident that everyone in a group is a refugee then there is no reason of principle why they cannot be recognised as such.

The 'two-pronged test', advocated by the UNHCR, has been criticised by one leading commentator as neither the correct interpretation nor defensible in practice.[10] The criticism is premised on the inherent difficulties involved in assessing the subjective element in asylum cases and on a reading of the 1951 Convention. This reading questions the use of the term 'fear' to denote a subjective state of mind. The criticism appears to be supported by the practice of states. The courts in the UK and other jurisdictions, while still stressing that there are two elements in the test, do in practice interpret it in a way which allows the objective element to 'trump' the subjective. This is because the subjective state of mind of the applicant is difficult to ascertain, and, further to this, there are some possible illogical consequences of strict application of a dual approach, in which neither branch of the test dominates.[11] For example, a person may be particularly courageous and not possess a fear of an objectively verifiable risk. In the absence of the subjective element, should this individual be deprived of protection? It would make little sense to deprive an individual of protection in such circumstances.

The leading UK authority on the proper test to be applied, and one that has been influential in other jurisdictions, is the House of Lords' ruling in *R v Secretary of State for the Home Department, ex p Sivakumaran*.[12] In that case the House of Lords considered, somewhat surprisingly for the first time in the UK, how the well-founded fear test should be interpreted and applied. The case involved six Sri Lankan Tamils who had fled to the UK because of alleged persecution by armed forces. Their applications for asylum were refused by the Home Secretary on the ground that they did not possess a well-founded fear of persecution. They sought judicial review of the decision, arguing that he had misapplied the test.[13] In the Court of Appeal Sir John Donaldson stated that the proper test

10   Cf Hathaway, note 4 above, p 65.
11   It would seem indefensible to suggest that a particularly courageous individual would be denied an otherwise good claim to refugee status because the requisite fear could not be demonstrated.
12   [1988] AC 958.
13   It is worthwhile noting that judicial review was sought because appeal on the merits was unavailable while the applicants remained in the UK. As will be discussed below, this gap in the appeal rights of applicants was eventually remedied in the Asylum and Immigration Appeals Act 1993. See Blake 'The Road to Sivakumaran' (1988) 2 I&NLP 13; Blake 'Life After the Lords' (1990) 4 I&NLP 7.

involved, first, proving an actual fear and, second, demonstrating good reason why that individual possessed such a fear:

> 'Fear is clearly an entirely subjective state experienced by a person who is afraid. The adjectival phrase "well-founded" qualifies but cannot transform the subjective nature of the emotion'.[14]

The Court of Appeal held that the Secretary of State had applied a primarily objective test which amounted to a misdirection. In the judgment of the Court of Appeal there were therefore two distinct aspects to the test and thus the subjective aspect could be qualified but not be 'trumped' by the objective. According to this test, the two approaches are essentially distinct. The House of Lords rejected the approach taken by the Court of Appeal. Lord Keith stated that it was a reasonable inference that the question of whether the fear of persecution was well-founded should be decided objectively:

> '[T]he general purpose of the Convention is surely to afford protection and fair treatment to those for whom neither is available in their own country and does not extend to the allaying of fears not objectively justified, however reasonable these fears may appear from the point of view of the individual in question.'[15]

He stated that the Court of Appeal's formulation would have the consequence that an individual whose fear was genuine would be granted refugee status even though it could be demonstrated, with reference to the conditions in her state of origin, that this fear was objectively unfounded. As Lord Keith stated, this would be an absurd application of refugee law and would in significant respects negate links to the broader issues of human rights violations in the state of origin. Refugee law, as a system of international protection, was designed to offer protection to those who are genuinely at risk of suffering persecution in their state of origin and not those whose fears were imaginary. As to the applicable standard he stated:

> 'In my opinion the requirement that an applicant's fear of persecution should be well-founded means that there has to be demonstrated a reasonable degree of likelihood that he will be persecuted for a Convention reason if returned to his own country.'[16]

This judgment was a strong defence of the objective basis of refugee protection. Echoing this, Lord Templeman emphasised

---

14 [1988] AC 958 at 964-965.
15 [1988] AC 958 at 992-993.
16 [1988] AC 958 at 994.

that the objective determination was not one that could be decided solely with reference to the individual's belief, but by an assessment by the Home Secretary on the available evidence.[17]   Lord Goff affirmed this reasoning, stating that the Convention was intended to provide protection only to those whose fear was 'in reality well-founded'.[18]   In other words, Lord Goff wished to reassert the primacy of the objective aspect of the phrase, and thus arguably provide a more 'workable' legal test than that stated in the Court of Appeal.

The judgment of the House of Lords represents a repudiation of the argument that 'well-founded' simply qualifies the term 'fear'. Rather, while the subjective fear of the individual must, it would seem, play a part, this is ultimately a limited part given that the test advocated by the House of Lords allows this subjective fear to be overridden by the objective aspect. Thus, in the UK the most significant factor in determining this aspect of refugee status is the Home Secretary's assessment of the applicant's statements viewed in relation to the conditions in the applicant's state of origin. It is to the objective conditions in the applicant's state of origin that decision-makers must look. The focus is thus on reconstructing the asylum seeker's narrative in the light of the available objective evidence on the present human rights situation. The key is the well-foundedness of the risk to the individual at the time her claim is determined. As Lord Slynn stated in *Adan v Secretary of State for the Home Department*:

> 'That well-founded fear must, as I read it, exist at the time his claim for refugee status is to be determined; it is not sufficient as a matter of the ordinary meaning of the words of the article that he had such a fear when he left his country but no longer has it.'[19]

The fear of persecution must be a current fear if it is to be well-founded.[20]

In addition to settling the question of how the phrase is to be interpreted in the UK, the House of Lords in *Sivakumaran* also addressed the issue of the standard of proof in such cases. How likely must persecution be before a fear is regarded as well-founded?   As a preliminary point, it is worth noting the well-established position that the initial burden of proving refugee

---

17 [1988] AC 958 at 996.
18 [1988] AC 958 at 1000.
19 [1998] 2 All ER 453 at 454.
20 Lord Slynn [1998] 2 All ER 453 at 454: 'The existence of what has been called an historic fear is not sufficient in itself, though it may constitute important evidence to justify a claim of a current well-founded fear.'

status rests on the asylum seeker. With respect to the standard of proof, as is well known, the normal civil burden of proof is on 'the balance of probabilities' and requires that the result be probable. Here the House of Lords addressed the question of whether this was an appropriate approach in asylum cases. The important point about asylum cases is that they involve an assessment of a future risk rather than being exclusively focused on past events. With reference to this, Lord Keith stated that he believed there should be a 'reasonable degree of likelihood' that persecution will take place upon return, as opposed to a probability of such ill-treatment.[1] Relying on the judgment of Lord Diplock in *R v Governor of Pentonville Prison, ex p Fernandez*,[2] Lord Keith agreed with his use of the phrases 'a reasonable chance', 'substantial grounds for thinking', and 'a serious possibility'. A lesser standard than the 'more likely than not'/ 'probable' approach was held to be required in these types of cases. Lord Goff additionally used the phrase 'real and substantial risk', which it must be stated does appear a somewhat higher standard than that mentioned by both Lord Keith and Lord Diplock.[3]

The formulation adopted by the House of Lords has been welcomed by some scholars, in particular in its disapproval of the ruling of the Court of Appeal.[4] Hathaway's argument, that the term 'fear', as used in the 1951 Convention, denotes prospective risk rather than a subjective state of mind is convincing, particularly given the weight attached in practice to this aspect of the definition.[5] Despite this argument, however, the courts in the jurisdictions under examination still 'play homage' to the subjective element in their judgments, even if it has little or no significance in the final decision. Thus, *Sivakumaran* supports the rule that the objective element of the test will override an individual fear, no matter how genuine this may be. This is broadly in line with a human rights-based approach, with the focus ultimately on the objectively verifiable conditions in an individual's state of origin rather than the particular

---

1   [1988] AC 958 at 994.
2   [1971] 1 WLR 987.
3   Cf *Soering v United Kingdom* (1989) 11 EHRR 439 para 53. See also UN Torture Convention, art 3.
4   Hathaway *The Law of Refugee Status* (1991) p 65. Cf Grahl-Madsen *The Status of Refugees in International Law* (1966) p 175. '*We cannot find a meaningful common denominator in the minds of refugees. We must seek it in the conditions prevailing in the country whence they fled.*' (My emphasis.)
5   Hathaway, note 4 above, pp 70–71. From his study of the application of refugee status in Canada he concludes that because of the inherently problematic nature of the subjective element it is always in practice objectively 'trumped'. In addition to this, he rejects the view that fear requires an assessment of the individual's state of mind, but rather that the term denotes the existence of a prospective risk.

subjective attributes of that individual.[6] In relation to the burden of proof, a lower standard than the normal 'balance of probabilities' or 'more likely than not' test is to be applied in asylum cases. This is a formal recognition of the importance of the process for the individuals concerned and the rights which are at stake.

There has been some discussion as to whether this lower standard should also apply to the establishment of past persecution suffered by the asylum seeker, in other words should the adopted approach be based upon a two-branch test or a unitary one. The issue was addressed by the IAT in *Koyazia Kaja v Secretary of State for the Home Department*.[7] The majority of the IAT, the President and the Vice President, stated that the better approach in these cases was the unitary one. They argued that the adoption of the two-stage approach would make serious inroads into the reasonable degree of likelihood test as expressed in *Sivakumaran*. This was particularly necessary in asylum cases where proving historical facts was often very difficult. As they noted, in some instances all the appellate authorities are presented with in asylum cases are the applicant's own story and reports by respected international human rights organisations such as Amnesty International and Human Rights Watch. The majority stated that this should not, however, lead to an ready acceptance of fact as established, but that there should be a more 'positive role for uncertainty' in asylum determinations:

> 'The applicability of the "reasonable degree of likelihood" approach to the whole recognises that an assessment of future likelihood cannot sensibly be separated from an assessment of the past and the present.'[8]

Therefore, in stressing the need for a unitary approach, the majority in the IAT acknowledged that any assessment of historical facts was likely to play a part in the assessment of future events. According to the IAT, it is inappropriate then to apply a two-stage approach with two different standards of proof. The minority strongly disapproved of the majority approach, arguing that any confusion which arose in asylum cases was mainly due to the

6   The adoption and use of such a test also highlights an under-utilised resource in the collection of information on the human rights conditions in certain states, ie the testimony and evidence presented in asylum cases. For the importance of country information generally, see *Report of the Consultative Group on Country Information and Documentation Centre* (December 1998). The report called for the establishment of an independent documentation centre in the UK. The Country Information and Policy Unit of the IND now produces country assessments.

7   [1995] Imm AR 1.

8   [1995] Imm AR 1 at 8.

disinclination to distinguish between the standard to be adopted when approaching past events and that to be adopted when assessing the possibility of events occurring in the future.

In *Sivakumaran* the Court of Appeal and the House of Lords both made reference to the US case *INS v Luz Maria Cardoza-Fonseca*, agreeing with the approach taken.[9] A brief analysis of the US position is necessary. In the US the Refugee Act 1980 amended the Immigration and Nationality Act (INA), with the addition of s 208 to include the granting of asylum to a refugee.[10] The Attorney-General is required, under the terms of the Act, to establish procedures by which an alien physically present in the US may apply for asylum. In cases where a deportation order has been made against an individual, asylum requests are dealt with under the withholding of deportation proceedings.[11] The *Cardoza-Fonseca* case was in many respects a landmark decision of the US Supreme Court.[12] The case involved a Nicaraguan visitor to the US who had overstayed. She argued that she was entitled to a withholding of deportation order under s 243(h) (that her life or freedom was threatened) and asylum under s 208(a) (well-founded fear). The Immigration Judge at the deportation hearing applied a 'more likely than not' test to both the grounds of the claim, stating that there was a lack of a clear probability of persecution taking place. The Supreme Court rejected this interpretation, stating that the 'clear probability' test, which did apply in s 243(h) cases,[13] did not apply in s 208(a) cases. The court reasoned, in contrast to some of the arguments discussed above, that s 208(a) contemplated a subjective element which was not entirely negated by the 'well-founded' element. Thus, an individual could have a well-founded fear based on a probability of less than 50%.[14] According to the court, it was enough, when applying the test, that

9   94 L ed 2d 434 (1987).
10   8 USC sec 1158. For an analysis of asylum law in the US, see Anker and Lufkin *The Law of Asylum in the US* (3rd edn, 1999); See Anker 'Discretionary Asylum: A Protection Remedy for Refugees Under the Refugee Act of 1980' (1987) 28 Va J Int L 1; Brill 'The Endless Debate: Refugee Law and Policy and the 1980 Refugee Act' (1983-1984) 32 Cleveland State LR 117.
11   8 USC sec 1253(h).
12   See Anker and Blum 'New Trends in Asylum Jurisprudence: The Aftermath of the US Supreme Court Decision in INS v Cardoza-Fonseca' (1989) 1 IJRL 67.
13   *INS v Stevic* 467 US 407 (1984).
14   467 US 407 at 447 (1984): 'That fear must be well-founded does not alter the obvious focus on the individual's subjective beliefs, nor does it transform the standard into a "more likely than not" one. One can certainly have a well-founded fear of an event happening when there is less than 50% chance of the occurrence taking place.'

persecution was 'reasonably possible'. While the court did mention the importance of the subjective element, it was not suggesting that this should be the only consideration taken into account. In *Cardoza* the court was much more concerned to clarify the standard of proof required to show that a fear was well-founded, rather than elaborating upon which of the branches of the definition was dominant.

In Canada an individual may claim asylum under the terms of the Immigration Act 1989. In *Chan v Minister of Employment and Immigration*[15] the applicant claimed to fear persecution on the basis that he would be subject to forced sterilisation if he was returned to China. As to the approach to the well-founded fear test, the Supreme Court stressed the importance of paying due regard to the two elements in the test. It was critical, for example, of the failure of the IRB to look specifically for the subjective element. Major J stated that the 'fear' must be shown to exist in the mind of the applicant. This would be demonstrated where she was a credible witness and her testimony was consistent. As to the assessment by the court of the objective element, relevant considerations included: the situation in the applicant's state of origin; the laws in that country; and their application. The Supreme Court ruled that in this case the applicant had failed to demonstrate that his subjective fear of persecution was well-founded. Important factors were his failure to provide any evidence to suggest that forced sterilisation was carried out in practice in his local area and that it was used against men. In *Re Adjei v Minister for Employment and Immigration*[16] the Canadian Federal Court of Appeal addressed the issue of the standard of proof required. A Ghanaian national claimed asylum under s 2(1) of the Immigration Act 1989. The Immigration Appeal Board had held that the test to be applied was whether there existed 'substantial grounds' to think that persecution would take place. The Court of Appeal rejected this formulation as being placed at too high a level. The court referred to *Sivakumaran* with approval, although notably Guigan JA questioned the reference by Lord Goff in that case to 'substantial grounds for thinking', which he correctly argued sounded too similar to the 'probability test'.[17] Instead, he preferred such phrases as 'reasonable chance' and 'reasonable or serious possibility'. The court thus adopted an approach similar to both the UK and US.

15 [1995] 3 SCR 593.
16 (1989) 57 DLR (4th) 153 (FCA).
17 (1989) 57 DLR 153 at 156.

An examination of these cases demonstrates that, in the three jurisdictions discussed, it is generally accepted that the 'more likely than not test' is inappropriate in asylum cases. In its place an approach which looks for a 'reasonable chance/possibility' or a 'serious possibility' of persecution is favoured. While the three jurisdictions adopt very similar tests, some of the comments of the House of Lords in *Sivakumaran* raise the question of whether the UK test is higher than that of the US and Canada. The use of the phrase 'substantial grounds for thinking' by Lord Goff in *Sivakumaran* does seem, as Guigan JA indicated, to resemble 'probable'. While he stated that even the use of 'serious possibility' might appear inappropriate, this was not the case as it still retained the link with possibility rather than probability. On the objective/subjective elements of the test, while the former appears to dominate the latter, the courts have not adopted an interpretation which negates the need for 'fear' to exist even though it tends to be imputed.

'Persecution'

The phrase 'well-founded fear' focuses on the conditions in the state of origin and thus the *possibility* of an individual encountering some form of ill-treatment on her return. This is, however, not the end of the story. The ill-treatment must be of a sufficiently serious nature if the individual is to qualify as a 1951 Convention refugee. It must constitute 'persecution' if the protection seeker is to overcome this legal hurdle. While protection is the primary purpose behind the 1951 Convention, this does not mean that refugee law offers protection to everyone who is likely to encounter human rights violations upon return. It does not, and its definition of entitlement is a limited one. Refugee law reflects a compromise between human needs and practical politics.

As the discussion of the case law above demonstrated, there has been a measure of consensus on the application of the standard of proof to the well-founded fear aspect of refugee status. This is not necessarily reflected in the approaches to the term 'persecution'. Persecution is notoriously difficult to interpret abstractly, often depending on the particular facts of a case. The essential problem rests on the attempt to classify types of treatment severe enough to merit being described as persecution. The process of interpreting persecution in refugee law is essentially one of reconstructing meaning. The most plausible defences of a framework of interpretation have been based on the explicit imposition of purpose. For example, Hathaway argues that:

'The challenge is to recast "persecution" in a manner which is consonant with modern political realities, and which genuinely enables governments to conceive of refugee protection as a humanitarian act which ought not to be the cause of tension between states.'[18]

Hathaway's framework is successfully deployed within states precisely because of the attractiveness of the reconstruction he defends. He offers a coherent way of understanding a rather slippery legal concept. His suggestion is that persecution is the sustained or systemic violation of basic human rights resulting from a failure of state protection.[19] The model has the advantage of linking persecution to the norms of international human rights law. Whether one agrees with Hathaway's hierarchy of human rights law is another matter entirely.

Despite contrary positions in some jurisdictions, international refugee law does not require persecution to have been carried out by the state.[20] Persecution can come from non-state entities as well, in the general context of a lack of effective state protection. The refugee must be 'unwilling and unable to seek the protection' of the state, the 1951 Convention does not specify that persecution should emanate only from the state. The UNHCR recognises that the agents of persecution need not be the state, but may be other groups within society which do not respect the standards established by the laws of the country.[1] As to the ill-treatment which will constitute persecution, the UNHCR *Handbook* is vague. While recognising the widespread existence of discrimination in many societies, the UNHCR notes that it will only, in very clearly defined circumstances, constitute persecution. The discrimination must, it stresses, have consequences of a substantially prejudicial character. In other words, the treatment must have serious implications for the individual.[2] On the often problematic question of when prosecution gives rise to persecution, the UNHCR notes that punishment may be overly excessive.[3] How is one to determine whether prosecution amounts to persecution? The UNHCR suggests that the authorities should refer to the laws in the country concerned.[4] The UNHCR's guidance is at times

---

18 Hathaway *The Law of Refugee Status* (1991) p 101.
19 Note 18 above.
20 See Van Der Veen 'Does Persecution by Fellow Citizens in Certain Regions of a State Fall within the Definition of Persecution?' (1980) 11 Netherlands Ybk Int L 167. Cf EU Joint Position, para 5.
1 UNHCR *Handbook* para 51.
2 *Handbook* para 54.
3 *Handbook* para 59.
4 *Handbook* para 59.

rather vague in this area and is a starting point only in interpreting this aspect of refugee law. The EU Joint Position, discussed in Chapter 3, offers guidance for the particular purpose of harmonisation of interpretations and is therefore of some use.

As to its interpretation in the courts, in *ex p Jonah*[5] Nolan J stated that persecution should be interpreted according to its ordinary dictionary definition. The OED states it may be defined as 'to pursue with malignancy or injurious action, especially to oppress for holding a heretical belief'. In stating this, he added, that the strength of the term had to be acknowledged in any interpretation. In *Sandralingham and Ravichandran v Secretary of State for the Home Department*[6] Staughton LJ stated:

> 'Persecution must at least be persistent and serious ill-treatment without just cause . . .'[7]

The ill-treatment must be particularly severe before meriting the name persecution. It would appear from the interpretations given by the IAT and the courts that persecution results when an individual is seriously and persistently abused. There appears to be a preference for treatment which is aimed at an individual or group and which poses some direct threat to her life or liberty, rather than that which disadvantages her in other less serious ways. This is a recognition of the exceptional nature of refugee status. While past persecution may evidence a possibility of future persecution, this does not necessarily mean that where past persecution has occurred the individual will be granted asylum.[8] The focus, as the discussion of the phrase 'well-founded fear' demonstrated, is on what is likely to happen in the future.

It is only through an examination of the case law that clarity can be achieved on the precise meaning of the term. In *Ravichandran v Secretary of State for the Home Department* Staughton LJ emphasised that a course of conduct must be consistent for it to constitute persecution.[9] The assessment must be a composite one rather than an examination of whether individual acts constitute persecution.[10] In *Faraj v Secretary of State for the Home Department*[11] the appellant was a member of the Islamic Party of Kenya (IPK) who was arrested, detained and beaten on account of his political

---

5 [1985] Imm AR 7.
6 [1996] Imm AR 97.
7 [1996] Imm AR 97 at 114.
8 *R v Secretary of State for the Home Department, ex p Halil Direk* [1992] Imm AR 330.
9 [1996] Imm AR 97 at 114.
10 Brown LJ [1996] Imm AR 97 at 109.

activities. He was refused asylum, and his appeal to a special adjudicator and the IAT was dismissed. One of the reasons given by the IAT was that any detention or beatings he had suffered were the result of an attempt by the police to keep the peace as part of their public duties. The appellant's appeal to the Court of Appeal was unsuccessful. The Court of Appeal, in distinguishing torture from persecution, stated that the latter involved a persistent course of conduct. Persecution arose from sustained or systematic failure of state protection as distinct from casual or random acts of violence against the general population. Isolated incidents of torture were not enough to constitute persecution. In *Demirkaya v Secretary of State for the Home Department* the appellant was a Kurd who was refused asylum.[12] The IAT found him to be a credible witness and accepted that he might be beaten at the airport on this return to Turkey and detained there. However, it stated that he would likely be released within two days and held that this would not constitute persecution. The Court of Appeal held that the IAT had not made clear in its determination the degree and severity of the beating which the appellant would suffer upon return and thus it was in error. On the issue of the standard of proof, the court ruled that the IAT had applied the wrong standard in its statement that the appellant would be released within two days. It had failed to apply the lower standard applicable in these cases.

The relevance of past persecution to the assessment of a prospective risk has arisen in many cases and has been mentioned above. Hathaway believes it is an 'excellent indicator' of what might occur upon the applicant's return.[13] The EU Joint Position provides:

'The fact that an individual has already been subject to persecution or to direct threats of persecution is a serious indication of the risk of persecution, unless a radical change of conditions has taken place since then in his country of origin or in his relations with his country of origin.'[14]

In *Adan* the House of Lords ruled that a historic fear was not sufficient to establish a claim to refugee status. However, Lord Lloyd, in agreement with Lord Slynn, stated:

'This is not to say that historic fear may not be relevant. It may well provide evidence to establish present fear.'[15]

11   [1999] INLR 441.
12   [1999] INLR 451.
13   Hathaway *The Law of Refugee Status* (1991) p 88.
14   Paragraph 3.
15   [1998] 2 All ER 453 at 463.

While past persecution will not by itself be enough to establish a claim to refugee status it provides a useful guide to likely future events. In *Adan* the House of Lords also addressed the issue of persecution emanating from rival clans during a civil war. Lord Slynn stated:

> 'Looking . . . at the language of the convention and its object and purpose I do not consider that it applies to those caught up in a civil war when law and order have broken down and where, as in the present case, every group seems to be fighting some other group or groups in an endeavour to gain power . . . In such a situation the individual or group has to show a well-founded fear of persecution over and above the risk to life and liberty inherent in the civil war.'[16]

Lord Lloyd stated:

> 'I conclude . . . that where a state of civil war exists, it is not enough for an asylum-seeker to show that he would be at risk if he were returned to his country. He must be able to show . . . a differential impact. In other words, he must be able to show fear of persecution for convention reasons over and above the ordinary risks of clan warfare.'[17]

The ruling follows the rather restrictive approach adopted in the EU Joint Position on this matter.

In *Ali (MMH)*[18] the applicants had fled Kenya because of its 'Africanisation' policy. The IAT held that, while the policy was discriminatory, it did not amount to persecution. This may be contrasted with *ex p Jeyakumaran*.[19] The applicant was a Sri Lankan Tamil who had been the object of continuous ill-treatment and harassment, including the destruction of his home, by the Sinhalese community and by the armed forces of the state. The High Court held that, in rejecting his claim to asylum, the Home Secretary had failed to take into account the personal violence and harassment which the individual had suffered. The context specific nature of persecution is evident in *Mohamed Ibrahim Hamieh v Home Secretary*.[20] Here a Lebanese citizen was forced to flee because of his refusal to join Hizbollah. The movement had threatened him with death. His application for leave to apply for judicial review was refused on the grounds that it was not unreasonable for the Home Secretary to conclude that the treatment was not persecution. It is clear from the case law that persecution

---

16 [1998] 2 All ER 453 at 455. Cf EU Joint Position para 6.
17 [1998] 2 All ER 453 at 463.
18 [1978] Imm AR 126.
19 [1994] Imm AR 45.
20 [1993] Imm AR 323.

need not only emanate from the state. An individual will be a refugee for Convention purposes where the ill-treatment emanates from non-state entities also. The focus is on the sufficiency of domestic protection and how effective the state is in protecting an individual from persecution.[1] Discrimination against an individual or group is transformed into persecution where evidence exists of a lack of state protection. In *Horvath* the IAT stated that there was a high threshold to be met in these cases.[2] On appeal the Court of Appeal held that state protection was sufficient if there was in force in the state a criminal law which made attacks punishable by a sentence commensurate with the crime. In cases such as *Horvath* the Court of Appeal held that the ill-treatment by non-state agents would have to be part of the prevailing political or social order. This ill-treatment would have to be encouraged or acquiesced in by the state, or be beyond its control, before it would amount to persecution.

Particularly difficult are cases where the individual claims that the law and its application in her state of origin amounts to persecution.[3] The maxim that prosecution is not in general to be regarded as persecution has already been recited. There are, however, exceptions to this general rule. In *Asante*[4] the applicant was thought, by the Ghanaian government, to be involved in embezzlement for the purpose of supplying funds to a dissident group. The applicant was arrested and subsequently released. Soon after this release he heard that the army was looking for him again. At this stage he decided to flee and seek asylum in the UK. The IAT held that the treatment did constitute persecution, as he feared persistent hounding on his return because of a belief on the part of the military regime that he had embezzled money. It is evident that the authorities were applying the law in this case in order to persecute an individual who they believed had been assisting dissidents in the state. In *Ameyaw*[5] the applicant based his claim on the argument that he would not receive a fair trial in

---

1   *Horvath v Secretary of State for the Home Department* [1999] INLR 7. The decision was upheld by the Court of Appeal: see *Horvath v Secretary of State for the Home Department* [2000] INLR 15. It has been affirmed by the House of Lords, see *Horvath v Secretary of State for the Home Department* (2000) Times, 7 July.

2   [1999] INLR 7 at 34: 'We have decided that he falls below the high threshold which we believe is required for international protection in a case where the fear is an accumulation of discriminatory acts and where it is alleged that there is not a sufficiency of protection from non-State agents.'

3   See EU Joint Position para 5.1.2.

4   [1991] Imm AR 78.

5   [1992] Imm AR 206.

Ghana. While Nolan J acknowledged that the lack of a fair trial, and malicious prosecution, might amount to persecution in certain cases, he held that the Home Secretary was entitled to make a distinction between prosecution and persecution in this case. In *Gulzar Ahmad v Secretary of State for the Home Department*[6] the appellants were citizens of Pakistan and members of the Ahmadi community. In 1984 the government enacted a decree which introduced a measure of discrimination against that community, in particular proselytising was forbidden. The Court of Appeal held that the Home Secretary had not erred in his approach when he rejected the claim. His duty in these cases was to examine the ordinance to establish its prohibitions and then find out the practical implications on members of the sect. The position of each appellant had to be considered against this background. In this case the evidence demonstrated that he had done this.

In *Secretary of State for the Home Department v Adrian Chiver*[7] the respondent was a member of a political party in Romania which opposed the Communist government. He was sacked from his job after taking part in a number of political demonstrations and was unable to secure further employment because of the government's refusal to give him a work card. The special adjudicator had held for the respondent, stating that he had a well-founded fear of persecution for a Convention reason. The Home Secretary, however, believed that what the respondent had experienced did not amount to persecution. The IAT upheld the decision of the special adjudicator, stating that if a person could show that he is unable to obtain employment resulting from his political beliefs then this would amount to persecution for a Convention reason. The decision of the IAT is a good example of the way economic and social rights may play a part in the consideration of refugee status.

In *R v Secretary of State for the Home Department, ex p Baljit Singh*[8] the applicant was a citizen of India who based his claim to asylum on the argument that the police in the Punjab had used improper means to enforce the law. He had been associated with a group in the Punjab which had been involved in terrorist activities. The court held that the Home Secretary had correctly borne in mind that a person who was associated with a terrorist group acting unlawfully in its own country should not normally be given refugee status. Again, a distinction was drawn between prosecution and

6   [1990] Imm AR 61.
7   (10758) IAT, reported in (1994) 8 I&NLP 148.
8   [1994] Imm AR 42.

persecution. The applicant was, the court stated, facing the legitimate processes of law in his own country, and it was reasonable for the Home Secretary to conclude in this case that they were being properly applied.

The obligation to perform military service is a good example of the difficulties which arise in drawing a distinction between persecution and prosecution. In *Dragi Petrovski v Secretary of State for the Home Department*[9] a citizen of the former Yugoslavia claimed asylum on the basis that he had refused to perform military service. The IAT held that refusal to perform military service and the punishment which followed could not ground a claim to asylum. This would only be the case where there was evidence that persecution would result from the refusal. Presumably, this means that where an individual is threatened with, inter alia, torture if she does not perform military service, this may amount to persecution, but where a measure amounts to simply a form of punishment, such as work for other areas of government, this will not. In *Adan v Secretary of State for the Home Department*[10] two of the appellants were Yugoslavian draft evaders. Brown LJ stated:

> 'In my view there can be no doubt that a person who on grounds of conscience objects to participating in an internationally condemned conflict can legitimately assert that the risk of prosecution for his actions amounts to a risk of persecution . . . However, I cannot accept that persons in the position of these appellants can claim to be in fear of *persecution* after refusing for extraneous reasons to fight . . It seems to me . . . that it is impossible sensibly to say that it is persecution on account of their political opinion.'[11]

As is evident from this statement, he did not accept that draft evaders were fleeing persecution for a Convention reason.

What is the position concerning the definition of persecution in other jurisdictions? In both the US and Canada the emphasis is again on persistent harassment, the same basic starting point as that adopted in the UK. In both jurisdictions it is accepted that the agents of persecution need not only be the state.[12] What is

9 [1993] Imm AR 134.
10 [1997] Imm AR 251.
11 [1997] Imm AR 251 at 273.
12 In the case of the US, see *McMullen v INS* 591 F 2d 1312 (9th Cir 1986). McMullen deserted from the British Army in Northern Ireland in 1972 and joined the IRA. After a number of years in the organisation he refused to take part in a kidnapping and the IRA sought to kill him. He fled to the US and sought asylum. The court in the case held that even though the persecution would come from a paramilitary organisation and not the state, that this could still ground a successful asylum claim.

apparent, however, is that there must be some connection to the state in the form of either state inability or unwillingness to offer protection. As Hathaway notes, 'there is a failure of protection where a government is *unwilling* to defend citizens against private harm, as well as in situations of objective *inability* to provide meaningful protection'.[13] Thus, he argues that the state fails in its most basic duty of protection and the need for surrogate protection arises.[14]

In the Canadian case *Zahurdeen Rajudeen v Canada (MEI)*[15] a Sri Lankan Tamil alleged persecution by Sinhalese Buddhists. The Federal Court of Appeal held that an individual could possess a well-founded fear of persecution where the police, who were of the same group as the attackers, took no active steps to prevent the assaults and were generally indifferent to the abuses. In another Canadian case, *Zalzali v Canada (MEI)*,[16] a Lebanese man, who had been harassed by a number of militias (with each one believing he belonged to the other) was held to be capable of having a well-founded fear of persecution. The court again stated that it was not necessary for there to be direct state involvement. Given the situation then existing in Lebanon, the government could not offer protection to its citizens. The court further noted, qualifying this, that a positive decision was less likely, first, where there was an internal flight option available or, second, where some form of protection was available from an established authority. The Canadian Supreme Court has addressed the question in the case of *A-G of Canada v Ward*.[17] The appellant, an ex-member of a paramilitary organisation in Northern Ireland, fled to Canada after he had contrived to assist hostages to escape. Members of the organisation sentenced him to death for this action. The appellant claimed refugee status on the ground that he would be persecuted by other members of the group if he returned. The Supreme Court, upholding the developed jurisprudence of the Federal Court of Appeal, held that direct state complicity was not required. The court defined the rationale of international refugee law as created to:

'provide refuge to those whose home state *cannot* or does not afford them protection from persecution.'[18]

---

13 Hathaway *The Law of Refugee Status* (1991) p 127.
14 Hathaway, note 13 above, p 128.
15 (1984) 5 NR 129.
16 [1991] FCJ 341.
17 (1993) 103 DLR (4th) 1.
18 103 DLR (4th) 1 at 17, per La Forest J.

The focus is thus on the inability or unwillingness of the state to offer protection from groups and individuals in society, as well as the more usual forms of state persecution. As La Forest J stated:

> 'The international community was meant to be a forum of second resort for the persecuted, a "surrogate", approachable upon failure of local protection. The rationale upon which international refugee law rests is not simply the need to give shelter to those persecuted by the state but, more widely, to provide refuge to those whose home state cannot or does not afford them protection from persecution . . . The state's inability to protect the individual from persecution founded on one of the enumerated grounds constitutes failure of local protection.'[19]

With respect to what level of treatment constitutes persecution, it is the general rule, as stated above, that prosecution for a criminal offence will not normally be regarded as sufficient. As with the UK there are, however, exceptions to this general rule. Prosecution may amount to persecution where it is discriminatory in nature and sufficiently severe in the context of the general approach to refugee law. In the US case *Dvomoh v Sava*[20] the applicant faced prosecution in Ghana because of his involvement in a coup against the established government. The court held that prosecution could amount to persecution because of the human rights situation existing then in Ghana, and because there was no other way in which political change could be achieved in the state. In another similar case, *Matter of Izatula*,[1] an Afghan citizen fled the country to evade arrest by the government. He had been accused of assisting rebel forces by providing them with supplies. The Board held that prosecution by the Afghan government amounted to persecution as, again, there was no other way to achieve political change. Thus, in the US example, prosecution may amount to persecution in cases where the individual who takes part in criminal activity had no other choices with regard to their political activity. This in effect requires an extensive assessment of the political situation within a state and ultimately a value judgment on the political situation pertaining there. This leaves substantial room for foreign policy considerations to enter the process.

In *Blanco-Lopez v INS*[2] a Salvodoran citizen criticised the government and was subsequently forced out of his job. In his new job a fellow employee informed the police, inaccurately, that he was a member of an armed opposition group. The police threatened

19 103 DLR (4th) 1 at 17
20 696 F Supp 970 (1988).
 1 (1990) BIA Int Dec 3127.
 2 858 F 2d 531 (1988).

to kill him if he did not confess to involvement. On his release he fled to the US. The court held that this treatment could constitute persecution and not prosecution as there had been no intention on the part of the police to bring a prosecution and the death threats which had been made in custody were enough to warrant a well-founded fear of persecution. This case may be contrasted with *Jan Kubon v INS*.[3] Here a Polish member of Solidarity had been detained by police for five days after a demonstration. He was interrogated and then released. No prosecution was sought by the police. The court held that brief periods of even arbitrary detention by a totalitarian regime did not amount to persecution. It would appear, therefore, that the detention itself is not persecution without some further ill-treatment, or threat thereof, while the individual is in custody. Further to this, the ill-treatment, actual or threatened, must be sustained and not sporadic, as it appeared to be in *Kubon*.

The assessment of whether actions under domestic law constitute persecution is more difficult when there is a state of emergency and the government is in conflict with paramilitary groups.[4] In the US case *Rajaratnam v Mojer* the petitioners were Tamils who had fled Sri Lanka following police ill-treatment.[5] The BIA had held that the Sri Lankan government was merely exercising its right to investigate terrorist activity, and was not engaged in persecution on account of their political opinion or ethnicity. The court reversed the decision of the BIA and stated that a right to investigate terrorism did not include the beating and torture of detainees. In *Singh v Ilchert* the petitioner was an Indian national refused asylum in the US.[6] He testified that he had been beaten and shot by the police, who were investigating Sikh extremists. He was accused of sheltering terrorists. The BIA held that the police treatment of Singh was prosecution within the scope of Indian anti-terrorist laws. The court rejected this conclusion, stating that the BIA had improperly characterised the Indian police's actions as legitimate. Beatings, torture and gunshot wounds were, it stated, not lawful government actions.

The US jurisprudence distinguishes between situations of general unrest and persecution directed against individuals or groups. For example, in *Lopez-Zeron v US State Department* the petitioners feared persecution by Nicaraguan contra guerillas who lived in the

3   913 F 2d 386 (1990).
4   See EU Joint Position para 5.1.1.
5   (1993) 832 F Supp 1219.
6   (1992) 801 F Supp 313.

Honduran border region, because they refused to support them.[7] The court held that their claims were based on a fear of general violence and unrest in Honduras and not persecution.

The Canadian authorities are willing to make extensive use of international human rights law in the development of their jurisprudence. The case law reveals that such an approach is possible and also desirable, given the need to emphasise the place of refugee law as an aspect of human rights law. Whether the use of international standards necessarily alters the practical result is another matter. In *Cheung v Canada (MEI)*[8] a woman from China claimed asylum on the basis that, as she had given birth to a second child, she would be forcibly sterilised in line with China's one child policy. The problem for the applicant in the case was the rule, accepted in a number of jurisdictions, that laws of general application do not prima facie constitute persecution. While the court acknowledged the existence of this rule, it was argued that this case could be distinguished. The court held that China's one child policy was not a law of general application, as it affected a small well-defined group only and not the entire population. Therefore, although ostensibly applying to the entire population, the law had a particularly negative impact on one distinct group. The court stated further, that the law itself was completely disproportionate to the aim sought. The forced sterilisation of women was, in addition, a violation of arts 3 and 5 of the Universal Declaration of Human Rights 1948, as the policy in effect amounted to cruel, inhuman and degrading treatment.[9]

In *Farah, Burdel and Burdel*[10] the Board addressed the similar question of the treatment of a divorced woman under Sharia law. The family had moved to the US from Somalia, whereupon the mother and two children, following divorce proceedings, left for Canada. Her claim was based on a number of grounds, one of which was that, as a married woman who had divorced her husband, she would, under Sharia law, lose her two children. Also she argued that, upon return to Somalia, there was a possibility that her daughter would be subjected to female genital mutilation and that the government offered no protection against these practices. The Board held that a divorced mother subjected to the

---

7 8 F 3d 636 (1993).
8 (1993) 102 DLR (4th) 214 (FCA).
9 See generally on the question of gender-related persecution, as interpreted by the Canadian authorities Immigration and Refugee Board of Canada 'Women Refugee Claimants for Asylum and Gender Related Persecution' (1993) 5 IJRL 285.
10 (1994) IRB T93-12198, T93-121199, T93-12197.

jurisdiction of Sharia law does not sufficiently enjoy her rights as a parent. Additionally, the Board held that female genital mutilation of a minor child amounted to a serious violation of human rights law, and thus also persecution, for which the Somali authorities offered no protection. While the Somali government disapproved of the practice, it was unwilling and arguably also unable to offer protection to the women involved.

Can any general themes be drawn from the case law on persecution in the various jurisdictions? Although there is a significant amount of variation, some basic issues seem settled. As to the agents of persecution, the better interpretation of international refugee law is that it does not need to be the state that is directly responsible for the persecution. Groups or individuals may persecute where the government in that state is unable or unwilling to offer protection. So although the state does not have to orchestrate the persecution, there must be some link in the form of lack of state protection. As to who specifically carries out the persecution, the case law suggests that this may emanate from: other ethnic groups in society; other members of paramilitary groupings; in the case of female genital mutilation, other members of society; and husbands in domestic violence cases.

The general position is less clear when one analyses the level of ill-treatment which will be taken to constitute persecution. Prosecution, while on the whole not to be regarded as persecution, may amount to such when the individual is being persistently targeted for a 'Convention reason'. In the US example it was shown that this might occur in cases where there is no other way in a state for an individual to vent political opposition to the government, and she is subsequently prosecuted or threatened with this action because of this. This raises the vexed question of which discriminatory laws in a state may amount to persecution. In this respect the Canadian authorities show the most advanced approach. While acknowledging that laws of general application are not usually to be regarded as amounting to persecution the courts have stated that there are some exceptions. Thus, where a law in a particular state seriously violates the rights of a defined group of individuals (thus distinguishing it from a law of general application), as in the Canadian example of Sharia law violating the rights of divorced women, then these laws may be regarded, in the appropriate circumstances, as capable of constituting persecution. The use of the proportionality test in the *Cheung* case is a particularly appropriate means to evaluate which laws in a state may be regarded as persecution. Given the nature of international affairs, the essential difficulty is ensuring that decision-makers are consistent in their approach. Possibly the most recurring criticism of asylum law is that it often simply acts in order to advance the interests of states by, for example, offering protection largely to individuals who flee unfriendly states.[11]   Although labelling the laws of other states may have political implications these may be avoided, to some extent, if a decision is anchored, like the Canadian jurisprudence discussed, in internationally recognised human rights standards. This will not answer all the difficult practical problems which arise in asylum cases but what it does permit is a more principled approach to asylum adjudication.

'Membership of a particular social group'

Not only must an individual demonstrate a well-founded fear of persecution, she must also show that this will occur for a 'Convention reason'. The reasons are: race; religion; nationality; membership of a particular social group; and political opinion. The intention here is to explore two grounds which have caused definitional problems: membership of a particular social group and political opinion.

One wonders whether those who drafted this aspect of the 1951 Convention realised the amount of time and effort that would be expended in trying to decipher its precise meaning. As the discussion on international refugee law in Chapter 2 indicated, the term 'social group' was added to the Convention at a late stage without much explanation. It has accordingly been the source of some debate.[12]   Because of its relatively open-ended nature it has attracted the hopes of those who wish to offer an inclusive vision of refugee law. The 'realists' in refugee law have tended to step in to deflate these hopes by claiming that they amount to wishful legal thinking.

---

11 See Tuitt *False Images: Law's Construction of the Refugee* (1996) pp 16-19.

12 See Haran 'Social Group for the Purpose of Asylum Claims' (1995) 9 I&NLP 64; Bamforth 'Protected Social Groups, the Refugee Convention and Judicial Review: The *Vraciu* case' [1995] PL 382; Fullerton 'A Comparative Look at Refugee Status based on Persecution Due to Membership in a Social Group' (1993) 26 Cornell Int LJ 505, 510; Graves 'From Definition to Exploration: Social Groups and Political Asylum Eligibility' (1989) 26 San Diego LR 740; Neal 'Women as a Social Group: Recognising Sex Based Persecution as Grounds for Asylum' (1988) Columbia Human Rights L Rev 1459; Gagliardi 'The Inadequacy of Cognizable Grounds of Persecution as a Criteria for According Refugee Status' (1987-88) 24 Stanford J Int L 259; Helton 'Persecution on Account of Membership of a Particular Social Group as a Basis for Refugee Status' (1983) 15 Columbia Human Rights L Rev 89.

The UNHCR has stated that it should refer to persons with 'similar habits, background or social status'.[13] The EU Joint Position provides:

'A specific social group normally comprises persons from the same background, with the same customs or the same social status, etc . . . Membership of a social group may simply be attributed to the victimized person or group by the persecutor. In some cases, the social group may not have existed previously but may be determined by the common characteristics of the victimized persons because the persecutor sees them as an obstacle to achieving his aims.'[14]

These are clearly inadequate as comprehensive definitions, but they do provide a useful starting point in charting the development of the concept in the UK. The meaning of the phrase has been addressed by the House of Lords in the *Shah/Islam* case discussed in detail in Chapter 4. As noted, the debate tends to oscillate between those who wish to see the adoption of an open approach and those who recognise that refugee law has clear limits.[15] Hathaway argues:

'The drafters of the Convention did not wish to avoid drawing distinctions among various types of putative refugees, but rather intended to establish a demarcation between those whose fear was attributable to civil or political status (refugees) and those whose concern to flee was prompted by other concerns.'[16]

In *Ochere*[17] the applicant had been an intelligence officer involved in collecting military intelligence for a previous regime in Ghana. He claimed that individuals involved in such a capacity in defeated regimes could constitute a 'social group'. The IAT expressed reluctance to give any general definition of a social group, but did state that the characteristic which defined the group must be one that an individual could not alter because it was fundamental to her individual identity or conscience. In *R v Secretary of State for the Home Department, ex p Binbasi*[18] the applicant claimed that he feared persecution because he was a homosexual. Kennedy J felt it was unnecessary to decide on the question of whether homosexuals were a 'particular social group' as there was no persecution in Cyprus against homosexuals who were 'not active'. However, he

13 UNHCR *Handbook* paras 77–79.
14 Paragraph 7.5.
15 Hathaway *The Law of Refugee Status* (1991) p 159.
16 Note 15 above.
17 [1988] Imm AR 21.
18 [1989] Imm AR 595.

acknowledged that the term would refer to groups whose common characteristics they could not change or could not be expected to change because they were fundamental to their individual identities. Reflecting an awareness of the possible extension of refugee status though the use of this category, he stated:

'In 1951 those who drafted the Convention were not seeking to guarantee all human rights. They had a more modest aim, namely to protect those who are genuinely fearful that if returned to their homeland they will be persecuted simply because of who they are or what they have done.'[19]

Despite this unwillingness to express a view it is the case that homosexuals are a 'social group' within the terms of the Convention. This position has been confirmed in the House of Lords' ruling in *Shah/Islam*.[20]

In *Secretary of State for the Home Department v Sergei Savchenkov*[1] the Court of Appeal addressed the interpretation of the phrase. The case arose from an appeal by the Home Secretary of a decision of the IAT that the respondent qualified for asylum. The respondent was one of a number of security guards at a hotel in St Petersburg. The mafia approached him and asked him to work as an informer. He refused and as a result was threatened with death. These threats were repeated on a number of occasions. A friend had already been murdered by the organisation. The issue which arose on appeal was whether he had a well-founded fear of being persecuted because of his membership in a particular social group. The IAT concluded that because of the extensive reach of the mafia in Russia, individuals who the mafia sought to recruit could be classified as a social group. Counsel for the Home Secretary, rejecting this approach, provided three types of instances where it was argued the phrase would apply:

'(1) membership of a group defined by some innate or unchangeable characteristic of its members analogous to race, religion, nationality, or political opinion, for example, their sex, linguistic background, tribe, family or class;

---

19 [1989] Imm AR 595 at 599.
20 *Islam v Secretary of State for the Home Department; R v Immigration Appeal Tribunal and Secretary of State for the Home Department, ex p Shah* [1999] 2 AC 629. See Bovey 'Out and Out: UK Immigration Law and the Homosexual' (1994) 8 I&NLP 61.
1 [1996] Imm AR 28.

(2) membership of a cohesive, homogenous group whose members are in a close voluntary association for reasons which are fundamental to their rights, for example, a trade union activist;
(3) former membership of a group covered by (2).'[2]

McCowan LJ stated that the social group for which the respondent contended in this case had no existence independent of the persecution feared. If he could claim refugee status then, he stated, any person persecuted could claim the same. He was critical of the approach adopted by the IAT, stating that a simple refusal to partake in unlawful activity could not make an individual part of a social group. Evans LJ agreed, stating that the group must exist independently and not be simply created by the persecution. Pill LJ indicated that this was not the sort of group to which the 1951 Convention was intended to apply. The law in this area has now been clarified in the House of Lords' ruling in the *Shah/Islam*.[3] This case has been examined in some depth already. The House of Lords rejected the notion of cohesiveness as determining a particular social group. While it was acknowledged that this might provide evidence for the existence of such a group, it was not limited in this way. The phrase extended to what was fairly and contextually within it and applied to any group which came within the Convention's anti-discrimination objectives. These were groups which shared a common immutable characteristic and were discriminated against in matters of fundamental human rights. A progressive approach was evident in the fact that the court ruled that women could constitute such a group where they came from societies such as Pakistan.[4] The ruling disapproved of aspects of the *Savchenkov* test. In *Ouanes v Secretary of State for the Home Department* an Algerian women, who had worked as a midwife, fled because of a fear of persecution by fundamentalists. The IAT held that Algerian midwives employed by the government in this context did constitute a particular social group. The

---

2 [1996] Imm AR 28 at 34. See also *Quijano v Secretary of State for the Home Department* [1997] Imm AR. The appellant's stepfather had refused to trade for a drugs cartel in Colombia. The Court of Appeal held that the appellant feared persecution because of his stepfather's actions and not because he came within a Convention ground.

3 [1999] 2 AC 629. See Lesley-Lloyd 'Shah/Islam: The Strangulation of Particular Social Groups' (1998) 12 I&NLP 8.

4 Lord Hoffmann, note 3 above, at 563: 'To what social group, if any, did the appellants belong? To identify a social group, one must first identify the society of which it forms a part. In this case, the society is plainly that of Pakistan. Within that society, its seems to me that women form a social group of the kind contemplated by the convention.'

Secretary of State appealed successfully against this decision to the Court of Appeal.[5]   The House of Lords' ruling in *Shah/Islam* provides welcome clarification of the meaning of the phrase. Notable in this ruling is the liberal interpretation applied.

In other jurisdictions an attempt has also been made to define a 'social group' more precisely. In the US case *Sanchez-Trujillo v INS*[6] the petitioners had fled El Salvador and claimed asylum on the basis that, as 'young urban working class males', they constituted a social group. The court developed a useful test for evaluating the cognisability of the group. Examining the UNHCR definition, the court stated that they found the definition 'unhelpful'.[7] Adopting their own approach, they concluded that the phrase:

> 'implies a collection of people closely affiliated with each other, who are actuated by some common impulse or interest. Of central concern is the existence of a voluntary associational relationship among the purported members, which imparts some common characteristic that is *fundamental to their identity*.' (My emphasis.)

Here the importance of the fundamental nature of the characteristic is emphasised. For illustrative purposes it compared this with a hypothetical statistical group, such as males over six foot. The latter group would not qualify as a 'social group'. The court stated that, here, 'young urban working class males' was much closer to their hypothetical example than the first. Such an approach is reflected in *Dilicia Reyes De Valle v INS*,[8] in which the wife of an army deserter claimed asylum on the basis that families of a deserter could constitute a 'social group'. The court rejected this argument, stating that this group of individuals did not share any common impulse or interests. In *Adebisi v INS*[9] a Nigerian citizen who had refused to participate in the hereditary traditions of his tribe claimed asylum on the grounds of membership of the tribe. On the question of 'membership of a particular social group', the court held that the problem was not his membership of the group but his refusal to participate in it. Thus, any persecution was not *because* of his membership of the tribe, rather it was the result of his refusal to join. In *Mohammed Bastanipour v INS*[10] an Iranian drugs

---

5 [1998] 1 WLR 218.
6 801 F 2d 1571 (9th Cir 1986). See *Matter of Acosta* (1985) BIA Int Dec 2986. See generally on US approach, Parish 'Membership in a Particular Social Group under the Refugee Act 1980: Social Identity and the Legal Concept of Refugee' (1992) 92 Columbia LR 923.
7 801 F 2d 1571 at 1576
8 901 F 2d 787 (9th Cir 1990).
9 952 F 2d 910 (5th Cir 1992).
10 980 F 2d 1129 (7th Cir 1992).

trafficker based his claim to asylum on the risk of persecution in Iran due to his membership of a group, in this case drug traffickers. The court stated that the intention was to offer protection to discrete, relatively homogeneous groups, who were targeted for persecution because of assumed disloyalty to a regime and not members of the 'criminal classes'.

It has already been stated that homosexuals should be considered a 'social group' for the purposes of the Convention. In this respect the US case of *Re Fidel Armando Tobosa*[11] was a landmark decision. In this case the Board held that a Cuban who feared persecution because of his homosexuality did so because of his 'membership in a particular social group'.

In the Canadian case of *Ward*, explored above, the Supreme Court provided a detailed assessment of the possible approaches to interpreting the phrase. The court stated that the limitations to the phrase could be derived from its connection to concepts within anti-discrimination law. The court stated:

> 'The meaning assigned to "particular social group" in the Act should take into account the general underlying themes of defence of human rights and anti-discrimination that form the basis for the international refugee protection initiative.'[12]

From the existing Canadian and US case law, the Supreme Court distilled a list of instances where a 'particular social group' would exist. They were:

> '1. Groups defined by an innate or unchangeable characteristic;
> 2. Groups whose members voluntarily associate for reasons so fundamental to their human dignity that they should not be forced to forsake the association and;
> 3. Groups associated by a former voluntary status unalterable due to its historical permanence.'[13]

The first basis is designed to refer to characteristics such as gender, linguistic background and sexual orientation, while the court stated that the second would include, for example, human rights activists. Applying these categories to this case, the court held that Ward could not be held to have been part of a 'particular social group'. The association of the paramilitary group, while voluntary, was not fundamental to his human dignity. Although it did possess political aims, the court stated that these aims could have been expressed in a non-violent manner. This classification is somewhat

---

11 BIA No A23 220 644 (1990).
12 (1993) 103 DLR (4th) 1 at 33.
13 (1993) 103 DLR (4th) 1 at 33–34.

more detailed and precise than that stated in *Sanchez-Trujillo* and allows for the inclusion of voluntarily associated groups.

The Supreme Court in *Ward* constructed its approach from a number of Federal Court of Appeal cases. In *Re Mayers*[14] the claimed group was Trinidadian women subject to domestic violence. The Federal Court of Appeal held that while it was not appropriate to label women as a 'social group', due to their numerical superiority, this caveat did not extend to this more specific and well defined group.[15] Thus, the court held that the decision-maker had not erred in law by finding that this could constitute a particular social group. In *Cheung v Canada (MEI)*[16] the appellant fled China because she had given birth to a second child, in violation of China's one child policy, and thus feared forced sterilisation. In finding that she was a member of a particular social group, the court stated that these women comprised a group who shared a similar social status and had certain basic characteristics in common.

'All the people coming within this group are united or identified by a purpose which is so fundamental to their human dignity that they should not be required to alter it on the basis that interference with a woman's reproductive liberty is a basic right "ranking high in our scale of values".'[17]

As in the US, the Canadian authorities have held that homosexuals constitute a 'social group' for the purposes of the Convention.[18] In particular, this has been linked to the individual's right to freedom of association as expressed in art 20 of the Universal Declaration of Human Rights.

Before concluding this examination of the case law, it is worth noting the Australian case *Morato v Minister for Immigration, Local Government and Ethnic Affairs*.[19] The applicant feared persecution upon return to Bolivia due to his high profile role as a police informant. The Federal Court of Appeal stated that the group had to demonstrate cohesiveness and homogeneity. However, in this case the applicant was a lone individual fearing persecution and could not be said to be a part of any clearly definable group. This can be contrasted with *A v Minister for Immigration and Ethnic Affairs*.[20] The claimed social group was people fleeing China's one

---

14 (1993) 97 DLR (4th) 729.
15 Cf Greatbatch 'The Gender Difference: Feminist Critiques of Refugee Discourse' (1989) 1 IJRL 518.
16 (1993) 102 DLR (4th) 214.
17 102 DLR (4th) 214 at 220.
18 *Talil Ali Said Al-Busaidy v Canada (MEI)* (1992) IRB Div No T91-04459.
19 [1992] 106 ALR 367.
20 (1997) 2 BHRC 143.

child policy who had one child and wished to have another and who were subject to forced sterilisation. The court held that they were not a social group because they were defined by the persecution and not independently of it. There was no characteristic which linked the couples and nothing external would mean they were perceived as a social group for Convention purposes.

The Canadian Immigration and Refugee Board, in a 1992 position paper,[1] recommended a test which utilises two distinct approaches. The first aspect it recommended is an examination of the existence of the internal characteristics which unite the group. These may be innate, such as gender, or, if not innate, immutable. Thus, a past aspect of a person's life, such as social position, cannot now be changed. Again, this may be a characteristic which is fundamental to a person's dignity. The second aspect of the test looks to the external perception, such as whether the group is regarded as threatening and whether it is in fact perceived to exist by external observers. This approach combines two distinct internal and external aspects.

Hathaway has attempted to provide a useful link to the human rights-based approach. He lists three types of groups which come within the phrase:

> '1. Groups defined by innate, unalterable characteristics;
> 2. Groups defined by their past temporary or voluntary status, since their history or experience is not within their current power to change;
> 3. Existing groups defined by volition, so long as the purpose of the association is so fundamental to their human dignity that they ought not to be required to abandon.'[2]

This is very similar to the test adopted in *Ward* and does provide a clearer framework than that offered by the UNHCR. Hathaway excludes groups whose characteristics are defined as capable of change, which will not require a renunciation of their basic human rights. The approach illustrated in the Canadian case law and advocated by Hathaway is useful in that it brings a measure of coherence to a difficult area. The approach attaches the interpretation to human rights standards while recognising that there are limits.

---

1 Preferred Position Paper *Membership in a Particular Social Group as a Basis for a Well Founded Fear of Persecution*, Immigration and Refugee Board, Ottawa, Canada, 1992.
2 *The Law of Refugee Status* (1991) p 161.

Political opinions

Although the politically active asylum seeker is often, in popular usage, the quintessential 'refugee', it is worth remembering that it is only one of a number of grounds for which refugee status may be granted. Note that the phrase refers only to the 'political opinions' and not to any action she had taken part in. If the persecution is directed at an individual's opinions, rather than her actions, then it will be enough to come within this ground. Hathaway has argued for the adoption of a broad characterisation of political opinion as 'an important means of maintaining the Convention's vitality in circumstances where the basis for oppression may not be readily ascertainable'.[3]

Nevertheless, if persecution is feared on this ground then one must presume that the political opinion has come to the attention of either the authorities in the state or the group carrying out the persecution.[4] The UNHCR recognises that the term presupposes that the applicant holds opinions not tolerated by the authorities, rather than simply possessing an opinion which is different from that of the government's.[5] In the majority of cases, the UNHCR states that some expression must be given to these opinions. The UNHCR states that an individual's beliefs may in many cases be so strong that they will sooner or later find expression.[6]

In *Asante* the IAT stated that the applicant did not have to possess the political opinions which were imputed to him, so long as the group carrying out the persecution believed this to be the case. In *Garces v Secretary of State for the Home Department* the appellant claimed asylum on the basis of an imputed political opinion.[7] She had witnessed the murder of a policeman in Colombia and had identified the murderer for the police. The murderer and his brother were part of a criminal gang who operated throughout the state. She had been threatened by this gang. A special adjudicator rejected her claim on the basis that it did not come within the 1951 Convention. The IAT, however, allowed the appeal on the ground that she was likely to be persecuted upon return because of imputed political opinions:

---

3 Hathaway, note 2 above, p 157.
4 UNHCR *Handbook* para 80.
5 UNHCR *Handbook* para 80.
6 UNHCR *Handbook* para 82.
7 [1999] INLR 460.

'The reason [is] that the appellant is seen to be on the side of law, order, justice and against disorder, chaos, injustice; and it is these dark forces that control government.'[8]

It is clear that some actual or perceived pattern of political activity or opinion must be established, and that this has come to the attention of the authorities. The issue of perceived political opinions which the applicant does not in fact hold can cause problems, but, as this case demonstrated, imputed political opinion is an established ground under the 1951 Convention. It has caused some notable problems for the US courts in particular. Further to this, another difficult question in these cases is whether certain political activity has been conducted deliberately to advance an asylum claim. A person may become a refugee as a result of her own actions outside of, as well as inside, her state of origin.[9] In the UK there is an evident suspicion of claims based on political activity which the individual had undertaken only upon arrival.[10] In *R v IAT, ex p B*[11] the applicant was an Iranian national with leave to enter the UK as a visitor. He applied for asylum on the ground that he feared persecution because of his political opinions. His political activities in Iran had been minimal. In the UK, however, he became the Chair of the Iranian Monarchist Society and was photographed by embassy officials attending various anti-government demonstrations. The Home Secretary refused the application, stating that the applicant's activities in the UK had been self-serving. In finding against the applicant the court stated that not all voluntary activity in the host state should be automatically disregarded in these cases, but that activity which was in all the circumstances of the case unreasonable could not be relied upon by the applicant. The court, in its judgment, advised all asylum seekers that they should ensure that, upon arrival in the UK, they do not necessarily enlarge the risk of future persecution. In *Mustapha Gilgham v IAT*[12] the applicant was a Libyan citizen who had been granted leave to enter. A request for variation of this leave was subsequently refused by the Home Secretary. The application for asylum was also refused and, after being served with

---

8 [1999] INLR 460 at 466.

9 UNHCR *Handbook* para 96.

10 See eg *Mustapha Gilgham v IAT* [1995] Imm AR 129. In this case the court held that where an applicant only engaged in political activity against the regime in his state of origin once he had come to the UK, it was open to the Home Secretary to conclude that these opinions were not genuinely held. See also *Ahmad Yavari v Secretary of State for the Home Department* [1987] Imm AR 138.

11 [1989] Imm AR 166.

12 [1995] Imm AR 129.

a notice of intention to deport, he 'went to ground'. When eventually arrested he made a second asylum application. The basis for the application was that he had joined a political organisation when he came to the UK and had taken part in various activities expressing hostility to the Libyan regime. He argued that his opposition to the government, which he had expressed within the UK, was well known to the authorities. The special adjudicator concluded that he had not been at risk when he left Libya and his activities in the UK were of a minor nature. The special adjudicator stated that, even if he was now at risk, this was attributable to his voluntary activities in the UK and, following *ex p B*, the applicant could not rely on those activities to found a claim for asylum. The Court of Appeal held that the fact that there was no evidence in existence that the applicant's activities had come to the attention of the authorities was sufficient to lead to the conclusion that there was no reasonable degree of likelihood he would be persecuted if returned to Libya. The court expressed some reservations concerning the decision in *ex p B*, but declined to state whether it was correctly decided. It did, however, hold that it was open to both the Home Secretary and the special adjudicator to conclude that, in cases where an asylum seeker does not engage in political activities against the regime until he has already decided to apply for asylum, those opinions were not genuinely held. The court was clearly concerned not to fix a rigid rule which stated that all unreasonable conduct should exclude the applicant from a positive claim to refugee status. Morritt LJ, for example, stated:

> 'I would find very great difficulty in accepting that unreasonable conduct could debar a claimant from the status of a refugee, even though, notwithstanding that unreasonable conduct, the Tribunal was satisfied that the conditions expressed in the Convention had been established.'[13]

With respect to the provisions of international refugee law, whether the activities of the individual took place at home or abroad should not necessarily disadvantage an application, although it is possibly not unreasonable for the Home Secretary to show initial suspicion, particularly where there has been no demonstrated political activity before arrival in the UK. Ultimately, however, difficult questions will arise in cases where the activity has been self-serving but the applicant still possesses a well-founded fear of persecution upon return. Therefore, it is suggested here that no matter how questionable the activities of the applicant (in terms of

---

13 [1995] Imm AR 129 at 141.

bringing her political activities to the attention of the authorities of her state of origin)[14] have been in the host state, if she demonstrates a well-founded fear of persecution for a Convention reason then the state is prohibited from returning her.[15] This position has been accepted and the Court of Appeal overruled *ex p B* in *Danian v Secretary of State for the Home Department*.[16] The appellant was involved with the Nigerian pro-democracy movement in the UK. His appeal against refusal of asylum was dismissed by a special adjudicator on the ground that his actions were calculated to enhance his claim. The IAT held that the protection of the 1951 Convention could not extend to an individual who had deliberately undertaken activities to advance his asylum claim, even if these had come to the attention of the Nigerian authorities. He successfully appealed to the Court of Appeal against this decision. The Court of Appeal ruled that those basing their claims on post-arrival activity carried out in bad faith should not be denied the protection of the 1951 Convention.[17] However, these cases merited the most rigorous scrutiny in order to ensure that the individual came within the 1951 Convention.[18] As the IAT had excluded the detailed documentary evidence from its consideration the case had to be remitted.

14 The position obviously differs in cases where the applicant has been engaged in serious political disturbances in the host state, and thus constitutes a threat to public order.
15 The response to this argument is usually framed in terms of the risk such a position may pose to immigration control, ie that a large number of individuals may deliberately set out to enhance asylum applications while in the UK. While there is some merit in this concern, even when the individual has engaged in political activity in the host state, she still has to fulfil the 1951 Convention criteria.
16 [1999] INLR 533. See also *Iftikhar Ahmed v Secretary of State for the Home Department* [2000] INLR 1. In this case the Court of Appeal held that although it might be reasonable for an asylum seeker to refrain from certain activity upon his return, if he would in fact act in a way that would result in persecution, he should be entitled to asylum. The important question, the Court of Appeal held, was whether there was a serious risk that upon return he would be persecuted for a Convention reason.
17 Brooke LJ [1999] INLR 533 at 557: 'Although his credibility is likely to be low and his claim must be rigorously scrutinised, he is still entitled to the protection of the Convention, and this country is not entitled to disregard the provisions of the Convention by which it is bound, if it should turn out that he does indeed qualify for protection against refoulement at the time his application was considered.'
18 The European Convention was also highly relevant: see Buxton LJ [1999] INLR 533 at 566: 'If there is a real risk of Mr Danian, on his return to Nigeria, being subjected to treatment that is contrary to art 3, then there is clear authority . . . that he cannot be returned there.'

In these types of cases it will be particularly useful for the asylum applicant to be able to demonstrate a link to prior consistent political activity or opinions before entry into the UK. However, the most important consideration in these cases is the risk which the individual faces upon return. If there is a real risk of sufficiently serious ill-treatment, then return should not be contemplated. In such instances the behaviour of the individual is not a material factor.

As noted, the UNHCR has stated that a person with strong political opinions will in many instances feel obliged, eventually, to give voice to these opinions upon her return to the state of origin. In *Viraj Mendis*[19] the applicant claimed to have a fear of persecution because of his well-known political beliefs, and because if returned to Sri Lanka he would be forced to speak out against the government. Balcombe LJ in the Court of Appeal questioned whether a person could claim to have a well-founded fear of persecution for reasons of political opinion on the basis that if he was returned he would speak out and offend the authorities in that state. In contrast, Staughton J refused to accept the argument that it could never be relevant to a claim to persecution on the grounds of 'political opinion':

> 'If a person has such strong convictions, whether on religious or other grounds, that he will inevitably speak out against the regime in his country of origin and will inevitably suffer persecution in consequence it may be said that he should properly be treated as a refugee. In such a case it could be questioned whether his conduct is voluntary in any real sense.'[20]

This approach, although not decisive in this case, is more in line with the purposes of refugee law. The differing approaches represent contrasting views of refugee law. Balcombe LJ might be said to have given immigration control considerations priority in his determination, while Staughton J placed greater emphasis on the importance of protecting the individual against future persecution.

Another issue which has arisen is whether the refusal to become involved with the militia in a state where there is a civil war constitutes a political opinion. In *Mohammed Hamieh v Secretary of State for the Home Department*[1] the applicant was Lebanese. He did not claim to be personally politically active, but argued that he had resisted pressure to join one of the militias then operating

19 [1989] Imm AR 6. See *Iftikhar Ahmed v Secretary of State for the Home Department* [2000] INLR 1.
20 [1989] Imm AR 6 at 22-23.
 1 [1993] Imm AR 323.

within the state. As a result of this he had been harassed by the group and his brother had been murdered. He argued that this resistance to pressure to join an organisation could amount to a political opinion. The Home Secretary rejected this, claiming that this was not a 'Convention reason' for persecution. The court, upholding the decision of the Home Secretary, stated that, given the facts of this case, it was not unreasonable for the Home Secretary to reach this conclusion. In a similar case, *ex p Hector Hernandez*,[2] the applicant, a Colombian citizen, claimed he had been obliged to supply drugs and medicines to a guerrilla group and he feared the consequences of this refusal. He had not requested the protection of the government but stated that they would have been unwilling to offer him protection. The High Court upheld the decision of the IAT to refuse leave to appeal from a negative determination of a special adjudicator. In doing so, the court agreed with the special adjudicator's conclusion that the activity of the applicant and the ill-treatment expected did not bring his application within the grounds stated in the 1951 Convention. Any ill-treatment (the court did not accept that he would be of any significant interest to the guerrilla group) which he would suffer was for the reason that he was a person who had access to drugs and not because of his political opinions. In *Quijano*[3] the applicant refused to co-operate with a drugs cartel in Colombia and had been threatened by them. The IAT held that any persecution which he would be likely to suffer would be the result of his refusal to perform a criminal act which did not amount to the expression of a political opinion.

In the US case law it has been generally accepted that such things as membership in a political organisation, or the voicing of a political opinion through membership in a political party, represent firm evidence of the existence of a political opinion. In *Ramirez-Rivars v INS*[4] the court held that even an association with a politically active family was enough to be attributed with a 'political opinion'. As with the UK cases noted above, there has been some dispute concerning the question of whether neutrality in a conflict may constitute a 'political opinion'. Over a number of years the courts had focused on the perception of the persecutor and not necessarily the individual's political beliefs. In other words, if the persecutor perceived a refusal to join an organisation

---

2   [1994] Imm AR 506.
3   (10699) IAT, reported in (1994) 8 I&NLP 99.
4   899 F 2d 864 (9th Cir 1990).

as an expression of a contrary political belief then this in itself could be regarded as a 'political opinion'. An illustration of this approach is *Bolanos-Hernandez v INS*.[5] Bolanos refused to join the guerrillas in El Salvador and feared persecution because of this refusal. Friends and relatives of his had been killed because they too had refused similar requests. The court held that this expression of neutrality could constitute a political opinion. The applicant did not have to become involved in the conflict for his actions to constitute a 'political opinion'; this was achieved by a refusal to partake.[6] Thus, neutrality in this line of cases could amount to a 'political opinion' where the persecutor perceived this to be the case. The US Supreme Court in *INS v Elias –Zacarias*,[7] however, significantly refined the test to be applied in these cases, stating that it should be focused more on the actual political opinions of the individual rather than, as they stated had been the case in the past decisions, assuming that neutrality in itself was, per se, a 'political opinion'. In that case Elias refused to join the guerrillas in Guatemala because they opposed the government, and he was afraid that due to his refusal the group might retaliate against him and his family. In contrast to the approach taken by the inferior courts, the Supreme Court actively looked for some political opinion on the part of the individual rather than solely relying on the perception of the persecutors. It was decided that his opposition had not been motivated by his political opinions and that there were explanations for his behaviour which were not political. The court stated that there was no evidence that the guerrillas had believed that his refusal was anything to do with politics. It is arguably the case that here the Supreme Court was acutely aware of the policy implications of an approach based solely on the perception of the persecutor. Applicants must show that they possess a 'political opinion' of which neutrality was a demonstration, or that the persecutors viewed this neutrality as a 'political opinion', for example, by believing that it represented support for the government. The two different approaches again indicate different attitudes towards the scope and function of refugee law. The case law of the lower courts, which tended to focus exclusively on the perception of the individual's behaviour, is based on giving prominence to the possible persecution, while 'downplaying' the role of cognisable grounds. In this conception the individual need

---

5   767 F 2d 1387 (9th Cir 1988).
6   See also *Maldonado-Cruz v INS* 883 F 2d 788 (9th Cir 1989).
7   122 S Ct 812 (1992).

not possess the opinion: for the purposes of refugee law she may be ascribed it by the group conducting the persecution. In this approach refugee law is conceived as primarily aimed at the protection of the persecuted. In the ruling of the Supreme Court, however, it was stated that such an approach is not in line with the actual requirements of the 1951 Convention. In its interpretation the existence of a political opinion is something which needs to be demonstrated independently of persecution and not derived solely from the perception of the persecutor. This approach would permit the rejection of an asylum application in cases where the applicant feared persecution but could not strictly show she had a political opinion which gave rise to this fear.

Exclusion and cessation

It is evident from the analysis thus far that refugee law has limitations. The legal definition of refugee is, for example, quite carefully circumscribed. Refugee law also provides for exclusion from refugee status.[8] Article 1F provides:

'The provisions of this Convention shall not apply to any person with respect to whom there are serious reasons for considering that:

(a) he has committed a crime against peace, a war crime, or a crime against humanity, as defined in the international instruments drawn up to make provision in respect of such crimes;
(b) he has committed a serious non-political crime outside the country of refuge prior to his admission to that country as a refugee;
(c) he has been guilty of acts contrary to the purposes and principles of the United Nations.'

Exclusion on the basis of art 1F(b) was considered by the House of Lords in *T v Immigration Officer*.[9] The applicant was an Algerian citizen who was excluded from refugee status by the special adjudicator because of his violent actions for the FIS in Algeria. The applicant admitted that he had been involved in a bomb attack on Algiers airport, which killed ten people, and he had been involved in the planning of a raid to seize arms, which led to one further death. His appeal against this decision was dismissed by the IAT and the Court of Appeal. Three of the judges ruled that, for a crime to be political, it had to be sufficiently close and directly

---

8   See UNHCR *The Exclusion Clauses: Guidelines on their Application* (1996) at para 6:
    'The logic of these exclusion clauses is that certain acts are so grave as to render the perpetrators undeserving of international protection as refugees.'
9   [1996] AC 742.

linked to the political purpose and thus not too remote from it.[10] Although there was no authority for the meaning of 'non-political crime' for Convention purposes, Lord Lloyd stated that it was common ground that it should be given the same meaning as in extradition law.[11]   Account had to be taken of the means used to achieve the political end. Important factors included whether the target was governmental or civilian and whether it was likely to cause indiscriminate killing of members of the public. In this case the attack on the airport had been indiscriminate and was bound to involve killing members of the public. The link between the crime and the political objective was thus too remote. Lord Mustill and Lord Slynn stated that acts of terrorism likely to cause indiscriminate injury to persons with no connection with the government were outside the scope of the phrase 'political crime'. They stated that the IAT had been correct to characterise these acts as terrorist offences.

In the Canadian case *Pushpanathan v Canada (Minister of Citizenship and Immigration)* the appellant was convicted for serious drug-related offences and excluded from refugee status by virtue of art 1Fc.[12] The Supreme Court, in allowing the appellant's appeal, stressed the importance of distinguishing between art 1F and art 33(2). The former was not intended to protect the host society from dangerous refugees, this purpose was fulfilled by the latter. Article 1Fc excluded those who were responsible for serious, sustained or systematic violations of fundamental human rights which amount to persecution in a non-war setting. This was not limited to those in positions of power. The Supreme Court stated that consensus in international law would be a good guide to whether acts constituted sufficiently serious and systematic violations of human rights. Where no such international consensus existed, then individuals should not be deprived of the protection

---

10   Lord Keith, Lord Browne-Wilkinson and Lord Lloyd.
11   [1996] AC 742 at 778, 786-787: 'Taking these various sources of law into account one can arrive at the following definition. A crime is a political crime for the purpose . . . of the Geneva Convention if, and only if (1) it is committed for a political purpose, that is to say, with the object of overthrowing or subverting or changing the government of a state or inducing it to change its policy; and (2) there is a sufficiently close and direct link between the crime and the alleged political purpose. In determining whether such a link exists, the court will bear in mind the means used to achieve the political end, and will have particular regard to whether the crime was aimed at a military or governmental target, on the one hand, or a civilian target on the other, and in either event whether it was likely to involve the indiscriminate killing or injuring of members of the public.'
12   [1999] INLR 36.

of the 1951 Convention. While the international community had taken measures to eradicate drugs trafficking, it was not apparent that it was a sufficiently serious and sustained violation of human rights so as to exclude individuals from the protection of the 1951 Convention. In another Canadian case, *Gil v Canada (Minister of Employment and Immigration)*,[13] the appellant was an Iranian citizen who had been involved in an anti-Khomeini group. He took part in five or six acts of bombing and arson. These resulted in injury and death to innocent bystanders. These attempts were directed at wealthy supporters of the regime and consisted of placing 'molotov cocktails' in their business premises. The issue for the Federal Court of Appeal was whether this was a 'political crime' and thus not a ground for exclusion under art 1F of the 1951 Convention. The court held that although Gil was politically motivated, there was no realistic rational connection between damaging business premises and bringing about an overthrow of the government. The means used to achieve the objective were also disproportionate to any legitimate political objective. On this the court stated that it was not merely the fact that some of the victims were innocent that was material. It was that the attacks were not carried out against armed adversaries and thus were bound to injure the innocent. In the US case *McMullen v INS* the petitioner had left the British army and joined the Provisional Irish Republican Army (PIRA).[14] As a member of this organisation he was involved in several bombings. However, he later resigned from the PIRA because of his disillusionment with its methods. He later became involved again and then subsequently fled to the US. The court held that the approach of the BIA was consistent with the 1951 Convention. It had adopted a balancing approach which looked to the proportionality of the offences and their atrocious nature. The court held that the PIRA's random acts of violence against citizens of Northern Ireland and elsewhere were not sufficiently linked to their political objective. In addition, the acts were so barbarous and disproportionate to their political objects that they were serious non-political crimes for the purposes of asylum law.

As a surrogate form of international protection it is eminently sensible to assume that, when conditions permit, return to the state of origin may be possible. Hathaway has even stated that the 1951 Convention conceives of refugee status as a 'transitory phenomenon'.[15] For the majority of refugees the principal aim is

13   (1994) 119 DLR (4th) 497
14   788 F 2d 591 (1986). See also *Quinn v Robinson* 783 F 2d 776 (1986).
15   Hathaway *The Law of Refugee Status* (1991) p 189.

to be able to return to their state of origin when the human rights situation allows. Refugee law provides in art 1C of the 1951 Convention for the cessation of refugee status in a number of cases and including when:

> '(5) He can no longer, because the circumstances in connection with which he has been recognized as a refugee have ceased to exist, continue to refuse to avail himself of the protection of the country of his nationality.'

The issue of cessation arose in *Arif v Secretary of State for the Home Department*.[16] The appellant was a national of Kashmir who had been involved with the opposition party, Azad Jammu and Kashmir People's Party (AJKPP). He was arrested, beaten and detained and fled to the UK. He was sentenced to seven years' imprisonment in his absence. During the process of seeking asylum in the UK the AJKPP came to power, leading the IAT to conclude that he would not be at risk of persecution. The Court of Appeal held that the burden of proving that the cessation clause applied fell on the Home Secretary. This would include showing that the appellant would not serve any or a significant part of his seven-year sentence. The Home Secretary had not shown this.

SAFE THIRD COUNTRIES

The 1999 Act makes specific reference to the safe third country concept. One of the arguments advanced in this work is that states have deployed a variety of concepts to achieve their objectives. One such concept, or notion, is that of safe third countries. The idea underpinning this concept is that asylum seekers should be required to seek protection in the first safe state that they reach. The asylum seeker does not simply lose the autonomy theoretically guaranteed within the citizen/state relationship when displacement occurs. Rules like this one seek to remove any element of choice that asylum seekers might exert over where they will travel to. It is as though displacement strips the asylum seeker of an autonomous existence. This international development has similarities with dispersal policies adopted within states. While the concept has solidified in the practice of states in Europe in particular, this requirement cannot be found in refugee law.

16 [1999] INLR 327.

Asylum law makes provision for the removal of asylum seekers to other states.[17] The rules distinguish between return to an EU member state under existing standing arrangements, such as the Dublin Convention 1990, and other safe third countries. The 1996 Act provided for certain conditions to be met before removal could take place. The 1999 Act removes these conditions in cases where the removal is to another EU member state. For other non-EU member states the 1999 Act recreates the effect of the 1996 Act with conditions attached to removal, including a recognition of constructive *refoulement*.[18] She cannot be returned if the government of the country she is being returned to would send her back 'otherwise than in accordance with the Refugee Convention'.[19] The rules make a clear distinction between EU member states and others, and reflect the trend of viewing other EU member states are presumptively safe for asylum purposes.

The application of the concept has been contested in the courts, with some success for asylum seekers challenging removal. The struggle over this aspect of asylum policy is illustrative of how the law and politics of asylum have decisively entered the courts. This success explains, for example, why the government has acted to remove conditions attaching to removal in some cases. The *ex p Adan* case was examined in Chapter 4 in support of the proposition that there has been increased judicial activity in asylum law generally.[20] The Court of Appeal in that case held that the Home Secretary was required to examine the practice in the third country in order to decide whether it was consistent with the true interpretation of the 1951 Convention. In stating this, a distinction was made between cases of interpretation and application. The case under examination was an interpretation case. Even where it was consistent he had to consider whether there were practical obstacles which would give rise to a real risk that the individual would be sent elsewhere contrary to the 1951 Convention. A country could not be regarded as safe if it adopted an interpretation which departed from the true meaning of the Convention. The scope of art 1A(2) of the Convention was a matter of law and the courts had made it clear that its protection covered those who

---

17 Immigration and Asylum Act 1999, ss 11 and 12. For an assessment of the compliance of the previous rules with human rights law, see Winterborne, Shah and Doebbler 'Refugees and Safe Countries of Origin: Appeals, Judicial Review and Human Rights' (1996) 10 I&NLP 123.

18 Section 12(7).

19 Section 12(7).

20 [1999] 4 All ER 774; [1999] INLR 362.

feared persecution from non-state agents. In these circumstances France and Germany had departed from the true meaning of the Convention and thus certification was unlawful.[1]

'If a signatory state were to take a position which was as a matter of law at variance with the convention's true interpretation, and act upon it, it could not be regarded as a safe third country: not merely because the "real risk" test was breached (though it certainly would be) but because in the particular case the convention was not being applied at all.'[2]

The willingness to stress the constraints of legality is illustrated in *ex p Adan* and also in cases such as *R v Secretary of State for the Home Department, ex p Gashi* where the certification was successfully challenged.[3] The appellant was an ethnic Albanian from Kosovo who had sought asylum in Germany unsuccessfully and then travelled to the UK to make another application. The Home Secretary certified that he could be returned to Germany without substantive assessment of his application. The Court of Appeal allowed his appeal, stating that the Home Secretary could not rely on a general assumption that the 1951 Convention was properly applied in Germany. This assumption could not be based on an assessment of the German jurisprudence alone. The Home Secretary had to go beyond this to explain, for example, the statistical disparity between recognition rates in Germany and the UK. In these cases the court had to subject the decision to anxious scrutiny and this involved assessing whether there was a real risk that the asylum seekers would be returned to another country contrary to the 1951 Convention.[4] It would be misleading to suggest that the courts were over anxious to intervene in these cases. For example, in the earlier case *R v Secretary of State for the Home Department, ex p Canoblat* the Court of Appeal held that the Home Secretary was entitled to reach the conclusion that France was a safe third country.[5] The applicant was a Kurd who had passed through Paris

1   This case can be contrasted with *Kerrouche v Secretary of State for the Home Department* [1997] Imm AR 610 where the argument against return was that France took a narrower view of political crime in relation to art 1F(b) of the 1951 Convention than the UK. The Court of Appeal dismissed the appeal. See also *R v Secretary of State for the Home Department, ex p Elshani and Berisha* [1999] INLR 265; *R v Secretary of State for the Home Department, ex p Iyadurai* [1998] INLR 472.
2   [1999] INLR 362 at 383.
3   [1999] INLR 276. Note that most of these cases did not involve a successful challenge to certification: see eg *R v Secretary of State for the Home Department, ex p Mbanja* [1999] INLR 390.
4   Buxton LJ [1999] INLR 276 at 299.
5   [1998] 1 All ER 161.

on her way to the UK. Her argument was that, in practice, claims for asylum were often ignored by French officials and orders for removal served contrary to proper procedures. The case highlighted the practical difficulties for an asylum seeker in seeking to challenge the certification in judicial review proceedings.

In *R v Special Adjudicator, ex p Lindsay Kandasamy*,[6] in relation to the words 'opportunity to' in the old rules[7] the court stated that it was sufficient that the applicant knew that he was no longer in the state in which he feared persecution. It was stated that a legal test was unnecessary but the court approved of the respondent's description of the present approach:

> 'a person has an opportunity to apply for asylum if he is aware that he is outside the country in which he fears persecution, he is physically able directly or indirectly to contact the authorities of the state in which he finds himself and there is no reason to believe these authorities would not receive an application.'

It is apparent that almost any form of contact with a third country will result in the likelihood of return as the concept is presently applied in the UK. In *R v Secretary of State for the Home Department, ex p Musa*[8] the applicant was a Turkish Kurd whose plane had landed in Germany on its way to the UK, and who stated that he had no knowledge of landing in Germany or of getting off the plane. The court rejected the applicant's claim on the grounds that the action of the Secretary of State could not be described as unreasonable. However, the court did demonstrate some uneasiness with the proposition that even unconscious contact with a state could constitute an 'opportunity' to seek protection.

There has clearly been a struggle waged between the courts and the government over the application of the safe third country concept. The interest of the government is to ensure that cases are rapidly dealt with. As the case law reveals, this has meant that the constraints of legality have been neglected. The approach of the Court of Appeal in *ex p Adan* illustrates the problem with any 'blanket' assumption that even EU states are safe for refugee law purposes.[9]

---

6 [1994] Imm AR 333.
7 (1991-1992) HC 251 para 180.
8 [1993] Imm AR 210.
9 [1999] 4 All ER 774.

THE INTERNAL FLIGHT ALTERNATIVE

Another concept that has been increasingly drawn upon in the UK and elsewhere is the internal flight alternative. As the Michigan Guidelines on the Internal Protection Alternative (Michigan Guidelines) state:

> 'In many jurisdictions around the world, "internal flight" or "internal relocation" rules are increasingly relied upon to deny refugee status to persons at risk of persecution for a Convention reason in part, but not all, of their country of origin.'[10]

As the Michigan Guidelines note, contemporary practice has evolved to take account of regionalised variations of risk within the asylum applicant's country of origin.[11]   While the safe third country rule can have the effect of regionalising displacement, this concept may internalise displacement. The basic idea is to encourage asylum seekers to seek protection in other parts of their state of origin where it is safe and where they can be reasonably expected to go. The problem with the application of the concept arises when it is used to deny access to refugee status determination.[12] It is instructive that Hathaway addresses what he terms 'regionalised failure to protect' within his analysis of persecution.[13]   He argues that the principle of internal protection should be restricted to:

> 'persons who can *genuinely access* domestic protection, and for whom the reality of protection is *meaningful*.'[14]

The Michigan Guidelines state:

> 'A refugee claim should not be denied on internal protection grounds unless the putative asylum state is in fact able safely and practically to return the asylum-seeker to the site of internal protection.'[15]

They further provide that, because this concept applies only following the establishment of a well-founded fear in one area of

---

10 Agreed to at the First Colloquium on Challenges in International Refugee Law, 9-11 April 1999.
11 Note 10 above, para 3.
12 UNHCR Position Paper *Relocating Internally as a Reasonable Alternative to Seeking Asylum* at para 2.
13 Hathaway *The Law of Refugee Status* (1991) p 133: 'A person cannot be said to be at risk of persecution if she can access effective protection in some part of her state of origin. Because refugee law is intended to meet the needs only of those who have no alternative to seeking international protection, primary recourse should always be to one's own state.'
14 Hathaway, note 13 above, p 134.
15 Note 10 above, para 9.

the state of origin, the burden of proof must lie with the putative asylum state.[16]

Where it is reasonable to expect an asylum applicant to seek protection in another part of her state of origin then the Home Secretary may refuse an asylum claim.[17] Prior to the 1993 Act it was not specifically mentioned in the immigration rules. Although it is given separate treatment here, the concept should be considered as an aspect of refugee status. It makes little sense to distinguish the assessment of persecution from the internal flight test. In practice this can amount to another subtle way of undermining refugee protection. The assessment of the internal flight alternative should be viewed as part of the overall claim to refugee status and the same standards applied.

In *R v Secretary of State for the Home Department, ex p Robinson* the special adjudicator refused the applicant's claim on the ground that he could safely return to Colombo in Sri Lanka, an area which was controlled by the government.[18] The special adjudicator did not expressly deal with the issue of whether it was reasonable to expect the applicant to settle in Colombo. Lord Woolf in the Court of Appeal stated:

'... if a question arises whether an applicant for asylum might reasonably live in another part of his home country where he has no present fear of persecution, the answer to this question goes directly to the issue whether he should properly be treated as a "refugee" within the meaning of the Convention . . .'[19]

Lord Woolf further stated:

'It follows that if the home State can afford what has variously been described as "a safe haven", "relocation", "internal protection", or "an internal flight alternative" where the claimant would not have a well-

---

16 Note 10 above, para 14.
17 Paragraph 343. The concept is also applied in other jurisdictions such as Canada; see eg *Thirunavukkarasu v Canada (MEI)* [1994] 109 DLR (4th) 682. A Tamil who had experienced problems with various Tamil factions in the north of the state fled to Colombo, in the South. He was arrested there and subjected to beatings by the police. The Refugee Panel had held that while he had the requisite fear in the north this was not the case with respect to the south of the country, and therefore there was an internal flight alternative (IFA). The Court of Appeal stressed that the IFA had to be realistic and accessible and that it must be reasonable to expect the asylum seeker to go there. The court held that in this instance the Panel had erred as the appellant had a well-founded fear in both the north and the south of the country. See generally Storey 'United Kingdom case law on the "Internal Flight Alternative"' (1997) 11 I&NLP 57.
18 [1997] 4 All ER 210.
19 [1997] 4 All ER 210 at 217.

founded fear of persecution for a Convention reason, then international protection is not necessary. But it must be reasonable for him to go and stay in that safe haven . . .'[20]

He further stated that in making the assessment a decision-maker had to take into account all the circumstances of the case 'against the backcloth that the issue is whether the claimant is entitled to refugee status'.[1] While the court surveyed a number of tests that could be applied, it cited Canadian authority for the test of whether it would be 'unduly harsh' to return the individual to a less hostile part of her state of origin.[2] The Court of Appeal also emphasised the usefulness of the EU Joint Position.

In *Ahmed v Secretary of State for the Home Department* the appellant was a Pakistani Ahmadi who regarded peaceful propagation of his views as indispensible activity.[3] The activity was, however, illegal in Pakistan and he had been persecuted prior to his flight. The IAT had allowed the Home Secretary's appeal on the basis that the special adjudicator had failed to consider the internal flight alternative. The Court of Appeal allowed the appellant's appeal on the basis that they thought that the special adjudicator had considered and rejected this option, given that the appellant would be persecuted wherever in Pakistan he returned to. But even if this was not the case the court held that the IAT could not, on the basis of the evidence, find that such an option was available there.

In *R v Secretary of State for the Home Department, ex p Celal Yurekli*,[4] a case decided before the 1993 Act, the court in judicial review proceedings held that it was not unreasonable for the Home Secretary to take into account that there was another part of the applicant's state of origin where it was possible for her to live. In *R v Secretary of State for the Home Department, ex p Hidir Gunes*[5] the applicant had fled from a village in Turkey to Istanbul, where he had lived peacefully for some months. The Home Secretary concluded that it was clear from his application that he could live peaceable in another part of his state of origin. Following *Yurekli*, the court held that the Home Secretary was entitled to adopt this position.

In *Secretary of State for the Home Department v Sachithananthan* the respondent, a Tamil asylum seeker, had successfully appealed

20   [1997] 4 All ER 210 at 216.
1   [1997] 4 All ER 210 at 218.
2   *Thirunavukkarasu v Minister of Employment and Immigration* (1994) 109 DLR (4th) 682. See *Karanakaran v Secretary of State for the Home Department* [2000] 3 All ER 449.
3   [2000] INLR 1.
4   [1990] Imm AR 419.
5   [1991] Imm AR 278; *R v Secretary of State for the Home Department, ex p David Vigna* [1993] Imm AR 93.

to a special adjudicator against a refusal by the Home Secretary.[6] He had fled Sri Lanka after he was arrested and detained and asked to report weekly at a Colombo police station. He had previously fled from Jaffna to Colombo to escape the military conflict there. The issue was whether his return to Colombo would be unduly harsh. The IAT held that he did not have a well-founded fear of persecution and his return would not be unduly harsh. It stated that there was no evidence that he would be subjected to extortion or that accommodation would not be available for him there. The fact that he might be arrested in some future round-ups by the security forces did not render return unduly harsh. The reasoning of the IAT was approved by the Court of Appeal in *Gnanan v Secretary of State for the Home Department*.[7] In this case, involving a Tamil asylum seeker, the IAT had appeared to state that it could not consider the cumulative effect of relevant factors when deciding on the internal flight alternative. The Court of Appeal held that cumulative factors could render return unduly harsh. However, it stated that each case should be decided on its own facts:

'What may be factors in one case will not necessarily be factors in another. Factors taken individually or cumulatively may tip the balance in one case but not necessarily do so in another.'[8]

RECOGNITION AS A REFUGEE

The law has a symbolic and instrumental importance. The legal construction of refugee status matters because of the practical consequences which follow from recognition or non-recognition. Those recognised as refugees have entitlements which do not apply to those granted complementary forms of protection. The number of those recognised as 1951 Convention refugees is relatively small, although there has been substantial fluctuation in the rates recently. For example, between January and November 1999, 43% of applicants were recognised as refugees, a marked increase on previous periods.[9] Where an individual is recognised as a refugee she is given leave to remain in the UK for a period of four years.[10] After this period of time she may claim residence in

---

6 [1999] INLR 205.
7 [1999] INLR 219.
8 Tuckey LJ [1999] INLR 219 at 225.
9 Refugee Council *In exile* (January 2000).
10 The first systematic research on the settlement of refugees in the UK is published in *The Settlement of Refugees in Britain* Home Office Research Study No 141 (1995).

the UK if she wishes. The refugee benefits from the protection provided in the 1951 Convention. All the benefits of being a national are extended to the refugee, except the right to vote, unless she is a Commonwealth citizen. Potentially, the most important benefits are the right to family reunion and the right to a Convention Travel Document which allows her to travel to other states. It is notable that the principle of family unity is not included in the Convention, although it is addressed specifically in the Final Act of the Conference, which:

> 'Recommends governments to take the necessary measures for the protection of the refugee's family, especially with a view to:
> (1) Ensuring that the unity of the refugee's family is maintained particularly in cases where the head of the family has fulfilled the necessary conditions for admission to a particular country.'

The Executive Committee of the UNHCR has also stressed that every effort should be made to reunite separated families in these circumstances and it advocates a liberal criteria when identifying which family members may join a recognised refugee.[11] The UK has traditionally approached the interpretation of the family, for the purposes of immigration law generally, in a restrictive manner. However, in cases where asylum is granted, the UK adheres to the policy of family reunification,[12] as recommended by the UNHCR.[13] Refugees experience particular problems in areas such as finding accommodation and in access to community services. In a 1995 report for the Home Office it was noted that the majority of recognised refugees (85%) resided in London.[14]

Exceptional Leave to Remain

Where an asylum applicant is not granted asylum, on the basis of failure to be recognised as a refugee, there is still the possibility that the Home Secretary may decide to grant Exceptional Leave to Remain (ELR). The existence of other forms of protection highlights why formal recognition matters for the refugee, for often complementary forms of protection are less secure than 1951 Convention refugee status. In *ex p Verich Ramarajah*[15] the court held

---

11 Conclusion No 24 (XXXII) *Family Reunion* (1981). See also Council of Europe, Committee of Ministers, Recommendation No 23 (99), 15 December 1999.
12 HC Hansard Vol 34 col 304, 20 December 1982.
13 UNHCR *Handbook* para 183.
14 Home Office Research Study, note 10 above, pp 61-76. See also Home Office *A Consultation Paper on the Integration of Recognised Refugees in the UK* (October 1999).
15 [1994] Imm AR 472; *Laftaly* (9661) IAT, (1993) 7 I&NLP 106.

that, for the purposes of seeking judicial review, there was a material difference between the grant of asylum and ELR. This form of protection is a common feature of a number of European asylum determination systems. It is generally regarded as an appropriate response in situations where an individual does not fulfil the Convention definition, but where return would be inadvisable on more general humanitarian grounds. However, it must be noted that the Home Secretary has traditionally refused to elaborate upon the specific grounds on which it is granted.[16] In figures published by the UNHCR in October 1999, other humanitarian forms of protection were clearly a dominant factor in the EU generally.[17]

If ELR is granted, then the individual is given leave to remain in the UK for one year.[18] At the end of the first year the individual re-applies and any further leave to remain is for a period of three years, following which she may apply for a further three-year extension. After this period of time, seven years in total, indefinite leave to remain in the UK may be granted. Dependants of those granted ELR have no right to enter the UK to join that person.[19] A period of four years must elapse before this is permitted, although this requirement may be waived in exceptional cases. In *R v Home Secretary, ex p Feyzullah Muslu*[20] the applicant, who had been granted ELR, challenged in judicial review proceedings the Home Secretary's refusal to allow his dependants to enter the UK. The court stated that they could not intervene in such cases where the policy of the Home Secretary had been publicly announced and there was no evidence in this case to show that this policy was unreasonable.

REFUGEES, ASYLUM SEEKERS AND THE STRUGGLE FOR HUMAN RIGHTS

The Human Rights Act 1998 will have a significant impact on asylum law. When it enters into force all public authorities will be required to act compatibly with the selected provisions of the European Convention on Human Rights.[1] The Immigration and Asylum Act 1999 contains direct reference to the 1998 Act. For

16 HC Hansard Vol 225 col 435, 24 May 1993.
17 UNHCR *Trends in Asylum Applications, Refugee Status Determination and Admission in the European Union 1989 – September 1999* (October 1999).
18 HC Hansard Vol 209 col 521, 17 June 1992; HC Hansard Vol 138 col 424, 28 July 1988.
19 *Somasundaram v ECO, Colombo* [1990] Imm AR 16.
20 [1993] Imm AR 151.
 1 See Wadham and Mountfield *Blackstone's Guide to the Human Rights Act 1998* (1999); Lester and Pannick (eds) *Human Rights Law and Practice* (1999).

example, a person may appeal to a special adjudicator on the ground that an authority, acting under immigration legislation, has breached her human rights.[2] Although the Human Rights Act 1998 is an ordinary statute, it is evident that it will assume the role of a special constitutional measure. It has generated a substantial amount of interest and will lend further weight to the attempt to 'take rights seriously' in the UK. It will alter the nature of the legal conversation about human rights in a fundamental way. Whether it will have a significant impact on the British constitution is another matter. Domestic courts are under an obligation to take the Convention jurisprudence into account.[3] The interpretative obligation may encourage the development of 'Strasbourg-style reasoning' in domestic courts. The 'democratic necessity' test will introduce its own problems and the courts will have to engage, in a coherent way, with the balancing processes that this will require. On the substantive Convention rights, it is likely that arts 3 and 8 will figure prominently in asylum and immigration cases. Before examining the content of the rights, this section explores the politics of human rights in the UK and how this impacts upon the legal protection of asylum seekers.

The politics of human rights law

The development of human rights law coincides with attempts at democratic renewal in the UK. There is heightened interest in forms of deliberative democracy and the concept of citizenship. This renewed concern with deliberative democracy occurs at a time when rights-talk now governs significant strands of legal scholarship. Yet for those interested in how this impacts on asylum law it is unclear precisely how democratic and human rights theory would deal adequately with the issue. For the asylum seeker in practice lies on the intersection of a politics of citizenship and a politics of human rights. She does not 'belong' in a strong enough sense for the purpose of citizenship, but she is a person within the jurisdiction of another state for the purpose of rights discourse. Communitarian discourse, with its emphasis on the responsibilities as well as the rights of citizenship, can function in exclusionary ways. This politics can promote the drawing of distinctions based upon status and thus departs from the postnationalism of human rights discourse. It is easy to dismiss this as the narrow exception to the rule, and regard it as a subject that tells us little or nothing

2   Section 65.
3   Section 2.

about mainstream legal debates. This view is profoundly mistaken. For the asylum seeker occupies that social and legal space between a concept of citizenship that must, if it is to be meaningful, draw a line between 'us' and 'them' and human rights discourse which transcends the local context to an understanding of entitlements that attach to personhood. The problems faced in trying to 'fit' the experiences of the refugee and asylum seeker within mainstream debates in public law can be viewed as part of the traditional difficulty of addressing 'peripheral peoples'.[4] It remains surprising that so much talk about constitutionalism and human rights, at whatever level, continues with little or no reference to who is being talked about. There is a tendency to assume that boundaries are drawn and known, or that the matter of making distinctions is something best not discussed. For if the legitimacy of legality rests, as many now argue, in the democratic process, then some analysis of the exercise in boundary drawing is required. What this chapter is concerned with are the marginalised groups rendered invisible by many standard accounts of law. If the process of drawing boundaries, and making distinctions, does underpin any discussion of legal and democratic theory, then it has an importance that in practice is often neglected. This is not to say that political theorists are unaware of the problem. There are numerous examples of attempts to rethink citizenship, membership and belonging in post-conventional and multicultural societies. Participation is widely believed to be the value that moves the focus away from the *ethnos* to the *demos*. In fact it is a value that is rapidly gaining the status of a universal good. Much work has been undertaken to explore how migrant and ethnic minority communities can participate more fully in the political community. Underpinning this emphasis on participation is the belief that the legitimacy of the process of policy formation rests in consulting with affected groups. Walzer does, for example, recognise the importance of boundary drawing when he notes that distributive justice presupposes a bounded world and the fact that choices about membership structure all other distributive choices.[5] The distributive

---

4   See Formet 'Peripheral Peoples and Narrative Identities: Arendtian Reflections on Late Modernity' in Benhabib (ed) *Democracy and Difference: Contesting the Boundaries of the Political* (1996) pp 314-330.

5   Walzer *Spheres of Justice: A Defence of Pluralism and Equality* (1983) p 31. Cf Carens 'Aliens and Citizens: The Case for Open Borders' in Kymlicka (ed) *The Rights of Minority Cultures* (1995) pp 331-349. He argues that borders should generally be open and he claims that his argument is strongest when applied to the migration of people from the 'third world' to the 'first world'. He does not believe that Walzer's theory provides adequate support for the right to exclude. For Carens, border controls are like feudal barriers to mobility which protect unjust privilege. His argument is that open borders would affirm, rather than undermine, the liberal character of community.

state thus presupposes the existence of membership rules within a political community. The problem which theorists have grappled with is an ethically defensible conception of membership. If the bounds of the political community cannot be ethically justified, what impact, if any, does this have on our understanding of democratic citizenship and human rights law? This issue is conveniently neglected in many standard accounts of law, but there is a real problem here for citizens who are disturbed by the ethically questionable nature of the rules which structure exclusion and inclusion. The problem for liberal constitutionalism is that universal claims are often made for the values reflected in the structures of individual states. In seeking entry an asylum seeker is thus requesting that a state lives up to its own basic values in practice. In this understanding restrictive regulation of borders is part of the modern anxiety about mobility which stems from the desire to protect privilege.[6] The values which underpin modern constitutionalism thus undermine arguments for restrictive border controls.

Human rights discourse can be tied to the constitutional traditions of a particular state but tends to point beyond the local context. Rules with a human rights content usually protect both members and non-members, or at least provide the means for contesting the ill-treatment of non-members. While this no doubt can be reconciled at the conceptual level, the tension which this reflects is inscribed in practical legal discourse. The point is important, for it can help us understand why some strategies of legal argumentation prove more fruitful than others in the asylum debate.

Models of deliberative democracy are useful in this process. In particular, by defending decentralised models of democracy they more accurately capture the fluidity of the public sphere. In addition, this work also has considerable explanatory power in relation to human rights discourse. Rights are not to be thought of as either citizens' rights or universal rights. 'Empowering rights' are in fact integral to the very possibility of democracy.[7] Political communities are not hermetically sealed geographical entities but 'multiple overlapping networks of interaction'.[8] The emphasis on networks of interaction, and the intersecting nature of modern legal orders, is a productive way of grasping the modern reality of human rights struggles. The focus on legal and

6   Carens, note 5 above.
7   Held *Democracy and the Global Order: From the Modern State to Cosmopolitan Governance* (1995) pp 223-224
8   Held, note 7 above, p 225.

other discourses assists in locating the strategies of refugee networks as they increasingly draw upon different forms of legal argumentation. In this way they point towards the systems and networks which intersect and collide. The contours of this essentially cosmopolitan understanding of law and democracy are evident. This is a framework which places weight on an activist understanding of democracy and the multiple public spheres that exist within a democratic political community. The decentralised understanding of the state and society which it promotes has implications which go beyond the nation-state.

Much legal scholarship in public law still relies on outdated assumptions about the politics of membership and belonging. There are understandable reasons for this. For when some of the orthodox positions are probed in any depth, their explanatory power can be found wanting. To these scholars the mythical nature of the legal construction of membership is thus useful and best left as it is. The suggestion here is that this is an unwise strategy. If the political dimensions of human rights discourse are not confronted, then we lose the frameworks within which legal argumentation takes place. We therefore lose a valuable insight into what is occurring in this legal sphere.

Complementing protection

Refugee lawyers have struggled for some time with the inherent and the inherited limitations and weaknesses of the 1951 Convention and its 1967 Protocol. The most well-established shortcomings are claimed to be: the limited scope of the definition; the exceptions (even to the principle of *non-refoulement*);[9] the art 1 exclusion clauses;[10] and the lack of procedural standards, as well as the absence of an authoritative international supervisory

---

9 Article 33(2) provides: 'The benefit of the present provision may not, however, be claimed by a refugee whom there are reasonable grounds for regarding as a danger to the security of the country in which he is, or who, having been convicted by a final judgment of a particularly serious crime, constitutes a danger to the community of that country.' See also art 32(1). Cf UN Convention Against Torture and Other Cruel, Inhuman or Degrading Treatment or Punishment 1984, art 3(1): 'No State Party shall expel, return (*refouler*) or extradite a person to another State where there are substantial grounds for believing that he would be in danger of being subjected to torture.'

10 Article 1(F).

mechanism.[11]   Human rights law has, however, always had the potential to remedy the deficiencies of refugee law.[212] Developments in international human rights law have increasingly come to supplement refugee protection in a most useful way.   While a teleological approach to the interpretation of the 1951 Convention is recommended, as one way to confront its limitations,[13] it is clear

11 The United Nations High Commission for Refugees (UNHCR) assumes the function of *international protection*, as well as seeking permanent solutions, see Statute of the Office of the High Commissioner for Refugees 1950, Annex UNGA Res 428 (V), 14 December 1950. '8. The High Commissioner shall provide for the protection of refugees falling under the competence of his Office by: (a) Promoting the conclusion and ratification of international conventions for the protection of refugees, *supervising their application and proposing amendments thereto . . .*' (My emphasis.) See also the 1951 Convention, art 35(1) and (2). See Anon 'The UNHCR Note on International Protection You Won't See' (1997) 9 IJRL 267, 267-268: 'In order to reinvigorate its mandate, UNHCR should consider refocusing its efforts on States of asylum, rather than States of origin.'

12 See Goodwin-Gill 'Who to Protect, How..., and the Future?' (1997) 9 IJRL 1, 6-7; Hathaway and Dent *Refugee Rights: Report on a Comparative Survey* (1995) p 45.

13 Cf Fitzpatrick 'Revitalising the 1951 Refugee Convention' (1996) 9 Harv Human Rights J 230, 231, mounting a strong defence of the 1951 Convention while recognising its weaknesses. 'The end of the Cold War has done less to alter the nature of refugee flows than to transform the political context within which the Convention is applied. A crisis exists not because the Convention fails to meet the needs of asylum-seekers, but because it meets them so well as to impose burdens that are no longer politically tolerable to the State parties involved.' Fitzpatrick is right to caution against the possibility of undermining refugee law's established protections. In the absence of an authoritative supervisory mechanism, this body of law is always open to abuse by states which adopt excessively restrictive interpretations of its provisions. Cf Hathaway *The Law of Refugee Status* (1991) p 232: 'The first purpose of this book has been to suggest ways in which a philosophy of humane protection can reasonably be accommodated within the framework as adopted.' The author has argued elsewhere for a recognition of the importance of interpretative strategies which would help to counter these restrictive trends and create a more inclusive approach to the application of refugee law: see Harvey 'Restructuring Asylum: Recent Trends in UK Asylum Law and Policy' (1997) 9 IJRL 60. This is not, however, an argument for an inappropriately expansive conception of judicial power. The implications of the theoretical distinction between norms, principles and values still must be accepted. In addition, interpretations elaborated by the courts, which may well emphasise a humane approach to the interpretation of refugee law, must find their way into real institutional practices. *It is perhaps one of the principal lessons of the twentieth century that the most worthy theories and objectives may be subverted by either an absence of institutional imagination or institutional cultures and practices which actively undermine stated ideals.* See Unger *What Should Legal Analysis Become?* (1996); Unger 'Legal Analysis as Institutional Imagination' (1996) 59 MLR 1, 23: 'Our interests and our ideals remain wedded to the cross of our arrangements. We cannot realise our interests and ideals more fully, nor redefine them more deeply, until we have learned to remake and to reimagine our arrangements more freely. We must win it in the here and now of legal detail, economic constraint, and deadening preconception.' Unger's emphasis on the importance of institutional imagination, *as well as* effective rights protection, is certainly relevant to current debates in refugee and asylum law. For criticism of his position, see Christodoulidis 'The Inertia of Institutional Imagination: A Reply to Roberto Unger' (1996) 59 MLR 377.

that links to other areas of international human rights law are essential to the future development of the protection of forced migrants.[14] The European Convention on Human Rights is proving to be a valuable protection for asylum seekers.

Given that many European states have often quite elaborate status determination systems, it is important to explore the role of the Convention system as a indirect supervisory mechanism in this area, and ask questions about its appropriateness for this task as well as considering the impact it will have on domestic law and practice.[15] How, for example, may the Convention most effectively advance protection goals in the UK? It would be misleading to suggest that it is only after the Human Rights Act 1998 enters into force that the Convention will have an impact in the UK. As a result of, for example, the *Chahal* case, domestic law and practice was altered.[16] The Convention has already had an impact on law and practice. The argument here is that this impact is likely to be more significant in the future.

Beyond refugee law

The Convention contains several provisions which are of direct relevance to refugees and asylum seekers. However, it is perhaps art 3 which offers the most important guarantee. Central to any effective protection regime is the guarantee against return to face sufficiently serious human rights violations. In international refugee law this is reflected in the fundamental nature of the norm of *non-refoulement*. As is well known, the European Convention includes no direct reference to the right to seek asylum.[17] The European Court of Human Rights has consistently stated that, as a matter of well established international law, and subject to their obligations under the Convention, states have the right to control the entry, residence and expulsion of aliens. In line with its dynamic approach to the interpretation of Convention rights, the court has, however, extended the scope of art 3 to include the protection of those who are to be extradited, expelled or removed.

14 Cf Hathaway 'Reconceiving Refugee Law as Human Rights Protection' in Mahoney and Mahoney (eds) *Human Rights in the Twenty-First Century* (1993) p 659.
15 See Goodwin-Gill 'Who to Protect, How . . . , and the Future?' (1997) 9 IJRL 1, 7, in relation to the development of common approaches in Europe, he makes the argument for a 'coherent model of due process that national systems strive to emulate and by which their success in progressing towards or achieving internationally required results can be measured and accounted.'
16 See Special Immigration Appeals Commission Act 1997.
17 Cf Universal Declaration of Human Rights 1948, art 14(1).

The legal position is that responsibility is engaged where '*substantial grounds* are shown for believing [that an individual] will face a real risk of being subjected to treatment contrary to art 3 if removed to another country'.[18] The post-*Soering*[19] jurisprudence of the court has seen the steady clarification of its position in relation to these art 3 cases.[20] What is apparent from the outset is that the court, following the long-standing approach of the commission, has indirectly fostered the protection of asylum seekers, notwithstanding the absence of any reference to this group in the European Convention. The willingness to adopt a dynamic interpretation of art 3, to ensure that it is both practical and effective, has resulted in an expansive approach to the provision. However, there are important differences between the application of the European Convention and refugee law which should not be discounted.

Treatment must reach a minimum level of severity before it will come within art 3. The minimum level is relative, depending on a number of factors such as: the duration of the treatment; its physical or mental effects; and in some instances the sex, age and state of health of the individual.[1] While the fact of expulsion itself

18 *Soering v UK*, judgment of 7 July 1989, Series A/161, (1989) 11 EHRR 439; *Cruz Varas v Sweden*, judgment of 20 March 1991, Series A/201, (1991) 14 EHRR 1; *Vilvarajah v the UK*, judgment of 30 October 1991, Series A/215, (1991) 14 EHRR 248

19 On this case see Schabas '*Soering's* Legacy: The Human Rights Committee and the Judicial Committee of the Privy Council Take a Walk Down Death Row' (1994) 43 ICLQ 913; O'Shea 'Expanding Judicial Scrutiny of Human Rights in Extradition Cases After *Soering*' (1992) 17 Yale J Int L 85; Lillich 'Notes and Comments: the *Soering* case' (1991) 85 Am J Int L 128; Van Den Wyngaert 'Applying the European Convention on Human Rights to Extradition: Opening Pandora's Box?' (1991) 39 ICLQ 757; Steinhardt 'Recent Developments in the *Soering* Litigation' (1990) 11 Human Rights LJ 453.

20 Although this chapter focuses on an analysis of the jurisprudence of the court and its role, as is well known, the commission has considered a large number of applications in this area and its decisions provide valuable guidance as to the scope of, inter alia, art 3: see eg *AG v Sweden No 27776/95*, (1995) 83 DR 101; *Lwanga and Sempungo v Sweden No 27249/95*, (1995) 83 DR 91; *H v Sweden No 22408/23*, (1994) 79 DR 85; *LI v Sweden No 21808/93*, (1993) 75 DR 264; *Voufovitch v Sweden No 19373/92*, (1993) 74 DR 199; *S, M and MT v Austria No 19066/91*, (1993) 74 DR 179; *L v France No 18807/91*, (1993) 74 DR 162; *A v France No 17262/90*, (1991) 68 DR 319; *Y v the Netherlands No 16531/90*, 68 DR 299 (1991); *A and FBK v Turkey No 14401/88*, (1991) 68 DR 188. These are only some examples of the vast number of applications dealt with by the commission. It is noteworthy that in a number of cases the application is withdrawn before a decision as to admissibility because an informal agreement is reached, demonstrating the practical impact which an application may have: see Harris, O'Boyle and Warbrick *Law of the European Convention on Human Rights* (1995) p 74. Cf *DR v France No 22903/93*, (1994) 76 DR 174; *D (No 2) v Sweden (No 21669/93)* (1993) 75 DR 257.

1 *Ireland* v *UK*, judgment of 18 January 1978, Series A/25; (1978) 2 EHRR 25, para 162.

may give rise to an issue under art 3, the principal focus in asylum cases is on the ill-treatment which the individual expects to suffer upon return to another state.

There are a number of straightforward differences between the coverage of the 1951 Convention and art 3 of the European Convention. The 1951 Convention permits a number of exceptions, even to the principle of *non-refoulement*.[2] While these exceptions should be interpreted in a restrictive manner, they exist in the text and thus place interpretative limits on it. Such exceptions are not to be found in art 3 of the European Convention.[3] The court has consistently stressed the absolute nature of this Convention provision. In other words, the guarantee permits of no exceptions[4] which relate to, for example, the behaviour of the individual.[5] The fact that no derogation is permitted from this Convention provision,[6] and that it is expressed in unqualified terms,[7] reflects the fundamental nature of this basic right.

In *Chahal* v *UK* the absolute nature of art 3 was challenged before the court by the UK.[8] The judgment provides valuable clarification of the present state of the law. *Chahal* is the first case where the court has found (following the commission) that art 3 would be breached in the asylum context. As to the facts, Chahal had been involved in political activities in the UK connected with the struggle for political autonomy for Punjab. He was charged and convicted of a number of offences. These convictions were later quashed by the Court of Appeal. Subsequently, under the provisions of the Immigration Act 1971,[9] his deportation was

---

2   Article 33(2).
3   Cf Council of Europe, Committee of Ministers, *Asylum to Persons in Danger of Persecution*, Res (67) 14, 29 June 1967, paras 2 and 3.
4   See *Tomasi v France*, judgment of 27 August 1992, Series A/241, (1992) 15 EHRR 1. The French government argued that account should have been taken, inter alia, of the fact that the applicant was suspected of participating in a terrorist attack. The court rejected this argument stating that the need to fight crime could not result in limitations to the protection of the physical integrity of the individual (para 115). Cf *Aksoy v Turkey*, judgment of 18 December 1996, (1996) 23 EHRR 553, para 62: 'Even in the most difficult of circumstances, such as the fight against organised terrorism and crime, the Convention prohibits in absolute terms torture or inhuman or degrading treatment or punishment.' See generally Warbrick 'The European Convention on Human Rights and the Prevention of Terrorism' (1983) 32 ICLQ 82.
5   *Ireland v UK*, para 163.
6   Article 15(2).
7   Harris, O'Boyle and Warbrick *Law of the European Convention on Human Rights* (1995) p 55.
8   Judgment of 15 November 1996, (1996) 23 EHRR 413. For extracts of the judgment see (1997) 9 IJRL 86.
9   Section 3(5)(b).

sought by the Home Secretary, on grounds of national security, and other political reasons, relating to the fight against international terrorism. He was detained in August 1990, and during this time he sought asylum. His claim was refused by the Home Secretary. He successfully challenged this refusal in judicial review proceedings.[10] However, a fresh refusal of asylum was eventually upheld by the Court of Appeal.[11] During his period in detention he made an application to the commission, claiming that a number of Convention rights had been violated.[12] One of the issues which arose in the case – and around which some uncertainty seems to have arisen – was whether national security considerations, and the threat posed by the individual, should play any part in an assessment of risk under art 3. In seeking to support the argument that this should be a material consideration, the UK relied on a statement by the court in *Soering*, where reference was made to the importance of the institution of extradition, and the fact that a fair balance was inherent in the whole of the Convention.[13] The UK cited the exceptions contained in arts 32 and 33 of the 1951 Convention, and maintained that the right of an alien to claim asylum was subject to such limitations. Alternatively, it stated that the threat posed by the individual to national security should at least be a matter which could be weighed in the balance in considering the risk of ill-treatment.

Following its well-established and consistent position on the absolute nature of art 3, the court did not accept this argument. It stated that it should not be inferred from para 89 of its *Soering* judgment that a balancing exercise was required.[14] The prohibition in art 3 was absolute, irrespective of the individual's conduct.[15] The rejection of the UK's argument provides welcome confirmation of the absolute nature of art 3. It also sweeps away any lingering confusion which may have followed some of its statements in the *Soering* case. When assessing the risk of ill-treatment, there is no

10 *R v Secretary of State for the Home Department, ex p Chahal* [1996] Imm AR 205, unreported).
11 *R v Secretary of State for the Home Department, ex p Chahal* [1995] 1 All ER 658, [1995] 1 WLR 526, [1994] Imm AR 107.
12 More specifically that his deportation to India would expose him to a real risk of torture or inhuman or degrading treatment in violation of art 3, that his detention had violated art 5(1) and (4), and that because of the national security element, and contrary to art 13, he had no effective remedy. All the applicants alleged that the decision to deport the first applicant would violate art 8.
13 *Soering v UK* (1989) 11 EHRR 439, paras 88 and 89.
14 Paragraph 81.
15 Paragraph 79.

room for an implied limitation to this right, or the striking of a balance between this risk and national security considerations.[16] As the court recognised, the result is that art 3 is a guarantee which is of wider scope than both arts 32 and 33 of the 1951 Convention. It is worth considering whether the drafters of the European Convention could have contemplated that it would eventually provide protection of wider scope than the subject-specific 1951 Convention. This demonstrates the significance of the dynamic approach to the interpretation of the European Convention adopted by the court. It also highlights problems with the present scope of refugee law. The exceptions which are contained in the 1951 Convention make a clear distinction between the 'deserving' and the 'undeserving' refugee.[17] Human rights lawyers are not comfortable with this distinction, tending instead to concentrate on personhood as the absolute guide to rights entitlements.

While issues of balance are appropriate in considering the weight to be attached to other rights, this is not the case in relation to *non-refoulement*. Others have recognised that refugee law has serious limitations if viewed from the perspective of human rights law.[18] These limitations must, however, be contextualised. The standard is higher than usually applied in 1951 Convention cases and the European Convention is not a status-granting mechanism. Refugee law remains relevant.

---

16 Paragraphs 80 and 81.

17 Cf Tuitt *False Images: Law's Construction of the Refugee* (1996) p 7: 'The main argument in this chapter is that the overriding aim of refugee law was at its inception and continues to be the reduction of the external costs of refugee-producing phenomena. Contrary to popular belief, refugee law is not motivated by exclusively humanitarian concerns - indeed, if the concerns of the law are humanitarian this is only marginally and incidentally so.' See also Tuitt 'Defining the Refugee by Race: The European Response to "New" Asylum-seekers' in Ireland and Laleng (eds) *The Critical Lawyers' Handbook 2* (1997) p 96; Tuitt 'Racist Authorization, Interpretive Law and the Changing Character of the Refugee' in Fitzpatrick (ed) *Nationalism, Racism and the Rule of Law* (1995) p 45. Arguments such as this often attract criticism from a hermeneutic position, or more plainly from those who draw a sharp distinction between the participant and the external perspective when it comes to the interpretation of a social practice: see eg Dworkin *Law's Empire* (1986) pp 76-86. It is suggested here, however, that these perspectives do not stand in opposition to one another, but are in fact relational. Both are partial perspectives which cannot on their own provide a comprehensive, or sufficient, critical perspective on law and policy. Central to the critical project is the ability to adopt different perspectives and thus to map the immanent tensions between them. Therefore, both internal and external perspectives are valuable but partial, if each is taken as an exclusive guide to critical analysis.

18 See eg Hathaway 'A Reconsideration of the Underlying Premise of Refugee Law' (1990) 31 Harv Int LJ 129.

It is noteworthy that in the joint, partly dissenting, opinion of seven of the judges,[19] it was stated that in its extra-territorial application the state should be permitted to strike a fair balance between the threat to its national security and the potential ill-treatment of the individual. In the opinion of these members of the court there was a material difference between ill-treatment which took place within the jurisdiction of the host state, and that which occurs in the state of origin. In other words, expulsion cases should be distinguished for the purposes of art 3 because of the extra-territorial aspect. If one examines other cases where the absolute nature of art 3 has been the subject of a challenge, such as *Tomasi*,[20] the ill-treatment occurred within the territory of the state. Should the fact that the ill-treatment will occur in another state be a material factor when assessing the risk under art 3? It is evident that some extremely difficult issues of responsibility are raised in the post-*Soering* jurisprudence. In its progressive development of art 3 in these cases it is apparent that the court is operating at the boundaries of this Convention provision, and thus will often attract the criticism that its dynamic interpretation has gone too far. However, while one can understand the problems experienced by states in these situations,[1] it is still difficult to agree with this dissent. The adoption of this 'bifurcated approach' to the interpretation of art 3 would erode the absolute nature of the prohibition in an unacceptable way. States should not be permitted to indulge in such 'balancing exercises' when the right is as fundamental as that contained in art 3. This reasoning is equally applicable to expulsion cases. The Convention regime can therefore perform a useful function in ensuring that core protection needs are respected even when national security considerations arise.

The issue arose again in *Ahmed v Austria*.[2] The applicant was a Somali citizen who arrived in Austria in October 1990. He applied for refugee status in November 1990, and was eventually granted it in May 1992. His family had been subject to persecution on account of their suspected involvement with the United Somali Congress (USC), and as a result he fled because of his fear of possible arrest and execution. In 1994 the Federal Refugee Office ordered the forfeiture of the applicant's refugee status after he had

---

19 Judges Golcuklu, Matscher, Freeland, Bakam, Gotchev, Bonnici and Levits.
20 (1992) 15 EHRR 1.
 1 One central aspect of establishing a human rights regime is the fact that when substantive norms are enumerated, sacrifices must be made by states with respect to preferred policy positions.
 2 (71/1995/577/663) judgment of 17 December 1996.

been sentenced to two and a half years' imprisonment for attempted robbery. After a successful appeal his expulsion was eventually stayed in November 1995 for a renewable period of one year. In December 1994 Ahmed had applied to the commission alleging that his expulsion would be contrary to art 3. The commission expressed the unanimous opinion that there would be a violation of art 3 if the applicant were to be deported to Somalia.

Both the court and the commission rightly attached particular weight to the fact that he had been granted refugee status, and that he lost this status solely because of his criminal convictions. In assessing the risk the court noted (on the basis of the finding of fact contained in the commission's report[3]) that the situation in Somalia had hardly changed at all since 1992, and that there was no indication that the dangers faced by the applicant had ceased to exist, or that any public authority would be able to offer him protection.[4] The country remained in a state of civil war.[5] Before the court the Austrian government did not contest the applicant's submission that the position had not improved. Taking these factors into account, the court found that there would be a violation of art 3 if the applicant were to be expelled. In its judgment the court stated that this conclusion was not invalidated by the applicant's criminal record, or the absence of a state authority in Somalia.[6] While this provides another example of the court's willingness to uphold the absolute nature of art 3, it also supports the proposition that the ill-treatment need not emanate from a state authority.[7] The ill-treatment which Ahmed feared arose as a consequence of civil war and the actions of hostile militias. This judgment will hopefully dispel the mistaken belief that simply because a civil war exists an individual should not qualify for protection.

---

3   The Commission was particularly influenced by information requested from UNHCR on the situation in Somalia: Commission Report, para 67.
4   Paragraph 44.
5   Paragraph 44.
6   Paragraph 46. Note the following statement by the Commission (para 68): 'The position of the Austrian authorities that there is no substantial risk for the applicant since the State authority had ceased to exist in Somalia cannot be accepted. *It is sufficient that those who hold substantial power within the State, even though they are not the Government, threaten the life and security of the applicant.* That is clearly the position in the present case given the powerful position of General Aideed.' (My emphasis.)
7   This is the well-established position in refugee law (despite the practice adopted in some jurisdictions): see UNHCR *Handbook* para 65; Goodwin-Gill *The Refugee in International Law* (2nd edn, 1996) pp 70-73.

Although not specifically concerned with the issue of asylum, the judgment of the court in *D v UK*[8] provides further evidence to support the absolute nature of art 3 in this general context. The case also illustrates how a more expansive approach to art 3 could be developed by domestic courts in the UK. As a preliminary point it is worth noting the court's statement that the developed jurisprudence under art 3 applied to physical presence in the state. It was irrelevant to the assessment of the art 3 claim that the applicant never entered the UK in the technical sense. His physical presence meant that he was in the jurisdiction of the state for the purpose of art 1.[9] The applicant was in the advanced stages of a terminal and incurable illness. However, his removal was sought following imprisonment for drug offences. Again, the court stated that art 3 was absolute and therefore applied irrespective of the behaviour of the individual. In the exceptional circumstances of the case, the court unanimously held that the decision to remove the applicant, if implemented, would violate art 3. A material factor was that he was to be returned to St Kitts, where the medical facilities to deal with this illness were inadequate. This raises the issue of violations of economic and social rights giving rise to an issue under art 3.

In *HLR v France*[10] the issue of responsibility for the ill-treatment and the applicability of art 3 was again addressed by the court. In this case the applicant was convicted of an offence under the misuse of drugs legislation and sentenced to five years' imprisonment. His exclusion from French territory was also ordered. The Aliens' Deportation Board, however, expressed the opinion that the applicant should not be deported because he did not constitute a serious threat to public order. The Minister for the Interior none the less issued an order for the applicant's deportation. An application to have the deportation order rescinded was rejected and the judicial review application challenging this decision was unsuccessful. While in custody he had helped the police with their investigations, leading to the arrest and conviction of HB for drugs-related offences. HB was subsequently deported to Columbia in April 1990.

HLR applied to the commission claiming that his deportation would be contrary to art 3. He argued that because of his convictions for drugs-related offences, no other country would accept him. As

---

8 (1997) 24 EHRR 423.
9 Paragraph 48.
10 (1997) 26 EHRR 29.

to the possible agents of ill-treatment, this would be other drugs traffickers because of his status as a known informer. The commission concluded that there would be a violation of art 3 if the applicant were to be deported.[11]

Before the court the government, in addition to contending that HLR had not shown a real and serious risk of ill-treatment, claimed that art 3 did not apply where the risk emanated exclusively from private individuals and groups. The French government maintained that by adopting this position the court would be considerably extending the scope of the European Convention. In somewhat cautious language, the court held that, due to the absolute character of the right, it 'does not rule out the possibility that art 3 of the Convention may also apply where the danger emanates from persons or groups of persons who are not public officials'.[12]   It is noteworthy that this point appears to have been impliedly accepted in *Ahmed*, where the expected ill-treatment would have resulted from the actions of militia in a state where there was an ongoing civil war. The distinguishing factor was, however, that in *Ahmed* no public authority existed which could offer protection, and the ill-treatment was feared by a powerful faction then existing within the country. In this context it is clear that the actions of non-state entities may bring an application within art 3. The guarded language again reflects the underlying tensions which fuel the court's incremental development of this right.

The court in this case placed the weight of its judgment on the fact that it did not believe that a real risk had been shown to exist. As to the possibility of protection by the Colombian authorities, the court stated that it was aware of the problems they faced. The applicants had not, however, shown that they were incapable of affording him appropriate protection.[13]   In the light of these factors (and others discussed below), and unlike the commission, the court concluded that there would be no violation of art 3 if he were to be deported.[14]

One of the more interesting aspects of the court's recent jurisprudence, from a refugee law perspective, is that it has recognised explicitly that art 3 is of wider scope than arts 32 and 33 of the 1951 Convention. The practical result is that some of the limitations of refugee law are exposed and remedied. States are

11   19 votes to 10.
12   Paragraph 40.
13   Paragraph 43.
14   15 votes to 6.

effectively obliged to offer protection not solely to refugees.[15] The provision applies irrespective of the applicant's conduct, and although the ill-treatment must reach a certain minimum level of severity, the applicant is not required to demonstrate that the ill-treatment will take place because of her race, nationality, religion, political opinions or membership of a particular social group.

In adopting a teleological approach to art 3 the court developed the Convention right considerably. It is unlikely that the drafters of the European Convention would have contemplated this end result. Justification for this 'progressive development' of the Convention jurisprudence may be provided by a recognition that instruments which protect human rights have a special quality. This is particularly the case with regard to the quasi-constitutional Convention system. This means that an interpretative strategy is required which gives priority to its object and purpose. The reasoning adopted by the European Court of Human Rights is likely to have a significant impact on domestic courts. It will be worth watching the approach of domestic courts in the UK in these art 3 cases.

A real risk of sufficiently serious ill-treatment

In order to gain the protection of art 3 there must be substantial grounds for believing that there is a real risk of treatment in violation of art 3 taking place. In making this assessment, the court is concerned with the forseeable consequences of return. It is now well established in the jurisprudence of the court that art 3 is absolute, and that the behaviour of the individual should not be weighed in the balance in an assessment of the risk of possible ill-treatment. This is clear from what is argued above. The problem which then arises is how to assess this risk. In other words, what are the evidential tests which the applicant must meet before she may successfully make out an art 3 claim? It is with this standard that the underlying politics of asylum in Europe becomes plain. For the court, as an institutional actor in the European polity, is evidently conscious of striking an effective balance with the status determination systems in states. By setting this at a relatively high level the Convention system is able to permit some level of

---

15 In the UK context a report by JUSTICE, the Immigration Law Practitioners' Association and the Asylum Rights Campaign *Providing Protection: Towards Fair and Effective Asylum Procedures* (July 1997), has, for example, recommended (Recommendation No 4) that the UK's immigration rules should define criteria for granting protection on grounds of torture or inhuman or degrading treatment as well as the UK's other international obligations.

'deference' to national level decision-making. An indication of the level of the standard of proof is that the applicant must provide 'substantial grounds for believing' that there is a 'real risk' of ill-treatment. This may be contrasted with approaches to the 1951 Convention definition of refugee.[16] One of the implications of delegating the application of refugee law to individual states is that interpretations can differ markedly. As the examination of EU law and policy suggested, this can be problematic. As Goodwin-Gill has noted, given the problems faced by refugees, and the centrality of protection, the approach to the standard of proof must be a cautious one.[17] This is reinforced if one considers that any assessment of the well-foundedness of a fear of persecution, or a real risk of ill-treatment, is difficult given that it involves the prediction of future events.[18]

The basic starting point is that it is within individual states that refugee status is determined in accordance with the provisions of refugee law. It has already been noted that refugee law does not exhaust the protection needs of asylum seekers, or even provide an inclusive approach to the protection of the forcibly displaced. Perhaps aware of the problems involved in becoming a potential 'surrogate' form of international supervisory mechanism, both the commission and the court have displayed some caution in this area.[19] An obvious factor is that the Convention institutions do not wish to usurp the functions of asylum determination systems within states. As art 1 of the European Convention makes clear, it is for states to secure to everyone within their jurisdiction the Convention rights and freedoms.

The willingness of the court to follow the reasoning of the commission in *Chahal* suggests, however, that it has abandoned its

---

16 For a recent comparative study see Carlier, Vanheule, Hullman and Galiano (eds) *Who is a Refugee? A Comparative Case Study* (1997). This includes detailed comparative analysis, based on national reports from Austria, Belgium, Switzerland, Canada, Germany, Denmark, Spain, France, Greece, Italy, Luxembourg, the Netherlands, Portugal, the UK and the US, on the approach to the definition of refugee in each state.

17 Goodwin-Gill *The Refugee in International Law* (2nd edn, 1996) p 35.

18 Note 17 above, p 39. He refers to the weaknesses of a system of protection which is based on 'essays in prediction'. Cf Hathaway *The Law of Refugee Status* (1991) pp 75-80, esp p 80: 'Because the risk of persecution will never be definitively measurable, decision-makers should ask whether the evidence as a whole discloses a risk of persecution which would cause a reasonable person in the claimant's circumstances to reject as insufficient whatever protection her state of origin is able and willing to afford.'

19 See Mole *Problems raised by certain aspects of the present situation of refugees from the standpoint of the European Convention on Human Rights* (1997) p 45.

'non-interventionist position' in refugee and asylum cases. Domestic courts will not be concerned with these international issues and may opt for a more progressive interpretation of this aspect of the Convention. Given that it is the right to life of the asylum seeker which may be at risk, decision-makers should adopt an appropriate standard in these cases.

It is time to return to consideration of the tests the asylum seeker is required to meet under art 3. While the judgments of the court in *Chahal* and *Ahmed* are most welcome, sight should not be lost of the fact that the test remains a demanding one. In *Vilvarajah v UK* the court considered that the personal position of the applicants was not any worse than that of other members of the Tamil community.[20] The 'mere possibility' of ill-treatment was not enough to give rise to a breach of art 3.[1] The second, third and fourth applicants in the case were subjected to ill-treatment upon return to Sri Lanka, but the court held that there was nothing to distinguish the cases of these applicants, and the Secretary of State could not have foreseen that this would be the result.[2] As in *Cruz Varas*,[3] the court attached importance to the knowledge and past experience of the UK authorities in dealing with asylum applications.[4] The court and the commission[5] have exhibited a readiness to respect the expertise of public authorities in dealing with asylum applications. Even states with considerable experience of processing applications from a particular country have problems with their determination systems.

In its argument in *Chahal* the government made reference to the internal flight alternative. The UK offered to return Chahal to a part of India of his choice. Further to this, the government argued that, contrary to some of the information contained in reports by Amnesty International, there had been a substantial improvement in the situation in Punjab. The Commission accepted this, noting in particular the establishment of the National Human Rights Commission (NHRC). However, it was unable to find 'solid evidence' that the police had been brought under democratic control, or that the judiciary had been able to assert its own independent authority in Punjab.[6] The government and the

---

20　(1991) 14 EHRR 1, para 111.
1　14 EHRR 1, para 111.
2　Paragraph 112.
3　Paragraph 81.
4　Paragraph 114.
5　Eg *LI v Sweden* (1993) 75 DR 264 at 273.
6　Commission Opinion, para 111.

commission differed on the impact which Chahal's notoriety would have on the likelihood of his future ill-treatment. The UK argued that the Indian government, aware that international attention would be focused on this case, would seek to ensure that he was protected, while the commission was of the view that, as a leading Sikh militant, he was likely to be of particular interest to the security forces, no matter where in India he was returned to.[7] In its assessment the court attached weight to, inter alia, the reports of Amnesty International, in particular those documenting the practice of extra-judicial killings alleged to have been carried out by the Punjab police outside of their home state. Further support for this was to be found in assertions accepted by the IAT, in the 1995 US State Department Report on India, and the 1994 NHRC's report on Punjab. The court was persuaded by this and other objective evidence that elements of the Punjab police 'were accustomed to act without regard to the human rights of suspected Sikh militants and were fully capable of pursuing their targets into areas of India far away from Punjab'.[8] Note that the court accepted the 'internal flight alternative' in the sense that it felt compelled to examine the situation throughout India. While it was prepared to acknowledge that there had been an improvement in the situation, the problem persisted.[9] The most significant factor for the court was that no concrete evidence had been produced to demonstrate that there had been any fundamental reform or reorganisation of the Punjab police.[10] The problem was, however, not confined to Punjab. Noting the comments by the United Nations' Special Rapporteur on Torture, that the practice of torture was still endemic against those in police custody, the court attached significance to the fact that human rights violations had been carried out by the police elsewhere in India.[11] Assurances given by the Indian government did not negate the fact that violations of human rights by members of the security forces in Punjab and elsewhere were still an enduring problem.[12] The court concluded that the assurance did not provide the applicant with an adequate guarantee of safety.[13]

In its previous case law the court has looked for an aspect of the applicant's plight which distinguishes her from the general

---

7 Commission Opinion, para 112.
8 Paragraph 100.
9 Paragraph 102.
10 Paragraph 103.
11 Paragraph 104.
12 Paragraph 105.
13 Paragraph 105.

population. As noted, when examining the forseeability of the ill-treatment in *Vilvarajah* the court stated that there was nothing to distinguish the applicants from the rest of the Tamil community. In *Chahal* the court was also influenced by the high-profile nature of the case. In particular, the applicant was well known as a Sikh political activist, and the allegations by the UK that he was a terrorist were likely to increase the risk to him; effectively making him a target for hard-line elements in the security forces.[14] In the light of the factors discussed, the court held that there was a real risk of treatment contrary to art 3 if he were to be returned to India.[15]

There are a number of elements which combine to make *Chahal* an exceptional case. It is apparent that the high profile nature of the applicant's activity was significant for the court. In response to the argument that this was the major distinguishing factor, it may be noted that the court expressly stated that it was particularly influenced by the well-documented activities of the Punjab police, and the violations of human rights carried out by members of the security forces elsewhere.[16] It is arguably best to view this as an example of how both the objective background human rights situation, and the particular circumstances of the individual's case, may be combined to make a successful art 3 claim. However, it does appear that the court is still wedded to an overly individualistic conception of risk. This conception appears to focus on evidence which demonstrates how the applicant's case 'stands out' from the general position in the state.[17] As a leading political activist, Chahal certainly could meet this test, but it is worth considering the wider group of individuals who are exposed to human rights violations who might not, and yet remain in need of some form of protection. There is no principled reason why art 3 should exclude groups of similarly situated applicants. This tendency of judicial and other decision-making bodies to search for personalised factors, which distinguish the applicant's case from others, appears to be an

14 Paragraph 106.
15 Paragraph 107.
16 Paragraph 107
17 Cf Crawford and Hyndman 'Three Heresies in the Application of the Refugee Convention' (1989) 1 IJRL 155, arguing that a 'singling-out' requirement is a misinterpretation of the 1951 Convention definition. See also Plender 'Summary of the Closing Session' UNHCR *The European Convention on Human Rights and the Protection of Refugees, Asylum Seekers and Displaced Persons* (1995) pp 77–78, he argues that the court's words in *Vilvarajah* should not be read as supporting a 'singling-out' requirement. Certainly they *should* not be read in this way, but it does appear from the case law of the court that it is looking for some especially distinguishing factor which makes the applicant's plight distinctive in some sense.

endemic problem which has been criticised heavily in the context of refugee law.[18] In relation to the European Convention system, it possibly arises from an underlying desire, noted above, not to assume the function of a surrogate supervisory mechanism. Again, one can see here a tension between the human rights mandate of the Convention bodies and 'functionalist-inspired' reasoning about the appropriateness of its role in this area.

A distinguishing factor in the *Ahmed* case was the fact that the applicant had been previously granted refugee status, and had only lost that status because of his criminal conviction.[19] This may be contrasted with the approach in the *HLR* case. Here the court noted the general situation of violence existing throughout Colombia, but emphasised that this in itself was not enough to bring the claim within art 3.[20] The evidence produced by the applicant showed the extent of the difficulties and tensions in the country, but the court noted that it did not reveal any situations which were like his own.[1] This suggests that evidence which demonstrates that individuals in a similar position have been subjected to ill-treatment will lend considerable weight to an application. It further stated that he had provided no documents to suggest that his plight was any worse than that of other Colombians.[2] The court concluded (in language that is reminiscent of that used in *Vilvarajah*) that no substantial grounds had been established for believing that the applicant would be exposed to a real risk of treatment contrary to art 3, if deported.[3] The case provides a useful contrast with both *Chahal* and *Ahmed*, and demonstrates again the significant evidential hurdles which the applicant must overcome if she is to be successful in an application under art 3.

The judgments of the court in *Chahal* and *Ahmed* suggest that even though a high standard of proof is demanded, this may be met in practice with the provision of sufficient supporting evidence. What factors contributed towards the success of the applicants in these cases? In *Chahal* it is clear that there was authoritative evidence from a number of objective sources that ill-treatment of

18 Note 17 above. See also Hathaway *The Law of Refugee Status* (1991) pp 91-97.
19 Paragraph 42.
20 Paragraph 42.
 1 Paragraph 42.
 2 Paragraph 42.
 3 In the dissenting opinion of Judge Pekkanen (joined by Judges Thor Vilhjalmsson, Lopes Rocha and Lohmus) this case could not be distinguished from *Chahal*, and they reached the same conclusion. Judge de Meyer agreed with this aspect of the dissent, as did Judge Jambrek.

Sikh political activists by the police and security forces was a problem in Punjab and throughout India. As noted in the examination of *Vilvarajah*, the objective human rights situation is, however, not enough to bring a claim successfully within art 3. The added component in *Chahal* appears to have been the high profile nature of his political activity. This reinforces the argument that an individualistic conception is being adopted by the court. *Ahmed* is rather more straightforward, in that he had been granted refugee status on the basis of persecution feared as a result of his suspected involvement with the USC. The commission had noted that the situation had not altered in Somalia, therefore the risk of ill-treatment remained. *HLR*'s case differed to the extent that he was not able to demonstrate, to the satisfaction of the court, that there was a real risk that drugs traffickers would take revenge on him. The court acknowledged that this sometimes happened, but he had not shown that the risk was 'real', or that his plight was different from that of the general population. He had also not been able to demonstrate that the Colombian authorities would not be able to provide him with appropriate protection.

As stated above, even following *Chahal* and *Ahmed*, the position remains that the test, as applied by the court, is a reasonably stringent one. In setting the evidential test at this level the court is showing a willingness to allow states a 'margin of appreciation' in the operation of their asylum determination systems even in art 3 cases. This is not how the court views this mechanism but it is one explanation for its use. In the absence of an international supervisory mechanism for refugee law, and taking into account some of the arguments discussed here, perhaps the court is concerned that the European Convention institutions do not end up filling this gap.

Detention and international zones

The detention of asylum seekers has already been examined. The use of detention against those who seek asylum has always been a controversial aspect of law and policy. There is a well-founded suspicion that the intention is to deter future asylum seekers. The fact that persons who flee persecution in one state might eventually find themselves in detention in another is ironic, but is a result of familiar concerns of states in this area. Refugee law offers only limited protection to the refugee who is detained.[4] Article 5 of the European Convention governs the right to liberty and security of

---

4   See art 31(1) and (2); Goodwin-Gill *The Refugee in International Law* (2nd edn, 1996) pp 247-251.

the person, and (importantly for the detained asylum seeker) requires the provision of a remedy to challenge detention.

In *Chahal* the applicant challenged his detention under art 5(1), and also claimed that there had been a violation of art 5(4). The commission was of the opinion that the proceedings were not pursued with the requisite speed and therefore art 5(1) had been violated.[5] The commission felt that the complaint as to the adequacy of the remedy was best dealt with under art 13.[6] The court, however, came to a different conclusion. It emphasised the importance of ensuring that these cases are thoroughly examined by the domestic courts.[7] Therefore, it did not regard the periods complained of as excessive, either taken individually or together. As to the guarantees against arbitrariness, the court stated that the special advisory procedure[8] provided an important safeguard. The detention therefore complied with art 5(1)(f). Unlike the commission, the court did consider the art 5(4) complaint. Here the national security element was decisive in the court's finding that there had been a violation. The domestic courts were not in a position to review whether the detention was justified on national security grounds, and the special advisory procedure could not be considered a 'court' within the meaning of art 5(4).[9] The court pointed out that the applicant had not been entitled to legal representation, he was only provided with an outline of the reasons for his deportation, the advice of the panel was non-binding and it was not disclosed.[10] Significance was attached to evidence presented concerning Canada's response to this problem.[11]

In an attempt to control the entry of asylum seekers, some states have made use of the concept of international or transit zones.[12] Even though individuals are physically present on state territory,

---

5 Commission Report para 122.
6 Paragraph 127.
7 Paragraph 117.
8 See *R v Secretary of State for the Home Department, ex p Hosenball* [1977] 3 All ER 452; *R v Secretary of State for the Home Department, ex p Cheblak* [1991] 2 All ER 319. For an outline of the procedure HC Hansard Vol 819 col 357 ff, 15 June 1971. Note that the newly elected UK government initiated reform following the *Chahal* judgment.
9 Paragraph 130.
10 Paragraph 130.
11 Paragraph 144. See Leigh 'Secret Proceedings in Canada' (1996) 34 Osgoode Hall LJ 112.
12 See Recommendation No R(94)5 of the Committee of Ministers on *guidelines to inspire practices of the member states of the Council of Europe concerning the arrival of asylum seekers at airports.*

this concept can be deployed to withhold formal admission. The issue of the compatibility of holding asylum seekers in these zones with art 5 arose in *Amuur v France*.[13] The applicants, who were Somali nationals, were held at the airport following their arrival in France, having travelled via Syria. They were refused leave to enter and returned to Syria. Before their removal they had applied for asylum, but the relevant authority ruled that it lacked jurisdiction because they had not been granted a temporary residence permit. Their application to a tribunal to challenge their detention was successful. They had, however, been returned two days before its decision. An appeal to the Refugee Appeals Board against the initial refusal of leave to enter was unsuccessful. The commission was of the opinion that the period spent in the international zone,[14] and the conditions they were held in, were equivalent to 'detention' in the ordinary sense of the term.[15] The commission concluded that art 5(1) was not applicable, as the degree of constraint required was not present.[16]

The court differed in its approach. It stated that keeping asylum seekers in the international zone involved a restriction on liberty, but this was not the same as holding them in detention centres.[17] Confinement in the international zone was acceptable for the purpose of controlling unlawful immigration. However, it stated:

> 'States' legitimate concern to foil the increasingly frequent attempts to get round immigration restrictions must not deprive asylum seekers of the protection afforded by these[18] Conventions.'[19]

The court stated that such holding should not be prolonged excessively, and that speedy review by the courts was required. Particular significance was attached to the need not to deprive asylum seekers of the right to effective access to the refugee determination procedure.[20] The court also found the absence of

---

13 Judgment of 21 June 1996, (1996) 22 EHRR 533. See Kokott 'International Decisions' (1997) 91 Am J Int L 147, 156: 'The *Amuur* judgment is another example of the indirect way the European Court of Human Rights ensures certain guarantees for asylum seekers despite the fact that the ECHR contains no explicit right to asylum.' Cf *S M and MT v Austria No 19066/91* (1993) 74 DR 179 at 186, confinement in a special transit area did not violate art 3.
14 From 9 to 29 March 1992.
15 Commission Report para 46.
16 Paragraph 50. Cf Dissenting Opinion of MM H Danelius, C L Rozakis, S Trechsel, H Schermers, Mmes G H Thune, J Liddy, MM J-C Geus, N Bratza, D Svaby and G Ress.
17 Paragraph 43.
18 The court had previously referred to both the 1951 Convention and the ECHR.
19 Paragraph 43.
20 Paragraph 43.

legal and social assistance for these asylum seekers to be significant.[1] The court rejected the government's argument that the fact that the asylum seekers were free to leave France was material. That they could go elsewhere did not exclude the possibility of a restriction on liberty.[2] The return of applicants to another country, in this case Syria was, for the court, dependent upon the 'vagaries of diplomatic relations', and the court attached significance to the fact that Syria was not bound by the 1951 Convention.[3] The court concluded that art 5(1) was applicable to this case.

In assessing whether there had been a deprivation of liberty the court stated that despite its name the international zone did not have extra-territorial status.[4] With regards to the law existing at the time of the applicant's confinement, it was not of sufficient quality for the purpose of art 5(1).[5] At the time in question the law did not permit the ordinary courts in France to review the conditions of confinement, or to impose limitations on the length of detention. Again, the court emphasised that no provision was made in the rules for legal, humanitarian and social assistance, providing further support for the argument advanced above about giving substance to these rights.[6]

Mention of a right to effective access is more significant than it might at first appear.[7] It has a role in building a robust proceduralism in this area. It is too easy to dismiss proceduralism as a relic of traditional models of constitutionalism. However, the right to effective access in asylum law can be developed into a substantial procedural right. A basic feature of a process-based approach is a guarantee of effective access to a fair, efficient and effective determination procedure. It is worth considering how far this notion of effectiveness might be extended. Does it, for example, extend to the provision of social assistance in order to give substance to the right? The court in *Amuur* referred specifically to

---

1 Paragraph 45.
2 Paragraph 48.
3 Paragraph 48.
4 Paragraph 52.
5 Paragraph 53.
6 Contrast this with the decision of the English Court of Appeal in *R v Secretary of State for the Home Department, ex p JCWI* [1996] 4 All ER 385, 401, per Simon Brown LJ: 'I would hold it unlawful to alter the benefit regime so drastically as must inevitably not merely prejudice, but on occasion defeat, the statutory right of asylum seekers to claim refugee status.'
7 Cf Marx 'Non-Refoulement, Access to Procedures, and Responsibility for Determining Refugee Claims' (1995) 7 IJRL 383, 401, he argues that the necessity to establish procedures is inherent in the *non-refoulement* principle.

the absence of legal and social assistance while the applicants were being held in the international zone.[8] Given the plight of the asylum seeker upon arrival in the receiving state, it is important that access to determination procedures is something more than a merely formal 'right'. The counter-argument against open access, in this holistic sense, is that this will leave too little scope for states to address abuse of the system. It is suggested here that apprehension regarding manifestly unfounded applications is best addressed by encouraging the development of fair, efficient and expeditious asylum procedures, and not by targeting the economic and social needs of asylum applicants.

Safe third countries and the European Convention on Human Rights

The issue of the compatibility of the safe third country concept with the Convention was tested in *TI v UK*.[9] The applicant left Sri Lanka and sought asylum in Germany. His application was unsuccessful and he travelled to Italy before arriving in the UK in September 1997. The UK requested that Germany accept responsibility for the asylum claim pursuant to the Dublin Convention 1990. Germany accepted this and the Home Secretary then sought his removal on safe third country grounds. His judicial review was unsuccessful. Following the judgment of the Court of Appeal in *ex p Adan* his representatives requested that the Home Secretary reconsider his decision. The issue for the European Court of Human Rights was whether the applicant's return to Germany would violate art 3. The court held that the indirect removal of applicants was the responsibility of the removing state for Convention purposes. The UK could not rely on the adoption of the Dublin Convention 1990 in order to absolve itself of responsibility under the European Convention. While the court accepted that the Dublin Convention may pursue laudable objectives, its effectiveness could be undermined by the differing approaches between states. Although the court had not heard substantive arguments from either the UK or Germany on the merits of the asylum claim, it stated that it had concerns about the risks upon his return to Sri Lanka. As to its role in asylum cases, the court emphasised that it was not prepared to examine asylum claims or to monitor the operation of the 1951 Convention. The

---

8   Paragraph 45.
9   Appl No 43844/98, judgment of 7 March 2000.

fact that Germany excluded persecution by non-state agents from the Convention definition was not directly relevant. The court would focus on whether procedural safeguards of any kind existed within the state to protect the applicant from being return to Sri Lanka. It accepted that, upon return to Germany, there was considerable doubt whether he would be granted another asylum hearing. However, it noted the existence in Germany of other complementary forms of protection that might fill this 'protection gap'. In the light of this, and the likelihood of the applicant's claim coming within this category, the court stated that the possibility of removal had not been shown to be sufficiently concrete or determinate. On the issue of whether judicial review was an effective remedy, when raised in art 3 cases, it found no reason to differ from its previous case law. The court, in past cases, has found judicial review in the UK to be an effective remedy in this context. The application was rejected as manifestly ill-founded.

The case is a reminder that the international human rights mechanisms are not proper or effective mechanisms for indirectly monitoring asylum practices. In the absence of an international tribunal or court dedicated to refugee and asylum issues, the asylum seeker must rely on bodies such as the European Court of Human Rights. It is noteworthy that the fact that Germany had a different approach to the interpretation of the 1951 Convention than the UK was not its primary concern. The court is thus concerned not with the true meaning of the 1951 Convention but the general procedural safeguards which exist for asylum seekers to protect them against return.

Expulsion, public order and family life

Article 8 of the European Convention will be relevant to asylum law even though the majority of decided cases have addressed the expulsion of migrants.[10] The cases under art 8 have tended to involve threatened deportation following criminal prosecution. On expulsion, asylum seekers will normally rely on art 3. However, the art 8 jurisprudence will be examined here to illustrate the scope of the provision in immigration cases and the possible relevance where expulsion threatens the right to family life in asylum cases. As this is not an absolute rights protection, the issue of balance becomes important. The case law reveals how the European Court

---

10 See Lambert 'The European Court of Human Rights and the Rights of Refugees and Other Persons in Need of Protection to Family Reunion' (1999) 11 IJRL 427

of Human Rights has addressed this issue and its approach will be of some relevance to domestic courts. The general pattern is for deportation cases to revolve around the public interest exceptions, and more specifically, whether deportation is 'necessary in a democratic society'. It is fair to state that the 'democratic necessity' test has caused the court considerable practical problems. The court has struggled to construct coherent explanations for its activity. There are fewer problems on the other aspects of this provision. For example, the 'legitimate aim' pursued by government in seeking deportation is the maintenance of public order through the 'prevention of disorder' and 'crime'. In *Berrehab v Netherlands* the court noted:

> 'In determining whether an interference was "necessary in a democratic society", the Court makes allowance for the margin of appreciation that is left to the Contracting States'.[11]

In this case the first applicant was a Moroccan citizen who was refused a residence permit after his Dutch wife divorced him. In making its assessment the court placed emphasis on the fact that this was not an admission case and the extent of the first applicant's real family ties in the Netherlands.[12] His close connections with the second applicant (his daughter) were also material in this case.[13] *Berrehab* marked a departure and signalled that the court was willing to challenge deportation within a rights framework.

In *Moustaquim v Belgium* the applicant was a Moroccan national who had lived in Belgium from the age of one.[14] He committed a series of offences in Belgium, including 26 aggravated thefts. The Belgian Advisory Board on Aliens acknowledged that his deportation would be lawful, but believed that it would be inappropriate because of his youth and the fact that all of his family lived in Belgium. A deportation order was, however, served on Moustaquim which included reference to the 147 offences he had admitted to committing. Following his deportation, in 1989 the order was temporarily suspended and he was later granted a residence permit. The court noted that his alleged offences had a number of 'special features'.[15] Although over 100 offences had been listed, criminal proceedings were brought in only 26 instances.[16] These were spread over a short period and the domestic

11 (1988) 11 EHRR 322, para 28.
12 Paragraph 29.
13 Paragraph 29.
14 (1991) 13 EHRR 802.
15 Paragraph 43.
16 Paragraph 44.

Court of Appeal had acquitted him of four of these offences.[17] His last offence was committed in December 1980 and the deportation order issued in February 1984.[18] The applicant was in detention for at least half of the intervening period.[19] The court further noted that when the order was made all his close relatives lived in Belgium.[20] As to the applicant, he had arrived very early in his life and had lived in Belgium for 20 years.[1] He had in this period been to Belgium twice on holiday.[2] His family life was severely disrupted and it is interesting that the court made reference to the recommendation of the Advisory Board on Aliens to support this. The court held that the means employed were disproportionate to the end pursued and thus that art 8 had been violated. The dissenting opinion of Judges Bindschedler-Robert and Valticos places greater weight on the applicant's criminal offences. They argue that these offences were 'more serious than is indicated by paragraph 44 of the judgment, which in our opinion glosses over it'.[3] The court placed greater weight on the family ties than on the public interest exceptions. In order to achieve this result it made reference to some 'special features' of the applicant's case. It did not, however, provide detailed reasons for the conclusion reached. This is not an isolated example.

In *Beldjoudi v France* the first applicant was an Algerian by birth who had lost his French nationality.[4] During his time in France he was convicted and given custodial sentences on several occasions. This included imprisonment for assault and battery, the acquisition and possession of weapons and aggravated theft. A deportation order was issued against the applicant on the ground that he constituted a threat to public order. The commission stated that in these cases the state was required to take into consideration the consequences of deportation. This was particularly necessary in cases such as this one where the applicant did not speak the language of his country of origin and had no family ties or links with that country.

---

17 Paragraph 44.
18 Paragraph 44.
19 Paragraph 44.
20 Paragraph 45.
 1 Paragraph 45.
 2 Paragraph 45.
 3 (1991) 13 EHRR 802 at 819: 'No doubt the measure may be regarded as severe in relation to a young man who has spent most of his life in Belgium and who would certainly have encountered great difficulty in adapting in his country of origin or other countries. However, we cannot go so far as to conclude that the Belgian State was not within its rights to take measures which it had urgent grounds for regarding as necessary for national security, public safety and the prevention of disorder or crime.'
 4 (1992) 14 EHRR 801.

'In such a situation, an order for deportation to that country is in general a measure of such severity that only in exceptional circumstances could it be justified as being proportionate to the aim pursued under art 8(2).'[5]

While the commission was prepared to attach significance to the offences of the first applicant, these were not of such a nature that public order consideration would outweigh the 'family considerations'.[6] The commission noted the failure to enforce the deportation order and the fact that the first applicant's presence in France was tolerated. The commission, clearly according significant weight to the interest of the first applicant in his family life, could find no exceptional circumstances which would justify the deportation to Algeria.[7]

The government argued that his offences were of a serious nature and were spread over a 15-year period. As to the gravity of the offences the court noted that his criminal record appeared much worse than that of Moustaquim.[8] The court however found a violation of art 8. How did it arrive at this conclusion? It is not entirely clear from the judgment. It listed several factors which were significant. For example, he had married a French woman and spent his whole life in France. Further to this, he did not speak Arabic and did not appear to have any links with Algeria. Mrs Beldjoudi, a French national, would experience great difficulty in relocating to Algeria and the interference might 'imperil the unity

---

5   Paragraph 65.
6   Paragraph 67. On the seriousness of the offences the commission noted that these had been committed when he was of full age and even after he had been served with the deportation order.
7   Paragraph 68. Note the concurring opinion of H G Schermers, joined by G H Thune p 827: 'The real reason for the inadmissibility of deportation is the fact that the first applicant is a second-generation immigrant. His ties with France and the absence of ties with Algeria are such that much stronger arguments are necessary to justify interference with his right to respect for his private life. A second-generation immigrant is so firmly integrated into his new homeland that deportation will inevitably destroy his private life.' Contrast this with the dissenting opinion of J C Soyer, joined by G Sperduti, A S Gözübüyük and A Weitzel (at 829): 'It is clear, from the actual practical consequences of this opinion for the social order, that the Commission is setting out a normative solution, namely a rule of law to the effect that second-generation immigrants cannot in practice be deported. Such a solution seems to me to ignore the letter and the spirit of the Convention. The Commission's opinion seems to me to imply consequences which–whether ill-considered or not considered at all-could be unintentionally harmful to the host community, a community which, on a balanced view, should not be alone in having obligations.' The final comment is revealing and is evidence of a clear concern about the duties of immigrants in host communities. The case reveals, again, substantive disagreement on the nature of rights protection.
8   Paragraph 75.

or even the very existence of the marriage'.[9] Judge Pettiti, in his dissenting opinion, distinguished *Moustaquim* and *Beldjoudi*. He noted that the applicant in *Moustaquim* was an adolescent with no roots outside the country.[10] This was not the case with *Beldjoudi*, who as an adult was a repeat offender and who came within the class of legitimate deportations.[11] His argument is premised on the right of the state to deport criminals even if they have lived continuously in the host country. The only general defence against the expulsion of criminals should, he stated, be art 3.[12] He also noted the glaring absence of precision in the court's judgment:

> 'In this judgment there is no definition of the threshold of risks and level of re-offending which should determine whether or not criminal aliens are to be deported . . . Each member-State remains the master of its own criminal policy, just as it retains the right to define the severity of sentences. In many States deportation is an exemplary penalty in addition to the sentence. In countries with a high proportion of aliens in the population, it is deportation much rather than the threat of prison which is a safeguard against repeated offending and strengthens the national consensus in favour of welcoming immigrants of good character who by their work share in the prosperity of the nation.'[13]

Judges Martens, in his concurring opinion, would have 'preferred its decision to have been based on . . . a less casuistic reasoning'.[14] His reasoning feeds into a general debate about the rights of second-generation immigrants.[15] From this perspective, drawing a sharp distinction between nationals and second-generation immigrants, or 'integrated aliens', is a mistake. Judge Martens stated that he would have preferred it if the court's decision was anchored in this principle. This, he suggested, would advance the cause of legal certainty in this field.[16]

---

9 Paragraph 78.
10 (1992) 14 EHRR 801 at 836.
11 (1992) 14 EHRR 801 at 836.
12 (1992) 14 EHRR 801 at 837.
13 (1992) 14 EHRR 801 at 838.
14 (1992) 14 EHRR 801 at 840.
15 (1992) 14 EHRR 801 at 840-841: 'In my opinion, mere nationality does not constitute an objective and reasonable justification for the existence of a difference as regards the admissibility of expelling someone from what, in both cases, may be called his "own country". I believe that an increasing number of member-States of the Council of Europe accept the principle that such "integrated aliens" should be no more liable to expulsion than nationals, an exception being justified, if at all, only in very exceptional circumstances.'
16 (1992) 14 EHRR 801 at 841.

In *Nasri v France*[17] the applicant was an Algerian national who had come to live in France in 1965. During his time there he was convicted of a series of criminal offences. For example, in May 1986 he was sentenced to five years' imprisonment for gang rape and in December 1990 he was sentenced to six months' imprisonment for theft with violence and receiving stolen goods. In seeking his deportation the government highlighted his long criminal record 'which included some thirty arrests and ten or so convictions over the period from 1981 to 1993'.[18] The principal reason for the decision to deport him was his conviction for rape.[19] In argument the applicant pointed to the fact that he was deaf and dumb and illiterate. He had no command of sign language and, he argued, that he would have severe problems communicating outside of his family circle. He had in this regard always lived in his parent's home and had no knowledge of Arabic. The commission regarded the threatened deportation as so serious that it would give rise to inhuman treatment under art 3. On art 8 it believed that the measure was so severe as to be disproportionate to the legitimate aim of maintaining public order. In its decision the court noted that the 'perpetrator of such a serious offence may unquestionably represent a grave threat to public order'.[20] However, the court stated that there were other factors to take into account, including the fact that the applicant had not been the instigator of the offence and had not re-offended since the commission of the offence.[1] But the most important other factor was the applicant's handicap. For a person such as the applicant, the court stated, the family was of added importance.[2] Interestingly, the court was prepared to take into account the fact that proximity to his family might prevent him re-offending.[3] In his concurring opinion Judge Pettiti again stressed the importance of specificity in these judgments.

In *Boughanemi v France*[4] the applicant was a Tunisian national who complained of an art 8 violation on being deported from France for the second time in 1994. He was convicted of a number of criminal offences including burglary. The commission found a

17 (1995) 21 EHRR 458.
18 Paragraph 40.
19 Paragraph 40: 'In short, the serious and repeated breaches of public order committed by the applicant outweighed the protection to be accorded to his family life, the reality of which appeared in any event disputable.'
20 Paragraph 42.
 1 Paragraph 42.
 2 Paragraph 43.
 3 Paragraph 43.
 4 (1996) 22 EHRR 228.

violation of art 8.[5] The court, however, held that the circumstances in this case differed from the other deportation cases. In this instance, and unlike its previous jurisprudence, the court was prepared to place particular weight on the applicant's criminal convictions. The reasoning is unclear and it is difficult, from the justification provided, to make a principled distinction between this and other cases. In his dissenting opinion Judge Martens viewed the uncertainty as an inherent aspect of the 'traditional approach'[6] adopted by the court.[7]

'National administrations and national courts are unable to predict whether expulsion of an integrated alien will be found acceptable or not. The majority's case by case approach is a lottery for national authorities and a source of embarrassment for the Court. A source of embarrassment since it obliges the Court to make well-nigh impossible comparisons between the merits of the case before it and those which it has already decided.'[8]

This is an important criticism precisely because the court places so much emphasis on national legal systems. If the court's jurisprudence is characterised by uncertainty, this hardly aids national decision-makers trying to act compatibly with this aspect of the Convention. As Judge Martens asked:

'Should one just make a comparison based on the number of convictions and the severity of the sentences or should one take into account personal circumstances?'[9]

His belief that the court has opted for the latter was well founded. One suggestion for the removal of uncertainty was that the court should conclude that the expulsion of 'integrated aliens' is contrary to art 3. Expulsion would constitute a violation no matter what crimes were committed by the applicant. If art 8 remained the principal provision under examination, then the court, he suggested, should:

---

5   Paragraph 78: 'Examining the interests at stake in the present case, the Commission considers that in spite of the serious nature of the convictions which gave rise to the deportation order, a fair balance has not been struck between, on the one hand, those considerations inherent to the prevention of disorder and of crime, and on the other hand, compliance with the applicant's right of respect for private and family life.'

6   This approach is that the Convention does not protect even integrated aliens from expulsion. They can rely on the Convention to the extent that their family life is interfered with contrary to art 8. The Court then must look at whether any interference is justified under art 8(2).

7   Note 4 above at 249.

8   Note 4 above at 249.

9   Note 4 above at 249-250.

'accept that expulsion of an integrated alien as a rule constitutes a lack of respect for his private life, but may exceptionally be justified where the alien is convicted of very serious crimes, such as serious crimes against the State, political or religious terrorism or holding a leading position in a drug trafficking organisation'.[10]

This is a clear statement of the nature of the public order issues to be considered under art 8. This dissent places the public order exception at a particularly high level applying specifically to only the most serious crimes. Given the interest of immigrants in security of residence, and the importance of a multicultural and pluralist European polity, this interpretation makes sense. While deportation may be one penalty which states can bring to bear against immigrants, it should be remembered that it is not the only one. Judge Baka, in his dissenting opinion, argued that the applicant should 'enjoy treatment not significantly less favourable than would be accorded to a national of the country. He committed crimes and he has been sentenced for that'.[11] To add an expulsion order to the punishment already received would be, he stated, to 'overemphasise heavily the general interest in the prevention of crime and disorder as against the protection of the individual's right to private and family life'.[12] Both these dissents are inspired by a general concern about the distinctions made between nationals and immigrants or 'integrated aliens'. The position is that deportation following criminal conviction may simply be a wholly disproportionate response to second-generation immigrants. There is considerable merit in this view. One must not forget that the state is not without the means to punish offenders. It is difficult to see why deporting an individual solves any of the problems involved. What it does do is divest the expelling state of responsibility. In reality this is about the assertion by states of authority, and ultimately, sovereignty. In this age of globalisation, when many states are experiencing a loss of regulatory control, this is perhaps an area where they believe they can continue to be assertive.

In *Bouchelkia v France*[13] the applicant had arrived in France at the age of two with his mother and his elder brother. In 1996 he married a woman of French nationality with whom he had had a relationship since 1986. They had a child in 1993. In 1988 he had been sentenced to five years' imprisonment for rape with violence.

10 Note 4 above at 251.
11 Note 4 above at 251.
12 Note 4 above at 252.
13 (1997) 25 EHRR 686.

Other criminal proceedings where later taken against him for insulting a public official and staying illegally in France. The deportation order against the applicant was issued in 1990. The commission noted that while the applicant's most important family connections were in France, he had retained links with Algeria. On the seriousness of the applicant's offences the majority of the commission concluded that they were severe enough to outweigh private and family considerations. The state's interest in public order 'trumped' the individual's right to family life.[14] The court stated that it attached:

> '[G]reat importance to the nature of the offence which gave rise to the deportation order. While it is true that the applicant was a minor aged 17 when he committed the serious crime of aggravated rape, that fact . . . does not in any way detract from the seriousness and gravity of such a crime.'[15]

The issuance of the deportation order was not rendered unjustified because he had built a family life thereafter. The court found that a fair balance had been struck. The judgment of the court is much less clear on the balancing issue than that of the commission.[16]

In *Dalia v France*[17] the applicant arrived in France from Algeria when she was seventeen or eighteen. Her family had all either French nationality or were residents. The applicant married a French national in 1986. She was convicted of drug offences and orders were made for her deportation. She left the country but returned in 1989 to visit her mother and in the same year she was divorced. In 1990 she gave birth to a child in France. While the court noted that her family ties were essentially in France, it distinguished this case from the expulsion of individuals born in

---

14 Cf dissenting opinion of H G Schermers, G H Thune, M M F Martinez and I Cabral Barreto: 'While accepting the serious nature of the convictions which give rise to the deportation, we have on balance reached the conclusion that it cannot justify the serious interference with his private and family life in France.' This differing approach to the balancing exercise places greater weight on the rights of the individual.

15 Paragraph 51.

16 Cf dissenting opinion of Judge Palm: 'I cannot agree with the majority's finding that the deportation was necessary. I find it in principle difficult to accept that a country can be justified under the Convention in expelling a second-generation immigrant to his country of origin because of his behaviour when almost all his ties are with his new homeland. In my opinion there must be much stronger reasons than those advanced in the present case to justify such action. As a rule, second-generation immigrants ought to be treated in the same way as nationals. Only in exceptional circumstances should a deportation of these non-nationals be accepted.'

17 Judgment of 19 February 1998.

the host country or who arrived there as young children.[18] It highlighted several factors: she had lived in Algeria until the age of seventeen or eighteen; she had maintained family relations; spoken the local language; and established social and school relations.[19] The court noted that in this case 'her Algerian nationality is not merely a legal fact but reflects certain social and emotional links'.[20] Further to this, the court noted that she relied on the fact that she was the mother of a French child but that she formed this link while in France illegally.[1] In the view of the court she 'could not be unaware of the resulting insecurity'.[2] The situation was thus held not to be decisive. The court was clearly influenced by the nature of the offence committed:

> 'Furthermore, the exclusion order made as a result of her conviction was a penalty for dangerous dealing in heroin. In view of the devastating effects of drugs on people's lives, the Court understands why the authorities show great firmness with regard to those who actively contribute to the spread of this scourge. Irrespective of the sentence passed on her, the fact that Mrs Dalia took part in such trafficking still weighs as heavily in the balance.'[3]

The court held that the refusal to lift the exclusion was not disproportionate. The majority were influenced by the nature of the drug trafficking offences and thus we can derive some insight into its view of 'public order'.[4] Where the offence is sufficiently serious, it appears that state action will be more likely to be adjudged 'necessary in a democratic society'. Again, however, precision is lacking and we see a reluctance to interfere with the decision of the state. This also raises the issue of which offences are sufficiently serious. The court will tend to defer to the sentences imposed by domestic courts as evidence of their seriousness. It has not been prepared explicitly to question the designation of an offence as serious. The applicant also raised the issue of a possible violation of art 3. Both the commission and the court concluded

18 Paragraph 53.
19 Paragraph 53.
20 Paragraph 53.
 1 Paragraph 54.
 2 Paragraph 54.
 3 Paragraph 54. Cf dissenting opinion of Judge De Meyer, joined by Judges Bernhardt and Levits: 'As the minority of the Commission observed, without being contradicted by the Government, the applicant had had nothing more to do with the drugs world and her presence in France, where she lives with her family and child, no longer prejudiced public order in any way.' Given the decisive nature of her involvement with drugs trafficking for the majority this is a marked difference of view within the court.
 4 See also *Djaid v France*, Judgment of 9 March 1999.

that 'renewed enforcement of the exclusion order would [not] cause the applicant suffering of such intensity as to constitute "inhuman" or "degrading" treatment'.[5]

More examples of the body of art 8 jurisprudence can be provided. In *El Boujaïdi v France*[6] the applicant was a Moroccan national who had been living with his family in France since the age of seven. He was subject to a permanent exclusion order. He had convictions for dealing in and trafficking heroin and for robbery. During domestic appeals against the enforcement of the exclusion order the applicant became a father. The court noted that, although he had claimed not to have close family connections in Morocco, he had not argued that he knew no Arabic, or that he had never returned to Morocco before the enforcement of the exclusion order.[7] It also stated that he seemed to show no interest in gaining French nationality.[8] The court held that it was thus not established that he had lost all links with Morocco.[9] Again, however, it was the seriousness of the offences, combined with the fact that he continued to engage in criminal activity while illegally present in France, which counted 'heavily against him'.[10] The enforcement of the exclusion order was thus held not to be disproportionate to the legitimate aim.[11]

In *Mehemi v France*[12] the applicant, an Algerian national, was born in France and was the father of three children of French nationality. He was sentenced for possession and illegal importation of drugs. In finding a breach of art 8 the court noted that he was born in France and had lived there until the age of thirty three. In addition, his close family all lived there, as did his wife and three minor children. The children were all born in France and had French nationality. The court found that it had not been established that the applicant had links with Algeria other than the legal fact of his nationality. The court's rejection of the government's assertion that he was part of a 'trafficking network' is important. These are assertions which are often made in the migration field without much empirical evidence to support them. The applicant's

5 Paragraph 58.
6 Judgment of 26 September 1997.
7 Paragraph 40.
8 Paragraph 40.
9 Paragraph 40.
10 Paragraph 40.
11 Cf dissenting opinion of Judge Foighel: 'The criminal law of the country of residence should normally be sufficient to punish criminal acts committed by an integrated alien, in the same way as it is deemed sufficient to punish criminal acts committed by a national.'
12 Judgment of 27 September 1997.

criminal activity was held to weigh heavily against him. However, the court stated:

> 'Nevertheless, in view of the applicant's lack of links with Algeria, the strength of his links with France and above all the fact that the order for his permanent exclusion from French territory separated him from his minor children and his wife, the Court considers that the measure in question was disproportionate to the aim pursued.'[13]

The conclusion can be contrasted with *El Boujaidi* where the individual's interest was held not to outweigh the serious criminality.

The continuing willingness to conceive of deportation as a legitimate and proportionate response to criminality was further evidenced in *Baghli v France*.[14] The applicant, an Algerian national, arrived in France at the age of two and remained there until May 1994, when he was deported to Algeria following conviction for drugs-trafficking offences. He had, however, gone back to undertake his military service between 1984 and 1985. All of his family lived in France. The court held that he had retained ties with Algeria, notably the language and his decision to do his military service. France was, the court noted, entitled to take a firm line with those convicted for drugs trafficking. The applicant was single and he had not retained close ties with his relatives in France. The relationship with his partner had not started until after the exclusion order had been made. Unlike other members of his family, he had retained his Algerian nationality and had not shown any desire to be a French national when he was entitled to it. He had retained links with his country of birth which went beyond mere nationality. The ten-year exclusion order was held not to be disproportionate.

Challenges to deportation are not confined to art 8. As noted above, art 3 has also been used. It is in national security cases that other difficult legal issues arise. When national security is raised, courts are likely to exercise an increased measure of deference toward the primary decision-maker.[15] The European Court of Human Rights has however been prepared to find against states, even when national security is raised as a defence. In *Chahal*[16] the

---

13 Paragraph 37.
14 Judgment of 30 November 1999.
15 In the UK see Nicol 'National Security Considerations and the Limits of European Supervision' [1996] EHRLR 37, 37: 'This reticence to scrutinise national security decisions can also be seen in immigration cases. Gulf War detainees and those allegedly involved in international terrorism have likewise been unable to persuade the courts to examine with any rigour decisions taken against them in the name of national security.'
16 (1996) 23 EHRR 413.

applicant was deemed a threat to national security and detained pending deportation. The commission found a violation of art 8 on the ground that the interference with family life was disproportionate. The court, because of its finding under art 3, felt it was unnecessary to deal with the issue.

These are only some of the cases under art 8 involving deportation and there is no attempt to be comprehensive here. The summary of the case law is used to illustrate the wider argument advanced in this chapter on the struggle for human rights protection. The cases examined demonstrate the problems and competing pressures which confront the court in this area and will confront domestic courts in the UK. My suggestion is that we should be concerned about the lack of clarity and consistency in decision-making, but not excessively so. The interpretation of art 8 will evolve if the court is to 'do justice' in the individual case. The court must provide enough coherent justification to permit a conversation over the meaning of the right to continue. I view this as an open-ended process. However, even within this understanding of legal interpretation there is reason to be dissatisfied with the current approach. The incoherence that is part of the jurisprudence undermines the notion of legality as it applies to migrants in Europe.

There is a tendency for the court to avoid raising serious questions about the nature of the criminal offences. It is generally accepted that, in seeking deportation, the state is pursuing a legitimate aim. The aim being the maintenance of public order. In measuring the proportionality of the action taken by the state, the court has been willing to recognise 'special cases' which mitigate this general public order concern. However, the court has not probed in any great depth the concept of public order advanced by states. In many of the cases examined it accepted the designation of the offence as serious. It has focused on the proportionality of the deportation without much in-depth consideration of the public interest exceptions. There is some evidence that the court does have a view of what is and what is not a public order matter which justifies deportation. As has been noted, it would be difficult to argue that a serious crime in itself would be enough to justify deportation.[17] The impact must, it would appear, reach a certain level of seriousness (terrorism or drug trafficking for example) before it would have the necessary impact on public order.[18] In practice, a balancing exercise would not be possible without some

17 Harris, O'Boyle and Warbrick *Law of the European Convention on Human Rights* (1995) p 352.
18 Note 17 above.

consideration being given to the severity of the offences. In conducting this exercise, the court is engaged in an assessment of the seriousness of a particular offence. In *Dalia*, for example, the majority were evidently influenced by the nature of the applicant's drug trafficking offences. The suggestion is that an offence must have a sufficiently serious impact and a demonstrable effect on public order before it can meet this Convention standard.

It is certainly possible to be quite critical of the court's approach in these cases. The general failure to establish clarity is problematic. However, one should not lose sight of the context which the court is operating in. This is an area which has traditionally been the exclusive prerogative of states. There is a tension between the desire of the court to make rights practical and effective and its continuing legitimacy. Nevertheless, one can still be critical of the current jurisprudence. The court should be responsible for setting down relatively clear criteria for the important balancing exercise that has to be undertaken. Given the importance of pluralism and multiculturalism in modern Europe the court should avoid any hint of arbitrariness in its decision-making. This is admittedly not an easy task. The court should 'flesh out' a coherent justification for its role in modern Europe. In this it must attempt to reconcile a commitment to human rights protection with the European tradition of political democracy. It is not the place to elaborate on this issue here, but what this requires is a paradigmatic understanding of the judicial role. This search for coherence will involve: a clear statement of how the court views the regulated population (in other words what view of modern European society does the court possess); how it views its place in this context; and the theory of rights it is committed to. Ultimately, it may be that these are answered differently by individual judges. Even then we will not have the level of clarity sought. In the end we may simply have to accept that contestation will remain at the heart of the interpretative process. This is not something that we should necessarily fear, so long as the judges ensure that there is sufficient coherence to permit the conversation to continue. For this is a dialogue about the content of the rights that make political democracy possible and sustainable.

The court has clearly struggled with the precise meaning of art 8 in deportation cases. The art 8 cases are notable for their lack of clarity and precision. This casuistic approach may well allow the court to 'do justice' in individual cases but the absence of a coherent justification remains problematic. The European Court of Human Rights has a fundamentally important role in the new European constitutional order. It must take responsibility for setting out clear standards and justifications for them if it is to continue to enjoy the respect and legitimacy it currently possesses. In an area where instrumental thinking can dominate, it is for the court to uphold the value of human dignity and the importance of rights which attach to personhood and not status. This will not, of course, end the conversation. This jurisprudence demonstrates the problems that surround the limitations to Convention rights. The suggestion here is that when domestic courts in the UK come to interpret and apply this provision they must adopt a coherent justification for their role in these cases based upon a clearly articulated normative framework.

RECONSTRUCTING REFUGEE STATUS AND HUMAN RIGHTS

This chapter has concentrated on the legal construction of refugee status and the relevance of European human rights law. The law's image of the refugee matters. It has both a material and symbolic significance. Material benefits flow from gaining access to the status. The establishment of other forms of protection is an attempt to inject a level of flexibility into the protection of the displaced. In other instances barriers are placed in the way of access which effectively restrict the grant of refugee status. This is a process of undermining the principle of legality as it applies to the protection of refugees and asylum seekers. The emergence of a law of human rights in the UK, with the Human Rights Act 1998, will have an impact on this area. The jurisprudence of the European Court of Human Rights demonstrates the relevance of the Convention provisions. These human rights protections may be used productively by refugees and asylum seekers struggling against restriction and deterrence in the UK.

Chapter 6

Conclusion

LEGAL REGULATION AND SOCIAL COMPLEXITY

In this final chapter an attempt will be made to draw together the major elements in this work and reach some conclusions about the present state of, and future prospects for, refugee and asylum law. While the overriding concern of this work is to stress the complexity of forced migration, this is not to suggest that a humane response is beyond us. Complexity does not overburden the medium of law and we can construct processes of law and policy that are fair and effective. That many states fail to do this is because of current practices rather than the inherent weaknesses of the legal form. Legality matters for refugees and asylum seekers. The attempts made by states to undermine legality have had a negative impact on refugee protection. It is worth reiterating the point made at the beginning: that it is necessary, when seeking to understand and evaluate this area of domestic law and practice, to map international and European developments. Although law and policy gains real meaning for the individual at the local level, the discourses of asylum law and practice are shaped by transnational conversations on the most effective way to address migration. This is not only the case with asylum law. Many areas of public law and human rights law can only be comprehensively understood as an interaction between intersecting legal, political and social orders. Mapping these processes and their impact will be a considerable challenge for the critical tradition in modern law.

THE LIMITS AND POTENTIAL OF REFUGEE LAW

The definition of refugee status contained in the 1951 Convention, widely adopted and applied by states, was drafted in a specific historical context. It is a limited conception of the refugee which is at variance with the reality of modern forced migration. The law's image of the refugee reflects both a desire to control and to protect. In the process many fall outside this legal category. The error that occurs here is the reification of a narrow approach to the image of the refugee. The practical result is that this legitimises the crude distinctions and the 'demonisation' of those individuals and groups which fall outside its scope. This instrumentalist thinking results in the eventual neglect of the humanity of the displaced. A critique of the international legal position is therefore central to an analysis of refugee law. One should not simply accept the attempt by states to perpetuate a crude distinction between the 'genuine refugee' and the economic migrant. The 'genuine refugee' is a legal construction, which is reflected in the 1951 Convention. Failure to qualify for this privileged status, however, tells us little, if anything, about the increasingly large number of individuals who do not.

It is apparent that forced migration has achieved a permanence and a universality not reflected in the international legal response until the 1960s. While the international legal regime developed as a specific response to refugee movements in Europe, it has since then evolved into a regime of universal applicability. Therefore, a conception of refugee status which was drafted with European concerns in mind has become the international legal definition. This is a problematic development. The definition of refugee status contained in the 1951 Convention is limited to those who possess a well-founded fear of persecution for a 'Convention reason'. The definition invites individualised assessment and the reduction of a complex global problem to a constricted conception of refugee status. While the 1951 Convention and 1967 Protocol may have gained substantial international recognition, international refugee law reflects quite specific notions of what it is to be a refugee, for example, the 'Convention reasons' are linked exclusively to civil and political rights. The exclusion of economic and social rights leaves international refugee law as a flawed human rights regime for the protection of refugees. The retort that economic and social rights relate solely to economic migration is inadequate and inaccurate. It is suggested here that serious violations of these rights which lead to flight should, in any comprehensive refugee law regime, entitle an individual to the title 'refugee'.

Much that has followed the adoption of the 1951 Convention has lent credence to the argument that the 1951 Convention definition is inadequate; the most notable examples being the conclusion of agreements in other regions which include more inclusive definitions of refugee status. Unsurprisingly, given the scale of the refugee movements in the region in the period that followed, the first such agreement, the 1969 OAU Convention, was adopted in Africa. The OAU members states found that the 1951 Convention definition was simply inadequate, on its own, as a means to address their needs. Further developments in Central America have added impetus to calls for reform of the definition contained in international refugee law.

As noted, refugee law limits refugee status to those expected to suffer persecution for listed reasons. Possibly the most ambiguous of these reasons is the phrase 'a particular social group'. Unsurprisingly, given the limitations of the other aspects of the Convention, some commentators have argued that this phrase should be used as a 'catch-all' which would aid in a teleological approach to the interpretation of refugee status. Thus, the term might be used to make the refugee definition more relevant to modern forms of forced migration. This position springs from an understandable concern with the implications which flow from the narrow scope of conventional refugee law. While this argument is extremely attractive, there is one notable flaw. If the term is applied as a 'safety-net', which incorporates all claims which fall outside the other grounds of persecution, why, it may be asked, did the drafters include a list of grounds at all? While it is important in the human rights law context to encourage purposive interpretation, an abandonment of the need to demonstrate that an applicant was persecuted for a 'Convention reason' would conflict with the text of the 1951 Convention. It is evident that states which drafted the Convention (but also the states that have subsequently become parties to it) wished to specify, as precisely as possible, to whom they would owe obligations. They sought to apply this essentially limiting mechanism solely to those fearing persecution because of the denial of prescribed civil and political rights. Thus, while a purposive approach to the definition of refugee status is one that is attractive, it must not go so far as to remove the definition completely from its context within the scheme of non-discrimination and civil and political rights.

It has been consistently argued throughout this work that, while the 1951 Convention does not directly refer to the right of a refugee to some form of protection, such a duty may be derived from a combination of obligations in international refugee and human rights law. The principal obligation of a state party to the 1951 Convention is not to return a *refugee in any manner whatsoever* to a state where her life or freedom is threatened. This obligation has subsequently been reinforced by developments in international human rights law, which have emphasised the importance of non-return and the right of the individual to seek asylum. The long-standing debate in refugee law as to whether the word 'refugee', as used in art 33 of the 1951 Convention, should be considered declaratory or constitutive has therefore been largely overtaken by these developments. However, it is worth restating the position that the term 'refugee' must be seen as declaratory if the obligation in art 33 is to be practically effective. While the focus of the principle is on the return of the asylum seeker, this is deceptive, as the obligation clearly has implications for states' admission policies. It is suggested here that states are obliged to offer, at minimum, de facto refuge to the asylum seeker, who has not travelled through a safe third country, until some consideration has been given to her application. Once this process is completed, and appeal procedures have been exhausted, then return becomes an option for the state. Any other interpretation would seriously call into question the utility of the present international legal regime for the protection of the human rights of refugees and asylum seekers.

Although refugee law has problems, it is essential that the normativity of existing law is not abandoned. Refugee law remains an important status-granting mechanism which attaches significant entitlements to a defined status. At a time when many states are suspicious of the concept of legality as it applies to asylum seekers, it is worth reasserting the importance of refugee law. It is a flawed yet fundamentally important legal regime.

The discussion thus far has focused on asylum. Modern refugee law has seen a movement away from exclusive concern with asylum as the only solution to the refugee problem. Traditional refugee law has been accused of possessing an 'exile bias' leading to the neglect of the root causes of refugee movements. It is questionable whether this can be described accurately as a 'bias'. The legal regime which emerged reflects legal realities; in particular, a context where protection could only be conceived as external. This reorientation in approach has had a number of welcome results. By pointing to the root causes of flight, the inadequacy of modern international refugee law becomes evident. There are a variety of other violations of international human rights law which give rise to forced migration. A consequence of this is the recognition of the need for a more comprehensive response to refugee movements. This helps to explain why, for example, the internally displaced have received increased attention in recent years. The key term in this emerging debate is prevention. Prevention discourse is not confined to refugee law. It is playing a significant part in new thinking in international law and politics and follows the sensible logic that prevention is better than cure. For European states, prevention discourse has proved attractive. While the elimination of root causes is eminently desirable, acknowledgment should continue to be given to the pragmatic needs of refugees and asylum seekers. External displacement is a reality of modern life. If the right to seek asylum is undermined, then this new approach may simply legitimise the present trend in state practice towards the containment of refugee flows. Root causes must be addressed, but the right of the individual to seek asylum must also be asserted. An overemphasis on root causes can have a distorting impact on the refugee debate.

LEGAL AND POLITICAL STRUGGLE WITHIN THE 'FORTRESS'

The EU has begun to take on the appearance of a 'protective state'. The regulation of external borders in order to secure freedom of movement for some is inscribed in the process of supranationalism. The EU has adopted a defensive strategy, aimed at limiting the number of asylum seekers entering the region. This initial focus on restrictive measures has resulted in a 'lowest common denominator' approach to the harmonisation of asylum law and practice. This is most evident in the acceptance and extensive application of concepts such as that of safe third countries. These have the practical effect of limiting the responsibilities of member states in problematic ways. The claims, for example, that instruments such as the Dublin Convention 1990 are intended to guarantee the asylum applicant consideration of her application are contradicted by the fact that member states are still legally permitted to apply the safe third country concept. The widespread application of concepts such as this raises the possibility of the *refoulement* of asylum seekers, and as yet there does not exist adequate safeguards to protect the asylum seeker against this.

Problems may also arise in the EU harmonisation process where, as at present, the objective is only partially achieved. From this perspective the problem is not the process but its partial implementation. If an asylum seeker is only permitted one asylum application within the territory of the EU, and there is a marked variance in the practice of states, then unfairness is the result. This points to the lack of choice for the asylum applicant in the present EU arrangements, but also to the problems which exist when harmonisation is only partially complete.

The main difficulty with the present EU policy, as indicated, remains the substantial judicial and democratic deficits. In effect, within the EU, the provisions of asylum law are becoming 'internationalised'; however, the protection for the asylum seeker which presently exists does not reflect this fact. If, as has been noted, the EU develops more fully toward a 'constitutional system', then it must not be based upon the present restrictive constitutionalism.

The picture which emerges from the EU is grim. The asylum seeker is routinely constructed as a threat to the area of freedom, security and justice. There is resistance to the direction of law and policy and it would be inaccurate to concentrate solely on the repressive nature of current practices. There are, for example, new transnational political and legal spaces being created by migrant networks in the EU. These networks present a challenge to the dominant logic. The hope for a more humane policy must rest with those social movements in the EU struggling for the protection of the rights of refugees and asylum seekers.

ASYLUM AND THE FRAGMENTING STATE

Asylum is a dominant issue in legal and political discourse in the UK. Both Labour and Conservative governments have failed to make asylum law and policy work in a way that is perceived as legitimate by all affected groups. The system has correctly been described as a 'shambles' and a 'mess'. There are few who would strongly disagree with this assessment of the operation of asylum law and practice. The asylum debate reveals a high level of anxiety about the threats posed by forms of international mobility. As with the other EU member states, the UK is a party to the 1951 Convention and the 1967 Protocol. In fact, the UK played a leading role in drafting the 1951 Convention. It was one of the states at the time which argued strongly for an inclusive regime of international protection. Although in practice asylum law in the UK is intertwined with general immigration law, an attempt has been made in recent years to give it a substantial measure of distinctiveness. Asylum law has emerged as another distinct legal regime. As noted in this work, the system created to deal with asylum seekers has not functioned well. An atmosphere of hostility to asylum seekers has fuelled a general culture of disbelief which has impacted on the treatment of this group. While the UK continues to affirm its commitment to the 1951 Convention, the message underpinning policy development is one of deterrence. In this the UK is similar to other European states that are disoriented by the loss of autonomy which follows in the wake of global mobility.

PROSPECTS

There is little sign that forced migration will end. Human society is conflictual in nature and, as history shows, power struggles can become violent and force people to flee their homes. Internal and external displacement will continue to be as much a feature of the coming century as it was the last. Dealing with forced migration will also lead to just as many tragic choices. Refugee populations are not all the same and the political, social and legal dynamics will vary depending upon context. Refugee populations can contain victims of internal armed conflict as well as those responsible for genocide. An awareness of context is thus invaluable to the fair and effective treatment of refugees.

Refugees will continue to require forms of international protection. The rhetoric of prevention should not disguise this fact. The point is not to discourage the enforcement of human rights and humanitarian law. Rather, it is to stress that states must begin to recognise that forced displacement is here to stay. The challenge is to construct mechanisms of refugee protection which accord due respect to human dignity and the autonomy of the displaced. Too often in the UK and the EU the full humanity of the displaced is lost in purely instrumentalist discourses of exclusion. The challenge will be to ensure that the humanity of the other is not buried in the law and politics of restriction and deterrence.

Index